Rallying for Immigrant Rights

The publisher gratefully acknowledges the generous support of the Anne G. Lipow Endowment Fund for Social Justice and Human Rights of the University of California Press Foundation, which was established by Stephen M. Silberstein.

Rallying for Immigrant Rights

*The Fight for Inclusion in
21st Century America*

———

Edited by

Kim Voss and Irene Bloemraad

UNIVERSITY OF CALIFORNIA PRESS

Berkeley   Los Angeles   London

University of California Press, one of the most distinguished university presses in the United States, enriches lives around the world by advancing scholarship in the humanities, social sciences, and natural sciences. Its activities are supported by the UC Press Foundation and by philanthropic contributions from individuals and institutions. For more information, visit www.ucpress.edu.

University of California Press
Berkeley and Los Angeles, California

University of California Press, Ltd.
London, England

Library of Congress Cataloging-in-Publication Data

Rallying for immigrant rights : the fight for inclusion in 21st century America / edited by Kim Voss and Irene Bloemraad. — 1st ed.
    p. cm.
    Summary: "From Alaska to Florida, millions of immigrants and their supporters took to the streets across the United States to rally for immigrant rights in the spring of 2006. The scope and size of their protests, rallies, and boycotts made these the most significant events of political activism in the United States since the 1960s. This accessibly written volume offers the first comprehensive analysis of this historic moment. Perfect for students and general readers, its essays, written by a multidisciplinary group of scholars and grassroots organizers, trace the evolution and legacy of the 2006 protest movement in engaging, theoretically informed discussions. The contributors cover topics including unions, churches, the media, immigrant organizations, and immigrant politics" — Provided by publisher.
    Includes bibliographical references and index.
    ISBN 978-0-520-26754-1 (hardback) — ISBN 978-0-520-26755-8 (paper)
    1. Immigrants—Political activity—United States.   2. Immigrants—Social networks—United States.   3. Protest movements—United States.   4. Immigrants—Civil rights—United States.   5. Immigrants—Government policy—United States.   6. United States—Emigration and immigration.   I. Voss, Kim.   II. Bloemraad, Irene, 1972–
    JV6477.R34 2011
    323.3'29120973—dc22   2011000293

Manufactured in the United States of America

20 19 18 17 16 15 14 13 12 11
10 9 8 7 6 5 4 3 2 1

This book is printed on 50# Enterprise, a 30% post-consumer-waste, recycled, deinked fiber and processed chlorine free. It is acid-free, and meets all ANSI/NISO (Z 39.48) requirements.

CONTENTS

ILLUSTRATIONS

TABLES

FIGURES

Five years have passed since millions of people wearing white shirts marched for immigrant rights across the United States. Their activism secured one of the demonstrators' immediate goals: to prevent Senate passage of the Border Protection, Antiterrorism, and Illegal Immigration Control Act, a bill approved by the House of Representatives in December 2005. The marchers also succeeded in bringing attention to a group of people who live and work in communities throughout the country but who often seem invisible and voiceless. As Roberto Suro puts it in his contribution to this volume, immigrants, and especially those without proper documentation, came out of the shadows and into the light during the spring of 2006.

So far, however, those who took to the streets in 2006 have failed to achieve some of their broader goals, notably passage of federal legislation that would provide a path to legalization for the almost twelve million unauthorized migrants living in the United States. Even more modest versions of a legalization program fail to get congressional approval year after year. The DREAM Act, legislation that would provide permanent residency to people brought to the United States as unauthorized migrant children by their parents, has been regularly introduced in Congress over the past ten years but has been stalled or voted down each time.

Deportations, meanwhile, have risen. U.S. Immigration and Customs Enforcement (ICE) officers carried out an increasing number of deportations in the final years of the Bush presidency, a trend that continues under the Obama administration. In 2007, there were 319,382 people "removed" from the United States; by 2009, the number stood at 393,289 (Office of Immigration Statistics 2010, 4). Administration officials predicted that deportations would reach a new high in 2010.

What the numbers do not reveal is the fear ICE raids have produced among immigrants, particularly in Latino communities. In the Bay Area, where we live, Mexican immigrants tell stories of federal officials detaining parents at soccer games, apprehending people picking up children from school, or deporting people without warning in the middle of the night after a 1:00 a.m. knock at the door.

The widespread perception that immigration reform has stalled at the federal level has opened the door to local activism. Those who support deportations and feel governments need to attack unauthorized migration into the United States have taken their activism and concerns to city councils and state legislatures. The move to local activism was heralded by the debate and media attention that followed passage of the Illegal Immigration Relief Act by the city council of Hazelton, Pennsylvania, in 2006. This municipal ordinance, passed in a town of about 25,000 residents, fined landlords who rented property to illegal immigrants and business owners who hired them. More recently, local activism culminated in the Arizona state legislature's approval of S.B. 1070, a law that, among other provisions, requires law enforcement officials to check the legal residency status of anyone they suspect of being undocumented.

Both laws, and many others like it, have been enjoined or declared unconstitutional by the courts, in part because the U.S. Constitution assigns control over immigration to the federal government. Concerns about racial and ethnic profiling also figure prominently in opponents' criticism of these local legislative efforts. Nevertheless, a clear trend emerges. To overcome jurisdictional conflicts, ICE has entered into partnerships with state and local law enforcement agencies to train local officers to enforce immigration law under Section 287(g) of the Immigration and Nationality Act. In 2007, 1,059 immigration-related bills and resolutions were introduced in state legislatures nationwide (Laglagaron et al. 2008). While only a minority were passed into law, over half sought to reduce migrants' rights or to regulate access to employment, education, housing, and the like. Similarly, at the local level, Ramakrishnan and Wong (2010) enumerate ninety-eight municipalities that tried to pass restrictionist ordinances in 2007, and seventy-eight municipalities that proposed expansive or supportive policies. The trend is clearly toward both a mentality and reality of enforcement and restrictions. Few politicians or government officials still take up the cause of comprehensive immigration reform, and their numbers are likely to decline further now that Republicans have regained a majority in the House of Representatives following the 2010 midterm elections.

It is hard to find a silver lining among the gathering storm clouds, especially given the sense of hope and collective power that animated the 2006 protests. But protest might very well matter. While more restrictionist bills and ordinances were proposed at the state and local levels in 2007, a higher percentage of legislation *favorable* to immigrants actually became law. For example, Ramakrishnan and Wong (2010) report that 74 of 78 promigrant municipal ordinances passed in 2007, compared to only 55 of 98 restrictionist measures, and they find that places with immigration protests were more likely to pass ordinances favorable to immigrants. At the same time, many believe that Arizona's hard turn against immigrants, epitomized by S.B. 1070, was in part a reaction to the highly visible protests of 2006. Both academics and activists need to better understand the role of protests in furthering political agendas and in driving backlash or countermovements. This is especially crucial at this political moment when hard-line advocates of immigration enforcement are ascendant in the new Congress. After all, it was the introduction of a draconian anti–illegal immigration bill that sparked the protests in 2006.

We also need to ask whether we are witnessing a new type of protest dynamic. Social movements in the United States have always been about political outsiders, whether progressive or conservative, challenging the established political system. But immigrants, due to their lack of citizenship, hold a fundamentally unequal position in such contests. They cannot transform street-based protest into action at the ballot box. Arguably, their moral claims to legitimacy and standing in the political system also become more difficult to make given a lack of citizenship or even legal residency. We thus find clashing frames of what is at stake. Are immigrant protestors illegal lawbreakers who take the jobs of American citizens, or are they human beings who contribute to U.S. society through their work and family values? A clear legacy of the 2006 immigration rights protests is the call to a new politics of inclusion, one that is being challenged by alternative visions of exclusion and expulsion. This is a story, and a political battle, that will continue in years to come.

ACKNOWLEDGMENTS

As is fitting for a book about a mass mobilization in the new millennium, the inspiration for this volume grew out of an e-mail exchange. In mid-April 2006, after weeks of immigration protests in cities across the United States, Roberto Suro, then of the Pew Hispanic Center, began an exchange with Kim Voss, Marshall Ganz, and Sidney Tarrow about whether we were seeing "the beginnings of something that might become a social movement." As the number of people drawn into the protests climbed and the geographical sweep of the demonstrations expanded, the number of questions we had also multiplied. How were so many undocumented people being drawn in? Who were the main actors driving the protests? What would the likely effects of the protests be? It soon became clear that answers would be elusive until more actual research about the marches could be undertaken.

Academic conferences are one of the best organizational devices we have for encouraging research on new issues. To encourage that research and to bring together scholars of the protests from different academic disciplines and different parts of the country, Voss agreed to take the lead on organizing a conference in spring 2007 in Berkeley, California, the site of major social movement activity forty years earlier. As she discussed with her e-mail partners how to bring together a dream team of researchers, Irene Bloemraad's name came up immediately as someone who would be ideal for bridging scholarship on social movements with the scholarship on immigration. She soon agreed to be a co-organizer of the conference, and eventually she also agreed to coedit this book. The collaboration has been a fully equal one and, to signal our equal effort, we have reversed the order of our names on the title page and on the introductory essay.

As anyone who has organized an academic conference knows, they sometimes "click," with people pushing their thinking and developing their ideas in new directions, and sometimes they don't. Our April 2007 conference clicked, and the participants came away inspired to continue work on their projects in light of the engaged interaction we all experienced at the conference.

This volume reflects both the learning we all did at the conference and our subsequent research and revisions. In putting it together, our goal has been to provide a broad, multidisciplinary account of what happened during the immigration rights rallies, protests, and boycotts of spring 2006, and to consider the consequences of the protests for academic theorizing as well as for American politics. To help meet that goal, we solicited two additional chapters from Luisa Heredia and Randy Shaw to fill in gaps in the research originally presented at the conference.

This book reflects the advice and spirit of colleagues who shared their research or provided advice and criticism along the way but who for one reason or another do not appear in the table of contents. Maria Echaveste, S. Karthick Ramakrishnan, and Jonathan Simon gave conference presentations that shaped our understanding of the protests significantly; Robert Mickey and Rachel Moran gave comments on conference presentations that have shaped several chapters of the book; Carlos Muñoz generously shared his insights and intellectual support for this project; conference participants debated the content and implications of the presentations with energy and acumen; and Marshall Ganz and Sidney Tarrow helped inspire our undertakings. Hana Brown provided expert and generous research support.

The Institute for Labor and Employment and the Pew Hispanic Center provided the financial support that made the conference possible. We thank them—and especially Michael Reich and Roberto Suro—for their generosity. We also are grateful to the Abigail Reynolds Hodgen Publication Fund for helping with publication costs. We owe a deep debt to Naomi Schneider at UC Press, for believing that this book is an important project, intellectually and as part of a larger debate about U.S. politics present and future, but also for pushing us to make it better. We end by noting that while the long-term prospects of what might be called an immigrant rights movement remain highly uncertain, the site of our conference, Berkeley, California, was at the vanguard of other transformative movements in the 1960s and 1970s. What made the 2006 protests so remarkable was the lack of a single center, but perhaps the spirit of the earlier period will play out again in the future.

What Happened?

The Historically Unprecedented Mobilizations
of Spring 2006

May Day march, Los Angeles, 2006. Photograph by David Bacon.

The Protests of 2006

What Were They, How Do We Understand Them, Where Do We Go?

Irene Bloemraad, Kim Voss, and Taeku Lee

In a short span of twelve weeks between mid-February and early May 2006, an estimated 3.7 to 5 million people took to the streets in over 160 cities across the United States to rally for immigrant rights.[1] Marches and demonstrations were organized from Anchorage, Alaska, to Miami, Florida, and forty-two states in between. The marches brought together groups large and small, from the 24 people counted at a protest in Anchorage to as many as 700,000 people in the streets of Chicago and Los Angeles. Often wearing white T-shirts, waving American flags and, at times, flags from their homelands, the marchers included people of all ages, from babies in strollers and teenagers walking with their parents to gray-haired seniors in wheelchairs. The marchers spanned economic conditions and came from all walks of life, from day laborers and janitors to professionals and politicians, including the future U.S. president, Barack Obama. Together, they chanted slogans such as "Today we march, tomorrow we vote," and "¡Sí, se puede!" (Yes, we can!). The majority of those who took to the streets were Latino, but people of European, African, and Asian heritage marched too. The group of "Latinos" who participated was diverse, including immigrants from over a dozen Spanish-speaking countries, their U.S.-born children, and Chicano or Hispanic Americans whose families' U.S. roots stretch back a hundred years or more.[2]

The sheer scope of the protests and the numbers involved are of historic proportions. During the heyday of the civil rights movements, in 1963, 250,000 people flocked to the Mall in Washington DC to hear Martin Luther King Jr. (JBHE Foundation 2003). In 1969, those who marched on Washington to protest American involvement in Vietnam numbered between 250,000 and 320,000 (Cicchetti et al. 1971). Looking back to the nineteenth century, some 300,000 to 500,000 people took to the streets to militate for labor rights, culminating in the famous Chicago Haymarket protest of 1886 (Avrich 1984; Foner 1986). Strikingly, none of these prior protests—historic moments in the annals of contentious politics in the United States—matched the largest May 1 rallies for immigrant rights in 2006.[3]

Beyond the United States, the marches of 2006 were likely the largest protests over immigrant rights seen in the world, and they probably figure among the largest demonstrations held in Western nations in recent decades.[4] Especially noteworthy, the 2006 U.S. mobilizations were peaceful and without a major violent incident: there were no demonstrator/police melees, not a single person died, and not a single car was burned, unlike other twenty-first-century protests and riots over immigrant rights and race relations in cities such as Birmingham, Paris, and Sydney.[5]

The scope, scale, and peaceful nature of the protests demand explanation; this is one of the goals of our volume. Activism outside "normal" electoral or institutional politics suggests that standard political science accounts of behavioral politics or Latino/minority politics must be expanded beyond voting or contacting elected officials to include contentious action. At the same time, the protests do not quite fit within existing social movements scholarship: the strategies used were tried and true tactics employed by past social movements, but the nature of the 2006 mobilizations was unusual. The protests rapidly ballooned to unimagined proportions, were sustained for about three months, but then collapsed as quickly as they started. Why, like a July 4 fireworks display, did the marches end as abruptly as they began? It is unclear whether the 2006 protests better represent "spontaneous" collective action, as articulated by an older generation of social scientists and recently retheorized (Killian 1984; Biggs 2003, 2005), or a "sustained" movement in line with most contemporary political process and new social movement models of contentious action.

Much of the research reported here suggests that the rapid, large-scale mobilization arose, in part, due to the loose network of local groups who received support from actors like the media or Catholic Church, organizations that could send widespread messages about the protests. We also suggest that the protests were animated by an almost paradoxical mix of threat—from legislative action against undocumented immigrants and anti-Latino or anti-immigrant sentiment more generally—and faith in the political system. Perhaps for this reason, there is evidence that some of the energies animating the 2006 street protests became channeled into 2008 electoral participation. These dynamics, if accurate, reinforce social movement scholars' argument about the importance of organizations for contentious politics. However, they challenge the idea that, for mobilization, social movements need openings in the political opportunities structure—2006 was more about threat than opportunity—and they challenge hard and fast distinctions between contentious and electoral political engagement.

The 2006 protests were remarkable in another way: they focused on, and were in substantial part animated by, people without citizenship in the political system they challenged. Most studies of formal politics take for granted the citizen-actor, an individual who holds political rights and who may act independently, as a voter, or in a collective, as part of a civic association, political party, or interest group. Those who are foreign-born, particularly those without citizenship and *especially* those without legal residence, are absent from standard, institutional accounts of political engagement.

Noncitizens also tend to be absent from studies of social movements. Social movement scholars devote their energies to studying the political actions of those who, in the classical language of social movements, are "challengers," forced to engage in contentious action because they see few opportunities in the formal political system (Tilly 1978). This characterization perfectly suits noncitizens' activities, yet the assumption undergirding most studies of social movements is one of the protesting *citizen*. Protesters might have second-class citizenship, as was the case for African Americans, but they are nationals of the countries where they advocate for change. They can be jailed, attacked, and obstructed in their protest activities, but they cannot generally be thrown out of the country altogether.[6] This is the case for a noncitizen migrant.

In the United States, an estimated 11 to 12 million unauthorized migrants lived in the country in 2006, and another 14 million noncitizen legal residents—from international students to permanent residents who have made the United States home for decades—face an additional form of repression not seen in most social movements. They can be summarily removed from the society in which they are protesting and be deported, ripping families apart and tearing a person away from his or her livelihood and community. What would possess people who have everything to lose by coming out into the limelight to march, even though the cost could be permanent and definitive exclusion? Noncitizens are invisible from most political struggles in the United States, but the 2006 protests rendered them visible.

The language of visibility—what worked to frame these individuals' struggles, and what didn't—deserves careful attention. Our preliminary conclusion is that the most successful framing of the movement centered on American values of family and work: immigrants are members of families and hard workers who do not deserve to be seen or treated like deportable criminals. In contrast, frames that hinted at foreignness, such as appeals to home-country pride, America's immigration history, or even human rights, found limited traction in the court of public opinion and mainstream media coverage of the protests. The American public, it seems, need immigrants to make appeals to their Americanism. From the viewpoint of some contributors to this volume, the 2006 rallies also mark a crystallization of a new Latino identity that brings together multiple generations whose roots in the United States might date from a few years to more than a century.

In the remainder of this chapter, we provide some background to the events of 2006, and we make the case for why the immigrant rights rallies offer an important lens onto critical questions of citizenship, social movements, politics, and identity. We sketch out key ways to understand the protests and highlight the various institutions and processes involved in this moment of mass mobilization. We then take a step back and ask about the consequences of the protests, for American politics and for immigrants and Latinos in the United States, as well as for academic scholarship within sociology, political science, and related disciplines. In doing so, we highlight the contributions of the other chapters in this volume, which address the question of why and how the protests occurred as well as their consequences for the future. In a world where globalization has spurred dramatic increases in the number of international migrants, even as immigration policies grow more restrictive in many places, the practical and theoretical issues raised by the 2006 protests present pressing dilemmas for scholars and citizens around the world.

BACKGROUND: THE EVENTS OF 2006

The immediate catalyst of the 2006 spring protest wave was the passage of the Border Protection, Antiterrorism, and Illegal Immigration Control Act, also known as H.R. 4437, on December 16, 2005. Representative F. James Sensenbrenner, a Republican from Wisconsin, first introduced the bill on December 6; ten days later it passed the House of Representatives with a vote of 239 to 182. The bill, which the Congressional Budget Office estimated would cost almost $2 billion dollars between 2006 and 2010 alone, counted among its provisions a substantial investment in border security, including almost seven hundred miles of double-layer fencing, increasingly high-tech document control, more cooperation between the Department of Homeland security and local law enforcement, and stiffer penalties for employers hiring illegal migrants.[7] Even in the context of greater congressional concern over security and border control in a post–September 11 environment, the bill was widely perceived as draconian, in no small part because it would make living in the United States without valid legal documentation a crime rather than the civil offence it currently is.[8] The provision would have not only criminalized anyone who committed an immigration violation, even a technical one without intent to violate the immigration laws, but it also threatened to criminalize anyone who assisted illegal aliens, including those working for religious, humanitarian, or social justice organizations that might offer legal aid, social welfare, or sanctuary to people without proper documents.

Passage of H.R. 4437 sent ripples of anxiety through immigrant rights, union, and religious networks across the country. By February 11, 2006, roughly five hundred Latino leaders from labor unions, churches, community-based organizations, advocacy groups, and universities met in Riverside, California, to plan a nationwide series of protests (see Wang and Winn, this volume). These activists wanted to influence the expected spring debate over immigration legislation in the U.S. Senate.

The ripples rapidly grew in amplitude and began to be visible to the wider public. The first wave of protests reported in the media occurred between February 14 and 22 in Philadelphia, Georgetown, Delaware, and Fort Myers, Florida, drawing between 1,000 and 5,000 participants. On March 1, Cardinal Roger Mahony of Los Angeles used his Ash Wednesday address—a choice that was a striking religious and symbolic message—to call on Catholics and other concerned citizens to defy H.R. 4437 should it become law. The wave of protests then grew at a furious pace, with 20,000 to 40,000 rallying in Washington DC on March 6, followed by a massive demonstration of 100,000 to 300,000 protesters in Chicago on March 10. The storm of immigrant rights rallies had begun.

Upwards of 260 separate demonstrations occurred in the subsequent two months, with most clustering around three distinct time periods: March 23–31, April 9 and 10, and May 1. Table 1.1 highlights the largest twenty demonstrations that occurred between March 23 and May 1, 2006. Eight of these rallies attracted at least 100,000 participants, with perhaps half to three-quarter million people marching in the streets of Chicago and Los Angeles on May 1. The symbolism of May 1 might have been lost on some American observers, but the date is highly significant: currently known as International Workers' Day, this day of labor protest and celebration of workers' rights originated in the United States with the Haymarket Riots of 1886 in Chicago. The theme of work, and the economic contributions made by immigrant workers regardless of legal status, was a prominent theme on placards held by demonstrators and in speeches addressed to the marchers. As one banner said, "We are workers, not criminals!" (Reid 2006).

The wave of protests also spread to new places not historically known for activism around immigrant rights or, for that matter, not known as places of migration at all. During the spring of 2006, demonstrations occurred in towns large and small across the South and Midwest. Tens of thousands took to the streets in Fort Meyers, Florida, and in Atlanta, while smaller rallies occurred across the Carolinas, in Tennessee, as well as in rural Nebraska and Kansas. For example, Schuyler, Nebraska, a small town of 5,300 souls, saw 3,000 people rally for immigrant rights (Wang and Winn, this volume). The broad geographic scope of the demonstrations, shown in figure 1.1, reflected the new and growing dispersion of immigrants,

TABLE 1.1 Turnout for Spring 2006 Immigrant Rights Marches, Top Twenty Cities

City	Date of Event	Media Estimate of Participants	Sources
Los Angeles	5/1/06	650,000	*Los Angeles Times*
Los Angeles	3/25/06	500,000	*Los Angeles Times*
Chicago	5/1/06	400,000	*Chicago Tribune*
Dallas	4/9/06	350,000	*Dallas Morning News*
Washington DC	4/10/06	180,000	*New York Times*
Chicago	3/10/06	100,000	*Chicago Tribune*
New York City	4/10/06	100,000	*New York Times*
Phoenix	4/10/06	100,000	*Arizona Republic*
San Jose	5/1/06	100,000	*San Jose Mercury News*
Fort Myers	4/10/06	75,000	*Orlando (FL) Sentinel*
Denver	3/25/06	50,000	*Denver Post*
Denver	5/1/06	50,000	*Denver Post*
Detroit	3/27/06	50,000	*Detroit Free Press*
Houston	4/10/06	50,000	*Houston Chronicle*
San Diego	4/9/06	50,000	*San Diego Union Tribune*
Atlanta	4/10/06	40,000	*Atlanta Journal-Constitution*
Las Vegas	5/1/06	35,000	*Las Vegas Sun*
San Francisco	5/1/06	30,000	*San Francisco Chronicle*
Washington DC	3/6/06	30,000	*Chicago Tribune*
St. Paul	4/9/06	30,000	*Minneapolis Star-Tribune*

SOURCE: Xóchitl Bada and Jonathan Fox's revised calculations, based on a database originally compiled by Xóchitl Bada, Jonathan Fox, Elvia Zazueta, and Ingrid Garcia Ruiz, available at Wilson International Center for Scholars, www.wilsoncenter.org/migrantparticipation. Estimates are the minimums reported by leading English-language daily newspapers.

and especially Latino migrants, throughout the United States (Singer 2004a; Zúñiga and Hernández-Léon 2005; Massey 2008).

As with many powerful storms, this one died quickly, at least from the public eye. Indeed, the demobilization of the marchers was as dramatic as their mobilization. Few rallies of substantial size occurred in the months and years following May 2006.[9] The immediate goal of many marchers—to kill H.R. 4437—succeeded. The Senate refused to consider the legislation. But the marchers failed to spur more proactive legislation. On May 26, 2006, the Senate passed S. 2611, the Comprehensive Immigration and Reform Act, which would have created a path to legalization for undocumented migrants, but the bill died and alternative bills during the summers of 2006 and 2007 suffered a similar fate. At the time of this writing, in spring 2010, there still has been no comprehensive immigration reform. President Barack Obama has signaled an interest in pushing for such a bill, but responding to the severe economic recession, foreign policy, and health-care reform have taken center stage early in his administration.

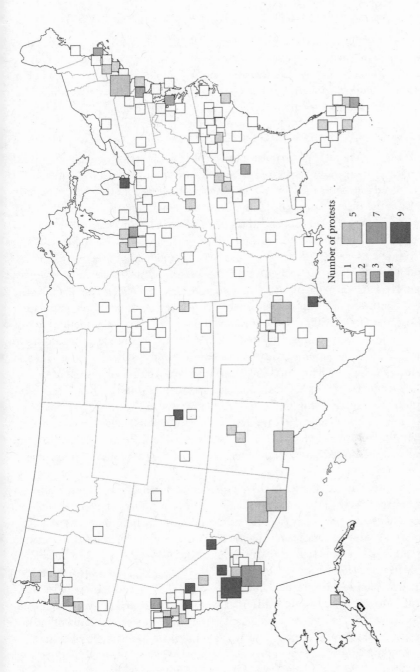

FIGURE 1.1. Immigration protests map, 2006.

PLACING SPRING 2006 IN HISTORICAL CONTEXT

Just as no one predicted the fall of the Berlin Wall in 1989, no scholar or political commentator predicted the scale and scope of the spring 2006 protests. With the benefit of hindsight, however, we can identify a number of precedents, including Chicano, worker, sanctuary movement, and immigrant rights activism, which laid the groundwork for 2006.

Legacies of Activism

"Latinos"—ranging from Spanish speakers of Spanish heritage to those of mixed or largely indigenous background born in the Spanish-speaking Americas— have lived in what is the United States since before the country's independence. Substantial incorporation of Latinos only occurred, however, with the Treaty of Guadalupe Hidalgo that ended the Mexican-American War of 1846–48. The treaty ceded significant proportions of Colorado, Arizona, New Mexico, and Wyoming, as well as all of California, Nevada, and Utah, to the United States, and it forced Mexico to recognize the Rio Grande as the border between Texas and Mexico.[10] In 1850, an estimated 80,000 Mexican Americans lived in the U.S. Southwest, accounting for about 20 percent of the region's population (Nostrand 1975).[11] Although the border was relatively open and unpoliced in this period, migration of Mexicans to the United States was modest. According to official records, 728,000 Mexican moved to the United States between 1901 and 1930 (Bean and Stevens 2003, 49). These migrants, combined with people born in the United States of Mexican heritage, accounted for the 1,423,000 Mexican- origin individuals living in the United States in 1930 (Bean and Stevens 2003, 53). This number would decrease over the subsequent two decades as older gen- erations passed away, new migration was reduced by economic depression and war, and the United States forcibly returned hundreds of thousands of people to Mexico.

Despite significant cases of discrimination and strong anti-Latino sentiment in the Southwest in the early twentieth century—including the forced deporta- tion of anywhere between 350,000 and 2 million Mexican immigrants and U.S.- citizen Mexican Americans during the Great Depression—there are few accounts of large-scale Latino collective action until the 1960s (Gómez-Quiñones 1990; Balderrama and Rodriguez 1995). In 1929, the League of United Latin American Citizens (LULAC) was formed in Corpus Christi, Texas, the nation's oldest His- panic advocacy organization still in existence today. In the ten years following World War II, Mexican American activists, working through organizations like LULAC and veterans' associations, won a number of important legal battles, in- cluding the landmark 1954 ruling *Hernandez v. State of Texas,* which declared Mexican Americans entitled to equal protection under the Fourteenth Amendment of the U.S. Constitution (M. T. García 1989). Few of these efforts involved mass protest or contentious political action.

What many call the Chicano civil rights movement originated in the 1960s, drawing inspiration from the black civil rights movement. The Chicano movement encompassed three streams. One stream centered on the struggle of the United Farm Workers (UFW), founded in California's Central Valley in 1962 and composed of Mexican, Mexican American, and Filipino migrant farmworkers who used nonviolent direct action to agitate for the right to organize and earn a living wage. At its height, the UFW unionized thousands of farmworkers and recruited and trained hundreds of community organizers and activist leaders. It also reinvigorated social movement tactics like the boycott and hunger strike, and as a result won the passage of the 1975 California Agricultural Labor Relations Act, the only law protecting the collective bargaining rights of agricultural workers in the continental United States (Ganz 2009; Shaw 2008).

The second stream was the Chicano nationalist movement, which started in Denver and New Mexico and was committed to etching a new collective understanding of the once-pejorative term *Chicano*. It also fought for the property rights guaranteed to Mexican citizens living in the Southwest when the United States signed the Treaty of Guadalupe Hidalgo in 1848. The Chicano nationalist movement drew many with its push for political and social inclusion and it helped to spark an artistic renaissance, yet its efforts to unify Mexican Americans around a single collective identity proved an elusive goal.

The third stream was the Chicano student movement, which erupted in 1968 when East Los Angeles high school students walked out of their schools. Though student protests were especially visible in California, they also occurred in Texas and New Mexico as well as in Phoenix, Chicago, and Denver. The student blowouts, as they were called, involved thousands of Chicano students protesting against their crumbling schools and the failure of the public education system to reflect their experiences in course material and teaching staff (C. Muñoz 1989; Gómez-Quiñones 1990).

From the context of 2006, two important points stand out about the 1960s period. First, the activism of that time largely revolved around the concerns and aspirations of U.S.-born citizens of Mexican or Chicano heritage.[12] These protests were *not* about immigration. The United Farm Workers, as a union, took stances hostile to immigration in the 1960s and early 1970s. Frustrated at the refusal of the Immigration and Naturalization Service to stop growers from bringing in undocumented immigrants to do the jobs of striking union members, Cesar Chavez testified before Congress in support of employer sanctions in 1966 for those employing illegal immigrants and endorsed tough immigration restrictions proposed in Congress in 1973. Although Chavez later became a strong supporter of immigrant rights (his anti-immigrant stance might more accurately be characterized as "antistrikebreaker"), in its heyday, UFW activism was not focused on immigration (Shaw 2008). Similarly, students agitating for a Chicano curriculum and Latino teachers appealed to the long-standing history of Mexican Americans in the United States, not the plight of new migrants from Mexico and other Spanish-speaking countries. In 1970, only 17 percent of the total U.S. Mexican-origin population was born in Mexico; more than four in five were U.S.-born citizens (Bean and Stevens 2003, 54).

A second lesson, however, is that the movements of the 1960s forged a generation of activists who learned to organize, protest, and mobilize people for a cause, and the earlier period provides a historical touchstone to which contemporary activists can appeal. We have some evidence that those active in the UFW and student movement during the 1960s later shifted their energies and organizational skills to take on the issues of immigrants, including the undocumented. In his contribution to this volume, Randy Shaw contends that there is a direct link between the young activists in the UFW and the contemporary immigrant rights movement in Los Angeles, a link also hinted at in this volume's chapters by Ted Wang and Robert Winn and by Luisa Heredia. Lisa Martinez's chapter on Denver alludes to the symbolic importance of the 1960s era for today's activists, reminding us that Denver was home to Rodolfo "Corky" Gonzales's Crusade for Justice in 1966. The Chicano movement and UFW also inspired other activists, such as those who mobilized for Puerto Rican rights and independence in the 1960s and 1970s (Torres and Velasquez 1998), generating organizational activism and norms of contentious political engagement up to the present.

Some of those active in these decades also became involved in the sanctuary movement of the 1980s, a concerted mobilization by churches and other groups to assist Central Americans fleeing civil war and to speak out against U.S. foreign intervention in the region (Chinchilla, Hamilton, and Loucky 2009; Coutin 1993; C. Smith 1996b). The sanctuary movement, and the broader Central American peace and solidarity movement of which it was a part, also mobilized new activists, including middle-class Americans with no personal experience with migration. These people, spurred on by humanitarian concern over the fate of Central American migrants, and also often by political views opposing President Reagan's policy in Central America, engaged in a concerted program of civil disobedience. They created various refugee and immigration organizations in the process, built transnational ties to activists in Central America, and adopted religious understandings to frame their actions. All of these activities would find parallels, though in new ways, during the protests of 2006.

Contemporary Migration and Recent Anti-Immigrant Politics

If the 1960s focused on the U.S.-born Hispanic, and the 1980s on Central Americans fleeing political conflict, today's activism centers on the Latino migrant, especially the undocumented. The shift in focus arose in large part due to the dramatic change in the Latino and Mexican-origin populations that occurred around 1970, as one wave of semiregulated temporary Mexican migration ended and the contemporary wave of diverse, large-scale legal and unauthorized Latino migration began.

The first postwar wave of migration began in 1942, when the U.S. government began what would be called the Bracero Program, a series of agreements with Mexico and Caribbean countries to import temporary foreign labor to fill war-related employment shortages, especially in the agriculture and railway sectors. From 1942 to 1964, when the program was formally ended, approximately 4.6 million Mexican-born workers came to the United States through official or informal channels (Calavita 1992; Tichenor 2002, 210). The Bracero Program instituted a pattern of temporary, cyclical migration, largely of male laborers, on which U.S. agricultural interests came to rely. It also generated a "culture of migration" (Kandel and Massey 2002; Massey et al. 1998) that established a norm of migration to "el Norte" for certain Mexican communities. The end of this program laid the groundwork for contemporary, large-scale undocumented migration (Massey, Durand, and Malone 2002).

Despite bracero migration, in 1970 those born in Mexico only made up about 8 percent of all foreign-born individuals living in the United States, while Latinos (then commonly referred to as Hispanics) numbered about 9.6 million out of a total U.S. population of about 206 million, or 4.7 percent (Bean and Stevens 2003, 22). By 1980, the proportion of Hispanics had increased more than 50 percent; by 1990 the number reached 22.3 million; and by 2000, 37.7 million (Bean and Stevens 2003, 22). High fertility rates among those of Hispanic or Latino origin accounted for part of the rise, but immigration was a major motor: considering just Mexican migration, in 2000 there were 8.8 million Mexican-born individuals living in the United States, who made up about 29 percent of the total immigrant population and also accounted for 41 percent of the Mexican-origin population in the United States (Bean and Stevens 2003, 54).

The dramatic increase in Mexican migration is part of a more general surge in immigration to the United States over the last four decades. In 1965, American immigration law underwent a radical overhaul after Congress passed the Immigration and Nationality (or Hart-Cellar) Act. This act restricted, for the first time, migration from the "Western Hemisphere," which included Mexico, Central America, South America, and the Caribbean, imposing a ceiling of 120,000 legal permanent resident visas per annum.[13] Conversely, the law removed discriminatory quotas on the rest of the world, or the "Eastern Hemisphere," finally opening the door to large-scale Asian migration. It also opened the door, outside the annual admission ceilings set by Congress, to the spouses, minor children, and parents of U.S. citizens.

The 1965 act allowed many people previously shut out of the United States to migrate legally, especially through the use of family sponsorship provisions. Immigrants from around the world, including from Mexico and Latin America, used family reunification to bring relatives to the United States. But the ensuing decades also saw a significant increase in undocumented migration. With the end of the Bracero Program, limited temporary work visas, a new Western Hemisphere ceiling, continued American demand for low-skilled labor, and limited economic development in Latin America, it is not surprising that undocumented migration began to grow.

This trend was exacerbated in the early 1980s when Central Americans, fleeing war and upheaval in El Salvador, Guatemala, and Nicaragua, came to the United States. Central Americans, seen by numerous civil society groups and by themselves as political refugees, were generally viewed by the U.S. government as economic migrants: less than 5 percent had their claims of asylum accepted in the 1980s (M. C. García 2006). Hundreds of thousands, unwilling to go back to war and persecution in their homelands, instead went underground, joining the burgeoning undocumented population. Later, after extended activism by churches, lawyers, and other civil society activists, many received Temporary Protected Status and related designations through special legislation passed by Congress or following the out-of-court settlement of a class action lawsuit that required the federal government to reopen 150,000 asylum cases (known as the ABC case, or *American Baptist Churches v. Thornburgh*). For some, these legislative and judicial victories led to permanent legal status, but others remain in a legal limbo between unauthorized status and legal permanent residence (Menjívar 2000, 2006).

The dramatic upsurge in undocumented migration led in 1986 to the first large-scale U.S. amnesty for those living in the United States without authorization. In 1986, Congress passed the Immigration Reform and Control Act (IRCA) which, depending on one's perspective, was a careful or convoluted compromise between a myriad of political actors and interests. Two main provisions were the introduction, for the first time, of sanctions for employers knowingly hiring undocumented workers and legalization of about three million people, approximately three-quarters of them born in Mexico (Martin 1994).[14] Quickly, however, evidence mounted that IRCA had not eliminated illegal migration. Researchers instead found weak oversight of employers and very little enforcement of IRCA in workplaces (Brownell 2005; Fix 1991). Further, as the U.S. government stepped up efforts to control the southern border through more border control officers, new fencing, and other techniques to deter clandestine entry, the cost of unauthorized border crossing—both financial and human—increased. This impeded historical patterns of circular migration and led families of undocumented migrants to risk deserts, mountains, and other dangerous crossing schemes to join those working—and now staying—in the United States (Cornelius 2001, 2005).

One of the states most heavily affected by migration, both legal and unauthorized, was California, and it is perhaps not surprising that this state would be home to the first volley of the anti-immigrant backlash of the 1990s.[15] In 1994, California voters overwhelmingly passed Proposition 187, an initiative to deny illegal immigrants all social services, including health care and public education. Championed by the incumbent Republican governor, Pete Wilson, as a central part of his reelection strategy, the measure was widely perceived as targeting all Latino migrants, not just undocumented, and it sparked the largest mass protests and school walkouts since the Chicano movement, by some estimates spurring 70,000 people into the streets (García Bedolla 2005, 29–31; McDonnell and López 1994). Although the initiative was later overturned by the courts as unconstitutional, its success at the polls emboldened conservative groups even as it spurred higher rates of naturalization, voter registration, and voter turnout among legal Latino immigrants (Pantoja, Ramírez, and Segura 2001; Ramakrishnan 2005). In 1996, some of the same Republican groups that had sponsored Proposition 187 penned Proposition 209, aimed at ending affirmative action in the state, which also won voter approval; then, in 1998, Proposition 227 ended bilingual education in the state, with a resounding 61 percent of the vote.

Although the anti-immigrant backlash began in California, the rapidly growing immigrant population and its spread to all areas of the United States had ripple effects on the national stage. In 1996, the U.S. Congress passed, and President Bill Clinton signed, two pieces of legislation with far-reaching consequences for migrants, both legal and unauthorized: the Personal Responsibility and Work Opportunity Reconciliation Act of 1996 (PRWORA) and the Illegal Immigration Reform and Immigrant Responsibility Act of 1996 (IIRIRA).[16] These laws marked two important turning points in the U.S. government's attitude toward noncitizen migrants: they underscored the importance of citizenship as the only secure protection against removal and exclusion from the United States as well as the only guarantee to social benefits, and they reinforced the marginal status of unauthorized migrants by making them ineligible for most social benefits as well as taking away the ability to appeal immigration decisions.

PRWORA, more commonly known as the Welfare Reform Act, was signed into law first, on August 22, 1996. Its stated purpose was to change the system of federal cash assistance to the poor by instituting lifetime limits to benefits and mandating new work requirements for those receiving benefits. However, an entire section of the act, Title IV, focuses on noncitizens, including legal permanent residents, refugees, and undocumented migrants.[17] The law effectively barred undocumented migrants from most forms of state support and ended a decades-old policy of treating legal permanent residents in the United States as citizens for social benefits like Supplemental Security Income, food stamps, Medicaid, and cash benefits (Singer 2004b). In sharpening the distinction between citizens and noncitizens, the United States bucked an apparent trend in other Western industrialized countries where social benefits depend more on long-term legal residence than citizenship, and where some rights rely on personhood rather than state-based membership through citizenship (Fix and Laglagaron 2002; Soysal 1994).

In parallel, congressional and White House attention to border control increased with IIRIRA, signed into law on September 30, 1996. It authorized substantial new hires of border control officers, new border control technology, and more money for fencing. It severely limited legal recourse against exclusion and deportation for apprehended undocumented migrants and for all noncitizen immigrants, legal or unauthorized, convicted of crimes.[18] The technical and legal nature of the law rendered it largely invisible to the public eye, but among legal experts it was seen as a radical change, leading some to talk about the criminalization of the U.S. immigration system (see, e.g., *Emory Law Journal* 2002). The trend toward criminalization gained further steam following the terrorist attacks of September 11, 2001, providing a decade-long precedent for the further criminalization of migration proposed under H.R. 4437, the immediate catalyst for the spring 2006 immigration rights protests.

As was the case in California, there is evidence that the federal attack on noncitizens' social and legal rights resulted in increased naturalization and the development of a new generation of immigrant rights activists across the country. Fix, Passel, and Sucher (2003) estimate that after a precipitous drop in immigrant naturalization levels from 64 percent of those eligible in 1970 to 39 percent in 1996, citizenship levels among legal immigrants rose to 49 percent by 2002.[19] The increase was likely fueled by noncitizens' fears over anti-immigrant legislation and facilitated by the greater attention to and funding for naturalization provided by nonprofit organizations and state governments after 1996. We also have piecemeal evidence that, as with the activists of the 1960s, some of the youth politicized by opposing anti-immigrant legislation in the 1990s went on to play a role in the mobilizations of 2006 (Oliver 2006; Wang and Winn, this volume).

Perhaps because of increased activism and growing political incorporation through naturalization, by the new millennium the pendulum on immigration reform seemed to swing away from restrictionism and toward an expansionary moment. For a while in 2000 and in the first eight months of 2001, large-scale immigration reform, including amnesty for the undocumented, appeared possible. The AFL-CIO made a 180-degree turn from its previous hostility to illegal workers to support legalization efforts and to encourage labor organizing among unauthorized workers. In a case of strange political bedfellows, a frequent phenomenon in immigration policy, the U.S. Chamber of Commerce also supported legalization. Newly elected as president, George W. Bush also signaled he was open to such an agenda, a position reinforced during state meetings with Mexican president Vicente Fox (Thompson 2001; Thompson and Greenhouse 2001).[20]

The political momentum behind legalization died on September 11 as abruptly as the thousands who lost their lives in the terrorist attacks. In the months and years following September 11, 2001, the legislative and executive branches drew additional boundaries between U.S. citizens and noncitizens. Noncitizens from specific countries were required to register with the federal government (Broder and Sachs 2002; Sachs 2003); foreigners were detained, without basic rights, at airports (Worth 2002); foreign-born residents were hauled in for questioning by American authorities with scant evidence of any link to foreign terrorists (Toner 2001). The distinction between citizens and noncitizens and between foreigners and the native-born—a distinction already evident in the 1990s—further hardened with the U.S.-led invasions and military operations in Afghanistan and Iraq.

Yet even as immigration reform stalled, the process of demographic change continued. Following a short hiatus immediately after the 2001 terrorist attacks, migration resumed. By 2006, foreign-born residents from all corners of the globe made up 12.5 percent of the U.S. population, accounting for 37.5 million people (Migration Policy Institute 2007a). Some of these immigrants live in the United States without authorization (about 29 percent in 2004), while legal foreign-born residents hold diverse statuses—each with different laws and regulations governing them—including naturalized citizen (32 percent), legal permanent resident (29 percent), refugee or asylee (7 percent), or temporary visa holder (3 percent) (van Hook, Bean, and Passel 2005).

The Latino proportion of this immigration is substantial. Forty-seven percent of immigrants reported being Latino or Hispanic in 2006 (Migration Policy Institute 2007a). Latinos are even more heavily represented among the unauthorized population. Demographers calculate that 57 percent of undocumented migrants were born in Mexico and that 24 percent come from Central and South America, suggesting that four of every five unauthorized migrants are Latino (van Hook, Bean, and Passel 2005; Passel 2005). At the same time, these estimates suggest that over 2 million illegal migrants are *not* Latino, hailing instead from Asia (9 percent of the total), Europe and Canada (6 percent), and Africa (4 percent).

While Latinos make up a significant proportion of all U.S. immigrants, immigrants make up a smaller proportion of the U.S. Latino population. In 2006, the Latino population was estimated to number 44.3 million people, almost 15 percent of the entire U.S. population, a proportion bigger than the non-Hispanic black population in the United States (Pew Hispanic Center 2008). Of this Latino population, those born outside the United States constituted 40 percent, or 17.7 million individuals. By far the largest contingent, 64 percent, was Mexican-origin, but Latino immigrants hail from twenty countries and speak not only Spanish but also dozens of indigenous languages.

The upshot of these statistics is threefold: not all immigrants are Latino, not all Latinos are immigrants, and not all Latino immigrants are undocumented. The U.S. immigrant population is diverse in its origins and its legal statuses, as is the Latino population in the United States. Diversity can serve as a barrier to political action—not all Latinos and not all immigrants necessarily have common interests—and it can impede solidarity under a common identity, be it as "Latino," "immigrant," or something else.

Although all immigrants, regardless of birthplace, are arguably affected in some way by anti-immigrant legislation, the 2006 immigrant rights protests generally did not reflect the full diversity of American immigration. Some activists and protesters were of European, African, or Asian origin, but the vast majority of participants were Latino, and the protests themselves were perceived as a Latino (or even Mexican) issue by much of the mainstream media and even by the ethnic press. Even in Chicago, where the protests appeared to draw a more diverse crowd than elsewhere, 76 percent of the marchers were Latino (Flores-González et al. 2006). A possible consequence of the 2006 marches, argued by Roberto Suro in this volume, is that Latinos of all immigrant generations feel increasing solidarity with each other due to the racialization of Latinos and the overwhelming association in the minds of many between undocumented migration and those of Latino origin.[21]

UNDERSTANDING THE MOBILIZATION PROCESS: WHAT EXISTING LITERATURES DO AND DO NOT EXPLAIN

On the eve of the first protests in February 2006, no one—from seasoned political observers to grassroots activists—predicted the magnitude or rapid spread of the immigration protests. This failure suggests that while existing social science frameworks offer some useful explanatory starting points—notably around the concepts of mobilizing structures, frames and identities—they must also be refashioned, especially to account for the participation of large numbers of noncitizens and to disentangle the meaning and implications of new narratives of membership outside formal, legal citizenship.

We focus on two sets of literatures. One literature, on political behavior, studies engagement in the formal political system, such as voting, campaigning, legislative agenda setting, and the like. A second literature, on social movements, views the formal political system as closed to new claims by less powerful actors, necessitating "contentious" or protest activity to effect political and social change. Much of the research on immigrants' political activities in the United States has taken

the political behavior approach, while that in Europe tends toward a social movement lens.

Why the difference? Historically, many immigrants in the United States accessed citizenship at relatively high rates, and the children of immigrants were
automatically U.S. citizens under the Fourteenth Amendment.[22] In theory, the
door to formal politics stood ajar to immigrants and their descendents. Many
European countries, in contrast, have had more restrictive naturalization regulations, which, in some cases, also applied to the children and grandchildren of
immigrants (Odmalm 2005). Faced with high barriers to citizenship and limited
opportunities for formal political participation, European scholars have viewed
migrants' mobilization as contentious politics (Koopmans and Statham 2001;
Koopmans et al. 2005).

We suggest that U.S. scholarship may need to take a "European" turn. Currently, three out of ten migrants in the United States have no chance at citizenship
due to their unauthorized status, and half of those legally able to naturalize have
not acquired U.S. citizenship. A social movements approach centered on political
"outsiders" is an important path for future theorizing, either in conjunction with
or parallel to the established behavioral approach.

What Do We Learn from a Political Behavior Approach?

Much of the political science literature seeks to explain the conditions under
which *individuals* make a decision to participate. It is a useful beginning, if only
to showcase how exceptional the protests were. This vast literature can be simpli-
fied into three key precepts: individuals act when they are properly *motivated* to
do so; individuals act when they have the *means* to do so; and individuals act
when they are *mobilized* to do so by political and nonpolitical actors and institutions. None of these three factors, taken in isolation, is a necessary and sufficient
condition to participation; but, in the view of political scientists, taken together
they explain whether and when political participation occurs.

Prior to 2006, the literature on Latino political participation, or on immigrant
political incorporation, painted a portrait of relatively low engagement in civic
affairs, formal politics, and contentious politics. Using the sort of mainstream
political activities that political scientists regularly monitor, such as voting, writing to an elected official, and contributing to political causes, immigrants of all
backgrounds and Latinos of all generations tend to participate less than native-
born non-Hispanic whites (Citrin and Highton 2002; DeSipio 1996b; Ramakrishnan 2005). However, much of the participation gap stems from lack of citizenship,
a younger age profile, and socioeconomic distinctions. For example, controlling
for Latinos' age, citizenship, level of schooling, and income, the participation gap
with native-born whites largely disappears. The same applies to contentious
activity—attending a rally or participating in a protest—though it is less clear

that demographic and socioeconomic controls completely erase the gap between Latinos and whites (Martinez 2005; Ramakrishnan 2005).[23]

The three foundation stones of behavioral political science—motivation, means, and mobilization—do a poor job of explaining the extent and timing of Latinos' *collective* response to H.R. 4437. When it comes to motivation, political scientists tend to use the language of instrumental reasoning, the careful weighing of probable benefits and potential costs. Yet instrumental reasons rarely account for risky behavior like protest participation. One person's involvement will only make, at best, a minute contribution to the demonstration; a single demonstration will typically make, at best, a minute contribution to the legislative debate on an issue like immigration reform. Given the typical costs of taking time off work, finding transportation to the rally, and the like, each individual is better off not participating: costs outweigh expected benefits. This logic holds especially true for undocumented immigrants, who face the far greater costs of exposure and deportation.

An alternative motivation, namely "solidarity" and "purposive incentives," only partially solves the problem. We can certainly tell a story about the camaraderie benefits of being among 100,000 marchers or the intrinsic benefit of feeling empowered during the protests. In the chapter by Irene Bloemraad and Christine Trost in this volume, they quote an undocumented Latina participant who explained, "I felt a great emotion when the mass of people met. . . . They clapped and I felt a great emotion, very nice, because as they were coming over, we were all united." It is unlikely, however, that this woman anticipated her emotional reaction in advance. Solidarity and purposive motivations help us to understand why someone may have taken part in the protests after the fact, but they are a poor predictor or explanation of why protests did not occur earlier, before 2006, or in the years following.

Instead of in motivation, perhaps the answer lies in means. Over several decades, political scientists emphasize the relationship between socioeconomic resources and political participation; study after study demonstrates that individuals with higher income, education, and status are most likely to be politically active (Verba and Nie 1972; Nie, Junn, and Stehlik-Barry 1996; Ramakrishnan 2005). This disproportionate representation of the highly educated and middle class is even true for contentious politics like riots, as studies of the U.S. urban rebellions of the 1960s have shown (Sears and McConahay 1973). A "means" story would predict that 2006 protesters were disproportionately well off. Yet the terms of H.R. 4437 largely affected less well-to-do immigrants in the United States, and news reports and the survey of the Chicago protestors done by Amalia Pallares and Nilda Flores-González in this volume paint a portrait of crowds of many individuals of modest means and education. Officials who spoke at the rallies may have been elites, but those that marched came from many walks of life.

Socioeconomic status is not the only kind of resource that matters. Political scientists distinguish between three kinds of resources—time, money, and civic skills—the latter typically defined as having civic knowledge, cognitive talents, expertise, and being embedded in participatory social networks (Verba, Schlozman, and Brady 1995). Researchers also often write of "group-based" resources—those resources accruing from group-based interests, identities, and institutions—most notably those related to race, ethnicity, and gender (Shingles 1981; Bobo and Gilliam 1990; Tate 1993; Leighley and Vedlitz 1999; Jones-Correa and Leal 2001; Burns, Schlozman, and Verba 2001; Stokes 2003; Ramakrishnan 2005; J. Wong 2006).

Civic skills and group-based resources are a promising lead in understanding the immigrant rights mobilizations, as evidenced by many chapters in this volume. The idea of civic skills highlights the role of institutions like churches, labor unions, ethnic media, community-based organizations, and other voluntary associations in developing participatory habits and abilities. The idea of group-based resources underscores the power of collective interests and identities—as immigrants, undocumented residents, Americans, Chicanos, Latinos, and so on. Still, from the perspective of a political commentator in 2005, the roles of civic skills and identities were not self-evident. For example, data from a special battery of questions on volunteering in 2002 found that Latinos, and especially Latino immigrants, are less likely to report formal participation in civic organizations than Asian-origin, white, or black residents (Ramakrishnan and Viramontes 2006, 4).

Finally, beyond means and motivation, political engagement also depends on whether you are asked. One study that examined the steep decline in U.S. voter turnout from the 1950s to the 1980s attributed more than 50 percent of the drop-off to declining personalized mobilization by political parties (Rosenstone and Hansen 1993).[24] Political parties have been glaringly absent as institutional loci of immigrants' political incorporation (Jones-Correa 1998; Ramírez 2002; J. Wong 2006), and there may well be incentives for parties not to appeal to the interests of immigrant communities (Fraga and Leal 2004; Kim 2007). If the agents of mobilization are extended to include nonpartisan civic organizations and ethnic media, we have a more plausible explanation. Ignored (or attacked) by formal political actors, we better understand why civil society groups encouraged immigrants and their supporter to take to the streets.

In sum, our accounting of the usefulness of the political behavior framework is mixed. The effectiveness of motivation, means, and mobilization explanations depends on how coarse or fine-grained a view we take. When the three are construed narrowly as material incentives, monetary resources, and partisan mobilization, the immigration protests are unfathomable. When they are construed capaciously—as solidarity and purposive benefits, resources based on civic skills, group interests and identities, and mobilization and recruitment by nonpartisan, immigrant and ethnic-specific institutions—we come closer to some compelling reasons for why a groundswell of immigrants took to the streets in 2006. Scholars working within the political behavior approach are unable to explain the timing, size, and demobilization of the protests.

Social Movements Literature: Contestation and Being an Outsider

If political behavior research is largely about "normal" politics, the premise underlying social movement scholarship is that people have grievances not addressed through formal, regularized channels of participation and representation, necessitating contentious protest. Grievances alone, however, are widely viewed as a very blunt instrument when it comes to explaining whether and when social movements happen: grievances are ubiquitous, but protests are rare. In the case of immigrants, for example, the criminalization of migration accelerated in the 1990s, but grievances only erupted into mass protest in 2006.

If political behavior research can be reduced to a triumvirate, the parallel threesome for scholars of social movements consists of mobilizing structures, political opportunity structures, and framing processes (McAdam, McCarthy, and Zald 1996). Formulated originally to explain the American civil rights movement (McAdam 1999), this conceptual tool kit has been used to elucidate other movements in various historical periods and national contexts, from the women's suffrage movement in Switzerland and the United States to peasant movements in Guatemala and El Salvador (e.g., Banaszak 1996; Brockett 2005). Each factor provides some purchase on the 2006 protests.

Mobilizing Structures. Overlapping political scientists' focus on civic associations and their role in mobilization and skill development, social movement scholars recognize the importance of "mobilizing structures." Grievances are translated into collective action, social movement scholars argue, when they are channeled through movement organizations and networks.[25] We similarly believe, and many of our chapters argue, that mobilizing structures provided critical scaffolding for the 2006 immigrant rights rallies. To illustrate the importance of mobilizing structures, we list some of the key types of organizations behind the 2006 protests. In doing so, we highlight some of the contributions from the chapters in the rest of this volume.

The constellation of mobilizing structures in 2006 appears a bit different from many prior social movements. In the case of the immigration protests, as Wang and Winn make clear in their chapter, no set of *national* organizations played a central leadership role, although Ricardo Ramírez hints that the syndication of some Latino radio shows served a quasinational coordinating role. Traditional Latino civil rights groups with national offices, such as the Mexican American

Legal Defense and Education Fund (MALDEF) and LULAC, were curiously absent in the initial months of spring 2006, although they later became involved in legislative lobbying around comprehensive immigration reform in the Senate. The lack of national centralization, especially in the field of immigration reform, is puzzling. Only the U.S. Congress—rather than state or local governments—has the power to pass laws pertaining to immigration. Even courts are wary about interceding in immigration issues, citing congressional "plenary power" to determine rules of entry and residence.[26]

Yet the empirical cases presented in this book, which include the cities of Los Angeles, Chicago, Denver, and Richmond, California, clearly document the leadership role played by *local* groups that came together in varying coalitions (and, sometimes, competitions) to organize the protests. In Chicago, where the first major demonstration took place on March 10, 2006, fifteen or twenty local Latino leaders, representing hometown associations, a local service employees union (SEIU), and an AIDS education community group, rallied to join a local Spanish-language DJ to bring out 100,000 marchers in three short weeks (Fornek 2006; Vargas 2007). In Denver, where the first of three major demonstrations took place two weeks later, the March 25 rally was coordinated by a handful of local groups, including two local immigrant rights groups, the local office of the American Friends Service Committee, a local SEIU union, and the Colorado Catholic Conference (Martinez, this volume). In Las Vegas, walkouts by middle and high school students on Cesar Chavez Day (March 28, 2006) prompted the involvement of several local organizations, including hometown associations, the Culinary Union, and church groups (Vargas 2007), ultimately bringing 63,000 protestors into the streets on May 1, 2006. In some cases, the local orientation of the groups flowed directly from service missions that are naturally centered on specific geographical communities, but in other cases groups were parts of larger networks that, nonetheless, saw leadership primarily at the local rather than national level.

Accounts of the marches almost always note that the high turnouts surprised the local organizers. Their unexpected size and the influence of the Spanish-language media have led some analysts to argue that the demonstrations were a "spontaneous" upsurge rather than organized protest (Vargas 2007; Hing and Johnson 2006). In a similar vein, early scholars of the civil rights movement saw the wave of sit-ins that swept through the South in 1960 as spontaneous. Conventional wisdom at the time claimed that college students in different cities engaged in sit-ins because they were emulating the actions of students elsewhere, rather than because of any coordination by national movement organizations like the Southern Christian Leadership Conference (SCLC) or the NAACP (Killian 1984; Oberschall 1989). Recent work by Andrews and Biggs (2006), however, shows that the sit-ins spread rapidly to places where newspapers provided information about events elsewhere and where there were core groups of *local* activists who were able to quickly take advantage of publicity without having to wait for approval from national leaders. A similar combination of media coverage and local organization seems to have fueled the rapid spread of immigration protests in the spring of 2006. In doing so, in line with the analysis by Andrews and Biggs, local activists might have been able to capitalize on the sense of being part of something bigger—feeding off others' successes and strategies—without being constrained by dictates from some large, central organization. Unlike in the 1960s, local activists' ability to coordinate and pull off widespread demonstrations also depended, in part, on new technologies. Faxes, text messaging, e-mail, websites, and blogs allow rapid diffusion of information and loose network coordination, as stories of "spontaneous" school walkouts fed by text messaging and cell phones suggest.

It is doubtful, however, that technology alone drove far-flung participation; mobilization usually requires some personal contact. Shaw, in this volume, suggests that the Immigrant Worker Freedom Rides of 2003 fed rapid, localized mobilization. Organized by two progressive labor unions, UNITE HERE and the SEIU, and sponsored by the AFL-CIO, the Immigrant Worker Freedom Rides were named after the 1961 Freedom Rides in which young black and white activists rode buses into the Deep South to challenge segregation in public transportation.[27] The 2003 rides largely escaped public notice, but Shaw claims that a key aim, and outcome, was to boost relationships among labor unions, community-based organizations, and religious, student, and immigrant-rights groups in the ninety-three cities and towns where the buses stopped.

Shaw may be right. Figure 1.2 maps out the cities where the Immigration Freedom Rides stopped and overlays this route with the cities where protests occurred in 2006. Nearly two-thirds (62.4 percent) of the cities where the buses stopped in 2003 had protests in the spring of 2006, supporting the claim that the Immigration Freedom Rides helped build the coalitional infrastructure that served as a backbone of the 2006 protests.

If no single national organization drove the 2006 protests, what *types* of local organizations facilitated the spread of information—about legislative proposals and the protests—and provided sources of leadership, resources, and centers of coordination? The Spanish-language ethnic media clearly played a critical role (Wang and Winn, Ramírez, both in this volume). Ethnic media publicized events, raised awareness about H.R. 4437, and conveyed information about protests across the country. As Hondagneu-Sotelo and Salas put it, "radio shows expanded from purely commercial entertainment venues to constituting nothing less than a big democratic town hall meeting on immigration reform" (2008, 222). A survey of participants in the huge May 1 rally in Chicago found that just over half heard about the march on television and radio (Flores-González et al. 2006, 3).

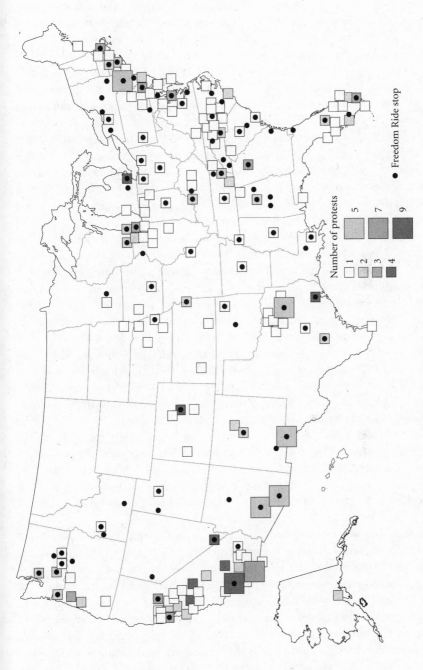

FIGURE 1.2. Freedom Ride stops in 2003 and immigration protests in 2006.

Wang and Winn single out key DJs on Spanish-language radio stations for generating massive turnouts in Chicago and Los Angeles, where their shows originated, but also for mobilizing Spanish-speaking communities across the country in their national broadcasts.

Unions, especially local SEIU and UNITE-HERE affiliates, were key actors in many cities. The groundwork for the union role was laid in the late 1980s when the SEIU created the Justice for Janitors campaign, which brought immigrant janitors into the Los Angeles labor movement and began to change organized labor's attitude toward immigrants (Fantasia and Voss 2004; Milkman 2006).[28] Building on the success of the Justice for Janitors campaign, a number of union activists, especially in California, began to push the AFL-CIO to change its historical opposition to amnesty for unauthorized immigrants and its reluctance to organize immigrants (Hamlin 2008). This campaign came to fruition in 2000 when the AFL-CIO reversed its anti-immigrant stance.

The Catholic Church also played a critical leadership role in some cities. The Church's importance lies, not only in its highly developed organizational infrastructure and the regular contact it has with Catholic parishioners, but also in its ability to invest protest with religious overtones, legitimizing engagement and imbuing it with symbolic meaning. As Luisa Heredia argues in her chapter, the Catholic Church in Los Angeles interwove religious references to holy days in its activities—as when Cardinal Roger Mahony vowed civil disobedience of H.R. 4437 on Ash Wednesday—and the Church used ritual to draw congregants into its activities for immigrant rights. While the use of religious narrative and ritual as a part of social protest also characterized the civil rights movement (Morris 1984; Garrow 2004), the United Farm Workers' movement (Ganz 2000), and the 1980s sanctuary movement (Chinchilla, Hamilton, and Loucky 2009; Coutin 1993), Heredia hints that the twenty-first-century activities of those within the Los Angeles diocese represent a two-decades shift away from a national, legislative orientation to more local contentious engagement.[29] If accurate, this move further highlights the puzzle of increasingly localized contestation around immigration despite a political system where authority for immigration legislation lies with U.S. Congress.

These big three—ethnic media, unions, and the Catholic Church—were joined by a host of smaller community-based organizations in cities and localities across the United States. Long-standing civic rights organization and new immigrant rights organizations were joined by nonprofit social service providers and legal assistance clinics that have sprung up in many cities to offer legal assistance with immigration, deportation and naturalization, translation services, bilingual health outreach, and a gamut of other services for groups that lack the language skills or legal status to access mainstream agencies (Cordero-Guzman 2005; de Graauw 2008). While their tax status as nonpartisan and nonpolitical 501(c)(3) organizations sometimes makes social service agencies reluctant to get involved in politics, the perceived legislative attacks on immigrants from 1996 to 2006 spurred partnerships with civil rights and immigrant rights organizations, as described in the chapters by Wang and Winn, Martinez, and Heredia.[30]

The contributors to this volume also underscore the work done by another set of institutions, not often analyzed in social movement scholarship: families and schools. Pallares and Flores-González draw attention to how discourses around the family—especially the wrenching effects of deporting undocumented parents who have American-born children—galvanized many in Chicago. The discourse on family not only applied to those who rallied for their own extended family members, but it was stretched to talk about the Latino community in familial terms, drawing links between those who have lived in the United States for generations and those who entered recently, becoming a call to civic responsibility and core U.S. values. Such appeals have resonance across the political spectrum, from political conservatives' talk of "family values" to the use of family frames by anti-Reagan activists during the sanctuary movement in the 1980s. Families also provided sites where different generations could talk about the protests and encourage each other to participate. As Bloemraad and Trost show in their chapter, parents used their experiences to make the immigrant rights rallies salient to their children, but children also encouraged parents to participate by bringing back information and excitement from schools and youth networks.

Schools, in particular, mobilized young people in many cities, from Los Angeles and the cities of the San Francisco Bay area to Las Vegas, Denver, and Chicago. Perhaps a quarter of those who walked in 2006, upward of a million marchers, were children and teenagers. It is unclear whether knowledge of the 1960s "blowouts" served as inspiration for the teenagers of 2006, or whether certain teachers in these schools had themselves participated in school-based protests in the 1960s or 1980s, but walkouts by students clearly swelled the numbers of protesters in spring 2006.

One additional mobilizing organization—hometown associations—also requires mention. Hometown associations (HTAs) are small organizations formed by immigrants to raise money for public works and other projects in members' communities of origin as well as to organize social events for those in the United States. Some worry that HTAs reinforce immigrants' ties to their homeland, undercutting engagement in the United States, but there is increasing evidence that HTAs build leadership, skills, and solidarity useful in the American context (Itzigsohn 2000; Viramontes 2008). In 2006, some HTAs provided key support for the marches, especially in Los Angeles and Chicago. As Jonathan Fox and Xóchitl Bada argue in this volume, HTAs are part of a larger binational migrant civil society, building migrants' capacity for self-representation. One could see this transnational activity and its influence on U.S. social movements as a new chapter in the binational activism some argue undergirded the Central American peace and solidarity movement (Perla 2008).

Political Opportunity Structures.   Mobilizing institutions clearly matter, but social movement scholars also emphasize the role of political opportunity structures. The essential insight here is that social movement politics are tied to the ebb and flow of regular institutional politics. Eisinger (1973), who first coined the term *structure of political opportunities,* did so to explain why some American cities experienced riots about race and poverty in the late 1960s and others did not. He found that cities with extensive channels for conventional political participation had no riots, nor did cities that repressed or effectively discouraged dissent. Instead, cities in the middle of the spectrum—between repression and formal access—experienced the most riots.

Scholars have built on Eisinger's work to show that social movements tend to emerge in periods when political opportunities are shifting and especially when they expand, as might happen when divisions develop among elites or when a government's capacity for repression decreases (Tilly 1978; McAdam 1999; Tarrow 1998; Meyer 2004). Most research over the past two decades has emphasized the precipitating effects of political openings and has discounted the triggering effects of political closings.[31] Recently, however, analysts have begun to challenge that consensus by noting that threats and periods of contracting opportunities sometimes spur collective action (Goldstone and Tilly 2001; Tilly and Tarrow 2007).

In the case of the 2006 protests, threat undoubtedly played a larger role than political openings: H.R. 4437 endangered the livelihoods of millions of undocumented immigrants, creating felons out of them as well as anyone who provided them with assistance. Moreover, in 2006, Republicans controlled the White House and Congress, arguably contributing to a feeling of political exclusion and a perception of limited legislative or lobbying options. The sense of political exclusion appeared even more dramatic juxtaposed with the hopefulness that many supporters of immigration reform felt just a few years before, in 2000 and early 2001, when George W. Bush met with Vicente Fox and the AFL-CIO reversed its long-standing opposition to amnesty. By 2006, the sense of threat was palpable, strengthened by the hard reality that undocumented immigrants targeted by H.R. 4437 were unable to vote.

Yet, as tempting as it might be to attribute protest activity simply to the threat of H.R. 4437, this explanation is insufficient if we consider that the same threatening shift in political opportunity structure might have opened the door to other kinds of protests in the early years of the second Bush administration—for example, antiwar, Social Security, environmental politics—yet mass protest did not materialize. Nor did it occur when the welfare system was overhauled in

1996. Reading across the existing analyses of 2006, in this volume and else-where, we believe that theoretical advances will require a more nuanced account of how threat and perceptions of threat play into the activities of mobilizing institutions.

For example, nuanced analysis of threat dynamics might help explain the disjuncture between federal policy and local activism. The "closed" arena of federal immigration politics, juxtaposed with the increasing spread of immigration across cities and towns throughout the United States, might help explain why immigration politics—either liberal or restrictive—are increasingly local. Some cities, from Oakland, California, to Takoma Park, Maryland, have formally proclaimed that they and their police forces refuse to work with immigration authorities to identify undocumented migrants. Other localities, epitomized by legislation and litigation involving Hazelton, Pennsylvania, have vowed to fight undocumented migration by enacting ordinances directed against unauthorized residents.

The particular threat embodied in H.R. 4437 might also have fostered stronger partnerships between immigrants and sympathetic allies than prior legislation. The proposed Sensenbrenner legislation not only targeted the undocumented but also all those who assisted them. The broad threat of this legislation likely propelled some Americans working behind the scenes for migrants' rights to trade backroom politics for the glare of television lights.

Finally, it is worth noting an interesting paradox highlighted by two chapters in this volume. Street-level protests are frequently taken as an indicator that "regular politics" is not working or that people are alienated from the political system. In such contexts, the threat of violence and mass disruption is, according to one social movement approach of long pedigree, the fundamental weapon of the weak and marginalized (Piven and Cloward 1978). Yet Roberto Suro's chapter recalls the peacefulness of the demonstrations and the absence of any palpable anger among the marchers. According to Suro, this reveals an enduring optimism among Latinos about the potential of American society to reverse discrimination and processes of racialization, an argument echoed in the chapter by Francisco Pedraza, Gary Segura, and Shaun Bowler. Pedraza and colleagues contend that participation in the marches reflects Latinos' *faith* in the U.S. political system rather than their disillusionment.

Framing/Identity.   The third linchpin of social movement explanations is the process of framing and storytelling that transforms grievances into "collective action frames." These entail the verbalization of unjust conditions, the development of a sense that things can be changed, the identification of a collective actor to pursue change, and the call for change in the public arena.[32] Identity and framing processes cannot be taken as given in the study of contentious politics around immigration (Koopmans et al. 2005). As we underscored earlier, multiple collective identities exist among immigrants and Latinos, shaped by the varying self-definitions that immigrants bring to the United States and by the national identity of the majority population. Identities need to be salient to those characterized as a group, and they must be recognized and acknowledged by those outside the group in order to carry political weight. In the case of immigration politics, both parts of this dynamic are in flux.[33]

As a group identity, *immigrant* has had relatively limited saliency, *Latino* somewhat more, but the latter is still hotly contested. As Lee (2008) points out, analysts cannot assume that individuals who share a demographic label, be it Latino, Asian American, or Arab American, share an identification with the label, share common political goals, or have an interest in acting together to pursue them. Activists influenced by the Chicano movement in the late 1960s were especially opposed to a pan-ethnic "Latino" identity until recently (J. Rodriguez 1998). On policy toward the undocumented, D. Gutiérrez (1995) documents widespread disagreement among Mexican Americans, historically and into the 1990s. A range of studies reveal deep divisions based on country of origin and cultural traditions in defining "Latinos," much less giving content to a unifying pan-Latino identity (Padilla 1985; Lopez and Espiritu 1990; L. K. Somers 1991; Calderon 1992; Portes and Macleod 1996).

In this context, an important question is whether the protests in 2006 were possible because they *built on* an already growing sense of common fate and solidarity among participants, or if instead they *created* a new sense of shared identity and collective interest. Suro, in his chapter, draws on public opinion polls to argue that the marches grew out of an emergent sense of common identity and ethnic solidarity first discernable in 2002 and 2004. Growing Latino unity, Suro suggests, built on a "broad and growing perception" that Latino advancement was being thwarted by discrimination.[34] The sense of discrimination, Suro argues, increases every time immigration restrictions are debated. Placed in a longer historical context, this implies that policies like California's Proposition 187 and the Illegal Immigration Reform and Immigrant Responsibility Act of 1996, although targeted at noncitizens, are read by a growing number of native-born and citizen Latinos as part of a racialization process, generating a sense of common fate that contributed to mass participation in 2006.

In the chapter on the Chicago protests, Pallares and Flores-González also argue that the immigration policies of the mid-1990s created a shared sense of injustice, but they emphasize the specific effects of deportations and family separations triggered by these policies. Support for family unity emerged as a new collective action frame and as a common referent connecting undocumented immigrants, legal immigrants, and the wider Latino community. For protestors who had at least one undocumented family member, the family unity frame packed an obvious emotional punch. But it also motivated those who had no undocumented kin, as the notion of "family" was redefined to include "my people." Pallares and Flores-González show, moreover, that this frame evolved into a critique of U.S. democracy for not valuing all families equally.

As the discussion by Pallares and Flores-González hints, the critique of U.S. democracy hinges on the appeal to a presupposed universal American value of family. This highlights the second part of any equation around identity work and framing: not only do identities and frames need to make sense to participants and sympathizers, they also need to resonate with opponents and the uncommitted. To the extent that politics is fought in part in the court of public opinion, frames and identities must have saliency and find purchase in the minds of those outside the movement.

One conclusion we draw from the 2006 protests is that more successful framing strategies appealed to bedrock American values: family and work. Appeals to America's experience with immigration, to immigrants' home-country pride or, even to human rights stood out as too "foreign"; such discourses found little purchase and often significant mainstream opposition.

The dance of collective action framing comes out most starkly in Martinez's chapter on Denver. Martinez reports that the frame of family reunification as an American value was evident in the Colorado protests. As one activist told her, "We're reclaiming the American flag . . . you can't say this is un-American because we're saying family reunification is about American values." Yet Martinez suggests that the link between flag and family emerged in Colorado partly in reaction to hostility from anti-immigrant activists. In the first major demonstration in Denver, on March 25, protesters framed their actions in terms of a common immigrant experience: they, like earlier generations of Americans, were hardworking people who had come to the United States for a better way of life. But because protesters carried Mexican flags as well as American flags, and they clutched signs written in Spanish as well as English, anti-immigrant activists were able to foment a backlash against the marchers, painting them as "lawbreaking criminals unwilling to assimilate." Portrayed as anti-American, organizers scrambled to reframe their claims to appeal to American values.

Martinez's chapter highlights the ways in which the development of political claims is an interactive process. Between the first protests in March 2006 and the final ones in May, it became clear that homeland pride had little legitimacy in mainstream American public discourse. Worse, it made the protesters easy targets in the framing war as disloyal and foreign, inherently *anti*-American. Protest organizers got the message. After the March protests, a sea of American flags drowned out Mexican flags, not only in Colorado but across the nation.

The flag and framing wars reveal the complexities faced by those who protest in the name of noncitizens. The civil rights movement highlighted how African

Americans (and Chicanos, Asian Americans, and American Indians) held "second-class" citizenship in their country. Demands for political change and calls for action rested on the appeal of full citizenship: to live up to the country's democratic values and the promise of the American dream, all *Americans* had to be given the chance and tools to access that dream.

The situation of noncitizen immigrants, and especially the unauthorized, is fundamentally different. The counternarrative, employed by those opposed to the immigrant rights movement, equates the act of being in the United States without proper documentation with un-Americanism: the unauthorized are breaking the law, not waiting their turn in the immigration queue, and, consequently, they prove themselves unfit for membership and citizenship. Appeals to inclusion are, prima facie, illegitimate because these people are illegitimate (Vargas 2007). Immigrants and their allies understand this counternarrative, as reflected in the many signs brandished by protesters that proclaimed, "We are not criminals."

Another narrative that fluttered on banners and was broadcast on loudspeakers centered on the economic contributions of immigrants. Such a frame sidesteps legal citizenship by underscoring another type of membership: as workers and consumers in the American economy. Highlighting the economic contribution of immigrants became a key tactic of some activists and led to debates and divisions over the advisability of calling on immigrants to engage in walkouts and boycotts. Those supporting economic frames appealed to a deep, historical theme of U.S. citizenship: membership occurs through one's ability to work. As Shklar has argued (1991), earning and controlling one's labor is not just about social rights but also about social standing, a source of public respect throughout American history. Highlighting immigrants' economic contributions shifted migrants' membership claims away from formal legal status, but it also fed into long-standing cultural and political notions of being a "good" American.[35]

Conceptually, the idea of "discursive opportunity structures" is helpful in thinking through these dynamics. Discursive opportunities influence which collective identities and substantive demands have a higher likelihood of gaining visibility in the media, resonating with other actors, and achieving legitimacy in public discourse (Koopmans et al. 2005, 19). At this juncture, frames and identities rooted in work, family, and minority racialization appear to have some saliency in the American context, and they represent framing strategies or identity work that seek to displace notions of illegitimacy, foreignness, or being an "alien," both legally and socially. Ominously, from the perspective of immigrant rights activists, all three approaches are rooted in and rely on a discursive opportunity structure that celebrates a particular notion of being or acting "American." This makes it easy for those opposed to unauthorized (or even legal) immigrants to label them as "others": noncitizens and non-Americans who have no rights.

How might immigration advocates circumvent the centrality of Americanism as a discursive template? The most expansive alternative would be a call for human rights or human security: citizenship becomes secondary as humanity provides a common bond and the basis on which to give rights. Pushed further, one could argue, in line with Carens (1987), that no one chooses their country of birth, so why not allow people to equalize their life chances by giving them access to stable, richer societies? Research in Europe and Japan purports to find that appeals to human rights offer powerful discursive and legal strategies to advance immigrant rights (Bauböck 1994; Gurowitz 1999; Soysal 1994; but see Koopmans et al. 2005). In the United States, Sassen (2006) has argued that a human rights frame might be the best way to understand claims making in the 2006 marches. At this juncture, however, despite banners sporting slogans like "No human being is illegal," the available evidence suggests that human rights discourses failed to resonate with the American public and did little to advance a political project around comprehensive immigration reform.[36]

In sum, drawing on political behavior and social movement scholarship, three key findings and concepts stand out to help make sense of the 2006 immigrant rights protests. First, local civil society groups such as unions, churches, ethnic media, advocacy organizations, and even schools and transnational hometown associations laid the groundwork undergirding the protests. We now need to better understand coalition building and the preconditions for a supportive, pro-immigrant groundwork in some places compared to others. Second, perceptions of threat and a closed political opportunity structure served to mobilize people in spring 2006. We need, however, further work on how perceptions of threat mobilized vulnerable populations without destroying all hope that political action could resolve perceived problems. Third, immigration politics cannot be understood outside the discursive contestation over identities and frames, which takes place within its own opportunity structure. We need further analyses of how identities and frames facilitated the 2006 protests and, perhaps more importantly, how they became recrafted during the movement. Did such reconstructions have any long-term effects, for example, by providing a starting point for identity appeals and collective action frames in subsequent years? It is to these consequences that we now turn.

REPRESSION, COUNTERMOBILIZATION, AND THE CONSEQUENCES OF 2006

The social movements literature is often more about origins than the subsequent development and fate of movement activism; much of our discussion thus far follows that trend. We have focused on finding conceptual tools to explain why, despite many anti-immigrant legislative actions from the 1980s through the

1990s, massive protest activity occurred in 2006, and how it was possible for this to occur. With the distance of time, however, another central puzzle for academics and activists is to understand the consequences of 2006. Why has so little mass mobilization for immigrant rights taken place since 2006? What effect did the protests have on politics and elections in the ensuing years? Here it is useful to distinguish between the response of civil society actors and the response of government and legislators.

Social movement scholars who examine interaction dynamics behind the rise and decline of protest point especially to the consequences of repression and countermobilization (e.g., Andrews 2004; Davenport, Johnston, and Mueller 2005; Meyer and Staggenborg 1996; Voss 1996; Zald and Useem 1987). As we have already noted, those opposed to amnesty and in favor of strong border control portrayed undocumented immigrants as lawbreakers and un-American. Yet while those opposed to the immigration protests often had their views reflected in the media, the number of counterdemonstrations was sparse and poorly attended. This was true even in Denver, which, as Martinez notes in her chapter, has the distinction of being "ground zero" for the anti-immigrant movement.

We also find little evidence that the protests had a strong effect on overall public opinion—in support or in opposition—during the spring of 2006. There is some evidence of sympathy for protestors: a Democracy Corps poll first conducted in late April 2006, then again in late May, found a slight increase in the number of respondents reporting that the marches made them "more sympathetic" to the plight of immigrants, 62 percent by the second survey. Yet public opinion also appeared to turn more restrictive on border control. Two *Time* magazine polls show a modest move toward more restrictive views, from 74 percent of respondents agreeing that the United States was not "doing enough to secure borders" in January 2006 to 82 percent in a late March poll. Following a similar line of questioning, a Fox News/Opinion Dynamics poll reported in April that 55 percent of Americans favored the use of the U.S. military to secure the border, a proportion that increased slightly by early June 2006 to 63 percent support. Ordinary Americans, at first blush, were not sure what to make of the sea of white shirts across the United States, neither reacting viscerally against the protestors, nor embracing their cause.

However, a broad sketch of the nation's reaction obscures significant local variations. There is some evidence that, in towns and areas where local residents had not given immigration much thought, the protests generated, in the medium term, increased hostility as residents suddenly became aware of significant numbers of migrants in their midst. For example, in Nebraska, the protests helped lay the groundwork for a nascent network of Latino civic organizations, but they also spurred the creation or expansion of anti-immigrant groups (Benjamin-Alvarado, DeSipio, and Montoya 2009). Such dynamics bring to mind the literature on "group threat" or "group position," which argues that when previously subordinate minority populations begin to challenge the status quo, majority members react to the perceived threat against their status position with increased prejudice and political hostility (e.g., Bobo and Tuan 2006). Such local responses are clearly an area for future research.

The consequences of the 2006 protests must also be understood in the reaction of government and legislators. In the short term, protestors won an important victory: H.R. 4437 failed, and those in Congress who favored increased border security took the criminalization of undocumented migrants off the table. During the rallies themselves, local police and federal immigration enforcement officers did not attempt to verify the immigration status of marchers, nor did they take immediate retaliatory action against marchers by engaging in mass deportations or preventing the rallies, a situation strikingly different from Southern police response to civil rights marchers in the 1950s and 1960s.

Yet, in the medium term, from summer 2006 to the end of the Bush presidency in January 2009, one can discern a pattern of blocked legislative progress and stepped-up immigration enforcement, which have acted to repress further organizing. In Congress, groups pushing for more restrictive immigration policies have successfully opposed any sort of amnesty; efforts to pass comprehensive immigration reform failed in 2007, just as they did in 2006 (see DeSipio, this volume). Immigration and Customs Enforcement (ICE) raids increased significantly in the wake of the protests, at workplaces, residences, and even in front of schools. Official figures show a sharp increase in deportations in both 2007 and 2008. In 2008, 358,866 individuals were expelled from the United States, over 100,000 more than the number of people removed in 2005, the year before the protests (Office of Immigration Statistics 2010, 4). Big raids on meatpacking plants in Iowa, Nebraska, and Wisconsin netted hundreds of undocumented workers, who were quickly deported. The raids also showcased a new enforcement strategy by ICE: for the first time federal officials used identity theft and forgery laws to charge undocumented immigrants with felonies.[37]

Such enforcement tactics have had a chilling effect on many would-be protestors, in part explaining the rapid demobilization of the movement following spring 2006. The lack of further protests also stems from the type of organizations that initially facilitated the protests. For some organizations, such as schools, churches, hometown associations, and ethnic media, protest activity is peripheral to their primary mission and thus they are poorly equipped to support a long-term social movement for immigrant rights. The organizations that were of a type that might sustain a movement, such as advocacy and immigrant rights organizations, tended to be smaller, with limited funding. While such organizations continue their activities into the present, the immigrant rights movement also has, like many other social movements, been divided by strong internal disagreements about tactics and goals, a conflict touched on in Heredia's chapter. An especially strong fissure, in 2006 and today, is between those national advocacy groups and some progressive unions willing to engage in a left-right compromise that might include enforcement provisions and local grassroots groups opposed to such trade-offs (Cho 2008).

Indeed, it is at the local level that political contestation around immigration has been most strongly felt in recent years. This can occur through local legislation or the activities of local anti-immigrant organizations like the Minutemen Project, which place ordinary citizens on the border to report undocumented border crossings. Meyer and Staggenborg (1996) point out that in federal political systems like in the United States, where power is divided between national and subnational governments, social movement conflict can be prolonged as movements and countermovements switch venues in their search for advantageous political opportunity structures. This has clearly happened in the conflict over immigration policy. Although Congress has plenary power over immigration policy, the political stalemate in Washington has pushed the struggle over policy to the state and local arenas. In the immediate aftermath of the protests of 2006 and the failure of H.R. 4437, no fewer than 1,059 pieces of immigration-related legislation were introduced in state legislatures, and 167 of those became law in 2007, more than double the number of immigration-related laws enacted in all of 2006 (Laglagaron et al. 2008). The battle in municipalities is even more intense as some communities have begun to compete to pass laws that will make them either like Hazelton, Pennsylvania, where the mayor brags that it is "one of the toughest places in the United States for illegal immigrants," or like Hightstown, New Jersey, with its pro-immigration sanctuary laws.[38]

From a social movement perspective, the rapid demobilization and poor showing at subsequent May 1 marches raises questions about whether we can talk about an immigration rights *movement,* a word that implies sustained activity and participation. But such doubts make sense only if we concentrate on street protests. Local political battles over immigration blur the boundaries between "regular" and "contentious" politics. Indeed, the battle over immigrant rights is also occurring at polling stations. Noncitizen immigrants cannot vote, but they can encourage their citizen family members, friends, and neighbors to cast ballots with immigration issues as a deciding factor, as can Latinos with no immigrant family members, if they equate anti-immigrant attacks with anti-Latino attacks. Strikingly, as Louis DeSipio enumerates in his chapter, politicians who ran on strong anti-immigrant platforms did poorly in the 2008 elections. Similarly, a significant proportion of the immigration-related bills introduced in state legislatures in 2007 sought to *expand* immigrants' rights and access to services (313 bills); such bills were passed at higher rates (19 percent) than bills that sought to contract immigrants' rights or that dealt with law enforcement (11 percent) (Laglagaron et al. 2008).

Can we take these electoral and legislative outcomes as evidence of Latino or immigrant power in the formal political system? Will contentious politics be abandoned as the formal political system accommodates new demands around immigrant rights? This conclusion is hinted at in the chapter by Pedraza, Segura, and Bowler, who document Latinos' faith in the U.S. political system. Indeed, exit poll data from the 2008 presidential election suggest a slight increase in Latino turnout, providing some support for protestors' claims that "Today we march, tomorrow we vote!"[39] In 2008, 9 percent of voters self-identified as Latino, an increase from 8.4 percent in 2004.[40] A 0.6 percent change may, in itself, seem small, but in raw numbers it represents an estimated 1.6 million new Latino voters in 2008.[41] The mobilization of Latino voters in 2008 is even more impressive in several key battleground states with large Hispanic populations. In New Mexico, for instance, Latinos were 32 percent of voters in 2004 and 41 percent in 2008. Similarly, in Colorado and Nevada, the proportion of that state's voters who were Latino jumped from 8 percent in 2004 to 13 percent in 2008 and from 10 percent in 2004 to 15 percent in 2008, respectively. The strong Republican showing in the 2010 midterm elections suggests, however, a new anti-immigrant turn among non-Latino voters and politicians.

There is also evidence that the Latino electorate is moving more strongly to the Democratic ticket and to a more uniform position on immigration issues. Such a shift could increase Latinos' voice by consolidating an "ethnic bloc," to which Democrats, in particular, would need to listen.[42] In 2004, roughly 53 percent of Latinos reported voting for the Democratic Party nominee John Kerry, while in 2008 exit polls reported that fully 67 percent of Latinos voted for Barack Obama.[43] Concerns about the war in Iraq and the economy clearly influenced Latino voters like many others, but immigration was also an issue. According to a Pew Hispanic Center poll conducted in the early summer of 2008, 75 percent of Latino registered voters viewed immigration as "extremely important" or "very important" to them personally.[44] The survey also showed that 59 percent thought Obama would do a better job on immigration; 19 percent favored McCain; 22 percent felt that "both would to the same job" or did not see a difference between the two. Of consequence to future elections, the shift in partisanship is again more pronounced in certain states. In Florida, where Obama's margin of victory was less than 200,000 votes, 57 percent of Latinos supported him, a marked change from 2004, when Kerry received only 44 percent of the Latino vote. Obama also enjoyed double-digit increases in shares of the Latino vote over Kerry in other battleground states like New Jersey, New Mexico, and Nevada (LULAC 2008; Lopez 2008). In the 2010 midterm elections, Latino voters in Nevada were credited with giving Senate Majority Leader Harry Reid the margin of victory in his tough-fought reelection campaign; according to exit polls, 90 percent of Latino voters chose Reid over his Republican opponent (Shaw, this volume).

Yet, despite evidence of increasing political voice among Latinos, immigrant advocates can, at best, harbor only cautious optimism. The final contributions to this volume speculate on the long-term impact of the 2006 demonstrations and what the protests might mean for electoral politics, the collective identity of Latinos in the United States, and the kind of mobilizing structures that were so important for coordinating the protests. DeSipio's assessment is that the demonstrations hardened attitudes and positions on all sides of the immigration issue, which will make the compromises necessary for comprehensive immigration reform more difficult, especially in light of the 2010 midterm elections. He suggests that legislative success rests on an energized and creative infrastructure of community-based organizations focused on immigrant incorporation and political engagement, underscoring the dynamic relationship between protest and old-fashioned politics.

In comparison, our final two contributors, Roberto Suro and Ruth Milkman, are more optimistic about the long-term impact of the protests, suggesting an alternative way of seeing the hardened attitudes and positions highlighted by DeSipio. According to Suro, Latinos' heightened sense of common fate, strengthened by the marches, will spur Latinos to become an energized voting block, with real electoral power. Milkman, focusing on the labor movement, draws parallels between the effects of the street protests against California's Proposition 187 in 1994. She argues that in 1994, the anti–Prop. 187 demonstrations spurred a wave of reactive naturalizations in California, which unions then mobilized to bring new voters into a progressive Latino-labor coalition that has reshaped California politics. According to Milkman, labor might well provide the infrastructure for immigrant incorporation and political engagement that DeSipio identifies as necessary.

Such a new progressive coalition would raise tricky questions about a key issue illuminated by the 2006 immigrant rights protests: the meaning of membership in a globalized world. Unions explicitly or implicitly link standing in society to work, which provides a wedge for those without legal residence to claim membership in the society that employs them and benefits from their labor. In making work a cornerstone of membership, however, certain equalities guaranteed by a focus on state-based citizenship are undermined. With citizenship, all citizens can claim equality in society and access to benefits regardless of their working status, a type of claims making that has been especially important for women.

If membership is not based on citizenship or work, what then? As we have argued, a cosmopolitan or human rights–based notion of membership and belonging gained little purchase in 2006, and, while civic binationality might exist in immigrant communities, it is not particularly well received by majority Americans. Given the tight link between citizenship and voting in the United States, there are few reasons to think a human rights view will expand American notions of membership to include all immigrants in the near or medium future. At the same time, if the immigrant rights movement does prove to be an ongoing movement, with the protests of 2006 merely an initial volley in a sustained contest over notions of membership and belonging, the conception of citizenship might well expand in future decades. Either way, the massive protests of 2006 will be looked back upon as a key moment in the development of immigration politics in the United States.

NOTES

1. These and other figures are drawn from accounts of the protests reported in local English-language newspapers across the country. We rely on two teams of researchers who combed newspaper stories on immigrant rights rallies: Wang and Winn (2006; see also their contribution to this volume) and Bada, Fox, Zazueta, and Ruiz (we use slightly revised calculations from their database, http://www.wilsoncenter.org/index.cfm?topic_id=5949&fuseaction opics.item&news_id=150685; see also Bada, Fox, and Selee 2006). Estimates are generally based on the minimum turnout reported and are subject to the biases inherent in relying on newspaper accounts of protest activity (McCarthy, McPhail, and Smith 1996; Earl et al. 2004). It is likely that in some cities, such as Los Angeles, individuals participated in numerous demonstrations; thus the same individual would be counted in successive protests. Double-counting inflates participant numbers, but relying on conservative, lower-bound estimates of turnout largely compensates for this.

2. We use the term *Latino* to talk about those from Spanish-speaking countries and their descendants, as well as those incorporated into the United States by American conquest of Mexican land. We recognize that some prefer *Chicano, Hispanic,* or *Hispanic American,* and that *Latino* obscures important distinctions between subgroups.

3. A few other marches in Washington DC likely equaled or surpassed the Chicago and Los Angeles immigrant rights rallies. For example, an estimated 750,000 to 1.15 million people attended a pro-choice March for Women's Lives on April 25, 2004, and over 800,000 probably participated in the Million Man March on October 16, 1995 (Barr and Williamson 2004). We use turnout numbers to illustrate the size of the 2006 protests. A careful analysis of protest turnout historically, however, requires standardization vis-à-vis the affected population or the population at the time.

4. It is difficult to gather accurate international data on demonstrations, but many consider the worldwide antiwar protests of February 15, 2003, to be among the largest in recent decades. The BBC reported between 6 and 10 million people marching worldwide, with between 750,000 to 2 million protesters in London and 650,000 to 3 million in Rome (BBC 2003).

5. A year later, on May 1, 2007, there was a violent confrontation between protesters and police at MacArthur Park in Los Angeles. Many observers reported that police used excessive force in trying to disband a pro–immigrant rights rally after about three dozen protesters began throwing objects at police. Dozens of people were hurt, including a number of media observers who helped bring attention to the event (Steinhauer and Preston 2007; Winton 2007).

6. In the few cases of documented noncitizen social movement activity, such as in transnational or international social movements (Tarrow 2005; J. Smith 2008), protesting "outsiders" largely live outside the context of protest, as when environmental activists in the global North help and express solidarity with indigenous peoples in the Amazon (Myers 1992; Keck and Sikkink 1998; Johnston

and Smith 2002). This is not the case for migrants: they live within the system against which they protest, but they do not have formal membership in that system. Removal from the country means separation from family, livelihood, and community in a way quite different from northern activists working in the global South.

7. See Holtz-Eakin (2005) for cost estimates, and for the full text of the bill see Sensenbrenner (2005).

8. In May 2008, Immigration and Customs Enforcement for the first time began charging undocumented workers with violating criminal laws against identity theft and document fraud for using false documents to obtain work. As the *New York Times* notes, this move signaled a sharp escalation of legal tactics against undocumented immigrants (Preston 2008c).

9. Journalists estimate that on May 1, 2007, only about 200,000 people rallied for immigrant rights across the United States, with by far the largest rally in Chicago (police estimated turnout at 150,000). On May 1, 2008, crowds were smaller still. For example, in Chicago, likely the biggest national event, 15,000 people participated. (See, e.g., Archibold 2007, 2008; Watanabe, Gorman, and Bloomekatz 2008; Olivo, Bauza, and Sadovi 2008.)

10. The United States acquired the remaining parts of what are today the states of Arizona and New Mexico under the Gadsden Purchase of 1853.http://www.indiana.edu/~jah/mexico/home.html.

11. As Nostrand (1975) notes, this is likely a conservative estimate, since it largely relies on the 1850 census enumeration, which probably missed some proportion of the population. It also does not include Indians and the few Spanish-speaking individuals in the region hailing from Peru, Chile, and elsewhere.

12. In a few instances, Chicano activists did join forces with Mexican immigrant activists around government efforts to identify and deport undocumented residents (see Flores 2003 for examples). However, as Flores suggests, tensions between Chicanos and Mexicans were more often the rule; the Chicano civil rights movements was focused primarily on achieving full social and political inclusion for Chicanos. (See also D. Gutiérrez 1995.)

13. This Western Hemisphere quota did not include the immediate relatives of U.S. citizens, who migrate outside the numerical limits of the annual ceiling.

14. There were two paths to legalization. I-687 was for those who had lived continuously in the United States since 1982 and could provide proof of their residence. I-700 (or SAW) was for agricultural laborers who had worked at least ninety days in 1985–86. About 1,760,000 individuals filed under I-687, 70 percent of whom were from Mexico, and about 1,270,000 applied under I-700, 82 percent of whom were Mexican (Martin 1994, 50).

15. For example, Martin (1994, 50) reports that just over half of all applicants for the 1986 IRCA legalization filed in California.

16. A third piece of legislation passed in 1996, often cited by legal experts for its detrimental effect on legal noncitizen permanent residents, was the Antiterrorism and Effective Death Penalty Act. It, combined with IIRIRA, substantially enlarged the government's ability to deport noncitizens, even longtime legal residents. Previously, a noncitizen convicted of a crime carrying a prison term of five years or more was deportable. After the 1996 law, noncitizens faced deportation for crimes that can carry a prison sentence of only a year or more, even if the defendant him or herself received a shorter sentence (D. Johnson 2001).

17. Fix and Passel (2002, 5) suggest that the focus on immigrants was not only a reflection of increasing anti-immigrant feelings, but was also because the noncitizen restrictions offered important financial savings for the government. A 1996 Congressional Budget Office report suggested that 40 percent of the Welfare Reform Act's overall savings, about $54 billion dollars, would come from immigrant restrictions, even though immigrants only made up 15 percent of all welfare recipients in 1996.

18. IIRIRA allowed immigration officials to summarily exclude and remove certain people at a U.S. port of entry without appeal or judicial review; made refugee and asylee claims more difficult; expanded the number of crimes that would lead to a migrant's removal from the United States; severely reduced noncitizens' ability to ask for a suspension of removal orders, for example, if the adult facing deportation has U.S. citizen children; made detention mandatory for those waiting removal; and severely limited judicial review of any decision or ruling related to migration (Yost 1997; Park 2008).

19. A 2007 report by the Office of Immigration Statistics of the Department of Homeland Security similarly finds that recent legal permanent residents (LPRs) are more likely to acquire U.S. citizenship within ten years of obtaining LPR status than earlier cohorts of migrants (Baker 2007).

20. For example, the founding director of Voces de la Frontera, a low-wage and immigrant workers' center with chapters in Representative Sensenbrenner's home state of Wisconsin, explicitly links her group's founding to the shift in the AFL-CIO's position as well as to the support for legalization by the U.S. Chamber of Commerce and the U.S. Catholic Conference of Bishops (Neumann-Ortiz 2008; see also "Essential Workers: Needed Workforce for the Future," www.uschamber.com/issues/immigration/essential-workers).

21. For more on the historical and contemporary tensions and commonalities between U.S.-born Mexican Americans and Mexican immigrants in the United States, see D. Gutiérrez (1995, 1999) and Jiménez (2008).

22. This divergence between U.S. and European scholars' approaches to immigrant political incorporation is also consistent with the emergence and dominance of the normative framework of pluralism and the empirical framework of behavioralism in American political science as a discipline between World War I and the mid-1950s, a "paradigm shift" less evident in European political science as a discipline (Farr 1995; Gunnell 1995).

23. Ramakrishnan (2005, 147) reports one exception to these trends of relatively lower Latino participation. Survey data collected by the Public Policy Institute of California in 2002 indicate that Latinos, from immigrants to those in the third and later generation, participate more than their Asian, white, and black coresidents when it comes to attending local meetings, perhaps reflecting relatively high levels of Latino participation in school meetings and PTA/PTO organizations.

24. The differential success of various approaches of direct and indirect mobilization and recruitment (door-to-door canvassing, mailers, phone calls, television ads) is at the heart of recent advances in research on mobilization (Barreto, DeFrancesco, and Merolla 2005; Gerber and Green 2000; Ramírez 2005, 2007).

25. In the American civil rights movement, black churches, the NAACP, CORE (Congress of Racial Equality), SCLC (Southern Christian Leadership Congress), and eventually SNCC (Student Nonviolent Coordinating Committee) mobilized blacks (and others) throughout the United States (Morris 1984; McAdam 1999).

26. For a good, succinct overview of the legal terrain undergirding the federal/local tug-of-war on immigration, see Romero (2008).

27. UNITE HERE is a union of hotel, restaurant, clothing, and laundry workers. In 2003 when the IWFR took place, the merger that created UNITE HERE had not yet happened, so the union was then known as HERE. We use the contemporary acronym.

28. Randy Shaw, in this volume, pushes the historical legacy of union activism back further, arguing that key participants in the boycotts and strikes of the United Farm Workers played central roles in the Justice for Janitors campaign, the crusade to get the AFL-CIO to reverse its policy on immigration, and in the 2006 protests in Los Angeles.

29. Non-Catholic religious groups played a role in some cities. For instance, Wang and Winn (this volume) note that the Dallas Area Interfaith Sponsoring Committee was a key member of the

coalition that brought out more than half a million demonstrators over the course of the spring protests in Dallas. It should be noted that although more than two-thirds of all Latinos are Catholic, 15 percent are born-again or evangelical Protestants, and nearly one in ten do not identify with any religion (Pew Forum on Religion and Public Life 2007).

30. Such social service and legal aid groups played a key role in helping millions of undocumented migrants legalize following IRCA in 1986 (Hagan and Baker 1993), and they facilitate naturalization and political incorporation generally (Bloemraad 2006).

31. Recently, scholars have begun to note that the concept OF WHAT itself has been so stretched that it is in danger of losing its coherence and analytical usefulness (see Meyer and Minkoff 2004; Meyer 2004).

32. The literature on "framing" within social movements is large and of distinguished pedigree. For an excellent review of this literature, by two of the central thinkers on the topic, see Benford and Snow (2000).

33. In comparison, the situation during the U.S. civil rights movement was quite different. One could reasonably argue that African Americans shared a "historically subordinate position within an on-going system of social stratification" and thus shared common political goals and an interest in acting in concert to pursue those goals (Morris and Braine 2001, 34). Explaining civil rights protests consequently centers on how the meaning of "blackness" was transformed in this period, not on the creation of brand-new communal identity ("cognitive liberation" in Doug McAdam's terms).

34. See also the arguments on increased Latino solidarity in Barreto et al. (2009).

35. Some activists inside and outside the immigrant rights movement worry that focusing on how immigrants take jobs "no Americans will take" also feeds invidious distinctions between "good" hardworking Latinos and "bad" lazy African Americans (Cacho 2008; Cho 2008).

36. Commenting on the White House proposal for comprehensive immigration reform, which included a significant guest-worker plan, Das Gupta notes, "The enormous appeal of the 'path to citizenship' embedded in President George W. Bush's guest-worker plan even among his usual detractors is symptomatic of the unquestioned legitimacy of citizenship that ties national belonging to rights" (2008, 406).

37. In May 2009, the Supreme Court, in a unanimous ruling, threw out an undocumented migrant's conviction for identity theft, placing into doubt ICE's ability to use this tactic against immigrants working without proper documentation.

38. Newspaper coverage of state and local immigration policies include Goodnough (2006), Faiola (2007), and Preston (2008a).

39. As we make clear above, not all Latinos are immigrants, and not all immigrants are Latino. Unfortunately, most exit polls do not ask voters whether they were born in another country, so the discussion here must rely on data for Latino voters.

40. Exit poll data are from Lopez (2008). These figures, based on national exit polls, often overestimate the share of the voting electorate that is Latino when compared to aggregated state-level exit polls or the November voter supplement of the 2008 Current Population Survey from the Census Bureau.

41. This 1.6 million figure is a rough calculation based on exit poll estimates of the proportion of voters who were Latino in 2004 and 2008, coupled with tabulations of the total number of voters in the two elections.

42. One could argue the opposite, that a divided Latino vote helps the Latino voice because it keeps the Latino vote "in play" between the two parties. At present, despite the tilt to Democrats, some Republicans continue to see courting the Latino vote as vital to their party's future, as witnessed in the internal dispute among Republicans over how the party should raise questions about Sonia Sotomayor's nomination to the Supreme Court.

43. Kerry's performance was a sharp decline from the 62 percent of Latinos who reportedly voted for Al Gore in 2000, leading to significant controversy among Latino organizations and scholars about the veracity of the 2004 exit poll data (e.g., Gimpel 2004; Fears 2004; Leal et al. 2005; Suro, Fry, and Passel 2005).

44. This is a very high proportion but not as high as education (93 percent), the cost of living (92 percent), jobs (91 percent), health care (90 percent), or crime (82 percent). The 75 percent figure equaled the importance placed on the Iraq War.

2
___

Groundswell Meets Groundwork

Building on the Mobilizations to Empower
Immigrant Communities

Ted Wang and Robert C. Winn

In the spring of 2006, millions of immigrants and their allies participated in hundreds of marches across the United States. The dramatic series of rallies brought a new dimension to the debate over reforming U.S. immigration policies, marking the entrance into the public eye of a large and vocal immigrant community claiming a right to be heard in the national dialogue over its fate. Despite some differences in strategy and approach, the mobilizations were held together by a sense of common purpose and were remarkable for their unity and dignity.

The themes and messages that spread through word of mouth, ethnic media, and advocates' outreach and organizing efforts had strong resonance for the larger immigrant community and helped fuel the momentum. The coordinated masses of white T-shirts, the heartfelt, multilingual slogans—"I am a worker, not a criminal," "Today we march, tomorrow we vote"—spoke to a deep reservoir of sentiment and potential capacity for action.

The scale, force, and spontaneity of the demonstrations surprised even longtime immigrant supporters, and organizers were often rushing to keep up with popular momentum. This groundswell, however, was also facilitated by the groundwork laid by advocates, community groups, and other organizations that have long worked together on issues affecting immigrants. Broad coalitions that had convened to support comprehensive immigration reform played important roles in mobilizing support for the demonstrations as well as coordinating and shaping public messages. In many regions, faith-based groups (particularly various Catholic Church archdioceses) and labor unions provided critical support. Hometown associations and other ethnic-specific organizations were also instrumental in reaching out to communities that typically had limited participation in the political arena.

The immediate aftermath disappointed many of the participants, to be sure. Although the mobilizations helped defeat legislation that would have turned unauthorized immigrants and their supporters into felons, their effect on the political climate was mixed. They did not prompt Congress to adopt comprehensive immigration reform, and immigrants have encountered backlash on many fronts. Harsh immigration enforcement measures at the national level have led to record numbers of immigrants arrested, detained, and deported. The failure of Congress to reform federal immigration policies led a number of state and local jurisdictions to adopt their own measures aimed at addressing unauthorized immigration.

Despite these challenges, the passion that was unleashed in these unprecedented demonstrations remains a potent force in shaping this country's future. While the following discussion is not an exhaustive history, it provides a glimpse of the dynamics and the constituencies involved in the events of 2006, and how they began laying the groundwork for future activities that could empower immigrants and strengthen the broader social justice movement. Our analysis is based on a review of news accounts of the mobilizations and interviews with over fifty individuals who helped organize these events across the country.[1]

H.R. 4437 SPARKS A GROUNDSWELL

The major catalyst for the groundswell was the U.S. House of Representatives' passage of H.R. 4437 in December 2005.[2] The bill's harsh provisions and enforcement-only approach to immigration reform touched a nerve and raised the stakes for a range of constituencies. Immigrants, both authorized and unauthorized, felt directly targeted by the legislation and the accompanying tide of anti-immigrant sentiment, prompting widespread indignation and a desire to rise up and claim their dignity. Many businesses, churches, social service agencies, and individuals, realizing their own potential liability under H.R. 4437's provisions that would criminalize assistance to unauthorized immigrants, also increased their participation in the debate over immigration reform.

In this environment, awareness of the perceived injustice of H.R. 4437 spread throughout immigrant communities. Ethnic media outlets—in print, on the radio and television, and online—were instrumental in informing immigrant communities of the issues at stake. Community-based and immigrant rights groups conducted public education campaigns about the implications of the bill. Public awareness of the draconian implications also grew when Los Angeles's Cardinal Roger Mahony became involved, for the first time asking the entire archdiocese to mobilize on a social issue. During a March 1, 2006 Ash Wednesday speech, he called for defiance of H.R. 4437 should it become law, stating that he would be willing to risk jail for his position and asking priests and faithful lay Catholics to do the same (Watanabe 2006).

Initially a number of communities held smaller local demonstrations following H.R. 4437's passage. However, the impetus for mass mobilizations gathered steam in early 2006 as local and national groups began to strategize a broader response. In one significant example, over five hundred Latino activists and academics from across the country met at the University of California, Riverside, on February 11 to consider a response to H.R. 4437. The event was convened by the National Alliance for Human Rights, an organization of Latino activists and academics founded by Armando Navarro, a UC Riverside ethnic studies professor with roots in the Chicano movement. Consensus was reached that mass action should be taken, and attendees from both Chicago and Los Angeles returned to their home cities and started working with coalitions that became the basis of the seminal mobilizations in those cities.

These efforts bore fruit in March as people drew together in a mass movement that steadily gained momentum. On March 7, a crowd of 20,000 to 40,000 (as estimated by officials and organizers, respectively) gathered in a Washington DC event organized by the National Capital Immigration Coalition, among other groups (Schwartzman 2006). On March 10, the rallying cry in Chicago was "El gigante despierta" (The giant wakes) as an estimated 100,000 to 300,000 marched through the streets in a record-breaking demonstration that put the rest of the country on notice (Newbart and Thomas 2006). Spontaneous student walkouts started across the nation, facilitated by MySpace.com and text messaging (Melber 2006).

Organizers of subsequent events across the country noted that each successful mobilization increased popular interest in the issue, and they often found themselves scrambling to respond in a very short time frame. For example, emboldened by the turnout in Washington and Chicago, Los Angeles geared up for its own Gran Marcha on March 25. Activists who had settled on the idea of a mass demonstration at the February 11 conference in Riverside, including Jesse Diaz and Javier Rodriguez, met with immigrant rights and community groups that were actively supporting comprehensive immigration reform and began organizing as the March 25th Coalition.

In addition to the efforts of activists and organizers, a crucial factor was the buy-in of Spanish-language DJs—most notably two nationally syndicated radio personalities, Renán Almendárez Coello ("El Cucuy") and Eduardo Sotelo ("El Piolín"). (El Piolín entered the United States in the trunk of a car in 1986 to become Los Angeles's highest-rated morning radio show host by 2006.) Immigrant supporters met with the DJs to provide them with background information and to lobby for their active involvement. After organizers convinced the DJs that this was an important moment, immigration reform and the upcoming rally were constant topics on their shows. They helped spread information about immigration reform, shared their own immigration histories, and drummed up support for the event, leading to a turnout on March 25 in Los Angeles estimated at 500,000 to 1 million (Watanabe and Becerra 2006a).

April saw efforts to continue the momentum as previously uninvolved community members and activists across the country added their voices to the chorus. The April rallies also reflected an effort to coordinate messaging, strategy, and support on a national scale as organizers at immigrant-supporting groups across the country—both national and local—conducted a flurry of conference calls and meetings that led to a National Day of Action in early April. Organizations such as the Center for Community Change's Fair Immigration Reform Movement (FIRM) and the Coalition for Comprehensive Immigration Reform arranged conference calls between national, regional, and local groups and created websites with scheduling details and logistical support. The main goal of the coordination was to increase the impact of the day's activity by having localities throughout the country present similar messages and goals. The "We are America" theme, for example, was encouraged through the umbrella organizations.

The resulting large and widespread demonstrations captured the nation's attention. Between 350,000 and 500,000 marched in Dallas's Mega Marcha on April 9, the largest civil rights march in the city's history (according to police estimates reported in *Dallas Morning News* 2006). The following day, organizers estimate that over 300,000 rallied in New York and hundreds of thousands more participated in over 170 events across the country. These mobilizations were remarkable not only for their scale but also their reach. South Carolina, with a relatively new immigrant population, drew unexpectedly large crowds (*The State* 2006); Schuyler, Nebraska, a town of 5,300, saw 3,000 people rallying for immigrant rights (*Columbus Telegram* 2006). The rallies also became more ethnically diverse as organizers reached out beyond the Latino communities and immigrant-supporting organizations to engage a broader range of allies.

As the number of individual and organizational participants grew, however, differences emerged in strategies and goals. The various groups involved brought a wide range of priorities and approaches to the table. The immediate concern faced by national groups was how the marches could influence the ongoing congressional debate on reforming U.S. immigration policies, with many hoping it would help persuade legislators to provide unauthorized immigrants with a path to legalized status. While this concern was shared by many grassroots groups, others prioritized the empowerment of immigrant communities over any legislative or policy goals. They viewed the marches as an important opportunity to broaden their base, engage new immigrant leaders, and highlight the economic and political power of their communities, with the goal of achieving more expansive reforms in the future.

Some of the challenges in building a broad coalition were evident in the planning of the May 1 rallies. These were also well attended around the nation, despite occasional strategic differences over whether immigrants and their supporters should participate in a one-day economic boycott, what supporters described as "A Day without an Immigrant." These differences included concerns about whether a boycott would create backlash against the movement generally as well as possible retaliation by employers against workers who chose not to work. In Los Angeles, for example, organizations and individuals in favor of a May 1 boycott and a more confrontational approach continued under the March 25th Coalition umbrella, including activists such as Javier Rodriguez, Jesse Rodriguez, and Nativo Lopez; they organized a midday rally on May 1. Established immigrant rights groups, most community-based organizations, the Los Angeles Archdiocese, service employees union SEIU Local 1877, UNITE HERE, and the Los Angeles County Federation of Labor formed the We Are America Coalition (a precursor to the national We Are America Alliance) to organize a late-afternoon march and rally timed to minimize conflict with participants' jobs. Many who attended the midday rally continued on to the second rally.

The May Day rallies represent the high-water mark of the mass mobilizations of 2006. Activists, organizers, and community members, having worked around the clock to organize and participate in these events, were exhausted by the effort and needed to tend to other responsibilities that had been placed on the back burner over the previous few months. In addition, debate began to grow within the immigrant rights movement over the most productive route to capitalize on the energy and attention raised by the mass mobilizations. Further efforts for additional mobilizations, for example, in September 2006, were not widely attended, as most organizers—and community members—focused on how to move beyond protesting H.R. 4437. The following sections discuss some of the factors behind the mass mobilizations as well as the challenges and opportunities moving forward.

WHY WERE THE MOBILIZATIONS SO BROAD?

A. *The people were ready.*   The unprecedented scale of the mobilizations took supporters, adversaries, and the mainstream public by surprise. A unique confluence of factors helped to create a movement that is still unfolding. To a large extent, the mobilizations were so well attended and spread so quickly across the country because the themes resonated deeply across generations within immigrant communities. There was a sense that the rallies were an organic and authentic expression of a long-suffering desire for respect, especially among Latinos. In a representative comment, one interviewee mentioned that it was not so much that the giant had been sleeping as it was that he had been busy working; now it was time for the giant to stand and speak. Participants and bystanders were swept up in the dramatic, peaceful, and celebratory tone of these demonstrations. Immigrant families were claiming their right to exist and be recognized. When asked about the factors underlying the tremendous turnout, Father Richard Estrada of La Placita Church in Los Angeles, an early meeting place of the March 25 planners, stated simply that "it was in the people's will already."

B. *Ethnic media played a pivotal role.*   Ethnic media closely followed the progress of immigration reform legislation and helped keep immigrant communities informed of the potential ramifications. As the mobilizations developed, Spanish-language media and several key DJs, in particular, were instrumental in raising awareness about the events. They publicized the rallies and, among other things, advised listeners to wear white shirts, downplay the Mexican flag in favor of the American flag, and present a dignified image to the rest of America. In Chicago, Rafael Pulido of WOJO-FM (nicknamed "El Pistolero") used his show to reach a large cross section of the Spanish-speaking community (Fornek 2006).[3] In Los Angeles, groups such as the Coalition for Humane Immigrant Rights of Los Angeles (CHIRLA) that had preexisting relationships with ethnic media helped engage the outlets as active participants. Two major Los Angeles–based radio personalities—Eddie Sotelo and Renán Almendárez Coello—challenged other radio hosts to join them in gathering support for the mobilizations. Because both Sotelo and Coello broadcast nationally, their messages regarding the March 25 march and subsequent events were also heard by a substantial portion of Spanish-speaking communities across the country.[4]

C. *Groundwork greased the wheels.*   While the organic nature of these events cannot be overstated, in many localities they were facilitated by the groundwork laid by advocates, community groups, and other organizations that have long worked together on issues affecting immigrants. In particular, organizations that had previously convened broad coalitions to support comprehensive immigration reform played important roles in mobilizing support for and shaping public messages generated by the public demonstrations. These groups included established immigrant rights coalitions in Chicago, New York City, San Jose, Boston, Southern California, and Maryland;[5] newer coalitions in Tennessee, Washington DC, Colorado, Washington State, South Carolina, Nebraska, Oregon, and other new immigration gateways;[6] and ethnic-based groups that organized rallies in numerous other localities.

These groups' existing relationships with immigrant communities and ethnic media, their familiarity with federal immigration issues, their experience working in coalitions, as well as their grassroots legitimacy, were all significant factors in the mobilization and planning of the 2006 events. Once they became aware of the groundswell, the core organizing groups worked around the clock to quickly call meetings, negotiate common positions, develop public messages, divide responsibilities for logistics and outreach, and call upon an extended network of organizations to bring more people out. Without much advance warning or preparation, representatives from these organizations were able to speak to both the mainstream press and to their grassroots constituents about the core issues of immigration reform in a way that resonated with large numbers of people. At the same time, these organizations were straining their capacity, driven by the urgency of the situation to capitalize on unfolding events.

In Los Angeles, for example, groups that had been working together in the Southern California Comprehensive Immigration Reform Workgroup— such as CHIRLA, the National Korean American Service and Education Consortium (NAKASEC), SEIU locals, the Korean Resource Center, the Central American Resource Center (CARECEN), and the Archdiocese Office of Justice and Peace—took the lead in coordinating the movement, especially after the initial March 25 demonstration. In New York City, the New York Immigration Coalition and other immigrant rights groups became the backbone for pulling together the April 10 mobilization and shaping the positive public messages conveyed at the rally. In less than two weeks, these groups in New York worked with unions and other allies to successfully organize the largest rally held during the National Day of Action.

Likewise, in Nebraska, an existing network of organizations participating in the Immigrant Rights Network of Iowa and Nebraska provided critical support for helping local immigrant groups to organize large-scale marches in several different cities.[7] In South Carolina, where the immigrant population and related organizations were still relatively new, groups such as Acercamiento Hispano (Hispanic Outreach) and the Coalition for New South Carolinians were able to draw upon relationships they had built up with community groups, service agencies, and churches to facilitate organizing for the April 10 mobilizations. In Dallas, the League of United Latin American Citizens (LULAC) took the lead in forming a coalition with the faith community (through the Dallas Area Interfaith Sponsoring Committee) to bring out more than half a million participants.

National coalitions and networks that linked many of these regional groups also played an important role in helping to turn what started as local rallies into nationally coordinated events. This was especially true of the April 10 and May 1 marches, in which a number of national networks provided coordination and communications resources. National groups and coalitions such as the Center for Community Change and FIRM, LULAC, the National Council of La Raza (NCLR), the National Immigration Forum, and the National Network for Immigrant and Refugee Rights arranged conference calls and helped coordinate logistical details and message framing. Websites were set up to disseminate information about times, meeting points, and organizers for events in major cities as well as small towns. Suggestions to wear white, to emphasize the U.S. flag, and to use slogans such as "We are America," spread through these organizations, helping to create a consistent image for the activities and thereby heighten their national impact.

D. The coalition broadened.   In addition to organizations that have typically focused on immigration issues, the mobilizations saw the increasing involvement of other stakeholders. In certain communities, faith institutions and leaders played major roles in organizing turnout and support for the mobilizations. The Catholic Church, in particular, provided critical support in a number of communities. The most visible example was in Los Angeles, where Cardinal Mahony's personal investment in the issue was a major factor in publicizing the harmful impact of H.R. 4437. The Church also played a significant role in mobilizing support in Chicago, Houston, Washington DC, and other metropolitan areas.

Hometown associations and other ethnic-specific organizations were also instrumental in bringing out crowds, both in established gateways and in regions that did not have immigrant rights organizations. These include groups such as Casa Michoacán in Chicago, which hosted early organizing meetings for the March 10 mobilization, Hermandad Mexicana chapters and other groups in Los Angeles, and groups such as Casa Guanajuato in Dallas. These associations typically focus on cultural and social activities, but they emerged as important players in mobilizing their communities during the marches.

Labor unions, especially in Los Angeles (SEIU Local 1877, UNITE/HERE, and the L.A. County Federation of Labor) and New York (SEIU Local 32BJ and SEIU Local 1199), also become increasingly involved in working directly with immigrant groups. Unions, with resources far greater than grassroots community organizations, were instrumental in providing key logistical and financial support as well as in bringing out the rank and file. In New York, for example, representatives from Change to Win (the labor federation formed in 2005) flew in from Washington DC to facilitate permit negotiations on an expedited basis. These unions also brought their organizing and mobilizing experience. Their involvement may also have been a factor in encouraging mainstream politicians to attend the immigrant rights rallies. At the national level, the SEIU played a central role in developing a new national coalition, the We Are America Alliance, to follow up on the mobilizations, with the goal of naturalizing and registering voters from immigrant communities and increasing their level of civic engagement.

In addition, efforts were made to engage communities and organizations beyond immigrants and their core supporters, including the African American community and social justice organizations that work on broader issues. This effort was based, in part, on the realization that a broader movement—focused on making America a better, more just place for everyone—would have greater appeal and a greater chance of success and could highlight the degree to which immigration and immigrants affect a wide range of issues.

BACKLASH

While the mass mobilizations were characterized by an unusually high degree of peacefulness, anti-immigrant forces used the images of the marches to galvanize their base and to advocate for more enforcement measures targeting unauthorized immigrants. Taking advantage of their access to conservative talk radio and cable television news shows, such as Lou Dobbs's nightly CNN show, restrictionist advocates launched multiple campaigns to convince the public and policy makers to turn against immigrants. While some of these efforts were thinly veiled attacks on Spanish-speaking communities (see, e.g., Center for New Community 2007), they were highly effective in persuading many elected officials in newer gateways to turn against immigrants because of perceived political gains or fear that constituents would be angered. For instance, many political observers believe that a key factor behind the Senate's failure to adopt comprehensive immigration legislation in 2007 was the unexpectedly strong efforts by restrictionist groups to oppose the bill. Many legislative offices found themselves inundated with anti-immigrant phone calls, e-mails, and faxes (Pear 2007).

Anti-immigrant groups did not limit their activities to the federal arena. They developed strategies to make immigrants' lives at the local level as miserable as possible, with the goal of having immigrants "self-deport." A leading restrictionist euphemistically described the policy as one involving "attrition, squeezing the illegal population through consistent, across-the-board law enforcement" (Krikorian 2004; see also *New York Times* 2007). Others were more explicit about their real goal. In a rally organized by the Federation for American Immigration Reform, anti-immigrant radio host Terry Anderson (n.d.) stated, "We've got to make it in this country so [unauthorized immigrants] can't exist here. . . . We've got to rattle their teeth and put their feet to the fire."

As part of this strategy, national restrictionist groups actively sought out state and local legislators to adopt anti-immigrant policies. They circulated "model" anti-immigrant laws designed to harass newcomers by requiring public agencies, private businesses, and landlords to check people's immigration status and to report such information to federal authorities (see, e.g., Immigration Law Reform Institute n.d.). They provided technical assistance to state and local legislators and offered to help municipalities defend their ordinances if challenged. Although courts have struck down many of these laws, immigrant leaders report that the growing anti-immigrant climate has had a devastating effect on their communities by directing distrust and hatred toward people perceived to be unauthorized. In some jurisdictions, large numbers of immigrants moved away following the passage of such laws, often resulting in harmful economic effects on the community that favored the anti-immigrant policies (see, e.g., Broder 2007, 15). In other places, policies that require government agencies to verify the immigration and citizen status of residents have resulted in numerous eligible citizens being turned away from government programs or being denied their right to vote (Broder 2007, 9). For example, following the passage of a state measure that required Arizona voters to first demonstrate their citizenship status, approximately five thousand eligible citizens were unable to register to vote (Diaz and Sherwood 2005).

Faced with criticism from anti-immigrant groups about its support of comprehensive immigration reform, the Bush administration stepped up its enforcement efforts significantly in late 2006. The Department of Homeland Security launched a new "interior immigration enforcement" initiative that included large-scale immigration raids targeting unauthorized immigrants who neither had criminal histories nor posed a danger to the public, and the agency increased criminal prosecution of immigration violations (see U.S. Immigration and Customs Enforcement 2006a). Though intended to appease the administration's immigration critics, the raids instead angered numerous state and local officials who criticized the administration's ineffective enforcement efforts for tearing apart families and for having devastating economic effects on local communities (see, e.g., Abraham 2007; Potter 2007; Rogers 2007; Bailey 2007; Boston Globe 2007).

For immigrant communities, the raids contributed to an already difficult situation. Many immigrants who were willing to step forward during the 2006 marches into the public arena have since retreated into the shadows for fear that they or their family members may be targeted for immigration enforcement actions. Latinos, in particular, have expressed pessimism about their situation in the United States in recent surveys. Nearly one in ten Latino adults—both native-born citizens as well as immigrants—reported in a 2008 study that within the past year the police or other authorities had stopped them and asked them about their immigration status. Worries about deportation as well as perceptions of discrimination in jobs and housing also color Latino perceptions of their status in the United States (Lopez and Minushkin 2008b).

IMPACT OF THE MARCHES ON POLICY MAKERS

The marches initially fostered great optimism among community members and immigrant supporters. "Today we march, tomorrow we vote," the slogan repeated throughout the demonstrations, framed the mobilizations as part of a political movement that promised to hold elected officials accountable to immigrant communities.

Many immigrant leaders and advocates shared this initial optimism. At the national level, discussions of immigration reform changed from an almost exclusive focus on enforcement to a growing realization by many legislators that comprehensive legislation must establish a path toward permanent residency and citizenship for unauthorized immigrants and future guest workers. The U.S. Senate ignored H.R. 4437 and adopted a comprehensive immigration reform bill, S. 2611, shortly after the initial marches.[8] While the Senate's legislation contained many worrisome enforcement provisions and restrictions, its passage illustrated the potential political power unleashed by the mobilizations.

This optimism, however, dissipated as comprehensive immigration reform failed to gain traction in a fiercely divided Congress. S. 2611 died after the House of Representatives refused to adopt similar legislation. In 2007, a comprehensive immigration reform bill developed by a bipartisan group of senators and the White House failed to secure the sixty votes needed to end debate and bring the bill for a vote before the entire Senate. Federal inaction, in the face of growing challenges, led a number of states and localities to enact their own policies in this area, including punitive laws aimed at deterring immigrants from settling in their communities.[9]

While the restrictionist forces initially had the upper hand immediately following the mobilizations, their ability to maintain these short-term gains is far from assured. Anti-immigrant forces have been largely unsuccessful in the electoral arena, their messages have not resonated with the broader public, and demographic and electoral trends are likely to undermine their restrictionist goals. For example, in the two years following the marches, a number of restrictionist candidates lost congressional and state legislative races to more moderate voices. In 2006, Representative J. D. Hayworth (R-AZ) and Arizona state legislator Randy Graf (a founder of the Minutemen) ran campaigns that had primarily anti-immigrant themes, and both lost. Likewise, two other prominent anti-immigrant legislators—Senator Rick Santorum (R-PA) and Representative John Hostettler (R-IN)—lost their reelection campaigns.[10] These losses have led even conservative political pundits to question the Republican Party's attempts to use immigration as a wedge issue, with some believing this strategy will eventually "destroy [the party's] future prospects in increasingly Hispanic, once-Republican states." (Kondracke 2007; see also *Wall Street Journal* 2007). Senator Mel Martinez of Florida noted that "the very divisive rhetoric of the immigration debate set a very bad tone for our brand as Republicans . . . there were voices within our party, frankly, which if they continue with that kind of rhetoric, anti-Hispanic rhetoric . . . we're going to be relegated to minority status" (Immigration Policy Center 2009).

THE EVOLVING LEGACY OF THE MASS
MOBILIZATIONS

The mass mobilizations of 2006 and the subsequent backlash highlight both the potential political force of newcomers and the distance they still must travel to become more influential in policy making. It would be a mistake, however, to assume that the energy of 2006 has simply dissipated. Rather, it has evolved. Many advocates have moved from the drama of mass mobilizations to the slow, hard, but necessary work of increasing immigrants' civic participation and alliance building to expand their base.

Whether the potential political power highlighted by the 2006 marches can be realized depends on how immigrant communities respond to their current challenging conditions. Interviews with a broad spectrum of immigrant leaders and advocates suggest that, in addition to responding to anti-immigrant proposals and attacks at the federal, state, and local levels, the period after the marches has seen a focus on building a movement through the following activities.

Naturalization.   Numerous organizations across the country have launched campaigns to help naturalize the approximately 9.4 million immigrants who are eligible for citizenship. The largest of these campaigns includes an innovative partnership between Spanish media giant Univision, the NALEO Educational Fund, NCLR, and other media and community-based organizations. Spanish-language television, radio, and newspaper outlets in eleven states actively promote citizenship and direct interested immigrants to organizations that provide assistance in their local region.[11] Data from the U.S. Bureau of Citizenship and Immigration Services indicate that such a program was highly effective in its initial region, doubling the number of citizenship applications in Southern California (Jordan 2007).[12] Nationwide, immigrants are applying for citizenship in record numbers. Citizenship applications in 2007 were up by more than 60 percent over the previous year and more than double those of 2005 (see, e.g., Ludden 2007; Gonzalez 2007; Quintero 2007). Political observers believe that many newcomers are motivated to naturalize because of the anti-immigrant climate. "A feeling has been created that maybe Hispanics are not welcome in this country," said pollster Sergio Bendixen, "and that the Hispanic culture is hurting the fiber of American society. And, of course, that has offended and insulted many Hispanics," motivating many to become citizens (Ludden 2007).

Voting.   Many groups that launched naturalization drives also are trying to turn the slogan of the mobilizations—"Today we march, tomorrow we vote"—into reality. During the 2006 election, immigrant groups launched large-scale voter campaigns in California, New York, Illinois, Tennessee, Washington State,

Arizona, and Nevada; many more participated in the 2008 presidential election. For example, the Univision/NALEO collaborative, mentioned above, focused its considerable media resources on registering and turning out new Latino voters. The We Are America Alliance, which emerged directly from the 2006 mobilizations, helped fund-raise, coordinated get-out-the-vote activities across thirteen states, and offered training and capacity-building assistance to organizations that mad a priority of increasing immigrant civic participation. These campaigns targeted not only immigrants but their children, family members, and others who share similar aspirations. A 2006 study highlights the potential political impact of mobilizing this constituency. There are approximately 14.25 million potential voters among (1) legal immigrants who are currently eligible to naturalize and (2) 16- to 24-year-old U.S.-born children of immigrants (Hoyt and Tsao 2006).

The results of the 2008 elections suggest that efforts to increase civic participation in immigrant communities are bearing fruit. Latinos, for example, voted in high numbers—the estimated turnout in 2008 was approximately 3 million more than the 7.6 million that voted in 2004 (America's Voice 2008). One in six Latino voters reported voting for the first time in a presidential election (NALEO 2008b). Of those who voted, 67 percent voted for Barack Obama and 31 percent for John McCain. The Latino shift toward the Democratic Party was particularly notable in Obama's victory in the battleground states of Colorado, Florida, New Mexico, and Nevada. Efrain Escobedo, director of civic engagement at the National Association of Latino Elected and Appointed Officials (NALEO), observed that "they really delivered. . . . This is an electorate that now understands the importance of voting, and they made a significant shift in the political landscape" (Preston 2008c).

Dispelling misinformation about immigrants.   Recognizing that many Americans have limited contact with newcomers and hold inaccurate beliefs about immigration and immigrants, newcomer groups are developing public education campaigns to dispel myths and stereotypes about newcomers, as well as to document their economic contributions to local communities. For example, the Tennessee Immigrant and Refugee Rights Coalition launched a Welcoming Tennessee Initiative in 2006, a public education campaign appealing to southern traditions of hospitality and building alliances with other communities. The success of the Tennessee campaign has led immigrant groups in other regions to develop a comprehensive nationally coordinated campaign called Welcoming America, with immigrant organizations leading the effort in the West, Midwest, Northeast, and the Southeast regions.

Leadership development and building alliances with other communities.   Another primary focus has been to develop the leadership within newcomer communities, including those who were drawn to the immigrant rights movement by the 2006 mobilizations. The Center for Community Change, for example, is collaborating with local organizations in five states to offer "democracy schools" to help newcomers learn about the U.S. political system, the broader historical and social context for immigrant rights, and to develop advocacy skills. At the local level, immigrant advocates are increasingly trying to work across racial lines with other disadvantaged communities to address shared concerns, such as creating better schools, high-paying jobs, or affordable health care for everyone. On immigrant issues, newcomers also have found allies in businesses, public health agencies, law enforcement officials, and others who have opposed anti-immigrant proposals at the state and local levels. By having newcomers work in coalition with other communities, these efforts help shift public thinking of immigration issues from "how to treat immigrants and what rights to give them, to defining the issue as how to reform immigration so that we build a stronger future for everybody" (Hong 2006).

Immigrant leaders and advocates view this set of activities as critical to recapturing the energy of the mobilizations and nurturing a nascent movement that has been under attack by anti-immigrant forces. They point to a number of factors that will help sustain their movement: the growing immigrant population across almost every region in the United States, the emergence of national coalitions to help coordinate advocacy, increased interest among immigrants in developing alliances with other communities, and the pressing need to develop more creative, proactive policies to help integrate newcomers so that they can fully contribute to U.S. communities.

Immigrant advocates acknowledge that their current work may not result in future large-scale mobilizations. But if done in a sustained and strategic manner, increased naturalization, voting, and civic engagement by newcomers may produce what the mobilizations ultimately did not accomplish—real reform of U.S. immigration laws and empowered communities that can hold lawmakers accountable for addressing the many challenges this country faces.

Grassroots immigrant-led groups, in particular, may provide touchstones to help maintain a clarity of vision and purpose as the movement goes forward. S. J. Jung of the Young Korean American Service and Education Center in New York offers an observation shared by many who took part in the marches: "By participating in this campaign, by going through this historic moment, I truly felt like I became a full member of this society. My participation in this rally was a declaration that I, as an immigrant, am ready to fully pursue responsibility while exercising my rights. Immigrants may emerge not only as a new political force, but as new guardians of justice in this society" (Jung 2006).

NOTES

The authors wish to thank the Four Freedoms Fund (FFF), which funded the research for this article. An earlier version was published by FFF and Grantmakers Concerned with Immigrant and Refugees in 2006 (Wang and Winn 2006). The authors are particularly grateful to Michele Lord, Taryn Higashi, Daranee Petsod, and Henry Der for providing comments on earlier versions of this article. They also wish to thank Naomi Abraham of FFF for developing a map of the mobilizations that is included here. The content of this article represents only the authors' views.

1. A list of people who were interviewed shortly after the initial marches can be found in Wang and Winn (2006).

2. The text and summary of HR 4437, primarily authored by Representative James Sensenbrenner (R-WI), is available at http://thomas.loc.gov. While the media's attention focused on the bill's attempt to criminalize undocumented immigrants and those who help these individuals, the bill contained a number of other harmful provisions, including those that would have dramatically increased passport and document fraud provisions, expanded mandatory detention to apply to more categories of immigrants, created new grounds of inadmissibility and deportability, and authorized state and local police agencies to enforce immigration laws.

3. Fornek (2006) quotes Emma Lozano, executive director of Pueblo Sin Fronteras, as stating that Pulido "was able to reach the factory worker in Waukegan and the person selling *elote . . .* on 18th Street and the woman who works as the cashier at the Dollar Store on 47th Street."

4. The significance of ethnic media is increasing. Univision, for example, is the fifth-largest network in the United States, and its primetime viewership among 18- to 34-year-olds has ranked as high as second overall, behind only Fox. Likewise, a 2005 survey by Bendixen and Associates and New America Media found that 51 million Americans, 24 percent of U.S. adults, are either primary or secondary consumers of ethnic media (Project for Excellence in Journalism 2006).

5. These immigrant rights coalitions included the Illinois Coalition for Immigrant and Refugee Rights, the New York Immigration Coalition, Services Immigrant Rights and Education Network (SIREN), Massachusetts Immigrant and Refugee Advocacy Coalition, Casa de Maryland, and the Coalition for Humane Immigrant Rights of Los Angeles and other groups working in the Southern California Comprehensive Immigration Reform Workgroup, as described later in the chapter.

6. The newer coalitions included the Tennessee Immigrant and Refugee Rights Coalition, the National Capital Immigrant Coalition, the Colorado Immigrant Rights Coalition, One America with Justice for All (in Washington State; formerly Hate Free Zone), Coalition for New South Carolinians, the Immigrant Rights Network of Iowa and Nebraska, and CAUSA in Oregon.

7. The existing network in Nebraska included Nebraska Appleseed, Omaha Together One Community, the Chicano Awareness Center in Omaha, and the Office of Latin and Latin American Studies at the University of Nebraska, Omaha.

8. In May 2006, the U.S. Senate passed by almost a two-third margin S. 2611, which would have offered a significant portion of the unauthorized population an opportunity to earn their way to legal status. Among other things, S. 2611 included a three-tiered legalization program available to unauthorized immigrants who had lived in the United States for (1) five or more years and (2) between two to five years, but these individuals would have had to first leave the country and receive a temporary work visa. Those here less than two years would have had to leave. See Title VI of S. 2611.

9. The National Conference of State Legislatures (2007) reported that more than 1,400 bills addressing immigrant and immigration issues were introduced in state legislatures in 2007. A significant number tried to help integrate immigrants by increasing their access to services or programs, but a majority were intended to restrict immigrants' access to jobs, economic opportunities or government programs.

10. In 2007, anti-immigrant candidates lost state elections in Virginia and New York State (Kondracke 2007).

11. More information can be found at the Ya Es Hora website, at http://www.yaeshora.info.

12. The number of applications for Southern California for the three months ending March 2007 was more than twice that for the same period in 2006.

Mobilization Dynamics

Why and How the Protests Happened

March 23 march, San Francisco, 2006. Photograph by David Bacon.

3

Mobilization *en Español*

Spanish-Language Radio and the Activation of Political Identities

Ricardo Ramírez

There is widespread agreement that Spanish–language radio played a key role in the massive turnout for the protests of spring 2006. As one producer of a popular Spanish radio show, *Piolín por la mañana*, noted at the time, "It's incredible, the people's response. Everywhere we go, they are talking about it, even at Disneyland. . . . We have been getting e-mails, telephone calls, faxes—everything" (Uranga 2006). Newspapers of the day also highlighted the phenomenon. On March 28, a headline on the front page of the *Los Angeles Times* proclaimed, "The Immigration Debate; How DJs Put 500,000 Marchers in Motion." Twenty-four hours later, the *San Francisco Chronicle* ran the headline, "Spanish-Language Radio Spread Word of L.A. Protest; Others Laid the Groundwork, but DJs Told the Masses." Moreover, researchers have backed up the claims of the newspapers and radio producers with systematic evidence. Analyzing a survey taken in the spring of 2006, Barreto and his coauthors (2009) show that Spanish-language TV and radio were significant agents for mobilizing support for the protests among Latinos across the country.

Perhaps because of the widespread agreement about the role of Spanish-language radio in the spring of 2006, some observers have similarly turned to the Spanish-language media when accounting for the significant drop-off in levels of participation since the 2006 protests. Gorman and Abdollah (2007) and Hernandez (2007), for example, in their analyses of reduced turnout in the May Day demonstrations of 2007, point to a seeming failure of disc jockeys to unite and mobilize their listening audience.

This chapter asks two important questions: First, what is unique about Spanish-language radio that allowed it to become a powerful resource for promoting political participation in 2006? Second, given its history of involvement leading up to 2006 and since, how does Spanish-language radio enable social and political incorporation by Latinos in the United States, and when is this capacity constrained?

In answering these questions, I challenge the conventional wisdom that non-English-language use inhibits political participation. Instead, I agree with Martin Johnson and his colleagues' controversial hypothesis that "choosing to speak a language other than English—in this case, Spanish—may represent an individual's access to social and community resources that enable, rather than impede, political participation" (2003, 413). I present a case study of Spanish-language radio since 1992 in Los Angeles that reveals a growing capacity to mobilize Latinos by appealing to and activating a common ethnic identity in response to external shocks or urgent needs of the community, including aiding those affected by natural disasters, spurring on the immigration protests, and supporting naturalization and voter registration drives. This same case study, however, also demonstrates that Spanish-language radio, as a mobilization resource, has limitations.

MEDIA AND POLITICAL BEHAVIOR

Scholars have long been interested in the effects of mass media on political behavior. Much of this literature focuses on public opinion and emphasizes either the priming or framing or the agenda-setting effects of mass media on political attitudes (Iyengar and Kinder 1987; Iyengar 1991; Zaller 1992, 1996; Mutz and Soss 1997; Peter 2004). There is also a great deal of attention paid to political participation, with conflicting views in this literature that can concisely be classified as either "media malaise" or "mobilization." The "media malaise" view argues that the proliferation of political cynicism and decline in turnout can be attributed to media use. The more media consumed, the less participation. In contrast, the "mobilization" view suggests that "media use contributes to political involvement, trust, efficacy, and mobilization" (Aarts and Semetko 2003, 760). This is consistent with social movement research that places radio at the center of participation in the southern textile worker insurgency of the late 1920s and early 1930s as well as in the civil rights movement of the 1960s (Roscigno and Danaher 2001; Ward 2004). Recent scholarship suggests that media has the power to both mobilize or depress participation, depending on media type, levels of exposure, and content (Prior 2007; Aarts and Semetko 2003; Newton 1999).

There are two significant oversights in this literature. First, the effect of media on political attitudes and behavior is overwhelmingly seen through the lens of mainstream mass media rather than alternative media (i.e., media outside of mainstream corporate control). Second, non-English-language mass media have been almost entirely overlooked by both political scientists and sociologists. These oversights are partly attributable to the fact that alternative media and non-English-language media affect only a subset of the population that either by choice or by necessity opt for something other than mainstream mass media. However, both forms of communication are growing in usage, as is evident in the rise of noncorporate online newsletters, newspapers, and Internet blogs as well as the increasing popularity of and demand for Spanish-language media in the biggest media markets in the United States. Thus, emerging studies of media and political behavior must incorporate these growing forms of communication if they are to remain relevant.

The most relevant literature for understanding immigrant rights mobilizations comes from analysis of the civil rights and labor movements. There is evidence that alternative media, mainly in the form of newsletters and newspapers, helped to mobilize supporters during the black and Chicano civil rights movements by providing relevant information and serving as facilitators of communication for civil rights leaders and organizations (Garland 1982; G. Rojas 1975). A recent study suggests that even mainstream radio stations were effectively used by labor during the southern textile strike campaigns of 1929 to 1934, when more than 400,000 workers throughout the South walked off their jobs. Roscigno and Danaher make the connection between radio and strike activity through a variety of sources to "show that the geographic proximity of radio stations to the 'textile belt' and the messages aired shaped workers' sense of collective experience and political opportunity: Walk-outs and strike spillover across mill towns resulted" (2001, 21). Radio was also used by African Americans during the 1960s civil rights movement to educate and inform both white and black radio listeners (Ward 2004). This literature is particularly well suited for an analysis of the role of Spanish-language radio.

In a very real sense, Spanish-language media have been the necessary alternative to mainstream English-language media for diffusion of information in the Latino community in the past decade. The immigration protests of 2006 were successful because Spanish-language radio transmitted information about when and where they were to take place. Community and national organizations provided some of the background information about H.R. 4437 as the impetus for action and also the necessary logistical support. However, it is not the case that Spanish radio stations were simply tools for information diffusion where national leaders and organizations could activate a captive audience. Unlike the civil rights movement, there are no national organizations or political leaders who command the type of consensus from the masses as was the case with Martin Luther King Jr. or more recently with Bill Clinton and Jesse Jackson. Without a national leader or even a national organization to frame a unified message or response, something else had to situate the issue and unify the response of millions of people throughout the United States. Through their syndicated morning shows, disc jockeys Eduardo "El Piolín" Sotelo and Renán Almendárez Coello "El Cucuy" were instrumental in activating a collective Latino identity, which spurred listeners to become engaged, either by participating in the immigration protest marches directly or supporting them in some other way.[1] The use of Spanish in this medium presents one significant alternative to the mainstream mass media, and one very important cultural process that induced "individual participation in collective action to ensure social solidarity, even in the face of harsh countermobilization" (Roscigno and Danaher 2001, 24).

However, it is one thing to examine the effects of alternative media, including non-English media, when they take the form of newsletters or community newspapers that help disseminate information and mobilize the audience at a localized level. It is wholly another proposition to consider what happens when the medium must inherently address the mass public, such as in radio or television. This is the case in mass Spanish-language media markets, such as in Los Angeles. Mass media open up opportunities for mass mobilization but also give rise to challenges. For example, increased ability to reach a wider audience necessitates a greater focus on raising money to cover increased costs. Organizations and social movements have to figure out how to deal with the trade-off between political effectiveness that could result from mass-produced and disseminated media and the increased costs associated with such mass-scale production and distribution.

This is a valid concern. In order to sustain expanded capacity, mass media must seek capital, often through commercialization to secure financial support, which then has the potential to deviate from grassroots origins or the desire to represent the community. As Hamilton notes, alternative media are faced with a dilemma where, "on one hand, they seek to become influential and powerful to help bring about changes to the current commercial media system and the society that supports it; yet, efforts to do so mean adopting the same large-scale, capital intensive, technologized means typical of mainstream media, which limits popular participation" (2000, 358).

Mass Spanish-language radio works within the same mass-culture perspective of mainstream mass media and therefore faces the dilemma of seeking mass distribution while maintaining a sense of commitment to the community. Thus, while Spanish-language radio stations may "seek to challenge the status quo, therefore appreciating rather than fearing the ability of mass media to organize popular social movements, they too often view their role more or less explicitly as one of educating and mobilizing the 'masses' in the service of the cause or movement" (Hamilton 2000, 359).

Some mainstream media accounts portrayed Spanish-language radio disc jockeys as leaders in the immigration protests. Yet the reality was less clear-cut. The disc jockeys complemented the efforts of grassroots organizations by framing the response to a perceived threat and mobilizing participation through the emphasis on collective identity, solidarity, and political opportunities. The radio hosts helped educate and mobilize the masses while organizations and other community leaders provided the requisite leadership and organizational capacity to carry out a mass-scale protest.[2] National survey data from the summer of 2006 reveal that media and this sense of solidarity were crucial, not only for participation in the protest marches, but also for support for them among those who could not attend (Barreto et al. 2009).

RADIO AS A MOBILIZATION RESOURCE

The role that Spanish-language radio disc jockeys played during the fight against H.R. 4437 was often characterized by mainstream media as new or unique. However, Ward (2004) makes the case that radio was also essential for mobilizing support for the civil rights movement. "By helping to publicize the goals and methods of the early movement beyond Dixie, radio contributed to a national process of legitimization that by 1965 had persuaded even some southern stations to allow pro–civil rights programming" (Ward 2004, 124). Moreover, the African American community in urban centers has a history of utilizing black radio for community mobilization and ensuring a strong link between black radio and the community (P. Johnson 2004; Squires 2000; Barlow 1998). There is, for instance, one account about Jack Gibson, a leading black disc jockey, who shared the microphone with Martin Luther King Jr. to rally listeners to attend meetings and become involved in the civil rights movement (Barlow 1998). Black radio served as a means to disseminate information and encourage a host of civic activities, ranging from attending meetings to taking part in voter registration drives. Again, it should be noted that disc jockeys in black radio stations facilitated the diffusion of information, but it was largely national leaders such as Martin Luther King Jr. who provided the rationale for the call to action.

The resulting effect on the listening audience would not have been possible if disc jockeys on black radio were unable to create an intimate relationship with their audience. Unlike the alternative media literature that questions the ability of mass media to avoid the pressures to corporatize and become disconnected from the community, black radio maintained a level of connection with the community through identity that is not readily available to other mass media. Squires argues black radio is an example of how "commercial media can play a positive role in forming and sustaining serious discourse within a subaltern public sphere, especially through a small market or niche format" (2000, 84).

More directly relevant to the case in Los Angeles, Phylis Johnson (2004) delineates the role of black radio in Los Angeles, especially in times of crisis. Her account of KJLH, a black-owned radio station in Los Angeles, suggests that it played a pivotal civic activist role in the aftermath of civil unrest that followed the May

1992 "not guilty" verdict of the police officers charged with the Rodney King beating.

Through its service to the community, KJLH-FM countered some of the negative images strewn across television. More important, the radio station became the focal point for discussion and implementation of nonviolent solutions to the social ills of southern Los Angeles and to the larger African American community across the nation. KJLH-FM's social and political identity, subsequently, was not merely established via on-air dialogue but also through the civic participation it inspired from its staff and community. The station's political activism appears as an important component of its larger community role both before and after the 1992 events. KJLH-FM listeners' interest and willingness to participate in rallies and voter registration drives became unifying forces within the Black community during 1992. KJLH-FM fostered a shared identity among its listeners as they called to voice their outrage with the Rodney King verdict. (P. Johnson 2004, 354)

Johnson and others make it clear, however, that 1992 was not the origin of this phenomenon. Rather, there is a history of such involvement in the preceding decades, including during the civil rights movement. This includes community-service efforts to raise money during the 1950s and 1960s, as a unifying force immediately after the assassination of Martin Luther King Jr., and through participation in voter registration campaigns that led to the election of black mayors for the first time in several cities, including Harold Washington in Chicago in 1983 and Willie W. Herenton in Memphis in 1991. Even as recently as October 27, 2000, there was an on-air one-hour conference call by Bill Clinton and Jesse Jackson to forty members of the National Association of Black-Owned Broadcasters to ask the listening audience to mobilize the black vote on election day. Others have noted that ethnic media have historically served a similar role for immigrants and ethnic communities: "For immigrant communities, these media . . . are often used as a means of mobilizing support or opposition. They also serve as a focal point for the development of a local consensus, and a means of expression of the community's demands upon the wider host community" (Gandy 2000, 3).

The role that Spanish-language radio played in Los Angeles in reaction to H.R. 4437 and anti-immigrant rhetoric is strikingly similar to the role that black radio has played, as well as reminiscent of the role of ethnic media among other immigrant communities, including Italian, German, and French (Gandy 2000). Tempting as it may be to see the decline in the number of protest participants and the diminished role of Spanish-language radio in the 2007 protests as a "return to normalcy," I argue that the swell of participation by protest participants and disc jockeys, and the noticeable drop in their participation, can be better explained by paying closer attention to the growth and evolution of Spanish-language radio in Los Angeles since the early 1990s. An overview of the contemporary development of Spanish-language radio in Southern California reveals various indicators of the potential role of this communication resource in the mobilization of immigrants, albeit ones that have gone largely unnoticed by political scientists and sociologists.

SPANISH-LANGUAGE RADIO, IDENTITY, AND MARKET-SHARE POLITICS OVER TIME

As noted earlier, communications scholars have made it clear that the community involvement by black radio in 1992 was rooted in a history of involvement since the 1960s. Similarly, an examination of the growth and evolution of Spanish-language radio yields a similar conclusion that contemporary involvement in community affairs is rooted in a history of earlier involvement. Without this historical perspective, any attempts to gauge the relevance of Spanish-language radio for the immigration protest marches will not capture the entire story.

This perspective, grounded in the history of Spanish-language radio, yields the incontrovertible fact that such broadcasting has grown dramatically over time and has been seen as a means to develop and enhance new modes of tapping into the growing Latino population in the United States. Since 1980, when there were only sixty-seven Spanish-language radio stations in the United States, the number has grown more than tenfold (Castañeda Paredes 2003; A. Starr 2006). This growth can be attributed to the existing practice of audience segmentation. According to Gandy, "audience segmentation . . . is both the product and the source of strategic information about individuals who share an identifiable status based on any number of attributes . . . or claimed membership in groups defined by race or ethnicity" (2000, 44). There are various ways of segmenting demographic minorities, but one of the most direct ways is through language. In the case of Latinos, even as they assimilate in the second and third generation and decrease their use of Spanish, the inflow of Latino immigrants has ensured the maintenance and growth of a sizable segment of a linguistically defined audience. The rapid growth in the number of Latinos, reached through Spanish-language radio on a daily basis, has not gone unnoticed by advertisers, as they realize that what was true in the 1970s is even more relevant today: "Every morning millions of persons across the United States wake up and turn to their radio for music, news and traffic reports. During the day they listen to radio as they drive to work, go about their daily tasks, and make their way home. For them radio is a 'constant companion', the communication medium that follows them wherever they go" (Gutiérrez and Schement 1979, 3).

In an age when the traditional English-language radio format has lost much of its audience to iPods and satellite radio, the characterization of Latinos from the late 1970s holds true today because Latinos listen to radio more than any other media and they listen more than non-Latinos. According to the 2007 Arbitron report *Hispanic Radio Today* "while TSL [time spent listening] for radio in general has struggled, not so in the Hispanic world." White-collar workers are often able to stay connected to the news during business hours through the Internet, but many Latino immigrants who work in the service sector listen to radio while they work and effectively "stay connected" throughout the day to Spanish-language news and entertainment.

In order to determine whether a communication resource can be used to mobilize Latino immigrants for a particular cause, it is important to recognize the nature of the radio industry and the factors that pushed Spanish-language programming into a prominent social, economic, and intermittent political role. In addition to considering the growth of Spanish-language radio in the FM stations in Los Angeles, the largest media market in the United States, it is also important to factor in the content provided by these radio stations. It is not simply that the "on-air" programs and advertisements are in Spanish, but the content often uses identity to appeal to and connect with a "subethnic" audience, thereby marketing to clearly defined consumer groups. For example, "advertising campaigns on Spanish-language radio can be developed with the subethnic in mind, such as Mexicans in Los Angeles or Cubans in Miami, each of whom has a unique set of Spanish words and cultural customs" (Castañeda Paredes 2003, 7).[3]

Subethnic marketing strategies and the creation of Spanish-language radio stations to reach Latinos are currently the accepted norm, but that was not the case twenty years ago, when this segment of the population was largely neglected by mass media. A series of events and recognition of shifting demographics changed this. One of the most cited stimuli was the transformation of the Los Angeles media market in 1992, caused by a new Spanish-language radio station seeking to capitalize on the presence of millions of Latino immigrants in Los Angeles. There was one FM station at the time, KLVE, and its programming could be characterized as soft adult contemporary music. The new radio station, KLAX, or La X, chose two relatively new DJs, who were former immigrant farmworkers, to head its morning show. More surprising was that it opted for an untested music format on FM in Los Angeles, consisting of Mexican regional and banda music. At that point, banda enjoyed no more acceptance in California than immigrants themselves.[4]

In a surprisingly short amount of time, by the end of 1992, KLAX captured the largest percentage of the radio market. While the accuracy of the Arbitron ratings was originally questioned by other stations, KLAX's continued success made it clear that its programmers had discovered a large and untapped pool of listeners consisting of recent Mexican immigrants, children of immigrants, and blue-collar Latinos who maintained Spanish competence.[5] The combination of ethnic pride in the music, the down-to-earth style of KLAX's disc jockeys, and concentration of the Latino population set the stage for the continued transformation of the largest media market in the country and for the influx of other Spanish-language radio stations throughout the United States.

The station's success surprised everyone, including the DJs, Juan Carlos Hidalgo and Jesus Garcia "El Peladillo," who were largely responsible for the dominant position of La X and the positive response from their listeners. As these two radio personalities boosted ratings through their focus on family values, they simultaneously built a relationship predicated on trust and reciprocity with their listeners, tending to the needs of their listeners and of the Latino community more broadly. By constructing and attracting a dedicated audience, they were able to create a media environment whose commercial and community goals overlapped (Squires 2000).

These disc jockeys also heavily criticized politicians whom they perceived as immigrant bashers. For example, they thought then-governor Pete Wilson blamed California's problems on illegal immigrants, and they took every opportunity to air those sentiments (Ginsberg 1994). They used the power of the airwaves to berate Wilson for using immigrants as scapegoats for California's struggling economy and for creating the perception that immigration was out of control and that most Latinos were in the United States illegally.

In her analysis of the role of the interaction between radio, music, and politics in California during the 1990s, ethnomusicologist Helena Simonett asserts that, "not only did recent immigrants feel unwelcome in California, but longtime Latino residents and Mexican Americans of several generations were also faced with growing resentment, open hostility, and hardly disguised racism" (2000, 2). Rather than sit on the sidelines or merely talk about empowerment, Juan Carlos Hidalgo and El Peladillo also set a precedent for direct involvement in real-world politics during the 1994 protest against Proposition 187. El Peladillo recalls that at that time he was unaware of the influence that came with his position as a popular DJ. His participation in the pro-immigrant marches in 1994 transformed him and further connected him to his audience: "El Peladillo gradually but increasingly identified with his audience and became 'raza,' seeking to help those who hear his show. . . . 'The first march that we took part in was in 1994 against Pete Wilson, that is how we came to identify as a united people'" (Radionotas 2006).

While the popularity of their morning show was evident in the Arbitron ratings, that their message resonated with their audience was more directly evident when Governor Wilson visited Los Angeles to give a speech at the opening of the new I-105 "Century Freeway." The disc jockeys asked any listeners who might be cruising nearby on the San Diego freeway (I-405) to honk in a sign of unity and protest to drown out Wilson's speech. In a pattern that would be replicated in 2006 and 2007, it appears that part of the reason why a Spanish-language station topped Arbitron's ratings has to do with its willingness to take on social and political issues that are important to its audience. However, after a reduction in the civic activist role of the radio station, the top spot was then achieved by another Spanish-language station that did not play this role. KLAX, which held top spot from 1992 to 1994, ceded its first-place rank to KLVE in 1995.

The emergence of other Spanish-language stations, such as KSCA and KBUE, in the Los Angeles media market in the mid-1990s cut into the KLAX's market share because they also used the Mexican regional music format. However, even with increased competition it is important to note that a Spanish-language radio station received the biggest audience share in Los Angeles from 1992 to early 2001. Despite losing the top spot in the summer of 2001, Spanish-language radio increased its total market share spread among multiple stations. According to Félix Gutiérrez (2006), an expert on Latino media, there was a transformation of Spanish radio during this time from a medium of chance to a medium of choice: "You listened to the radio station because you preferred Spanish or you only spoke Spanish, and you only had one or two choices. Now it's a medium that's replicated English-language media.... So whatever flavor you want in Spanish, you can get it."

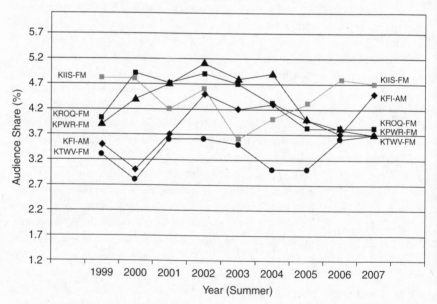

FIGURE 3.1. Top five English-language radio stations in Los Angeles by audience share, 1999–2007. Source: Author's compilations of published Arbitron audience share ratings, 1999–2007.

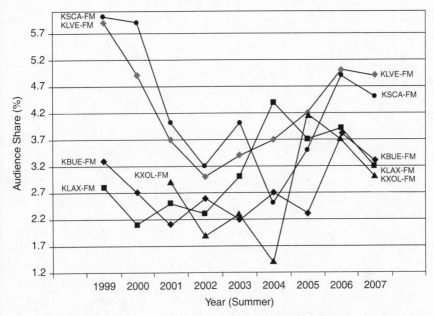

FIGURE 3.2. Top five Spanish-language radio stations in Los Angeles by audience share, 1999–2007. Source: Author's compilations of published Arbitron audience share ratings, 1999–2007.

The influx of new Spanish-language radio stations, change in ownership, and changing disc jockeys eventually resulted in greater volatility in the audience share of the Spanish-language radio stations as compared to the English-language stations (see figures 3.1 and 3.2). From 1999 until 2007, audience share of the top five English-language stations was between 2.8 and 5.1 percent. Audience share of the top five Spanish-language stations was between 1.4 and 6 percent. Variance between low and high audience share for the English-language radio stations was significantly less than for their Spanish-language counterparts. The most consistently rated English-language station varied 0.9 percent between its high and low points, while the least consistently rated station varied by 1.5 percent. By comparison, the most consistent Spanish-language station, as measured by the difference between low and high audience share, had 1.7 percent between the two points, or 0.2 percent more variability than the least consistent English-language station. The least consistent Spanish-language station, KSCA, experienced variance in audience share ranging from 2.5 to 6 percent, a difference of 3.5 percentage points. Interestingly, KSCA, and its morning DJ, El Piolín, was largely credited with bringing together the competing Spanish-language stations to mobilize their respective audiences and came within 0.1 percentage point of KLVE, the top station in 2006.

STRENGTH FROM WITHIN: IDENTITY AND NEW MOBILIZING OPPORTUNITIES

It is useful to compare Spanish-language radio to black radio for a better understanding the medium's potential as a resource for mobilization. Both black radio and Spanish-language radio have demonstrated a commitment to their communities and have built this capacity over time. Just as black radio mobilized around exogenous shocks or crises that have required community involvement, so too has Spanish-language radio been effective in developing a close connection with its audience. While this intermittent civic role may appear to be reactionary and haphazard, such an assessment does not fully encapsulate the opportunities and challenges faced by Spanish-language radio; one must understand the role of exogenous and endogenous factors in the decision to engage in civic activism. Exogenous forces include natural disasters and political threats that require engaging personalities that can motivate and mobilize the community for a specific outcome. There are instances when Spanish-language radio has been used outside of the political realm as a communication resource to diffuse information and others when it has independently sought to mobilize the community. For example, when communities in the United States and Latin America have experienced natural disasters, Spanish-language radio has a track record of raising funds to help the victims, even when there is no other grassroots organizational activity for this purpose.

While he was at KSCA and then at KLAX, DJ Renán Almendárez Coello "El Cucuy" devoted on-air programming and formed the El Cucuy Foundation to mobilize his audience to make financial and other contributions in reaction to natural disasters.[6] He helped raise hundreds of thousands of dollars for victims as well as for other notable public projects. For example, his efforts helped victims of major hurricanes in Honduras, Mexico, and New Orleans in 1998, 2002, and 2005, respectively, as well as the victims of major earthquakes in Latin America. There is a history in Spanish-language radio of mobilizing around a cause, and El Cucuy's appeals were infused with calls for Latinos to step up and help.

Another similarity between Spanish-language and black radio is that their social and political identity is inherently tied into the identity of the listening audience. Yet, there is one notable difference with respect to the role of identity. Barlow's account (1998) of black radio suggests that it is important to look at the construction of racial identity through voice. He explores the history of white DJs "passing" for black over the air and vice versa, a phenomenon dubbed "racial ventriloquy" (Watkins 1994; Barlow 1998). While both Spanish-language and black radio rely on and encourage identity formation, there is much less ambiguity about whether the Spanish-language DJs are Latino than about whether a DJ on black radio is black. In other words, by its very nature, the language of transmission ensures some common identity, with the mother tongue as a possible unifying mechanism.

However, while both black and Spanish-language radio rely on a strong identity connection with the audience to effectively transmit their messages, their target audiences and overarching goals were distinct. Black-oriented radio can be characterized as primarily having an information-diffusion and proselytizing function: "Although television and the print media were vitally important in promoting northern white and federal support for the attack on Jim Crow, movement workers also appreciated the unique potential of radio to help fashion favorable national attitudes toward the southern struggle" (Ward 2004, 116). The linguistic isolation of Spanish-language radio precludes any possible effort to build alliances and fashion favorable attitudes toward the immigrant struggle. While this might seem to hinder Spanish-language radio from becoming active in a cause, it is actually black-oriented radio that is more commonly under scrutiny. This was evident during the civil rights movement in the South: "Since many white southerners had originally become hooked on African American music by secretly listening to black-oriented shows. . . . this racially transgressive capability alone justified closer examination of what was being said, as well as what was being played, on southern radio" (Ward 2004, 117). In such circumstances, it is not surprising that black-oriented radio was careful of taking an explicitly activist tone and making direct calls to action. Unlike black radio the 1960s, when there was fear of immediate backlash and outside guests were the driving force in crafting the message, in 2006, DJs such as El Piolín, El Cucuy, El Mandril, El Pistolero, and Humberto Luna were able to use linguistic isolation to directly mobilize people to protest and were instrumental in formulating the symbols and message.

Another significant difference between black and Spanish-language radio has to do with the endogenous forces affecting the very nature of Spanish-language radio. The sheer size and concentration of the Latino population has allowed Spanish-language radio to achieve the top audience share in the largest media market in the United States. From 2005 to 2007 in Los Angeles, Spanish-language radio has had at least three stations in the top ten in terms of audience share. Moreover, according to the summer 2006 Arbitron ratings, five of the top ten Los Angeles stations were Spanish-language. This level of success has created an extremely competitive market for the Spanish-language radio audience, and this increased competition between Spanish-language stations has meant increased volatility in terms of audience share, which then has the potential to affect programming and marketing styles. Unlike the situation when there are only one or two black radio stations, the diffuse nature of the Spanish-language radio market requires extreme coordination and willingness to overlook the competition in favor of community needs, such as the immigration protests in 2006. This does not prevent any one station from taking on a civic activist role; it simply makes a unified response to exogenous shocks less likely, but still possible.

Spanish-language radio has evolved and grown so much that comparisons to black radio become limited. The level of commercial success achieved by Spanish-language radio puts it in uncharted territory. This success is directly attributable to the ease with which Spanish-language radio segments a linguistically- identifiable target audience. The challenge, however, is that despite its impressive combined market share, there is very little chance that Spanish-language radio and its listening audience will be fully integrated within the mainstream mass listening audience: the language barrier inherently prevents most Americans from becoming regular listeners.[7]

On a more localized level, there are similarities between black radio's civic activism in Los Angeles in the early 1990s and the contemporary successes of Los Angeles–based Spanish-language radio. These parallels include helping to disseminate information, relating the community's views (in 2006, on immigration), and strategically using political power to mobilize the audience into protest politics. The immigrant rights protests of 2006 were a cumulative response to a national anti-immigrant political environment and were coordinated by a partnership between civic and community organizations and the Spanish-language media. However, just because there is a capacity to mobilize does not mean that the radio stations are always in mobilization mode. To a degree, the stations have employed strategy and selectivity. One must also factor in the reality that, at its core, Spanish-language media is corporate mass media, and therefore this capacity is constrained to a greater degree than in locally owned black radio.

Owen and Wildman's insights (1992) about the nature of the television industry are instructive for those interested in the opportunities and challenges presented by Spanish-language radio. Their critique of television analysts is particularly useful if applied to the radio industry analysts: "The first and most serious mistake that an analyst of the television industry can make is to assume that advertising-supported television broadcasters are in the business to broadcast programs. They are not. Broadcasters are in the business of producing audiences. These audiences, or means of access to them, are sold to advertisers. The product of a television station is measured in dimensions of people and time. The price of the product is quoted in dollars per thousand viewers per unit of commercial time" (1992, 3).

With the caveat that Spanish-language radio is first and foremost a money-generating business, one can reconcile the fact that the disc jockeys were allowed to devote airtime to the immigration issue: doing so did not hurt ratings; on the contrary, it boosted them. This boost was evident in 2006 (see figure 3.2). However, after the protest marches, disc jockeys had to get back to their traditional format or face a potential loss of the core audience that tunes in for entertainment and general news and information. As the competition for audience share among Spanish-language radio stations increases, so too does the pressure for "commodification" of Latino identity expressly for commercial purposes, not for social and political ends. While these are not necessarily mutually exclusive, there are limits to the extent that Spanish-language radio can be used as a means to mobilize.

The short-sighted critiques levied at the disc jockeys and Spanish-language radio for their diminished role in the 2007 and 2008 protest marches fail to consider that, while radio format is at times bound by tradition and social and economic constraints, at other times radio is able to introduce innovation. When there are opportunities for innovation, radio is more flexible to engage a broad spectrum of people than existing grassroots organizations. The first innovation vis-à-vis the 2006 protests was the ability of disc jockeys from competing stations to come together to jointly mobilize the Latino community to participate and to help frame the response to the political threat with a sea of white shirts and American flags. Spanish-language radio did what would have likely taken months of negotiation for grassroots organizations with different goals and constituents. The difficulty in reaching consensus across organizations is evident in that various alliances or coalitions sprang up using the We Are America name, but each had its particular goals.

More recently, Spanish-language radio has again come to the forefront of Latino immigrant community affairs. Rather than focus on repeated efforts to protest in 2007 and 2008, both of the syndicated disc jockeys, El Piolín and El Cucuy, took to heart the slogan from the immigration protests: "Today we march, tomorrow we vote." On July 1, 2006, El Cucuy began a national voter registration drive called the Votos por America campaign, with the goal of registering one million new Latino voters. El Piolín similarly focused on two forms of nonprotest political engagement: contacting elected officials and promoting naturalization efforts.

Additionally, El Piolín initiated what has been called the largest letter-writing campaign on immigration, which consisted of a six-week effort to gather one million letters in support of immigration reform from citizens and legal residents that he then personally delivered to bipartisan members of Congress on June 14, 2007. He also sought to increase the pool of eligible voters by encouraging the citizenship-eligible Latinos to seek naturalization. In February 2007 he began an on-air contest called "Who wants to be a citizen?" in which listeners from around the country could win prizes for correct responses to questions found on the citizenship exam. He also further cemented the connection with his audience by sharing his own experience of going through the naturalization process between February 2007 and the naturalization ceremony on May 21, 2008.

In another scenario, El Piolín took part in the unlikely alliance between Spanish-language radio, television, newspapers, and national organizations to promote immigrant political integration. These very distinct entities came together to increase Latino political incorporation through the Ya Es Hora (Now Is the Time) campaign. The unique nature of this campaign is evident in its description and its relationship to the immigrant protest marches: Ya Es Hora is a historic and comprehensive civic participation campaign launched as a community response to the pro-immigrant mobilizations of 2006. The campaign represents the largest coordinated effort to incorporate Latinos as full participants in the American political process. Unlike past approaches, which focused on naturalization, voter registration, or get-out-the-vote drives, this campaign seeks to integrate these components into a comprehensive civic engagement strategy and under a recognizable action-oriented slogan: *ya es hora,* now is the time.[8]

A study of the citizenship workshops that took place at the Los Angeles Convention Center in 2006 found that Spanish-language radio and television were instrumental in getting thousands of people to initiate the citizenship process (Félix, González, and Ramírez 2008). The effectiveness of this campaign was recognized when Univision Communications, one of the partners of the Ya Es Hora" campaign, was honored in April 2008 with the prestigious Peabody Award.[9] Obviously, the campaign cannot claim full credit for the 702,589 and 660,477 successful naturalizations in fiscal years 2006 and 2007, respectively. Nor can it fully be credited with the 1,130,000 applications awaiting a decision at the end of fiscal year 2007. However, it is clear that the central role of Spanish-language media, in collaboration with hundreds of local organizations and several key national organizations, have been successful in getting more Latinos to apply for citizenship, register to vote, and turn out on election day. As Ayón aptly concludes, "The Spanish-language media has developed into an ethnic communications industry that is unique in American corporate history and in its voluntary commitment to public service. Taken together, these elements constitute a standing potential that can be activated at certain times by credible actors who have cultivated strategic relationships and share a common frame of reference" (2009, 15).

CHALLENGES AND UNCHARTED WATERS FOR SPANISH-LANGUAGE RADIO

Successful as Spanish-language radio has been before, during, and after the 2006 protest marches, it is important to have a balanced view of some of the challenges and limitations of this medium. In addition to some of the limitations that the mass broadcast media format inherently imposes on Spanish-language radio, it is possible that these stations will behave more like mainstream radio, in the sense that, at the end of the day, their primary goal is making money. It is likely the case that the very connection between the DJs and the protesters will become a means to compete for greater market share, thereby diminishing the possibilities for future mobilization efforts. If the primary goal of Spanish-language radio is to enable Latino social and political incorporation, why have radio stations shifted the programs and DJs that enabled the message framing and message diffusion during the immigration marches?

Currently, only one of the four principal morning DJs, El Piolín, is still on-air in the mornings in Los Angeles. In late 2006, Ricardo Sanchez "El Mandril" left KSCA and joined KLAX (now called La Raza), but in the afternoons. In mid-September 2008, El Cucuy left KLAX to pursue his own radio network. Around the same time, Chicago's famous morning DJ who helped mobilize people during the protest marches was moved to the afternoons to make room for El Piolín's further syndication throughout the United States. Finally, Humberto Luna left his long-running morning show in Los Angeles to join Clear Channel's La Preciosa network, which is syndicated in several cities but not Los Angeles. This volatility among the DJs is echoed in the volatility of ratings for individual radio stations in Los Angeles, where the total market share for the top five Spanish-language stations dropped by nearly 4 percent from the peak in 2006.[10]

The analysis presented here suggests that Spanish-language radio is indeed unique, relative to mainstream English-language media and even relative to the significant role that black-oriented radio has played since the 1960s civil rights movement. How then do we explain the mobilization and participation of immigrants in 2006 that will likely go down in history as some of the most significant moments of protest-event politics in the United States? Existing academic literatures fail to offer adequate explanations for the activation of immigrants and/or their sympathizers and the fact that non-English-language use and non-English-language radio enabled rather than inhibited participation. To be fair, scholars such as Verba, Schlozman, and Brady (1993) do indicate that protests are perhaps the exception to the rule that non-English-language use inhibits participation, and past assertions about the isolating effects of non-English media consumption were often made before Spanish-language stations reached the current level of success. However, even in the most mainstream political activities, like naturalization and voter registration, Spanish-language radio has prompted and encouraged greater participation through the activation of political identities. Studies about the effect of mass media on political behavior continue to largely overlook the Spanish-language media, much to their detriment. It is important that subsequent research incorporate the social, economic, and political changes that are underway as a result of the growing immigrant population and its established presence in the largest media markets in the country.

A more contemporary and realistic account of Spanish-language radio is that it is unique in its ability to selectively mobilize its listening audience, not just

through information diffusion, but through framing of the issues and collabora-
tions that have extended to local and national nonpartisan and nonprofit organizations. Spanish-language radio, because of its size and scope, has affected short-
term mobilization of protest participants and long-term efforts to expand the
citizen population. However, given its quick assent into prominence in key media
markets such as Southern California, another unique aspect of Spanish-language
radio has to do with the evidenced volatility and intense competition between and
among Spanish-language radio stations. This may constrain the medium's ability
to promote Latino social and political incorporation in Los Angeles and beyond.
This challenge should be placed in proper context. While market forces may create an only intermittent role for Spanish-language radio as a mobilizing agent,
this is still significantly more than extant scholarship would have predicted. The
revised account of Spanish-language radio presented in this chapter is one step in
a more accurate account of the forces that have helped shape the integration of
Latino immigrants in Southern California since the 1990s, and it simultaneously
raises questions about the long-term role that this new powerful agent can have in
the political discourse about immigration and politics.

NOTES

1. Many nonsyndicated DJs such as KSCA's El Mandril and KHJ's Humberto Luna were also
instrumental, but they were arguably secondary figures, whereas El Cucuy and El Piolín were much
more central to creating the initial frames surrounding the March 25 protest march in downtown
Los Angeles.

2. Several immigrant organizations obtained the necessary march permits from the City of Los
Angeles and paid for banners, posters, water, portable toilets, and the use of the microphones and
speakers. While it is unlikely that the turnout would have been as great without the help of the disc
jockeys, the actual planning and implementation of the march could not have happened without
established organizations and their leaders.

3. Interestingly, subethnic marketing, it is argued, happens less in the Spanish-language television format. Rather than emphasize or target specific Latino subethnic groups, Davila (2000) argues that there are efforts by Spanish-language television and marketing industries to forge a transnational diasporic culture of Latinidad that deemphasizes cultural distinctiveness across national
origin groups.

4. Banda music is a brass-based form of traditional Mexican music.

5. Similar to Nielsen media research on television audiences, Arbitron collects listener data on
radio audiences in the United States and reports the percentage of the radio market share garnered
by radio stations.

6. According to a Reuters press release on September 15, 2008, when the DJ left KLAX, "El Cucuy is going to follow his dream of building his own radio network."

7. The one possibility of fully becoming part of the mainstream is through bilingual stations
such as KXOL (Latino 96.3 in Los Angeles), whose disc jockeys broadcast mainly in English, with
some Spanglish, and play a variety of English- and Spanish-language music.

8. The Ya Es Hora campaign was led by a joint effort between national Latino organizations—
including Mi Familia Vota, the NALEO Educational Fund, and the National Council of La

Raza—and the Spanish-language media companies Entravision Communications, ImpreMedia, and Univision Communications. The campaign's strategy focused on removing barriers that have prevented many from becoming full participants in American life and activism.

9. Univision Communications is the largest Spanish-language media company, consisting of both radio and television.

10. Also, in mid-January 2009 yet one more English-language radio station in Los Angeles (103.1 El Gato) switched to the regional Mexican format.

4

Building the Labor-Clergy-Immigrant Alliance

Randy Shaw

In the spring of 2006, millions of Latinos and their supporters marched through America's streets to demand legalization for the nation's undocumented immigrants. Protests occurred in over two hundred cities, with turnouts of nearly 1 million in Los Angeles, 500,000 in Chicago, and 3,000 in the rural town of Garden City, Kansas, where 10 percent of the city's entire population took to the streets.

The marchers' most spirited chant in cities large and small across the United States was the same: "¡Sí, se puede!" (Yes, we can!). Cesar Chavez adopted these words as the United Farm Workers' rallying cry during his Arizona fast in 1972, and they soon became closely identified with the farmworkers' movement. That millions linked the cause of immigrant rights with Cesar Chavez and "Sí, se puede" is fitting, as the UFW helped lay the groundwork for today's immigrant rights movement.

Many factors contributed to the massive marches for immigrant rights in 2006. But central to the largest events in Los Angeles and elsewhere was the active support of immigrant rights by the labor movement and the religious community. Labor unions have become so identified with the immigrant rights movement that it is easily forgotten that organized labor had long opposed measures to protect undocumented immigrants; in 1986, the AFL-CIO even played a key role in passing federal legislation that imposed tough sanctions on employers of undocumented workers. Similarly, while the nation's religious community protected undocumented immigrants seeking political asylum from El Salvador and Nicaragua in the 1980s, relations between the Catholic Church—the most common place of worship for Latino immigrants—and progressive and labor activists became strained over a series of labor disputes starting in the late 1980s and continuing for over a decade. These disputes hampered the Church's ability to work in broad coalitions in support of immigrant rights.

In a little over a decade, prior to the mass marches of 2006, a conscious effort was made to connect labor unions, and to reconnect the religious community, to the immigrant rights movement. This effort was primarily focused in Los Angeles, where activists like Miguel Contreras, Eliseo Medina, and Fred Ross Jr., who got their formative training with Chavez's UFW, played key roles in mobilizing labor and religious support for immigrant rights. The building of an immigrant rights movement that included labor and the religious community in key roles was a multifaceted project that took many years and entailed changing the orientation of the national labor movement toward immigration. Los Angeles was central to this effort. The city's steadily growing immigrant rights movement saw massive public outpourings—from 200,000–500,000 on March 25, 2006 to an estimated 650,000 on May 1, 2006—that were among the largest demonstrations in the nation and the most racially diverse in the city's history. These mass protests came only a decade after UFW veterans in Los Angeles began building a labor-religious-immigrant alliance in the wake of the passage of the anti-immigrant Proposition 187 in 1994, a project culminating in the public unveiling of a powerful movement for immigrant rights on the streets of Los Angeles in 2006 (Bada, Fox, and Selee 2006; Goodman and Gonzalez 2006).

BUILDING THE LABOR-IMMIGRANT ALLIANCE

Los Angeles became the epicenter for the development of a mass immigrant rights movement for three chief reasons. First, the city had the nation's largest influx of undocumented Latino immigrants. Second, the November 1994 California ballot included Proposition 187, whose vicious attacks on undocumented immigrants angered the Latino community as never before. Third, Los Angeles in the mid-1990s was home to veterans of the UFW who knew how to translate this passion into effective action and how to forge labor-religious-community coalitions to bring about progressive change.

Miguel Contreras and the Los Angeles County Federation of Labor

The story of how Miguel Contreras used the UFW organizing model to help develop the Latino-labor alliance that boosted the cause of immigrant rights begins with his birth in 1952 in the small Central Valley farm town of Dinuba, California. Contreras and his five brothers worked with their parents in the fields, and when Contreras was a teenager his family became active with the UFW. He and his father were later elected union leaders at their grape and tree-fruit ranch, and Miguel was a picket captain during the strike that began in 1973 after grape growers across California refused to renew their UFW contracts. He was arrested eighteen times for violating antipicketing injunctions. These were days when the UFW was running multiple boycotts in addition to their organizing work in the fields, and Cesar Chavez was always on the lookout for potential leaders. Chavez asked Contreras to join the union staff, and he spent more than two years in Toronto, Canada, organizing for the grape boycott (A. Rojas 2006).

Contreras was supervised in Canada by two of the UFW's most talented strategists, Marshall Ganz and Jessica Govea. Ganz felt Contreras found his "calling" in Toronto, and when the Agricultural Labor Relations Act passed in 1975, Contreras joined other boycott staff in returning to the fields to organize farmworkers for union elections. He then became a UFW contracts negotiator, a departure from his organizing experience that soon led him to leave the UFW in 1977. Along with other farmworker staff he began organizing for the San Francisco Hotel Employees and Restaurant Employees union, Local 2 (HERE, the precursor to UNITE HERE). Contreras became staff director for HERE Local 2 and helped coordinate a citywide twenty-seven-day hotel strike in 1980. The strike produced the greatest wage and benefit increase in Local 2's history and led Contreras to be appointed to HERE's national staff (Ganz 2007).

In late 1980, Contreras was focused on rebuilding troubled HERE locals in San Francisco, San Diego, and Los Angeles. He also spent considerable time organizing undocumented workers in Las Vegas, which under the leadership of Vincent Sirabella and John Wilhelm soon became a HERE stronghold. Contreras noted that when he traveled throughout the nation organizing members and staffing picket lines for HERE, "It was an extension of Cesar. Everywhere I went I ran into farm worker organizers" (Ganz 2007). In 1986, Contreras was working for Sirabella and the HERE national staff when Ganz asked him to come to a meeting at his home on the California coast with a young union firebrand named Maria Elena Durazo (Ganz 2007; A. Rojas 2006).

Durazo was running an insurgent campaign to be president of HERE Local 11 in Los Angeles. Contreras came to Ganz's house to determine if Durazo was someone with whom the international union could work; she was there to assess the international's view of her candidacy, and to assess whether Contreras was someone she could trust.

The meeting went well. The Local 11 election was in March 1987, and after ballots were cast and Durazo seemed headed to victory, the national leadership halted the process and put the local into trusteeship. Bill Granfield, a UFW veteran who worked at San Francisco's Local 2 before becoming head of New York City's restaurant union UNITE HERE Local 100, became the trustee. But the person put in charge of the day-to-day running of Local 11 was Miguel Contreras, who quickly confirmed the sense that Durazo got from the Ganz meeting that he could be trusted. Durazo accepted an offer to join the union's staff, and after the trusteeship ended in May 1989, she was elected president of Local 11. She and Contreras eventually married, becoming the "dynamic duo" of the Los Angeles labor movement (Ganz 2007; Milkman and Wong 2001; Rabadan, Milkman, and Wong 2000).

Contreras was named political director of the Los Angeles County Federation of Labor (LACFL) in 1995. When the LACFL's leader died in 1996, Contreras became the first Latino elected to head the organization (and one of the few Latinos in the United States to head a county labor federation) (Meyerson 2005; K. Wong 2006).[1] Although LACFL had long engaged in electoral work, it had not built strong relationships with the rising number of newly arrived immigrant workers. LACFL did support a No on 187 rally at city hall in downtown Los Angeles, despite concern from many Democratic politicians that the Latino event would trigger a political backlash. Labor, immigrant rights groups, and the ethnic media turned out over 100,000 people, the city's largest rally in over fifty years. Prop. 187 galvanized the political consciousness of California's Latino community as never before and gave newly hired LACFL political director Miguel Contreras a motivated constituency from which to draw new progressive, prolabor votes. Contreras's ability to capitalize on the Latino backlash to Prop. 187 helped transformed Los Angeles into America's most politically potent union city, a sudden and dramatic political shift that would later make the city the national epicenter for the mass protests of 2006 (Frank and Wong 2004; Meyerson 2005).

Throughout the late 1990s, Contreras built a Latino-labor alliance that increased the political clout of both constituencies and brought unionization to increasing numbers of Latino immigrants. In 1999, LACFL helped the SEIU's Los Angeles health-care Local 434B win union recognition for 74,000 home health-care workers, the largest union organizing victory since the 1930s. In 2000, the SEIU's Justice for Janitors, whose membership was primarily Latino immigrants, engaged in a nearly three-week strike that foreshadowed the broad support for immigrant rights on the streets of Los Angeles in 2006. The strike saw virtually every elected official in Los Angeles—including the city's Republican mayor—speak out on the workers' behalf. The Los Angeles Archdiocese's Cardinal Roger Mahony, who embraced the cause of Cesar Chavez and the UFW while a Central Valley auxiliary bishop in the 1960s, conducted a public mass for thousands of striking janitors; Mahony even got arrested to show support. Several elected officials were also arrested, fulfilling Contreras's demand that the politicians LACFL supported be "warriors for working people." The janitors won wage hikes of 22 to 26 percent over three years, confirming to participants the value of UFW-style grassroots activism (Frank and Wong 2004).

In 2000, Contreras, HERE head Maria Elena Durazo, SEIU international vice president and former UFW Executive Board member Eliseo Medina, and Medina's assistant and SEIU regional coordinator Ben Monterroso created the Organization of Los Angeles Workers (OLAW) to strengthen the labor–Latino immigrant connection. Frank and Wong (2004) describe the joint effort that resulted:

> OLAW and the County Federation [LULAC] worked with Spanish-language Univision (channel 34) to conduct citizenship fairs. At [one] event, every consulate in Los Angeles set up a booth, and over 3,000 people attended to inquire about the citizenship process as it relates to their country of origin. Channel 34 set up call-in shows with a toll-free number into the SEIU Local 99 phone bank. Univision started conducting other call-in shows with Labor, marketing them *"Treinta Cuatro en Su Lado"* (Channel 34 on Your Side). They advertised and televised a question-and-answer session with immigration attorneys, and the union recruited fifty immigration attorneys to staff SEIU Local 99's call center. That session led to over 200,000 phone requests. For a question-and-answer session on L.A. schools, the union recruited school district and union representatives to field another barrage of questions, and a session on community–police relations filled the phone bank with LAPD community affairs representatives.

Describing the importance of such events, Eliseo Medina observed, "With the phone bank at Local 99, the TV has the SEIU logo behind all of the experts and people start to understand that labor has a role on all these key issues" (Frank and Wong 2004).

The AFL-CIO Joins the Immigrant Rights Movement

While Contreras and Medina were building labor-immigrant unity in Los Angeles, this alignment was counter to the AFL-CIO's history. Since the early 1900s the AFL-CIO consistently supported restricting immigration, claiming that the entry of foreign workers suppressed wages and slowed union membership growth. The AFL-CIO's position helped create a powerful political base against progressive immigration reform.

Starting with immigrant organizing drives by HERE and the SEIU in the 1980s—and the creation of the SEIU's Justice for Janitors campaign by UFW veteran Stephen Lerner in 1987—union attitudes toward immigrants began to change. At its 1995 convention, the labor federation passed a resolution that "the notion that immigrants are to blame for the deteriorating living standards of America's low-wage workers must be clearly rejected" (Briggs 2004).

Organized labor's stance toward immigration had thus somewhat shifted by the mid-1990s, but Medina and others were not satisfied. Medina saw immigrant workers as the future of organized labor, and he wanted labor to help lead the fight for immigrant rights, not simply stop bad proposals. Medina saw his chance to change the AFL-CIO's anti-immigration policy in October 1995, when SEIU president John Sweeney was elected to replace Lane Kirkland as president of the AFL-CIO. Medina believed Sweeney to be a strong supporter of immigrant rights but also knew that he liked to operate by consensus. This meant that Sweeney would not change AFL-CIO immigration policy until a broad consensus was organized from below. Medina took up the task of creating this popular groundswell, and as the newly elected executive vice president of the SEIU, and the highest ranking Latino in the labor movement, he used his new base in Los Angeles to make it happen (Medina 2007).

Medina had a vision of unifying labor with community, religious, and immigrant rights groups and spent 1997 and much of 1998 discussing with Contreras, Durazo, the UFW, and the United Food and Commercial Workers (UCFW) just how to realize this vision in Los Angeles. By late 1998, the group decided that Sweeney had been in power for three years and it was time to offer a resolution to the 1999 AFL-CIO convention to shift the labor federation's immigration policy (Medina 2007).

Two factors worked in the group's favor. First, the October 1999 convention was to be held in Los Angeles, so that union officials from across the country could see firsthand how a city's growing union-immigrant alliance was boosting labor's political clout. Immigrant janitors, drywallers, home health-care workers, and hotel workers had become the face of the city's labor movement, so that the convention could not have been held in a more receptive location for promoting immigrant rights. Second, HERE president John Wilhelm was achieving great success boosting his union's membership in the Las Vegas hotel industry and was close enough to Los Angeles to attend some of the reform group's strategy meetings. With Wilhelm and SEIU president Andy Stern growing in influence and both backing a new pro- immigrant policy, a shift in the AFL-CIO's long-standing position was at hand.

Medina took the lead in the debate on the resolution on the convention floor. He told the assembled leaders that his recent experience working with Los Angeles's unionized janitors showed the importance of aligning labor with the cause of immigrant rights. "While we do everything to bring justice and dignity to janitors in the workplace," he recalled saying, "the minute they leave the worksite they revert to their undocumented status" (Medina 2007).

In February 2000, on the committee's recommendation, the AFL-CIO Executive Board met in New Orleans and reversed its 1985 policy favoring employer sanctions for hiring undocumented immigrants. Since the AFL-CIO had extolled its support for this policy as recently as 1987, this reversal was dramatic. The AFL-CIO also called for a new system that ensured a level playing field for all employers, and the federation urged amnesty for the nation's estimated six million undocumented workers (Parks 2005).

The AFL-CIO's new immigration policy immediately changed the longstanding political calculus around legalization for undocumented workers. The federation's action also showed how the Los Angeles labor movement, with UFW alumni Eliseo Medina and Miguel Contreras playing key roles, was helping to strengthen the nation's immigrant rights movement.

BUILDING RELIGIOUS COMMUNITY SUPPORT FOR IMMIGRANT RIGHTS

The launching of the Active Citizenship Campaign (ACC) in 1995 bolstered efforts in Los Angeles to build a strong alliance between Latino immigrants and the religious community. The ACC was a national project of the Industrial Areas Foundation (IAF), and its goal was to encourage Latino immigrants to apply for citizenship and then to become "active" citizens by registering to vote and casting ballots. Its efforts in Los Angeles were spearheaded by four church-based groups, one of whom, Los Angeles VOICE, hired UFW veteran Fred Ross Jr. as its executive director. Ross, whose father, Fred Ross Sr., was working for the IAF when he trained Cesar Chavez as an organizer, had recently headed Neighbor to Neighbor, a national grassroots organization dedicated to stopping U.S. military aid to Central America (Villarreal 1995).

Under Ross's leadership, the ACC dramatically increased citizenship applications and fought with the INS to expedite their processing. As the backlog of applications grew, the ACC made it clear to the Clinton administration that this delay could prevent as many as 300,000 California Latino immigrants from voting in the November 1996 presidential election. The IAF's faith-based groups in New York, Chicago, and San Francisco joined the Los Angeles organization in the campaign, which bolstered church support for immigrant rights. This congregation-based support led Cardinal Roger Mahony to send a letter to Vice President Al Gore expressing a "sense of urgency" over the INS backlog. Mahony had a longtime relationship with Ross, dating from his days as an associate bishop in Fresno, when the powerful religious leader had been a close ally of Cesar Chavez (Kirschten 1997).

Ross's involvement also helped bring Eliseo Medina and Miguel Contreras into the struggle to secure citizenship for Latino immigrants in time for the November 1996 elections. Medina was eager to boost civic engagement among immigrant workers, and he saw the ACC's work as "empowering immigrant workers to have political power and create a much more progressive electorate in the state" (Barragan 2007). As is often the case with Medina's contributions, there is little public record of his role with the ACC. But VOICE leader Cecilia Barragan recalled that Medina "was very involved" in the ACC and that "Eliseo was someone who cared about our community and was always there for us" (Barragan 2007). Medina was a frequent speaker at VOICE events and helped secure critical financial assistance for the campaign from the SEIU's state and national offices. With Contreras's

LACFL providing local financial support for ACC's voter registration and out-reach efforts, and Medina bringing in state and national resources, organized labor played an important role in the citizenship campaign's success (Barragan 2007; Medina 2007; Ross 2006).

RESTORING THE CATHOLIC CHURCH–LABOR–IMMIGRANT ALLIANCE

While the ACC strengthened Catholic Church support for immigrant rights, outstanding issues still hampered the creation of a Church-labor-immigrant alliance. Cardinal Mahony was a close ally of Chavez and the UFW but had backed off from involvement in labor causes since his diocese successfully defeated efforts by the Amalgamated Clothing and Textile Workers Union (ACTWU) to unionize the Church's cemetery workers in 1989–90. Bad feelings from this dispute were exacerbated when, in 1997, the SEIU engaged in high-profile conflicts with Catholic Healthcare West (CHW) over its attempts to unionize hospitals. CHW fought back against the SEIU with full-page newspaper ads attacking the union's "corporate campaign" and "disruptive activities."

This conflict between labor and portions of the Catholic Church disturbed Medina, a deeply spiritual man whose UFW experience taught him the importance of labor-Church unity. In 1999, Medina reached out to Mahony, to help resolve the dispute. Some union activists accused Mahony of hypocrisy, but Medina understood how to approach Mahony and assure him that the labor movement needed, and would appreciate, his support. Mahony worked behind the scenes to pressure CHW to reach a "peace accord" with the SEIU in 2001, and by 2002 the SEIU had won contracts covering nine thousand workers at over twenty CHW hospitals. The "peace accord" between the SEIU and the hospital operator would have dramatic implications for the immigrant rights movement, as it repaired a rift and reunified two powerful forces for the cause of legalization (A. Jones 2001; Medina 2007).

THE IMMIGRANT WORKERS FREEDOM RIDE

Although Mexican immigrants were not associated with terrorist acts against America, 9/11 suspended progressive immigration reform efforts. An issue whose time seemed ripe for resolution prior to the tragedy suddenly shifted off the political radar screen. Medina and his allies had no choice but to wait out 9/11's aftereffects, but in 2003 they renewed progressive reform efforts by launching the Immigrant Workers Freedom Ride (IWFR).

The Immigrant Workers Freedom Ride was a nationwide event chiefly organized and sponsored by UNITE HERE, the SEIU, and the AFL-CIO. UNITE

HERE and the SEIU played a leading role in building a broad coalition of religious groups, students, immigrant rights organizations, and community groups in support of the event. The IWFR largely escaped national consciousness at the time, but it served a critical role in reenergizing and broadening America's immigrant rights movement, setting the stage for the mass marches of 2006.

The IWFR was named after the 1961 Freedom Rides of the U.S. civil rights movement in which student activists rode buses in the Deep South to challenge segregation on interstate transportation and in bus and train terminals. The chief organizer of the IWFR was Dave Glaser of UNITE HERE, who later went on to head the national Hotel Workers Rising boycotts. The national chair of the IWFR was Maria Elena Durazo, who believed that the IWFR would "take the fight for immigrant rights to a new level of unity and strength" and would show that "immigrants are also fighting for good jobs, access to health care and rights on the job—the same issues all workers are seeking" (Parks 2003; Parks provides an invaluable account of the IWFR). Miguel Contreras's LACFL showed its commitment by donating $100,000 to offset the cost of the Freedom Ride (Parks 2003).

A critical aim of the IWFR was to boost working relationships between labor unions and the many community, civil rights, religious, student, and immigrant rights groups that collectively comprised the nation's immigrant rights movement. The Freedom Riders included immigrants themselves, both documented and undocumented, as well as union and community allies, who planned to promote the need for immigration reform when stopping in dozens of communities across the country. The IWFR also hoped to return immigration issues to the national political agenda a year before the 2004 elections and to encourage greater civic participation by immigrants.

As the start of the IWFR approached, key relationships were being forged that would expand and strengthen the immigrant rights movement. In Chicago, a crowd of fifteen hundred rallied in support of immigration reform on August 9 before marching to the Congress Hotel, whose primarily immigrant workers had been on strike for eight weeks. Seattle unions used the IWFR to reach out to a diverse number of community groups, with Steve Williamson, executive secretary-treasurer of the King County Labor Council, noting, "Labor is saying that immigrant issues are union issues, and other groups are talking about unions as never before. The energy is growing exponentially" (Parks 2003). Houston's central labor council also sought new alliances in support of immigrant rights. "We are building ties with groups that have never had a relationship with the union movement before," said Richard Shaw, secretary-treasurer of the Harris County (Texas) Central Labor Council (Parks 2003)

The religious community was also gearing up. In Maryland and Washington DC, over Labor Day weekend in 2003, there was a Labor in the Pulpits program at 125 religious services emphasizing immigrant rights. "Just as the Freedom

Rides in the 1960s set the stage for a national movement to secure the rights of African Americans in this country, the Immigrant Workers Freedom Ride can create the platform for a real national dialogue about immigration reform," noted Fred Mason, president of the Maryland State and DC AFL-CIO (Parks 2003). Over 160 religious groups, including affiliates in the National Interfaith Committee for Worker Justice, endorsed the IWFR. Throughout the rides, meetings and rallies were often held in churches, just as they were during the UFW grape boycott (Parks 2003).

The buses carrying over nine hundred activists began departing on September 23, 2003, from ten major cities—Boston, Chicago, Houston, Las Vegas, Los Angeles, Miami, Minneapolis, Portland, Oregon, San Francisco, and Seattle—and planned to converge in Washington DC and New York in early October. The IWFR got off to a rousing start in Los Angeles, where an estimated ten thousand people gathered to send the riders off. Cardinal Roger Mahony held a service in the city's cathedral to offer his blessings to the riders and the event (Parks 2003).

The IWFR showed the diversity of cities in which a burgeoning immigrant rights movement was taking root. Tulsa, Oklahoma, Knoxville, Tennessee, Birmingham, Alabama, Grove Springs, Florida, Charleston, South Carolina, and Des Moines, Iowa, were not well known for immigrant rights activism, yet riders were warmly received by local supporters in each of these cities. At one level, the stops in over one hundred cities were simply a function of logistics: riders needed places to eat and sleep. And it was only logical that they would meet local supporters from labor, the religious community, and student and community groups while staying in or passing through town. But beyond the practical necessity, the plan represented a brilliant strategy for laying the groundwork for a national immigrants rights movement. By traveling through cities like Knoxville, Omaha, and Birmingham, the IWFR helped pave the way for large marches in these communities in 2006.

Eliseo Medina and Maria Elena Durazo recognized that the IWFR was less about pushing specific legislation and more about announcing the emergence of a larger movement. Medina stated, "We need to organize and use the power of our vote. That's the next step in the struggle. It's not just about immigrant workers rights, but about living wages, about decent education. This is the beginning of us taking back America" (Greenhouse 2003). Maria Elena Durazo, IWFR national chair and general vice president of HERE, predicted that the Immigrant Workers Freedom Ride was not an event "but the creation of a new movement. Immigrants now understand we are not alone, we have allies." As the crowd left, she urged them to become freedom fighters, "Whether you are second generation, or 14th," she said, "We have to build a new movement in the United States of America" (Greenhouse 2003).

SPRING 2006: THE MOVEMENT EXPLODES

After the IWFR helped establish the alliances necessary for a nationwide movement, Republican congressman James Sensenbrenner of Wisconsin introduced H.R. 4437 on December 6, 2005. This legislation, known as the Sensenbrenner bill, made it a federal crime to live in the United States illegally. Not content to simply criminalize between ten to twelve million hard-working immigrants, Sensenbrenner's bill also made it a felony to assist or offer services to undocumented immigrants. Nurses, teachers, and even priests could be sent to prison for up to five years, and have their assets seized, if they were convicted of offering help to undocumented immigrants.

The House of Representatives passed H.R. 4437 on December 16, 2005, only ten days after it was introduced. Sensenbrenner stated during the floor debate on the measure that he was making "unlawful presence" in the country a felony "at the administration's request." Accordingly, President Bush issued a statement that day to "applaud" what he described as a "strong immigrant reform bill." He also urged the Senate to take action on immigration reform so that he could sing a "good bill" into law (Swarns 2005; White House 2005).

House Republicans were so influenced by vocal anti-immigrant sentiments from right-wing media outlets that they failed to recognize how the immigrant rights movement had grown since the passage of California's Proposition 187 in 1994. When immigrant advocates learned of H.R. 4437's passage, the response was fast and furious. The U.S. Conference of Catholic Bishops sent a letter to members of Congress and President Bush urging them to publicly oppose the measure, and the bishops' spokesperson noted that the law "would place parish, diocesan and social service program staff at risk of criminal prosecution simply for performing their jobs" (Swarns 2005). An immigrant rights movement that now included labor unions and churches on its front lines, and that had solidified its infrastructure through the Immigrant Workers Freedom Ride, was ready for battle. As Eliseo Medina later observed that Sensenbrenner "could not have imagined the historic mobilization he would help spark when he introduced his bill to criminalize hardworking, taxpaying immigrants and the teachers, health-care professionals, clergy members and others who assist them" (Medina 2006).

The House passage of H.R. 4437 triggered a series of mass mobilizations and also set in motion plans by immigrant rights advocates to win Senate approval of a prolegalization bill. Eliseo Medina was the lead negotiator on the Senate legislation. The grassroots strategy for responding to the Sensenbrenner bill began to be conceived on February 11, 2006. Immigrant rights activists from across the country met in Riverside, California, to discuss a schedule for protest activities against H.R. 4437. The group decided to hold the first mass protests on or around March 25, the date on which most southwestern cities celebrate Cesar Chavez's birthday. The second event would be held on Monday, April 10, a workday. The third mass event would occur on May 1, International Workers Day, and would highlight the indispensable role undocumented immigrants play in the American economy.

But before any immigrants took to the streets, Los Angeles's Cardinal Roger Mahony sent a powerful message that foreshadowed the massive protests to come. Mahony's Archdiocese of Los Angeles was the nation's largest, and the cardinal had become the de facto American Catholic Church leader on immigration policy. This status made Mahony's statement on Ash Wednesday, March 1, 2006, particularly significant. He directed parishioners to spend the forty days of Lent in prayer and reflection on the need for humane immigration laws. He then announced that if the Sensenbrenner bill was enacted and providing assistance to undocumented immigrants became a felony, he would instruct both priests and lay Catholics to break the law.

As the *New York Times* put it, "It has been a long time since this country heard a call to organized lawbreaking on this big a scale" (*New York Times* 2006). Cardinal Mahony's pledge to ask even lay Catholics to violate a federal law considerably raised the stakes over H.R. 4437. Mahony's declaration made it clear to millions of Catholics that all of the services the Church was providing to undocumented Catholic immigrants—the job training, child care, counseling, emergency shelter, and much more—were now at risk. Mahony's solidarity with undocumented immigrants not only inspired action among the nation's Catholic clergy and congregants, but it particularly sent a message to Latino immigrants of that faith that the Church supported their taking to the streets to assert their rights.

On Saturday, March 25 in Los Angeles, the city whose labor-Latino alliance had sparked the AFL-CIO's shift toward a pro-immigration stance, between 200,000 and 500,000 people marched in one of the largest demonstration in the city's history. Organized labor and the Catholic Church played important roles in generating this turnout, but when an event that was predicted to draw 20,000 protesters mushrooms to 500,000, a new element is likely at stake. This element was the Spanish-language media, specifically popular radio hosts whose Spanish-language talk shows were among the city's highest rated in any language. Eliseo Medina had cultivated an alliance with Los Angeles's Spanish-language media when forming OLAW in 2000, and he had subsequently harnessed this power to boost attendance at the Sports Arena events following the AFL-CIO's adoption of a new immigration policy.

After being contacted by the SEIU and other protest organizers about the impact of H.R. 4437, Los Angeles's leading Spanish-language radio personalities went all out to mobilize their listeners. Eduardo Sotelo, known to listeners of his highly rated morning talk show as "El Piolín," or Tweety Bird, said he felt personally obligated to fight on this issue because he had entered this country illegally in 1986 and had only gained legal status as a result of the 1986 Immigration Control and Reform Act. Sotelo arranged for a March 20 summit on the steps of city hall that included such rival deejays as Ricardo Sanchez ("El Mandril," the Baboon) and Renán Almendárez Coello ("El Cucuy," the Boogeyman)—often described as the Latino version of Howard Stern. After these leading Spanish-radio personalities joined forces to promote the March 25 protest, momentum "just blew up." According to Mike Garcia, president of California's statewide janitors union, Local 1877, Sotelo, Coello, and their radio colleagues "were the key to getting so many people out. If you listened to Spanish-language media, they were just pumping, pumping, pumping this up" (Watanabe and Becerra 2006b).

While the mass protests in March involved different players, the spirit of Cesar Chavez dominated the marchers' call for amnesty for undocumented immigrants. Immigrant rights' marchers in 2006 repeatedly told the media that they saw their actions as carrying out Chavez's legacy. Many of the protests were consciously timed to coincide with Chavez's March 31 birthday, and his picture was pervasive. Latino marchers clearly identified Chavez and the UFW's struggle with their own, which is why in virtually every march, the major chant and the most common phrase on banners was the UFW's rallying cry, "¡Sí, se puede!"

Further, the peaceful nature of the marches—with few arrests and virtually no acts of violence—echoed the nonviolent UFW protests of the past, sending a clear message that America's immigrants were law-abiding. In this respect, the marches projected a much different tone from the "Battle in Seattle" protests against the World Trade Organization in 1999, the huge nationwide march opposing the Iraq war in 2003, and the mass demonstrations at the Republican National Convention in New York City in 2004. Although these demonstrations were primarily peaceful, media footage typically portrayed protesters battling police or engaging in conduct that detracted from their message. Activists often criticize the media for promoting such images, arguing that random acts are inevitable and cannot be controlled by event organizers. But such acts were absent from the immigrant rights marches of 2006.

One major reason was that the turnout was so much a product of the Latino-labor-Church alliance that also comprised the UFW's mass events. The SEIU's Eliseo Medina and the Catholic Church leadership sought to ensure that the marches would not convey a message linking immigrants with disorder, which is why in city after city the SEIU and other unions took responsibility for security. For example, at the massive March 25 protest in Los Angeles, SEIU Local 1877 trained nearly five hundred people how to deal with potential problems, and two dozen SEIU members wearing orange vests were posted on each block to ensure that marchers stayed on the prescribed route. In Phoenix, the SEIU took responsibility for security at an April 10 march that was projected to have 50,000 participants but over 200,000 showed up; according to SEIU state director Martin Manteca, "the event did not result in even one arrest" (Manteca 2007).

The immigrant rights marches also paralleled the historic UFW protest events by conveying an overtly patriotic message. Backers of the massive Los Angeles protest urged immigrants to wave American flags, and these flags became a potent and highly visible symbol in events across America. Deejay Eddie Sotelo, who played a major role in boosting turnout at all of the Los Angeles marches, explained, "We wanted them to show that we love this country. Bringing the U.S. flag, that was important. There are so many people who say 'I'm glad my parents came here and sacrificed like they did for us.'" Susan Meehan, a veteran antiwar protester who attended the April 10 national rally in Washington DC, noted, "I've been to 10 zillion marches and this is the first one with people shouting 'USA! USA!' and with so many American flags." Reflecting this conscious attempt to send a patriotic message, Jaime Contreras, formerly secretary-treasurer of SEIU Local 82 and then president of the National Capital Immigration Coalition, a lead organizer of the national event, ended his speech by leading the crowd in chanting "U.S.A.! U.S.A.! U.S.A.!" (all quotes from Goodman and Gonzalez 2006).

The UFW understood the symbolic potency of American flags, which were regularly seen at UFW marches and rallies in the 1960s and '70s. During the 1970 Salinas lettuce strike, the union's red flags with a black Aztec eagle were hung throughout a hundred-mile stretch from Watsonville to King City. The Teamsters and other UFW opponents attacked these "Red" flags and had their members waving American flags throughout the area. In response, Cesar Chavez told his staff to buy up every American flag they could get their hands on. Soon, the UFW strikers were also waving these flags and Chavez himself was photographed waving a huge American flag. The many U.S. flags at the immigrant rights events of 2006 were designed to show immigrants' allegiance to their newfound home. UFW veteran Fred Ross Jr. had used the same symbolism when he brought immigrants and their supporters to the INS Los Angeles headquarters as part of VOICE's Active Citizenship Campaign, and the hundreds present that day stood in the INS halls waving American flags (Ganz 2007).

Despite the positive message of the American flag, conservative opponents of legalization highlighted the presence of Mexican flags in the crowds to claim that those marching put allegiance to Mexico first. While Mexican flags never outnumbered the American flags, activists became conscious of the messaging and, after the initial group of rallies, encouraged protesters to leave their Mexican flags at home. Rafael Tabares, a senior at Los Angeles's Marshall High who helped plan that school's March 24 walkout, "ordered classmates to put away Mexican flags they had brought to the demonstration—predicting, correctly, that the flags would be shown on the news and that the demonstrators would be criticized as nationalists for other countries, not residents seeking rights at home." Although Mexican flags were not often seen in future marches, groups like the anti-immigrant Phoenix-based Minuteman Civil Defense Corps continued to insist that the sight of "people marching on the streets and waving Mexican flags" was resulting in "a quiet rage building" (Gold 2006; Watanabe and Becerra 2006a).

Patriotic spirit was also reflected in the rallies' support for veterans and current members of the military. Latinos accounted for 16.5 percent of Marine recruits at the time of the marches, a steady increase since 1997. Uniformed soldiers were sometimes singled out for applause, and military personnel were a "popular presence" at the immigrant rights rallies. Eliseo Medina noted that at the April 10 rally in Houston. attended by over 50,000, "speakers repeatedly pointed to people in uniform at a nearby bridge, and they received roaring applause" (Spagat 2006). According to Medina, "when [demonstrators] see people in uniform, it gives them tremendous pride and validates that we are contributing to this country." At San Diego's huge April 9 rally, Latino veterans carried signs, that read "We fought in your wars." Jorge Mariscal, a Vietnam veteran who went on to become director of Chicano studies at University of California, San Diego, observed that "after serving our country, to see our relatives criminalized through this legislation [H.R. 4437] is provoking a lot of people" (Spagat 2006).

In addition to marchers' identification with Cesar Chavez and the UFW's "Sí, se puede" spirit, their peaceful conduct, and their patriotism, the 2006 marches also resembled past UFW events both in their demographic composition—not since the heyday of the farmworkers' movement had so many Latinos participated in public protests—and in their ability to convey a powerful moral message about the function of immigrant workers in the U.S. economy. What had made the farmworker marches so compelling, in addition to the music, singing, and colorful religious imagery, was that workers were coming out of Central Valley fields to remind Americans that the fruit and vegetables on their dinner tables had been picked by human beings who should be fairly treated. California's Central Valley was far from major population centers, and the media rarely exposed Americans to the realities of the nation's agriculture system.

The undocumented immigrants who marched in 2006 left the shadows to publicly proclaim that the U.S. economy depended on them. They announced without apology that it was undocumented immigrants who worked in America's restaurants, cleaned America's buildings, cared for America's sick, and made much of America's food industry possible. The very sight of hundreds of thousands of Latino immigrants marching made a statement more powerful than any slogan on a banner. Not since UFW marches had the country seen a comparable type of protest event.

It was hard to imagine that the immigrant rights movement could top its hugely successful events in March and April. But the turnout of Latino immigrants on Monday, May 1 exceeded all expectations, with at least a million people walking through over two hundred American cities in a truly dramatic display of "people power." Once again, Los Angeles led the way with over 650,000 marchers. The city's usually active port was almost completely closed. Cardinal Mahony had urged immigrants not to risk losing their jobs by skipping work and had asked children not to miss school; the Los Angeles march was held in early evening to address these concerns.

While Medina and other labor officials downplayed the role of unions in the marches, the *Los Angeles Times* described labor's involvement in the Los Angeles events as "instrumental."[2] For the May 1 march and rally, labor raised most of the $85,000 needed for portable toilets, first-aid stations, and stages. Mike Garcia of SEIU Local 1877 and Jorge Rodriquez of AFSCME "managed the connections" between the many groups involved with the events. The Laborers' union handed out forty-five cases of bottled water and built the stage for the rally. The Communication Workers of America staffed media tables; the Teamsters joined with other unions in mapping out the marching routes and providing security; and Maria Elena Durazo, then interim executive secretary-treasurer of the L.A. County Federation of Labor, hosted the rally. The events demonstrated how the AFL-CIO's shift in support of amnesty for undocumented immigrants at its 1999 convention was providing a dramatic boost for the nation's immigrant rights movement (Watanabe and Mathews 2006).

The protests also made young people more eager to vote. Jessica Dominguez, who frequently spoke to student groups as head of the Los Angeles County Bar Association immigration section, noted, "My own 19-year-old son is so excited. He knows we are living through historic moments, and he can't wait" (Watanabe and Gaouette 2006). The major involvement of young people in the rallies was encouraging for the movement's future, as they used cell phones, e-mail, the Internet—including MySpace—and other twenty-first-century organizing techniques to organize school walkouts and boost attendance at rallies. Medina described the mass outpouring as "an incredible organic movement that's being born in this country. I have been organizing for 41 years, and I've never seen anything like it. Rather than organizers creating an activity, it's the activity creating the organization" (Althaus and Garza 2006).

The question on many minds, articulated by political scientist and longtime immigrant rights activist Armando Navarro, involved "the need to take this critical mass and organize it. . . . We need to harness this power" (Colias 2006). This led some to hope for the emergence of a single umbrella organization, or a "dynamic figurehead" like Cesar Chavez or Martin Luther King Jr. to lead the effort. But Eliseo Medina, who had seen firsthand both the benefits and downside of Chavez's charismatic leadership, described the successful events this way: "We are seeing hundreds of leaders coming together. Many of them are people nobody has ever heard of. This organic organization will outlive any one charismatic figure." Medina described the 2006 marches in a May 2 *Los Angeles Times* op-ed as "the birth of a national movement," but he was too modest to cite his own role in its creation (Medina 2006).

Medina was among the new generation of labor leaders who pushed unions to organize immigrants, and his success in Los Angeles became a national model. He had also led the fight to align the American labor movement with the cause of immigrant rights, which resulted in the AFL-CIO adopting a pro-immigrant policy for the first time in its history. In addition, Medina had created bonds of trust with Cardinal Mahony and the national religious community that encouraged the clergy's enthusiastic support for such activist events as the Immigrant Workers Freedom Ride of 2003 and the protest marches of 2006. Many allies joined Eliseo Medina in these struggles, but he clearly played the leading role in resurrecting the labor-clergy-community alliance that had brought success for the UFW in its heyday and that provided the vehicle for mass participation by Latino immigrants in 2006.

POST-2006: POLITICAL BACKLASH AND DREAMS DEFERRED

Progressive change does not occur in a straight line. Nearly a decade passed between Rosa Parks's refusal to go to the back of the bus in Montgomery, Alabama, in 1955 and the enactment of federal civil rights laws in 1964, and there was often little sense of progress during that period. Similarly, while many who marched in the massive immigrant rights protests of 2006 thought the outpouring would quickly lead to congressional passage of comprehensive immigration reform, such expectations were unrealistic while Republicans controlled the White House and Congress. In fact, congressional Republicans responded to the protests by demanding harsher crackdowns on immigrant workers. Latinos countered by helping defeat anti-legalization, Republican members of Congress in Colorado and Arizona in the November 2006 elections, confirming the protesters' vows that "Today we march, tomorrow we vote." But Republican political leaders remained far more focused on maintaining support of the party's harshly anti-immigrant right wing than on attracting Latino voters. Republican attacks on immigrants intensified in 2007 and 2008, causing great human hardship and moving Latinos en masse into the Democratic Party.

The November 2008 national elections appeared to represent a major turning point for Latino political empowerment and comprehensive immigration reform. Record Latino Democratic voter turnout helped Barrack Obama win four states—Nevada, Florida, Colorado, New Mexico—that Republican George W. Bush carried in 2004, and contributed to Democrats winning large House and

Senate majorities. The long-dormant Latino voting giant had finally awakened, and expectations were high for enactment of immigration reform during Obama's first two years.

Unfortunately, two factors changed this political calculus.

First, despite losing Latino voters in droves, the Republican Party continued its shift away from supporting any legislation that would grant undocumented immigrants a meaningful path to legalization. The party's rising anti-immigrant rhetoric was part of its racially coded attacks on the Obama administration and was fueled by claims following the onset of the 2008 economic crisis that undocumented immigrants were stealing jobs from U.S. citizens. As right-wing, anti-immigrant Republicans redefined themselves as the "Tea Party," they threatened Republican senators seeking reelection in 2010 with primary challenges if these senators supported immigrant rights. This dynamic even led Arizona senator John McCain, the 2008 Republican presidential nominee, to shift from cosponsoring the bipartisan Kennedy-McCain immigration reform bill in 2007 to becoming a strong opponent of any path to legalization by 2009.

Second, prospects for comprehensive immigration reform in 2009 were also derailed by President Obama's decision to put other major priorities aside until the passage of health-care reform. Immigrant rights advocates accepted Obama's timetable, but when the health-care fight continued into 2010, it meant that the opportunity to build on the momentum of 2008's large Latino voter turnout was lost.

The combination of intensifying Republican opposition and competing Democratic priorities resulted in no action on comprehensive immigration reform during a period in which Democrats controlled a large House majority and held fifty-nine Senate votes. In fact, progress appeared to be reversing, with Arizona in April 2010 enacting S.B. 1070, the Support Our Law Enforcement and Safe Neighborhoods Act. The act's strong anti-immigrant provisions, legally challenged by the Obama administration and immigrant rights groups for racial profiling, galvanized anti-immigrant activists. The legislation also put progressives on the defensive, as proponents of stricter enforcement pointed to the Obama administration's inaction on immigration reform since taking office.

Activists sought to respond to the Arizona law and rejuvenate the drive for comprehensive reform by using the November 2010 elections to again show anti-reform Republicans that they would pay a steep political price for betraying Latino concerns. And Latino voters responded. In Nevada, Senate Majority Leader Harry Reid won a tough reelection fight by securing 90 percent of the Latino vote, with Latinos making up a record 12 percent of the electorate. California Democratic senator Barbara Boxer won 86 percent of the Latino vote in a race where 18 percent of voters were Latino, and Democrat Michael Bennett survived a fierce battle in Colorado by winning 81 percent of the vote, with Latinos comprising

10 percent of all voters (Latino Decisions 2010). However, Latino voters could not alter a national election wave that saw Republicans take control of the House. This wave effectively ended any chances for comprehensive immigration reform in the near future.

Today's immigrant rights movement confronts a political environment as hostile to comprehensive federal reform as it was before millions took to the streets in the spring of 2006. Much has been learned about the risks of trusting politicians, and about relying on inside the Beltway strategies rather than on the type of grassroots activism that seemed to put reform on a path to passage following the 2008 national elections.

This reversal in reform's prospects is distressing and may lead some to conclude it is a hopeless task. But the road to social justice can be uphill and winding. When Cesar Chavez began a drive to organize California farmworkers in 1962, nobody knew it would take thirteen years to pass the California Agricultural Labor Relations Act, or even whether the movement he started would ever succeed. Veterans of the marches of 2006, and those who continue to work for comprehensive immigration reform, as well as the next generation of activists, remain driven by the "Sí, se puede" spirit and will work for legalization until it is achieved.

NOTES

Much of this chapter is excerpted from Randy Shaw's *Beyond the Fields: Cesar Chavez, the UFW, and the Struggle for Justice in the 21st Century* (University of California Press, 2008).

1. Harold Meyerson's columns on Contreras and the Los Angeles labor scene were invaluable to this chapter. Meyerson's work often echoes that of the also insightful UCLA Labor Center's Larry Frank, Ruth Milkman, and Kent Wong, and many of the chapter's citations reflect conclusions, analysis, and factual findings found in the writings of all four authors, as well as in those of labor activist and author Peter Dreier.

2. Miguel Contreras, who had also played such an important role, had passed away unexpectedly in May 2005.

5

From Prayer to Protest

The Immigrant Rights Movement and the
Catholic Church

Luisa Heredia

Undocumented immigration has been at the heart of contemporary legislative debates on immigration policy in the United States. In 2006, immigrants of all legal statuses were at the center of the mass mobilizations that responded to and affected these debates. In cities across the country, undocumented and documented immigrants, and their supporters, took to the streets to protest enforcement-only legislation, H.R. 4437 being the first of such bills,[1] and demanding immigration reform that included the legalization of undocumented immigrants residing in the United States. In the halls of Congress after the mass mobilizations, immigration debates immediately shifted and soon hinged on finding a way to provide a *pathway to citizenship* for all, or a portion of, the reported twelve million undocumented immigrants. As a swift response to the 2006 mobilizations, Immigration and Customs Enforcement (ICE) officials moved well beyond the border into the interior of the United States, embarking on a national campaign to raid workplaces and homes; to date, hundreds of thousands of undocumented immigrants have been deported.[2]

In Los Angeles, the immigrant rights organizational community—including religious, labor, and community-based immigrant rights organizations—mobilized the largest Latino civil rights demonstrations ever experienced in the United States, and despite splits over tactics and platform, this mobilization solidified L.A.'s role as the center of the immigrant rights movement (IRM). Of the various actors that have been involved in mobilizing for immigration reform in L.A., the Catholic Church has been especially visible.[3]

In this chapter I examine the Catholic Church's participation in the immigrant rights movement in Los Angeles during the 2006 campaign for immigration reform. First, I examine the literature on religion and political participation, arguing that past studies have failed to examine the role of religious values and practices, and also Church structure, in order to advance our understanding of how religious institutions reach out to and mobilize their members. Second, I discuss the Church's national Justice for Immigrants campaign and the impact of the national Catholic Church on the participation of its local parishes in L.A., specifically focusing on the union between the Church and the immigrant rights movement in Los Angeles. Third, I present the activities organized by the Church in its efforts to shape immigration reform, carefully considering the role of religious values in growing the types of mass-based activities in which individuals can participate. And finally, I end with a discussion of how the Church's efforts in mobilizing its base have fit into the divisions within the immigrant rights movement.

THE ROLE OF CHURCHES IN MOBILIZATION

The literature on religion and political participation highlights the importance of religious bodies as mobilizing institutions (Beyerlein and Chaves 2003; Verba, Schlozman, and Brady 1995). Churches are especially important for mobilizing Latinos and immigrants. In a recent study on immigrant mobilization, J. Wong argues that, in the absence of political parties, civic organizations and "religious institutions play a strong role in politically mobilizing immigrants" (2006, 116). Jones-Correa and Leal also argue that, "while churches play an important part in American civic life in general, in the absence of other civic associations they play a disproportionate role in the civic and political lives of Latinos" (2001, 763).

Existing studies have mostly been on the individual level however, linking Church membership to political activities by considering the likelihood of an individual participating in political activities (Brown and Brown 2003; Jones-Correa and David Leal 2001; Verba, Schlozman, and Brady 1995; Wuthnow 1999). I move beyond this vantage point to the organizational level and more broadly examine how religious institutions participate in social movements. In essence, my interest lies in how religious institutions mobilize their congregants, and to what forms of activities, as part of a social movement. In their study, Beyerlein and Chaves (2003) show that religious traditions engage in some political activities over others, reporting that the Catholic Church, more than other congregations, organizes demonstrations and marches and lobbies elected officials. This study contextualizes this finding by exploring the Church's efforts as part of the immigrant rights movement in the United States.

According to social movement theory, religious institutions are *mobilizing structures,* or "those collective vehicles, informal as well as formal, through which people mobilize and engage in collective action" (McAdam, McCarthy, and Zald 1996). Studies have shown that churches can provide social movements with a variety of resources, including material resources, leadership, and a mass base (Morris 1984; Munson 2003). Beyond the resources that individual churches may offer, some churches can also provide a standing organizational network to support political campaigns and social movements (Hertzke 1991; Morris 1984). However, most studies draw on the role of the black church in the civil rights movement; most of these churches acted as local, independent institutions and can therefore be treated likewise.[4] Consequently, scholars have sidestepped the fact that not all religious traditions are organized in this localized manner. For instance, one of the Catholic Church's most distinguishing characteristics is its immense hierarchic infrastructure.

I show that the Catholic Church in Los Angeles has served as a mobilizing structure, but I expand the aforementioned literature by considering *how* its immense infrastructure supports mobilization. I argue that, in support of the 2006 immigrant rights marches, the Catholic Church provided resources to lower levels of its hierarchy to activate those local resources and lower the expense of such mobilization efforts. This local-level mobilization, in turn, strengthened the political voice of the Church at the city, state, and federal levels. The Church's campaign to activate Catholics during the spring of 2006 solidified a Catholic-related sector of the immigrant rights movement that proved to have critical repercussions for the internal workings and trajectory of the movement.

Other studies have pointed to the importance of religion in mobilization. In this vein, Munson argues that religion provides social movements with "values, languages, and narratives that are legitimated by an understood tradition with a long historical pedigree, and a claim to the transcendental or sacred" (2003, 25). C. Smith (1996a) links the conception of religion as a set of beliefs to its potential to be disruptive; that is, the potential to challenge the social order. Still, researchers of social movements and immigrant political incorporation have continually failed to encompass religious values and practices in their research and to most importantly distinguish "what is distinctively *religious* about religious institutions" (Munson 2003, 20).

Taking up this question, this chapter presents evidence that the Catholic Church's religious values provide it with legitimacy when addressing the general public and policy makers. Furthermore, the Church's efforts to activate its members relied on the transmission of its religious values and on linking these values to political action on behalf of immigrants. For example, an important feature of the Church's participation in the 2006 protests was its reference to and incorporation of holy days and rituals when attempting to draw congregants to participate in the political activities it organized for immigrant rights, thus investing these activities with religious meaning. The Church played a leadership role in mobilizing its parishioners to participate in the IRM by adding a moral voice to immigration policy debates. Accordingly then, religion, when considered as a set of values, serves as the impetus and forms the parameters for the Church's activism and policy on immigrant rights.

The Catholic Church in Los Angeles

The most relevant geopolitical units of the Catholic Church are its dioceses, which are overseen by bishops directly appointed and supervised by Vatican officials. Each diocese is comprised of parishes that are dispersed over the geographic area the diocese encompasses. Each parish has its own congregation, typically comprised of individuals within the diocesan parameters. One step up from the diocese is the archdiocese, which spans a larger geographic area. The bishops from every diocese in the United States have formed a national body called the U.S. Conference of Catholic Bishops (USCCB).[5] There are also a variety of offices, such as Justice and Peace or Catholic Charities, within or affiliated with the Church that also share a similar national, state, and local organization. The Los Angeles Archdiocese spans three counties in Southern California and, at the time of this study, was headed by Cardinal Roger Mahony. Because of its size, the archdiocese is divided into five "pastoral regions" that are headed by bishops.

In L.A., the role of the Catholic Church as a mobilizing agent for immigrant rights is heightened because of the Church's large Latino membership in that city. Latinos comprise 70 percent of the Catholic population in L.A. (G. Rodriguez 2004), whereas nationally they represent only 39 percent of Catholics (USCCB 2007a). These numbers hold despite a decline in Catholic membership over generations—arguably because of the most recent influx of largely Catholic immigrants to the United States (Espinosa, Elizondo, and Miranda 2003). Accordingly, the Catholic Church continues to dominate the religious landscape among Latinos in L.A.

DATA AND METHODS: UNDERSTANDING THE CHURCH'S ROLE IN L.A.

The data used for this chapter were compiled from the spring of 2006 to the fall of 2007, and they draw on a variety of sources, including in-depth, semistructured interviews with both religious and community leaders; personal, organizational, and Web-based archive searches of different levels of the Catholic Church hierarchy; and participant observation of coalition meetings and collective actions relative to the legislative campaign during this period.

For example, I interviewed priests from the most renowned Latino immigrant parishes, including Our Lady of the Angels, better known as La Placita, and Dolores Mission. I attended the meetings and political actions of a variety of immigrant rights groups, including faith-based, grassroots, and professional organization coalitions.[6] To undertake archival research, I visited the California Catholic Conference Archives, the Archdiocese of Los Angeles Archives, and the Claretian Missionaries of the Western Province Archives.[7] Key informants also supplied documents from their personal files, and some informants led me to search official Church websites related to the different offices and campaigns of the Catholic Church.

ACTIVATING CATHOLICS TO THE STRUGGLE FOR IMMIGRANT RIGHTS

Justice for Immigrants: A Journey of Hope

In 2005, the USCCB launched the Justice for Immigrants: A Journey of Hope (JFI) campaign, which was "designed to unite and mobilize a growing network of Catholic institutions, individuals, and other persons of good faith in support of a broad legalization program and comprehensive immigration reform principles" (Kerwin 2005). The Church sought to add its moral voice to ongoing immigration policy debates to influence policy makers and the general public. The Church's organizational structure and its religious teachings were instrumental in reaching into the pews of every church in the effort to mobilize Catholics around immigrant rights. This mobilization strengthened and legitimized the national Church's political voice by increasing the number of movement participants and activating local clergy to take leadership roles within the broader immigrant rights struggle on behalf of the Church.

Dioceses were undoubtedly the central organizing units of the campaign to reach out to and mobilize Catholics. The Archdiocese of Los Angeles answered the call to join the national JFI campaign by forming a steering committee charged with developing and implementing the campaign. Mirroring the national campaign, the JFI steering committee sought to "mobilize large numbers of Catholics in favor of immigration reform" (Archdiocese of Los Angeles n.d.). Reaching parishes was to be the first step in that process. Local parishes were asked to participate by launching parish-level JFI campaigns through existing Justice and Peace or Social Concerns parish offices. Parishes, bolstered by the legitimacy provided by the national and archdiocesan campaigns, would then mobilize their parishioners to participate in actions that pushed a platform for comprehensive immigration reform.

To foster support and begin mobilizing for comprehensive immigration reform, the JFI campaign sought "to educate the public, especially the Catholic community, including Catholic public officials, about Church teaching on migration and immigrants" (Justice for Immigrants 2005a). Catholic social teaching—including biblical scriptures, bishops' statements, and papal statements—were all used to appeal to Catholics and to lay the foundation for the Church's activism on behalf of immigrants. Catholics were then asked to live their faith by actively participating in the struggle for immigrant rights. Bishop Gerald Barnes, in a letter introducing the JFI campaign to parishes, stated this sentiment clearly: "As your parishioners become familiar with the Scriptural and Catholic Social Teachings that inform Christian attitudes toward immigrants, it will be important to provide them opportunities to actively live their faith through acts of Christian charity and advocacy on behalf of immigrants" (Barnes 2006a). While some activist parishes and parishioners were already familiar with Catholic social teachings on immigration, others were not. The Church's strategy of educating Catholics on the religious foundations for "welcoming the stranger" provided legitimacy to the existing efforts of activist parishes. However, the Church also intended to reach beyond these parishes and took an active role in mobilizing Catholics who had not considered immigration to be a "Church issue." In this way, the Church sought to provide leadership on the issue of immigration by adding a moral voice to ongoing legislative debates, and in so doing it sought to reach beyond its parishioners to the general public and, most importantly, to policy makers.

The effects of the national JFI campaign were not unidirectional; rather, the national campaign also benefited from the activities of dioceses, parishes, and Catholic congregants themselves. The JFI campaign was launched to "maximize the Church's influence" in its effort to "make comprehensive immigration reform, with special emphasis on legalization, a major public policy priority within the Church" (Kerwin 2005). In order to reach its goals of affecting immigration reform policy, the national JFI campaign "reach[ed] beyond the networks of the participating national agencies . . . to enlist the support of *Catholic individuals and institutions* in dioceses throughout the country" (Kerwin 2005). Because the Catholic Church is territorially based, local parishes not only added voices to the Church's national campaign but they also directed their actions at local, state, and federal representatives. Therefore, the Church's top-down and bottom-up efforts were mutually reinforcing.

Religious and lay leaders at the archdiocesan and parish levels saw their activities couched within the national and archdiocesan JFI campaigns. Even for community-based activist parishes with a history of providing services and advocating for immigrants, the JFI campaign provided justification to continue and to expand their efforts in the struggle for just and humane immigration reform. Thus, the Catholic Church at the national level, by launching a national campaign aimed at involving its members, provided resources and legitimized local actions on behalf of the Church to educate and engage Catholics in activities on behalf of immigration reform. Those activities, in turn, strengthened the political voice of and provided legitimacy to the Catholic Church in the national arena. In the remainder of the chapter, I discuss more in depth these top-down versus bottom-up processes.

Resources: From the Top Down

To facilitate local-level participation, the national JFI campaign provided dioceses with resources, which in turn equipped their parishes with a vital educational and organizing apparatus. Although these resources were available to outside organizations and individuals, the JFI aim was to engage different levels of the Catholic Church hierarchy and to also consolidate a national Catholic voice relative to immigration reform. To realize its mission, the JFI campaign developed and communicated its official policy positions during the immigration reform debates. It also provided information pertinent to organizing political activities, including a series of how-to guides to assist dioceses and churches in involving their parishioners, which were transmitted through parish kits, a JFI website, and updated memos to dioceses.

A Common Platform. Although the USCCB has been involved in advocating for immigrant rights for some time, the basis for the national JFI campaign can most immediately be traced to a binational meeting between the bishops of Mexico and the United States on international migration. As a result of this meeting, in 2003 both conferences of U.S. and Mexican Catholic bishops released a pastoral statement titled, *Strangers No Longer: Together on the Journey of Hope.* This statement discussed the social reality of international migration, Catholic religious teaching on immigration, and areas of policy in need of reform. [8] Thus, the U.S. and Mexican bishops' pastoral statement provided the foundation for the policy platform the Catholic Church would later pursue.

The Office of Migration and Refugee Policy, housed within the USCCB Office of Migration and Refugee Services (MRS), "assist[ed] the bishops in the development and promotion of migration and refugee policy positions within the context of the Church's social and moral teaching" (USCCB 2007b). [9] Overall, the JFI campaign distilled a five-point legislative platform that encompassed "just and humane immigration legislation": "Just legislation should include a viable path to citizenship for undocumented persons residing in our nation; a temporary-worker program which protects the right of both U.S. and foreign-born laborers; reforms in the family-based immigration system by reducing backlogs and shortening times for family reunification; and restoration of due process protection for immigrants. Immigration enforcement also should be an important component of comprehensive immigration reform" (Barnes 2006b). The JFI campaign provided a unified legislative agenda to the Church leadership as part of its strategy to build a Catholic movement to influence immigration legislation. Furthermore, Church leaders were kept informed as debates on immigration reform progressed.

The MRS Office of Migration and Refugee Policy monitored pending national legislation and, through its ties to the JFI campaign, summarized the bills' provisions for local religious leadership, updating the leadership on where bills were in the legislative process and the Church's assessment and stance on these bills. The Office of Migration and Refugee Policy transmitted this information to religious and lay leaders through e-mails and an official JFI campaign website that included a section on "pending legislation."[10] The bishops supported or withheld support for pending legislative bills that were up for debate.

The USCCB came out strongly against H.R. 4437, the Border Protection, Anti-terrorism, and Illegal Immigration Control Act of 2005, an immigration reform bill that sought to criminalize undocumented immigrants and anyone that aided them, that authorized local law enforcement officers to enforce federal immigration laws and that would construct seven hundred miles of fencing along the Mexico-U.S. border. After the House passed H.R. 4437, the Senate began debating a series of bills in 2006, making the information provided to dioceses more crucial. The Catholic Church came out in support of several of these bills. The Church first lent its support to a 2005 bill sponsored by Senators Ted Kennedy and John McCain, S. 1033, the Secure America and Orderly Immigration Act.[11] Later it supported S. 2611, the Comprehensive Immigration Reform Act of 2006, as a bill from which to begin debate.[12] The Church also came out against H.R. 6061, the Secure Fence Act of 2006, which targeted the U.S.-Mexico border in the name of national security and authorized the construction of up to seven hundred miles of fencing (Skylstad 2006). The monitoring function of the Office of Migration and Refugee Policy and the updates provided by the JFI campaign made it easier for religious and lay leaders to remain involved by lowering the costs of closely following such debates amid their other obligations to their parishes and parishioners.

Political Activities. The national JFI campaign utilized "parish kits," or packets of information supplied to individual parishes that included documents on Catholic social thought, legislation, and activities. The parish kit contained how-to guides for writing letters to or visiting elected officials, writing op-ed pieces for local newspapers, and starting a JFI group in the parish.[13] The JFI website offered more timely information on legislation and activities via action alerts that provided sample letters and a search tool to find contact information for elected representatives. These parish kits, along with activities sponsored by the national-level campaign, provided resources to dioceses, churches, and parishioners, and therefore lowered the costs of organizing Los Angeles Catholics around immigrant rights in politically oriented local-level activities.

It is important to note that dioceses and parishes were not required to get involved in the JFI campaign, but their participation was strongly encouraged. For those bishops and cardinals that did engage their dioceses around immigrant rights, the national JFI campaign ensured the legitimacy and precedent with which to utilize the Catholic Church's infrastructure to engage the local community.

For instance, when local parishes in the Los Angeles Archdiocese became part of the national strategy to influence federal immigration legislation, the Church's participation gained local and national support by making the issue more visible in its localities—the L.A. efforts clearly strengthened the national-level campaign.

Strengthening the Catholic Presence in the Struggle for Immigration Reform. By putting forward an assessment of immigration and immigrant rights rooted in Catholic social teachings, the national Catholic Church hierarchy also played an essential role in legitimizing and promoting the involvement of Catholics who sought to affect the immigration reform debate. The national Church also provided information about organizing creative political activities to assist local churches that were attempting to draw parishioners into the immigrant rights struggle. During early 2006, the Los Angeles Archdiocese was able to noticeably reach beyond traditionally activist parishes to mobilize other parishes. This aided in solidifying the Church's presence within the broader immigrant rights movement in L.A. and further strengthened the Church's political voice at the national level.

Political Clout: From the Bottom Up

Mass-Level Politics.   In the 2006 campaign, the Catholic Church's presence was exemplified by the variety of faith-based activities it organized.[14] The first major action of the Los Angeles Archdiocese JFI campaign was initiated on March 1, 2006, by way of an important religious tradition, Lent, which marks the forty-day period of preparation before Easter, one of the most important periods in the Catholic religious calendar. Hence, when "Cardinal Roger Mahony called upon Catholics to commit their Lenten practices of prayer, fasting, and good works [during the month of March] to immigration reform," he signaled the religious foundation with which the Church was going to engage in the struggle for immigration reform (Archdiocese of Los Angeles 2006b). As a result, the first official action of the Church's campaign was solidly based in prayer and fasting, and it was widely publicized throughout the archdiocese and by Southern Californian media.

Parishes also participated by organizing their own faith-based political actions in response to the national and archdiocesan JFI campaigns. For instance, Dolores Mission, a local parish in the San Gabriel pastoral region, organized a month-long fast and prayer in support of immigrant rights and just immigration reform during February 2006, the month prior to the archdiocesan Lenten fast. Dolores Mission's action was connected to a larger statewide action endorsed by the California Province of Jesuits, the order that oversees the parish. The Los Angeles Archdiocese supported the Jesuit efforts, and Bishop Gabino Zavala, the bishop for the San Gabriel pastoral region, participated in a local press conference. An excerpt of the press release reads, "Hundreds of people from Dolores Mission Church, other churches, and Jesuit institutions across California have already committed to pray and fast during the month of February. The conference will serve the purpose of calling others to join in prayer and fasting for 11 million undocumented immigrants in this country, and for the enactment of just laws by congressional politicians" (Archdiocese of Los Angeles 2007).

The archdiocese also turned to its religious activities to organize events as part of the immigrant rights movement. For example, during a critical moment of legislative debate, Cardinal Mahony called for "a special day of prayer and fasting," on April 5, 2006 (Archdiocese of Los Angeles 2006e). Mahony celebrated a Mass at the Cathedral of Our Lady of Angels, asking Catholics to attend and pray for the legislators that were debating immigration reform and to fast in solidarity with the undocumented who would be affected by such legislation. Adding to their April 5 action, five days later on April 10, the archdiocesan JFI campaign and the organizations that would later form the Somos America Coalition (We Are America Coalition), under the banner of "Today we act, tomorrow we vote," · organized a candlelight vigil and procession as part of a larger National Day of Action, with marches scheduled across the nation.[15]

Again, Cardinal Mahony called on Catholics to join the vigil and procession and to pray for legislators who would be deciding the fate of immigration reform. The vigil and procession began at La Placita and ended with a rally at Fletcher Brown Square. This demonstration highlighted the religious dimension of standard protest events and of the movement more broadly in Los Angeles; though it took the similar form of a rally and march, faith leaders were key actors and the procession included "stations" of reflection and prayer, which drew from the Catholic tradition of Stations of the Cross. From its inception, the Los Angeles Archdiocese's JFI campaign used religious ritual and traditions in the struggle for immigration reform, laying the religious foundation for Catholics to act on immigrant rights and to actively practice their faith. These local-level activities strengthened the Church's stance within California and beyond. The Los Angeles Archdiocese also took its message directly to policy makers, and its parishioners were key to the Church's legitimacy and political clout.

The archdiocese used its infrastructure more actively in mobilizing congregants to lobby elected officials through local parishes. The Los Angeles Church actively organized national lobbying events through its affiliation with the Somos America Coalition.[16] As part of a postcard campaign, launched on May 9, 2006, by the coalition, the Los Angeles Archdiocese called on parishes to collect signatures after Sunday services before and after May 9 on form letters it provided (Mahony 2006). The postcards were addressed to then Senate majority leader Bill Frist and minority leader Harry Reid, who were targeted because the Senate was beginning debate on immigration reform. The postcards read: "I urge you to enact realistic and humane comprehensive immigration reform this year that: (1) includes a path to citizenship for hard working immigrants and their families, (2) provides an effective visa program for future immigrants that protects their rights and includes a path to citizenship, (3) keeps families together, (4) protects our civil rights and civil liberties, and (5) does not criminalize immigrants or their allies. Our immigration laws and our leaders should recognize that immigrants strengthen our economy and contribute to the fabric of this country" (We Are America Coalition 2006c).

Parishes throughout the Los Angeles Archdiocese participated in the action, compiling over 150,000 postcards (Archdiocese of Los Angeles 2006i). The postcard campaign was part of a larger action, National Lobby Day. The Catholic portion of the delegation from Los Angeles included Cardinal Mahony, Bishop Oscar Solis, and local parish leaders such as the pastor from Dolores Mission, Father Sean Carrol, and Father Mike Gutierrez, Saint Anne's pastor. Bishop Solis carried 10,000 postcards with him and helped to box over 120,000 more to be sent via mail (Doyle 2006). Thus, congregants knew that their signed postcards would be delivered directly to legislators by a delegation from the archdiocese. This action engaged Catholic congregants, irrespective of ethnicity, nativity, and legal status, in direct lobbying efforts; even if congregants could not lobby legislators in person, the postcard they signed linked their individual actions to the parish, the archdiocese, and finally to a larger Southern California delegation that represented their interests directly to legislators. Strategically, this campaign came on the heels of the May 1, 2006, mass mobilization and was intended to continue the momentum of these marches.

The activities described thus far were private and public forms of protest, which showed the strength of the Catholic Church's voice in sheer numbers. The Church also attempted to boost its political clout via more traditional electoral means. In order to increase the electoral power of Latino Catholics, the Church organized naturalization, voter registration, and get-out-the-vote (GOTV) activities. Part of the Somos America Coalition's agenda was also to convert the unprecedented numbers witnessed during the mass mobilizations on March 25, 2006, and on May 1, 2006 into electoral power by registering Latinos and immigrants to vote.

The archdiocese's naturalization efforts were coordinated through its affiliation with the Somos America Coalition and through local parishes' affiliations with secular immigrant rights organizations. Through its ties to the Somos America Coalition, the archdiocese participated in a Citizenship Day, held on July 1, 2006, designed to aid individuals in the naturalization process. As part of a national-level action sponsored by the Congressional Hispanic Caucus (Almada 2006), Citizenship Day was the launching event of Democracy Summer, an effort "to strengthen the power of immigrant communities and [their] allies at the ballot box by naturalizing, registering, and mobilizing thousands of new participants" (We Are America Coalition 2006d). An estimated 2,000 to 5,000 immigrants attended the Los Angeles Citizenship Day (Hidalgo 2006).

Although citizenship classes were not new to parishes, they had previously been inconsistent—but they gained a newfound prominence during the Church's immigration campaign. For example, two parishes with large Latino immigrant populations coordinated with community-based organizations to provide services to their congregants. Our Lady of the Holy Rosary, located in the San Fernando Valley, had ties to the group One Los Angeles, Industrial Areas Foundation (One LA-IAF); they had worked together on immigrant rights prior to the JFI campaign, and that partnership continued and helped Our Lady of the Holy Rosary as they began planning for administering the parish's citizenship classes (Zanotti 2006). The same held true for La Placita in downtown Los Angeles, with standing ties to La Hermandad Mexicana Transnacional, a community-based immigrant rights and service organization, when it organized and administered the parish's citizenship classes (Armenta 2006).

GOTV activities were organized nearer the November 2006 elections, several months after the mega marches in Los Angeles. The 2006 National Latino Congreso, held in Los Angeles in September, brought together Latino elected officials, activists, and organizational leaders from across the nation to discuss, debate, and develop an action plan and policy platform for the Latino community. The Somos America Coalition was a co-convener. Approximately one hundred community and religious leaders and community members attended the closing event, a Justicia for Immigrants rally followed by a procession to and vigil at La Placita. Speakers from national organizations emphasized their commitment to increasing and getting out the Latino vote. Voter registration forms as well as flyers for other immigrant rights events were made available to rally attendees. I discuss the divisions within the immigrant rights movement later in the chapter, but it is important to note here that, by this time, these divisions were deep and widely publicized, and the momentum behind the mobilizations had begun to lose ground.[17]

As the JFI campaign continued, local parish efforts gained more prominence. Local parishes worked with secular organizations to fuse the religious and political in service of immigrant rights. During 2006 and 2007, U.S. Immigration and Customs Enforcement (ICE), under the Department of Homeland Security, increased workplace and community raids and deportations, resulting in the separation of families. Family separation due to unjust immigration laws was a policy area of concern for the JFI campaign—it deemed ICE's actions a consequence of "unjust and inhumane" immigration policy. Drawing attention to this situation, leaders from La Hermandad Mexicana Transnacional and clergy from La Placita organized a month-long series of masses and processions during March 2007, the month of Lent, calling for an end to the ICE raids and detentions. Each Wednesday evening, Catholic faithful, members from La Hermandad, other religious leaders and members, and local activists from the March 25th Coalition and the coalition United for Immigration Reform met at La Placita for Mass. They would then process—armed with candles and roses, praying and singing, carrying an image of La Virgen de Guadalupe—to the ICE detention center, where they would worship together and then return to La Placita for a *convivencia*.

On a broader scale, in 2007 local parishes joined with other faiths to revive the old sanctuary movement as a strategy to provide a moral voice on the issue of family separation. The new sanctuary movement (NSM), spearheaded by Clergy and Laity United for Economic Justice (CLUE), was intended to put a face on the broken immigration system by highlighting the stories of mixed-status families, in which a parent with U.S. citizen children could be deported. As in the family framing work in Chicago, discussed by Pallares and Flores-González (this volume). L.A. churches, in line with the national movement, were asked to house mixed-status families for a three-month period or to become an "allied church" by providing resources and services to families in sanctuary. The NSM broke with the strategy of the earlier sanctuary movement, however, by declining to open the doors of participating churches to a host of undocumented individuals. Instead of stating an official position on behalf of the Los Angeles Archdiocese, Cardinal Mahony consented to individual parishes deciding if they would participate in the NSM. Several parishes have been very committed to the NSM effort since its inception, including La Placita, Saint Anne, and Our Lady of the Holy Rosary.

As part of the campaign to enact comprehensive immigration reform, the Catholic Church in Los Angeles organized and encouraged electoral and nonelectoral activities. In the electoral arena, the Church helped organize naturalization and GOTV drives as well as lobbying efforts. In the nonelectoral arena, the Church helped to organize demonstrations, marches, and a series of unique religious actions that linked standing religious traditions and/or activities to immigration reform, making the move from prayer to protest a reflection of faith for Catholics. These activities expanded the Church's presence in the immigrant rights movement by providing more opportunities for individuals to participate and, as a consequence, solidified a Catholic sector of the IRM.

THE CATHOLIC CHURCH AND THE IMMIGRANT RIGHTS MOVEMENT IN LOS ANGELES

During the 2006 immigrant rights campaign, the Catholic Church became involved in mobilizing its membership to engage in a variety of political activities, including marches, protests, and faith-based political actions, reaching out to a broad segment of the community. All of the activities the Church organized, whether at the archdiocesan or parish levels, strengthened the political voice of the Catholic Church in California and nationally. However, the Church was neither acting in a vacuum nor monolithically. Rather, it was acting within a long-standing movement for immigrant rights (Diaz 2010).[18] Thus, while the national JFI campaign sought to build and consolidate the Church's role within the immigrant rights movement, it also fostered divisions within the movement in Los Angeles, even though some parishes and clergy did not participate and others pursued activities outside of the archdiocese.

Unity and Division

The immigrant rights community in Los Angeles was intensely united on several issues: (1) it stood strongly against an enforcement-only policy, particularly H.R. 4437; (2) it agreed that the current immigration system was "broken" and in need of reform, demanding that a legalization provision be included in this reform; and (3) it agreed that the community needed its voice heard in the legislative immigration debates. Despite unity on these points, however, the immigrant rights community was also divided on issues of tactics and policy, and the Los Angeles Archdiocese was a forceful voice in these debates.

Strategy. The Catholic Church organized a variety of activities and reached out to Catholics, encouraging them to participate in achieving comprehensive immigration reform. At the same time, the Los Angeles Archdiocese did not participate in all of the marches organized by the immigrant rights community and was vocal in condemning the tactics of a segment of that community. Several examples highlight this dynamic.

The La Placita Olvera Working Group (LPOWG), a coalition of immigrant rights organizations working out of La Placita, organized the first major march against H.R. 4437 in Los Angeles on March 25, 2006. The Los Angeles Archdiocese, coordinating with United Farm Workers, had scheduled an annual procession and Mass to celebrate the life of Cesar Chavez one day later, on March 26. Voting against combining both events by a slim margin, the LPOWG continued to meet and organize from La Placita until the Gran Marcha was actually realized on March 25. For their part, the archdiocese put its efforts behind the Cesar Chavez procession and Mass that would "also serve as a call for action to follow in Chavez's example and work for just and humane immigration reform" (Archdiocese of Los Angeles 2006c). The Church's decision to combine its standing Cesar Chavez event with the struggle for immigration reform on March 26, instead of supporting a separate demonstration on March 25 against H.R. 4437, marked the beginning of a rift in the immigrant rights organizational community. These organizational splits would later be institutionalized through the creation of two separate coalitions the March 25th Coalition and the Somos America Coalition.

However, these splits were not all encompassing and did not present themselves throughout the entire Catholic Church. Indeed, though their participation was limited, Catholic clergy did participate in the March 25 march and rally.[19]

Tensions between the dominant coalitions organizing for immigration reform, the Somos America Coalition and the March 25th Coalition, also surfaced during the May 1 marches of 2006. The March 25th Coalition organized a national economic boycott, El Gran Paro Americano 2006: Un Dia sin Inmigrantes, in an effort to show the impact of immigrant labor and consumer power on the economy, to silence arguments that immigrants are a drain on the economy, and to defeat S. 2611. The Somos America Coalition, along with the Catholic Church, did not agree with the strategy of pushing an economic boycott, reasoning that it would hurt the national debate and that, without offering legal resources, could potentially harm immigrants' individual employment situations. Thus, in direct conflict with the March 25th Coalition's economic boycott and march, in a press statement, Cardinal Mahony asked students to go to school and laborers to go to work (Archdiocese of Los Angeles 2006g). As an alternative, the archdiocese and the Somos America Coalition took the lead in organizing an alternative march to be held in the early afternoon. Not heeding the divisions within the immigrant rights movement, boycott observers and marchers from the earlier March 25th Coalition action, including local Catholic religious leaders and parishioners, chose to continue participating in the day's events by joining the Somos America Coalition's march and rally in the afternoon (Diaz 2006).

The Los Angeles Archdiocese's stance on the student walkouts also divided the immigrant rights groups. Though Cardinal Mahony is credited with his forceful statement instructing religious leaders to engage in civil disobedience by defying H.R. 4437 were it to be enacted, he later condemned the student walkouts after the Gran Marcha on March 25 and again in preparation for the May 1 Gran Paro Laboral, two actions in which students were calling for immigration reform (Archdiocese of Los Angeles 2006d, 2006h). The reasoning behind the Church's stance was that such actions would polarize public sentiment about immigrants and immigration reform, doing more harm than good. Cardinal Mahony was not alone in his position; in the second round of student walkouts he was joined by Los Angeles mayor Antonio Villaraigosa and the superintendent of the Los Angeles Unified School District, among other Latino elected officials, in asking students to stay in school. Cardinal Mahony's press release regarding the walkouts makes this sentiment clear.

Our goal is a shared one: work together effectively to educate the entire community about the issues, join in efforts which help change people's minds and hearts to embrace sound immigration reform, and take only those steps that lead to this goal. In my opinion, student boycotts of school and other activities on our streets do not produce meaningful immigration reform. On the contrary, such activities tend to polarize groups in our community and to create a negative backlash against decent immigration legislation. Consequently, I am pleading with all of the students in both public and private schools across Southern California to go to school tomorrow, and stay in school during the entire school day. It would be far more effective to achieving our goal if the students remained in school, engaged in debate and discussion about immigration reform, and spent time writing letters to California's US Senators and House Representatives. Such activities will be effective in obtaining our overall goal. (Archdiocese of Los Angeles 2006d)

Policy.   The split in the immigrant rights organizational community in Los Angeles was also manifested in divisions over policy, for example, about whether or not to support S. 2611, the Senate's Comprehensive Immigration and Reform Act. The Catholic Church was a key organization in this division. Peter Schey, an immigration lawyer and a key supporter of immigrant rights who aided organizations in assessing policy, helped the March 25th Coalition in analyzing S. 2611, after which the coalition came out strongly against the Senate bill. Members of the Somos America Coalition were split, with some organizations pushing S. 2611 as a starting point and others arguing that they could not support the bill as it stood. Leaders in the March 25th Coalition worked in direct contrast to the Somos America Coalition during the National Lobby Day discussed earlier, lobbying against S. 2611 using a "Kill the bill" slogan (Diaz 2006).[20]

A particular provision in the 2006 legislative debates also caused conflict among the immigrant rights community in Los Angeles—the issue of temporary workers. Prior to the mass mobilizations fueled by H.R. 4437, in its 2003 *Strangers No Longer* document and up to 2006, the Catholic Church supported temporary-worker visas to increase legal avenues for immigration.[21] In the parish kits put together for the JFI campaign, the following position was expressed: "Because the US experience with temporary workers programs has been fraught with abuses, the bishops call for a temporary-worker program that includes: Path to permanent residency which is achievable/verifiable; family unity which allows immediate family members to join workers; job portability which allows workers to change employers; labor protections which apply to US workers; enforcement mechanism and resources to enforce workers rights; wages and benefits which do not undercut domestic workers; mobility between US and homeland and within US; labor market test to ensure US workers are not harmed" (Justice for Immigrants 2006). Although the temporary-worker program the Catholic Church envisioned has many provisions to guard the rights of both foreign-born and U.S. workers, throughout the 2006 and 2007 campaign the organizations that comprised the March 25th Coalition did not support any type of temporary-worker program. This issue continued to be debated, and in 2007 a broad group of leaders in the Los

Angeles immigrant rights movement, including Catholic religious leaders, issued a policy platform that came down against the expansion of temporary-worker programs.

In January 2007, Peter Schey, along with immigrant rights organizations, convened a working group in L.A. to develop this immigration reform policy platform. He brought together key organizations in the immigrant rights movement, including local priests, activists, labor unions, and community-based organizations to debate and develop an affirmative policy platform that organizations could push in their lobbying efforts instead of merely reacting to pending legislative proposals. Schey's intent was to convene the leaders of the IRM in Los Angeles, who had differed on tactics and strategy, to develop a policy platform around which to base their future activities.

The issue of temporary workers was debated and, after a smaller working group came together to debate and develop a proposal, the final platform emerged against expanding temporary-worker programs. But it also mirrored the Catholic Church's proposal by calling for a "pathway to residency." The platform, titled the "Unity Blueprint," was distributed to and signed by hundreds of organizations nationwide, and it was presented to members of Congress. A summary of the statement on future immigrant flows and temporary workers lists the following as goals: "Achieve a realistic legal framework for future migration. Restructure the immigration quota system to better match the known family and employment-based demand. Ensure that the issuances of permanent and temporary employment-based visas are determined by labor needs based upon reliable economic indicators, rather than an employer-driven system that is easily gamed. Temporary-worker programs should not be expanded and must be reformed to provide full labor rights and the ability to seek resident status after three years" (Unity Blueprint for Immigration Reform 2007).

CONCLUSION

This chapter has argued the importance of examining religious institutions as mobilizing agents. In particular, it challenges scholars to take seriously the organizational infrastructure and the religious values and practices of religious institutions in examining these institutions' impact on mobilization and political incorporation. Religious institutions not only mobilize but also affect the form and content of political activities. In one respect, the Catholic Church expands the opportunities for individuals to become involved; and on the other, it channels some of this participation into the divisions that are present within the larger immigrant rights movement.

Overall, the Los Angeles Archdiocese joined the U.S. Conference of Catholic Bishops' national Justice for Immigrants: A Journey of Hope campaign to achieve just and humane immigration reform. The national Catholic Church hierarchy offered legitimacy and resources—a religious foundation, legislative agenda, and political activities—lowering the costs of engaging local parishes as part of the Los Angeles Archdiocese's strategy to affect immigration legislation. At the local level, the Catholic Church organized electoral and nonelectoral activities that expanded the opportunities for Catholics to become politically involved. These local efforts mobilized Catholics to become politically engaged in the struggle for immigration reform, strengthening the political voice of the Catholic Church at the federal level. Thus, the national and archdiocesan campaigns consolidated a Catholic segment of the immigrant rights movement. At the same time, the Catholic Church's participation also added to the divisions found within that movement in Los Angeles.

The Catholic Church in Los Angeles persists in its struggle for immigrant rights by continuing its advocacy and providing services to the immigrant community. The archdiocese continues to call on Catholics to pray and advocate for immigrants. In his 2008 Lenten message, Bishop Solis provided recommendations "for a more meaningful Lenten spiritual journey," which included praying for "peace and justice, keeping in mind the Church's continued call for comprehensive immigration," and, as part of a postcard campaign, "send[ing] postcards to our government leaders in support of families torn apart by a broken system" (Solis 2008). Bishop Solis continues to reach out to different sectors of the archdiocese by giving talks about the Church's position on immigration (Solis 2009). In addition, local activist parishes, with their ties to other immigrant rights organizations, are continuing their efforts to stop ICE raids and to get immigration reform back on the agenda. RISE, a nonviolent action wing of the IRM, helped to organize a hunger strike and encampment at La Placita, from October 15 to November 4, 2009, in an "effort aiming to gather 1 million people committed to 'vote for immigrant rights, fast at least one day, recruit five family and friends to sign the pledge and take action to hold the new administration accountable for our votes'" (Muñoz 2008).

In a time of fear and uncertainty due to increased raids and deportations, and with no federal policy in sight, the Catholic Church is also reaching out to immigrant communities. As part of an interfaith immigrant rights coalition, the Church and other faith-based and immigrant rights activists launched a week-long series of events on International Human Rights Day to teach immigrants about their rights. The coalition aimed to distribute one million business-sized cards with information on undocumented immigrants' rights when confronted by an enforcement officer (Watt 2008). The Church leadership is also renewing its commitment to the struggle for pursuing comprehensive immigration reform. These activities are also occurring elsewhere. Father Sean Carrol, formerly with

Dolores Mission in East Los Angeles, is now executive director of the Kino Border Initiative, whose purpose is to "aid illegal immigrants deported from the United States to Mexico."[22]

The Catholic Church at the national level, along with the ebbs and flows of the immigrant rights movement, has shifted from broad, mass-based contentious collective action at the federal level to local activities (advocacy and service) aimed at the most pressing issues facing the immigrant community. Local activist parishes are still engaging in collective contentious actions with an eye toward stopping the raids and deportations and putting immigration reform back on the political agenda. Thus, the Los Angeles Archdiocese is still committed to the struggle for pursuing comprehensive immigration reform even if its strategies have shifted. Cardinal Mahony, in a 2008 address, renewed the Church's commitment to immigration reform and called on both presidential candidates to make reform a top priority in the new administration.[23] Denouncing the turn to enforcement-only policies, the increased anti-immigrant sentiment they engender, the inhumane treatment of immigrants, and the resulting fear within immigrant communities, Mahony (2008) proclaimed, "A human being's worth is defined by their God-given dignity, not by what papers they carry."

The questions raised in this chapter open new avenues for future research. First, the Catholic Church forms only part of the larger immigrant rights movement in Los Angeles. This account does not explore in-depth the role of other community-based immigrant rights organizations, which were vital in mobilizing the masses in Los Angeles. Second, although they captured the nation's attention, the mass mobilizations during the spring of 2006 were neither new nor impulsive but were only the culmination of a long history of immigrant rights activism in Los Angeles (Heredia 2008). This chapter employs data that are part of a larger study examining a longer history of the Catholic Church's activism on behalf of immigrant rights in Los Angeles—thus we need a longer view of the immigrant rights movement. Third, the Catholic Church is not a monolithic entity. This chapter gives a narrow glimpse of how the national JFI campaign affected the lower tier of the Church, but it is a top-down analysis with minimal discussion of dissent within the Church itself. A bottom-up analysis is still needed, with a discussion of divisions within the Church and the responses of local parishes and parishioners to the larger political milieu in which they were acting. And finally, this chapter does not give voice to those immigrants who took to the streets and struggled alongside one another to claim their political space in the United States, irrespective of their marginalized status and the increasing attacks on their communities. These stories should be told, these voices need to be heard.

NOTES

1. I will discuss this legislation in-depth later in the chapter. At this point I will say that H.R. 4437 represented enforcement-only legislation, meaning that its provisions were meant to bolster the enforcement side of immigration policy and did not include any type of legalization program, as did more comprehensive legislation.

2. Operation Return to Sender was an initiative instituted by ICE to raid and deport "criminal aliens." According to Homeland Security secretary Michael Chertoff, "Operation Return to Sender is another example of a new and tough interior enforcement strategy that seeks to catch and deport criminal aliens, increase worksite enforcement, and crack down hard on the criminal infrastructure that perpetuates illegal immigration" (Chertoff 2006). Though the operation was said to have lasted between May and June 2006, ICE continued its increased efforts to raid and deport immigrants beyond this date. Furthermore, ICE has increased apprehensions over time. According to the Migration Policy Institute (2007b), "Immigration and Customs Enforcement (ICE), the agency charged with enforcing immigration laws in the interior of the country, made 863 criminal arrests and 4,077 administrative arrests in fiscal year (FY) 2007 compared with 716 criminal and 3,667 administrative arrests in FY 2006. In FY 2005, those numbers were far lower: 176 criminal and 1,116 administrative arrests." For more information on deportation statistics, see U.S. Department of Homeland Security (2008).

3. Though the Catholic Church traces its activism on behalf of immigrants to early waves of Irish, Polish, German, and other European immigrants, it has a tumultuous historical relationship with Latinos, particularly with Mexicans and Chicanos. For example, in the first third of the twentieth century, early years the Catholic Church actually cooperated with immigration services to deport dependent Mexicans (C. Fox 2007). In Los Angeles in the late 1960s, a group of Catholic lay and religious leaders formed Católicos por la Raza to demand that the Catholic Church develop and appoint Chicano religious leadership to important posts within the institution. Other religious organizations such as PADRES and Las Hermanas were also organized, calling on the Catholic Church to be more responsive to the "Hispanic presence" (M. T. García 2005).

4. Even studies that examine the Catholic Church follow the model set forth by religious institutions in the civil rights movement by treating Catholic parishes as independent institutions. In this chapter, I show that even parish-level efforts occur within the Catholic Church's broader organizational context.

5. The USCCB is the national branch of the Catholic Church. "The USCCB is an assembly of the Catholic Church hierarchy who work together to unify, coordinate, promote, and carry on Catholic activities in the United States; to organize and conduct religious, charitable, and social welfare work at home and abroad; to aid in education; and to care for immigrants. The bishops themselves constitute the membership of the Conference and are served by a staff of over 350 lay people, priests, deacons, and religious" (USCCB n.d.).

6. These groups included the New Sanctuary Movement, the March 25th Coalition, United for Immigration Reform, and the We Are America Coalition.

7. The California Catholic Conference houses the state-level archives for the Catholic bishops of California and Catholic Charities. The Archdiocesan Archives house documents from the Los Angeles Archdiocese. The Claretian archives house the archives for a local parish, La Placita.

8. In that statement, the bishops argued that immigration policy needed to address the root causes of migration. They suggested that economic development in Mexico, with an emphasis on border communities, was a central issue. They argued for the creation of more opportunities for legal migration, including family reunification, a broad legalization program, and permanent and temporary employment-based visas. The bishops also suggested a reform in enforcement provi-

sions, including that only federal authorities be responsible for enforcement, the abandonment "of strategies that give rise to migrant smuggling operations and migrant deaths," that the border patrol aid immigrants in distress, and for more effective efforts to halt human trafficking. The bishops called for the right to due process for immigrants who have broken the law and, finally, they called for asylum seekers and refugees to "have access to qualified adjudicators who will objectively consider their pleas ... [and] to ensure that [they] ... have access to appropriate due process protections consistent with international law" (USCCB 2003, 46).

9. This sentiment was also corroborated in an interview with Kevin Appleby, director of the USCCB's MRS Office of Migration and Refugee Policy, September 12, 2007.

10. The official website as a strategy in the Church's campaign for immigration reform was aimed at expanding the Church's reach beyond the religious leadership, disseminating information on immigration legislation to individual congregants and interested parties. The use of technology in social movements merits further investigation, especially its use among religious and related organizations as a strategy for mobilizing participants.

11. The Secure America and Orderly Immigration Act was a comprehensive "compromise" bill that included border security, employer sanctions, earned legalization, and a guest-worker program. According to Cardinal McCarrick, "These elements [of immigration reform as proposed by the Catholic Bishops] are best embodied in S. 1033/H.R. 2330, the *Secure America and Orderly Immigration Act of 2005*. As the Senate Judiciary Committee and the full U.S. Senate begin consideration of a Senate bill, we ask that principles embodied in the *Secure America and Orderly Immigration Act* receive strong consideration and support" (McCarrick 2006).

12. The proposed Comprehensive Immigration Reform Act included a three-tiered "earned adjustment" provision, a temporary-worker program, the reduction of family-based immigration backlogs, "mandatory detention provisions, the expansion of expedited removal, restrictions on judicial review, and the increase in the authority of local law enforcement to enforce federal immigration law" (USCCB 2006).

13. Parish kits included documents like "Tips for Legislative Advocacy," "Communicating with Elected Officials," "Media Outreach Tips," and "Guide for Communicating with the Media." The JFI website posted similar but more comprehensive information, for example, time-sensitive action alerts.

14. This discussion includes Church immigrant rights activities from March 2006 to March 2007. I have written about other Church involvement elsewhere (see Heredia 2008).

15. Although the Los Angeles event was organized to have this religious dimension, this was not necessarily the case for the rest of the actions scheduled across the nation (Archdiocese of Los Angeles 2006f; We Are America Coalition 2006a).

16. The We Are America Coalition of Southern California is part of the national We Are America Alliance, a coalition of local community-based organizations that includes faith-based, immigrant rights, and labor organizations and hometown associations. Though these groups worked together to organize the April 10, 2006, procession discussed earlier in this chapter, they did not coalesce under the We Are America banner until afterward. The Los Angeles Archdiocese is part of the Southern California coalition's steering committee (We Are America Coalition 2006b). The We Are America Coalition was one of two major coalitions in Los Angeles. The March 25th Coalition, comprised of community-based organizations, including immigrant rights, leftist, educational, and labor organizations, was formed after these organizations worked together to organize La Gran Marcha on March 25, the first large-scale mass mobilization against H.R. 4437 in Los Angeles.

17. Though the larger actions were losing ground, this does not mean that undocumented immigrants and their supporters were not participating in protest events. Approximately one week earlier, the March 25th Coalition held a march in solidarity with Elvira Arellano, an undocumented

immigrant with a U.S. citizen son. Elvira was under order of deportation but sought sanctuary in a Methodist church in Chicago. Approximately 5,000 undocumented immigrants and their supporters marched in downtown Los Angeles. Leaders from the March 25th Coalition, attribute their higher turnout to their policy stance for legalization for all undocumented immigrants and against S. 2611, the Senate's immigration reform bill.

18. Ironically, Cesar Chavez, in his early years organizing farmworkers, organized against the interests of undocumented immigrants.

19. The data for this section come from a series of informal interviews held with Jesse Diaz, cofounder of the March 25th Coalition and a lead organizer in the La Placita Working Group. Further interviews with clergy and community leaders corroborate different points of this account.

20. Jesse Diaz, who related this information, was cofounder of the March 25th Coalition and went to DC as part of a group representing the coalition to lobby against S. 2611.

21. Though the Catholic Church has consistently taken this stance during recent immigrant rights campaigns, it has not always supported temporary-worker programs. In fact, during the campaign that led up to the Immigration Reform and Control Act of 1986, the Church was completely against temporary-worker programs (USCCB 1984).

22. The Kino Border Initiative was created by the Jesuits and will focus on direct service, education, and research. An outreach center is located in Nogales, Sonora (Caesar 2009).

23. In his address, Mahony stated, "While we acknowledge the right and the need for our government to enforce the law, we must remind our fellow Americans that man-made law does not permit the violation of God's law. And by repairing the law, we are better able to enforce it in a humane manner" (Mahony 2008).

6

Mobilizing Marchers in the Mile-High City

The Role of Community-Based Organizations

Lisa M. Martinez

In Denver, in the spring of 2006, close to 150,000 protestors took part in three major demonstrations. Although turnout in Los Angeles and Chicago was ultimately higher, the Denver marches marked the first time events of such magnitude had taken place in that city, with the exception of Pope John Paul II's visit in 1993. Because the public was mostly unaware that a battle was being waged to reform the immigration system, many believed the marches were purely spontaneous. The data and evidence presented here suggest otherwise.

This chapter focuses on the coalition of community-based organizations (CBOs) that drove the 2006 protests in Colorado and, specifically, in the city of Denver. By focusing on the coalition of organizers that mobilized Latinos and immigrants, I address the following question: How did CBOs mobilize thousands of protestors in light of opposition (by Latinos and non-Latinos, Republicans and Democrats, and anti-immigrant activists) and negative public perceptions that mounted during the course of the movement? Through fifty-five interviews with CBO leaders, activists, and elected officials, I find that the 2006 marches were carefully coordinated and would not have been as massive without the combined efforts of a coalition of immigrant rights groups, social justice organizations, the Service Employees International Union (SEIU), the Colorado Catholic Conference, and community activists.

The focus on CBOs is important because they have traditionally been viewed as the vehicle by which protestors—especially those that are outside mainstream politics and lack institutional resources—mobilize resources to achieve their goals (Gamson 1990; Morris 1993). Much like African American organizations during the civil rights era, Latino organizations are the vanguard of social, political, and economic opportunity for Latinos because they mobilize constituencies to obtain a collective good (Vigil 1987, 111). They are also important because they provide the "creation of commitment" (Gamson 1990), movement ideology (Okamoto 2004), and facilitating structures that make social change possible (McCarthy, McPhail, and Smith 1996; Okamoto 2004). CBOs in Colorado had long been working on immigrant rights issues, but the introduction of H.R. 4437 and a state-level initiative, Senate Bill 90, made their work all the more pressing.[1] By the National Day of Action on May 1, thousands of protestors, from Denver to Grand Junction and places in between, had been mobilized. But how did this happen in Colorado, a formerly red state known for its prominent anti-immigrant proponents?

Using political opportunity theory (Eisinger 1973), I describe how organizers mobilized protestors; the tactics, strategies, and frames they employed; and their response to the anti-immigrant countermovement. I also discuss why the protests were able to raise the salience of the immigration issue in the public's mind but were unable to influence public policy at either the state or national levels. Before addressing these issues, I situate the broader debate within the context of Colorado's activist roots and recent political history.

CONTEXTUAL DYNAMICS IN COLORADO AND THE MILE-HIGH CITY

The site of this study is important for several reasons. As Pallares and Flores-González (this volume) note, the magnitude of the marches took the public, the media, and even the organizers by surprise. Few people would have predicted that so many protestors would turn out. It is especially worth noting that the cities that staged marches ranged from large urban centers to small rural communities and to areas with small but significant Latino populations. Thus, the sites of the marches and the political contexts in which they took place are important because they influence the types of resources and opportunities that make protest possible (Martinez 2008b). But while many important studies have addressed Latino political mobilization and political action (see, e.g., Hardy-Fanta 1993; Ochoa 2004), most focus on major urban centers in California, New York, and Illinois, where Latinos are in greater proportion to the total population, are more ethnically diverse, and where political activism has longer-standing roots. Denver offers an opportunity to understand how contextual variation influences CBOs' ability to mobilize resources, especially in contexts that are more conservative or where Latinos are fewer in number. Consequently, Latinos may have established political structures in some contexts but lack the means to access them in others (Martinez 2008b).

The Denver case is also important given the city's history of Chicano activism. Denver was the birthplace of the Crusade for Justice, a Chicano social justice organization founded by the late Rodolfo "Corky" Gonzales in the 1960s. Gonzales is considered one of the founders of the Chicano movement and, aside from being remembered for his activism, he is well-known for embodying the spirit of the movement in the poem "I Am Joaquin." His work also lives on in the number of Latino and immigrant CBOs that have sprung up across the state. Though many are fairly new (most were formed less than ten years ago), they have been pivotal in opposing anti-immigrant and anti-Latino initiatives. For example, in 2002 Colorado voted against Amendment 31, which sought to eliminate bilingual education programs. The defeat of Amendment 31, also known as the English for the Children Initiative, marked the first time an Unz-sponsored immersion bill was defeated in any state (Escamilla et al. 2003, 357).[2] A significant Latino population alone does not explain why this would occur. Instead, Amendment 31 was defeated, in part, because of the efforts of local community-based organizations that successfully mobilized Latinos.[3] Finally, despite the state's conservative political leanings, voters elected Senator Ken Salazar (who became secretary of the interior in the Obama administration) and Representative John Salazar, two Latino Democrats (and brothers). And, in the 2008 presidential election, the state went to President Obama.

Colorado is also known for its conservative climate because, among other things, it is home to Focus on the Family, an evangelical group in Colorado Springs. The state also has the distinction of being "ground zero" for the anti-immigrant movement and the Minutemen, the organized group that espouses vigilante tactics, such as patrolling the U.S.-Mexico border and rounding up migrants. As the events of 2006 began to unfold, the Colorado Minutemen and similar groups descended upon the state to oppose any reforms that included guest-worker programs or paths to citizenship for undocumented workers. Backed by former congressman Tom Tancredo and Minutemen Project founder Jim Gilchrist, these groups called for more extreme measures that included building a wall along the U.S.-Mexico border and the immediate deportation of the approximately twelve million undocumented immigrants living in the country. Even though pro-immigrant organizers did not consider the Minutemen a real threat to the movement, the group's presence in the state was palpable as was its voice in the national debate (Martinez 2008a). For these reasons, Denver is an important case because it epitomizes protest politics in a highly polarized state.

POLITICAL OPPORTUNITY AND THE COLORADO PROTESTS

In the months leading up to May 1, 2006, discussion about immigrant rights and immigration reform dominated the national news. Although CBO leaders noted that they had been working on immigration issues long before that spring, the movement began to gather steam when U.S. congressman James Sensenbrenner introduced H.R. 4437 in late 2005. Though the bill failed to pass the Senate, one of the most striking provisions was the call to erect a fence along the U.S.-Mexico border, as anti-immigrant groups proposed. The bill would also have made it a crime for any agencies, including churches and charity organizations, to aid or assist undocumented immigrants, and it would have created stricter penalties for employers who knowingly hired undocumented workers. In response, local, state, and national immigrant rights organizations began a campaign to challenge these initiatives, bring greater awareness to the plight of undocumented immigrants, and to call for more humane immigration reform that included a path to citizenship.

The coalition of Colorado CBOs planned three major events that took place on March 25, April 10, and May 1, the National Day of Action. The groups also supported a walkout by Denver-area middle and high school students on April 19. Although the unanticipated turnout created a groundswell of support from segments of the community, debates about tactics, frames, and desired outcomes of the marches created divisions among coalition members, which ultimately affected its ability to challenge restrictive immigration legislation at the state level. Before describing the organizations involved, who they represented, their goals and targets, and their frames, I first turn to a discussion of how political opportunity theory is a valuable lens for understanding the protests in Denver.

Political opportunities are those elements of the political environment that provide incentives for collective action (Eisinger 1973; Tarrow 1994). The perspective holds that social movement activity is closely tied to more conventional political activity within institutional channels and is connected to exogenous factors that affect "activists' prospects for advancing particular claims, mobilizing supporters, and affecting influence" (Meyer 2004, 126). Exogenous factors include those that enhance or inhibit a movement's prospects for mobilization, claims making, the cultivation of alliances, use of particular tactics and strategies, and influence on institutional arenas (Meyer 2004). Because protest activities are viewed as bound by the political arena in which they take place, the perspective posits that protest will only occur if participants believe they will be successful or that institutional channels are least effective (Meyer and Staggenborg 1996). Thus, when state structures are open or receptive to challengers' demands, activists are more likely to mobilize collective action.

Among the political opportunity literature, Meyer and Staggenborg (1996) offer a refined, multidimensional approach. Their propositions account for the factors contributing to movement success, movement threats, the role of elite allies and sponsors, as well as the interplay between movements and countermovements within state structures. The authors note that movement actions create reactions to the extent that successes create opposition, threaten a segment of the population, and generate oppositional mobilization by political elites. Meyer and Staggenborg maintain that "movements that have shown signs of succeeding, either by putting their issues on the public agenda or by influencing public policy, are the most likely to provoke counter-movements. By raising the public salience of a particular set of issues, social protest can generate media interest, win the attention of policy makers, and more generally put an issue into play. Protest movements can open a 'policy window' creating an opportunity for institutional action, which in turn encourages a wide range of actors to mobilize on the issue in different venues" (1996, 1635). While open policy windows are important, Meyer and Staggenborg also note that a state's capacity to settle conflicts will affect whether or not a movement can make strides in the policy arena and, if not, the state will face sustained challenges by movements and oppositional movements. As I will show, polarization within the state apparatus made it difficult for challengers in Colorado to work with lawmakers in pursuit of immigration reform.

Another important proposition centers on the influence of movement frames and demands, which affect existing interests and values. Meyer and Staggenborg maintain that, "when movement issues seem to symbolize a whole set of values and behaviors, they are likely to threaten a broader range of constituencies who will be attracted to countermovement action for different reasons" (1996, 1639). Moreover, battles are likely to ensue if a movement begins to symbolize broader rights and cultural values. Indeed, the visibility of immigrants, especially from Latin America, has heightened public perceptions that immigration has run amok despite evidence that migration rates are comparable to those of earlier waves (Bean and Stevens 2003).

Third, as Meyer and Staggenborg see it, "a movement's strategies and tactics reflect choices about the venues of collective action, the forms of action employed, and the demands and collection action frames used" (1996, 1647). They argue that movement actors are most likely to choose a means of influencing policy and to maintain particular tactics and strategies, unless there are reasons to do otherwise. Should additional institutional venues for action be available, movements that are suffering defeats are likely to shift targets and choose venues that have a greater chance of success. As I note below, differences in strategies and tactics quickly surfaced in Colorado, with some CBOs wanting to pursue a policy-oriented target and others wanting to pursue more extreme, extrainstitutional measures, including walkouts and boycotts. Opposition groups also targeted the policy arena by encouraging lawmakers to pass the most restrictive immigration laws possible.

Finally, countermovements affect how movements respond to and frame their demands. Meyer and Staggenborg (1996) suggest that movements are forced to define claims in response to their opposition rather than to longtime supporters.

In addition, "frame disputes" (Benford 1993) create cleavages between moderate and more radical factions of a movement, which spill over and make it difficult to frame issues that appeal to the public and elite supporters. Because immigration is a cultural wedge issue, images of protestors carrying signs written in Spanish and waving Mexican flags soured the public's reaction to the marches. This allowed anti-immigrant activists to seize upon the images and shift the discourse away from CBOs' preferred frames of immigrants exercising their rights, being hard working, and wanting a better way of life, to frames that emphasized immigrants as lawbreaking criminals unwilling to assimilate. The media played a part in this as well. H.R. 4437 brought illegal immigration to the fore, and the media quickly seized the opportunity to highlight the growing immigration "problem" in their coverage of the protests (Martinez 2008a). CBOs realized the public was reacting negatively and decided to change frames over the course of the protests; however, in hindsight, some wondered if they had waited too long to "change people's hearts and minds."

With the introduction of H.R. 4437 and the state's S.B. 90, CBOs began mobilizing constituencies and worked, at least initially, to win the attention of policy makers in order to "put the issues into play." Negotiations between local and national CBOs and state and national lawmakers began in earnest, as did the coordination of protests across the country by pro- and anti-immigrant forces. As the number of protestors grew at each march and public attention began to sour over images of protestors carrying Mexican flags, state lawmakers became more disapproving of proposals that included paths to citizenship for immigrants and, instead, began to favor more restrictive laws. Although H.R. 4437 failed to pass the U.S. Senate, debates over tactics, frames, and outcomes created divisions among the coalition of Colorado CBOs and the policy window finally closed when S.B. 90 was signed into law. Nonetheless, CBOs were successful in mobilizing 150,000 protestors over the course of March, April, and May in a conservative state that was once known for its political activism. How did all this happen?

March 25

The first major protest took place on March 25 at Civic Center Park near the capitol in downtown Denver. The main catalyst for the event was H.R. 4437, which represented an open policy window. More than 50,000 protestors attended the event to oppose what they considered punitive immigration laws.[4] The size of the crowd took participants and even organizers by surprise. Prior to the event, Lily, the director of a human/immigrant rights organization in Denver, described how she and another member discussed the upcoming protest and the turnout in Chicago on March 10. They were cautiously optimistic about the national push on March 25. Lily commented:

God it was so much fun. And it was funny too because like we're talking to each other like Friday [March 24] and they're like, "Well, what do you think? What do you think?" And I said, "Well, I think we'll have done really well, we will have done a solid job if we get 3,000 people," because we had never had more than a thousand people for anything we had done around immigrant rights. I had heard about these amazing, amazing mobilizations, because Chicago had happened, and I thought, "We can blow the lid off this thing if we get 10,000 [laughs]. We planned for a couple thousand. So I knew my estimate was wildly off when I got the Greek Theater [at Civic Center Park] at 8:30 and the event wasn't supposed to start until 10:00, and there was people spilling out of the theater already. I thought "Ahhhh! We're going to be 3,000 maybe 10,000," but it was still more than I expected.

The March 25 event was the result of grassroots efforts including two immigrant rights groups, the local office of the American Friends Service Committee (AFSC), SEIU Local 105, and the Colorado Catholic Conference (CCC). The local and national Spanish-speaking media (mostly radio) played a significant role as well by informing the public about the event as well as the reasons behind it. Most of the planning meetings took place in Denver, but groups from across the state mobilized protestors for the event. And although participating CBOs represented different constituencies (immigrants, social justice advocates, the Catholic Church, organized labor, etc.), they all aligned on that day for the purpose of immigrant justice and used the frames "Ya es hora" (Now is the time), "It's time for immigration reform," and "Justice for immigrants" to mobilize protestors.

The frames were intentionally broad and simple because the issue (H.R. 4437) was viewed as an insult to the community, and organizers did not have to say more beyond that to motivate the Latino and immigrant communities. The agreed-upon target was H.R. 4437 and was entirely policy focused. In fact, tables were set up so that protestors could draft letters to state senators, letting them know that comprehensive immigration reform was needed and that H.R. 4437 was not the solution. They also wrote narratives to show state lawmakers the human side of immigration and included lines such as "I'm an immigrant and I want to provide for my family." Protestors carrying American and Mexican flags chanted "Sí, se puede (Yes we can)" as organizers rallied supporters and informed them about the potential threat H.R. 4437 posed to them and their families. For many, the human impact of H.R. 4437 was their motivation because they knew that immigration was a serious issue. For example, Lily explained that a member of her organization planned to protest because he knew firsthand the changing realities for undocumented immigrants. He shared that his sister-in-law had been deported and could not get back to her family. In response, he and members of his family passed out flyers to raise awareness about the issue and to mobilize others. Soon, he began attending planning meetings and brought friends to get in on the action too.

On March 26, events on the national scene were heating up. Lily remembers a gathering with members of her organization where she relayed news that Senator Kennedy had introduced language to potential legislation that was close to what advocates were hoping for. She described the feeling in the room as euphoric, because they believed they were making progress in the policy arena. But then the backlash began as public attention began to focus on Mexican flags and flags from other countries, and the state legislature followed suit. "The legislature was like, 'Forget this,'" Lily remembered, "and the Minutemen were starting to mobilize, lawmakers were getting called."

April 10

The next major event was a candlelight vigil that took place at Sloan's Lake Park in a predominantly Latino section of northwest Denver. The event drew between 7,000 and 10,000 people.[5] The purpose of the vigil was to remember immigrants who lost their lives crossing the border and to promote justice for immigrants. After listening to speakers, participants linked arms around the lake and then walked around the perimeter holding candles. Others carried small wooden crosses bearing the names of people who had died trying to enter the United States.

For the crowd that gathered at Sloan's Lake, it was a solemn event. For CBOs, it signaled the start of tensions among member organizations. The coalition started to splinter as differences about tactics, frames, and outcomes emerged. One of Meyer and Staggenborg's propositions (1996, 1641) holds that, during periods of heightened collective action, it becomes increasingly difficult for organizations to control the use of frames and demands that threaten powerful interests, especially as more radical factions splinter from more moderate groups. In the case of the immigrant rights movement, different groups began to take different approaches. Around the same time, student activists became more vocal and began organizing a series of walkouts and boycotts in response to the proposed immigration laws. Even though school administrators, the media, and some parents grew critical of the walkouts, student leaders began to favor increasingly aggressive tactics. Diverging perspectives about the purpose of the marches coupled with differences in tactics made it difficult for CBOs to unify on strategy at the local level and to keep up with calls to action at the national level. Jamie, the coordinator of an immigrant-driven CBO that works with several smaller immigrant justice organizations across the state, shared her take on the rift:

> What we felt, what we at [CBO name] felt, was that there were not very many organizations that were interested in actually consolidating organization around the mobilizations. We had a letter-writing campaign because we were capturing people's names and addresses to follow up with them later. The SEIU folks did give us some

assistance in capturing that information for us and they Xeroxed massive numbers of letters for us so that we could have copies and upload a database, but other organizations weren't thinking that way. They were just sorta like, "Okay, on to the next mobilization." And our members had a reaction to how they perceived other groups who were like, "On to the next mobilization," and they literally said, "We don't want to support other mobilizations, we want to be negotiating policy with these policy makers."

Jamie recalls passing out flyers after the March 25 event, inviting the immigrant base to a meeting on March 27 to discuss how the event had turned out and to propose strategies for moving forward. The 250 members from Jaimie's organization in attendance decided they (all) wanted to meet with former Colorado Speaker of the House Andrew Romanoff. Romanoff agreed to the meeting but suggested that a smaller group of representatives would be more desirable. Jamie made a call that they would not take all 250 members, a move that angered members because they felt that if the small contingency had not acted as powerbrokers, they might have turned the tide and made a stronger impact on lawmakers. Thus, rifts over differences about tactics and where best to put energies began to take hold. Some CBOs wanted to escalate the tactics, while others did not.

As John, an organizer with the AFSC noted, "Most people seem to think that mobilizations and marches are the end in and of themselves and I don't believe that and our members don't believe that." Moreover, he said, media coverage and attracting large numbers of protestors appeared to be other organizations' hallmarks of success rather than his group's focus, which was to "make change happen."

May 1

The largest of all three mobilizations took place on May 1 and was coordinated as part of a national call to action. Although organizers had been in constant communication with leaders of national immigrant rights organizations as to the movement's strategies, some leaders in Colorado increasingly felt frustrated that they were not "sitting down with the power players" in Washington DC. Nonetheless, organizers in Colorado continued to follow directives from the national organizations about aspects of the May 1 march. Still, as was the case in Los Angeles (see Wang and Winn, this volume), the Colorado movement began to splinter as differences arose about the purpose and goals of that march.

Immigrant rights organizations wanted the day to be about the march but, also, about the importance of immigrants to Colorado's economy. This shift departed from the movement's original frames. Some CBOs encouraged workers to participate in the boycott by taking the day off and not spending money. Pro-immigrant businesses were also asked to close their doors for the day or, at least, to allow their employees to take the day off. Some placed signs in their doors indicating that they supported immigrant rights. The dominant frames centered on the notions of immigrants as being "a powerful economic force and who, through hard work and respect for the country, are working for the American Dream." CBOs emphasized the vital role of immigrants in the economy and, although some business owners disagreed with the boycott, most (approximately two hundred in Denver) were supportive.

Protestors of all ages wearing white, waving American flags, and carrying signs that read "Somos America" (We are America), "I am not a criminal," and "This is what America looks like" began to line up at Viking Park as early as 7:00 A.M. As helicopters flew overhead, protestors patiently waited for the signal to begin the nearly three-mile walk from the park to the front steps of the state capitol. Few people could have known how many people were there until the line slowly began to move, around 9:30 A.M. It was not until protestors made their way across a bridge connecting North Denver to lower downtown that they could see the line snaking out in front of them. As people walked, they chanted "¡Sí, se puede!" while others sang songs. Some protestors pushed baby strollers while others escorted elderly protestors beside the line. Not only was the crowd multigenerational, it was also racially and ethnically diverse. As the marchers made their way past downtown landmarks and buildings, many people standing on the sidewalks clapped and cheered, while others booed and sneered. The end of the line reached the capitol just before noon.

The event was even more widely publicized than the other events and, yet, organizers were still surprised by the turnout. Manuel, a well-respected activist and cofounder of a local Latino social justice organization, said:

> We were like, "Aww, people aren't going to come, we'll be lucky if we get a few thousand." By two days prior to the march, our sense was that it was going to be the biggest march, that it was not gonna be no small march. And I was here the entire night prior to the march. I left here at midnight and I was getting phone calls [from] people that wanted to come by and pick up flyers. When I walked out of here a little after midnight there were still phone calls. And I was back here at four o'clock in the morning and people were calling then because they wanted fliers. And we distributed maybe close to 15,000 flyers, people coming in and they were taking them to other places and there were businesses making copies of the fliers. They would take 100 fliers and make more copies. So our 100 was tenfold. Yeah, so we had a pretty good sense that it's going to be the biggest march coming. But we could not have expected it was going to be 200,000 people.

When I asked Lily about the CBOs responsible for the May 1 march, she said, "It just went. Nobody had to organize it. We had a constant stream of strangers coming in, people we'd never seen, asking for flyers and saying, 'Give me a thousand.' And I believe they passed them all out. I've never been part of a bigger demonstration, it was incredible, it was beautiful." Still, Lily recognized that the May 1 march was not entirely spontaneous. She said that, although no one organization was responsible for the vast numbers, the fact that all three events went as well as they did was a tribute to the organizers: "The [success of the mobilizations] was due to the groundwork and the structures, and the processes, and the practices . . . of people who have been doing this work for decades, laying a framework that people could just funnel into it. In the planning of it, we had to tell people, 'You can't do that [have an open mic at the rally] and this is why . . .' and that stuff doesn't happen without organization."

Another organizer, Beth, described the scene as "amazing." She said, "It was exciting, you know, and it was just an amazing sight to be on the top of the capitol being able to see down and see that march snake into the streets." Jamie echoed Manuel's and Beth's insights that the marches exceeded everyone's expectations and said, "People from all these organizations were taking flyers and just dropping them off to all the local businesses, the churches, people on radio. It really was a mass effort."

Despite the massive numbers, a series of issues made the May 1 turnout bittersweet. One measure of an open opportunity structure is the support of elite allies, such as government authorities (Meyer and Staggenborg 1996). But CBOs had a difficult time gaining lawmakers' support, including Democrats, which ultimately affected the coalition's ability to change state laws. Others noted that allies' support came too late and, when it did come, it changed the nature of the march. Several organizers took issue with the fact that the immigrant base was only allowed to play a supportive role on May 1, especially because they were not the main speakers at the march, which had been the case at the other events. This raised the ire of more than a few organizers who felt that influential leaders, especially prominent Latinos, jumped on the bandwagon only *after* they realized the magnitude of the mobilizations. They pointed out that, prior to the May 1 march, elite allies were very hesitant to publicly support immigrant rights or, at the very least, to oppose H.R. 4437 and S.B. 90. Some organizers, like Jennifer, an organizer with an immigrant rights group in northern Colorado, shared that Latino leaders were approached early on about working on influencing lawmakers to oppose S.B. 90. She said they resisted until just before the May 1 march:

> As a result [of the April 10 rally] a lot of people came out of the woodwork . . . people who had been organizers in the past have changed their perspectives or spheres of influence came out of the woodwork again—like X, who is suddenly back on the scene, which is really good—there's a good infusion of resources, really good infusion of publicity and skill, so all of that was really good. But, at the same time, I think it's really important to maintain the immigrant voice in all of that and to not let the Xs of the world take over what could have been a really powerful movement and can still be a really powerful movement . . . by stepping into the

limelight and making really bad decisions that don't represent the wishes of immigrants, which is what X did, which is really frustrating.

Jennifer felt that community leaders acted opportunistically and that their involvement took the focus away from immigrants and immigrant rights. Thus, organizers including Jennifer felt that prominent Latino leaders could have helped the immigrant rights movement had they showed their support early on; their willingness to participate after "all the hard work had been done" led some to comment that the motivations of these elite allies were mostly self-serving and did not help the cause.

The march was also bittersweet because of the public backlash. Public perceptions grew increasingly negative as the media, in an effort to appear balanced, seized upon countermobilization efforts, even though their representatives were much fewer in number. By May 1, the debate had reached a fever pitch across the country, as pro- and anti-immigrant groups locked horns. The media sought out opposing interests and framed the debate as one between pro- and anti-immigrant groups rather than reporting on the intended focus of comprehensive reform. The media therefore shifted the debate from one about immigration reform to the problem of illegal immigration.[6] As such, Mexicans and Mexican Americans in particular became the targets of vitriolic sentiments. Rather than voicing opposition to the marches, anti-immigration advocates used the public backlash to their benefit. In an interview with a local newspaper, former congressman Tom Tancredo was quoted as saying, "Nothing that I've seen in the recent past could have helped our cause more than the display of hundreds of thousands of people waving Mexican flags and essentially demanding the right to violate the law. I hope they have one every weekend" (Hughes 2006). Anti-immigrant advocates also became energized, as the marches seemed to confirm their worst fears about the "browning" of America. But, on the whole, the Colorado Minutemen were not considered real threats by CBO organizers, at least at the state level. Although there were reports that hundreds of Minutemen were planning a counterprotest on May 1, those that did show up were outnumbered thirteen to one. Local conservative radio personalities were more reviled by CBO leaders because they reached a larger audience and believed that their views were less extreme than Minutemen groups.

As far as public opinion, CBO leaders did not anticipate that reactions would be as negative as they were. Given the public's reaction, however, they changed frames to appeal to American values. Julio, a member of an immigrant justice organization in Greeley, Colorado, said, "This is how we framed it at the meetings: We're reclaiming the American flag because you can't say that this is un-American because we're saying family reunification is about American values. We're not going to take this American flag and let you use it against us." Kara, a member of the same organization, explained how the changes to the frames came about:

> From the first marches to the May 1st march there were definitely discussions in the communities—from the planning side also from the community side, there were discussions about how do we present ourselves. There were discussions. And there were American flags in all the marches and rallies, and there were Mexican flags, and Cubano flags, all kinds of flags, but by May 1st there was still Mexican flags. But you know what, politically it was a better visual impact, it mollified some peoples' fears about Mexicans . . . but it did not change people's hearts and minds.

Those who participated in the May 1 march noted that there was a preponderance of American flags and fewer from other countries. Organizers had shifted strategies, tactics, and frames in order to appeal to the "moveable middle" and did so intentionally to assuage the public perception that immigrants were unable or unwilling to assimilate. When they realized after March 25 that middle America was not responding favorably to multinational flags, they decided to do something that was "more American."

While some organizers worked on redefining frames, others began to feel that their energies would be better served targeting different arenas, which sparked debates over tactics (Wang and Winn, this volume). By this point, the coalition of CBOs had virtually dissolved, as leaders and members continued to debate the utility of the boycott. Some CBOs, including the SEIU, supported the march but opposed the economic boycott. The CCC, the political arm of the Catholic Church, held a Mass commemorating the day but began to pull back from the movement as walkouts and calls for boycotts became more prevalent. In the CCC's view, the other CBOs' tactics were becoming more disruptive than productive. The CCC also felt the need to appease congregants who felt they were wrongfully supporting illegal activity. The SEIU and CCC also opposed the tactics because they felt they would continue to erode public support. Myra, who worked closely with an organizer with the SEIU said, "It's not that we didn't support it, it's just that we didn't think it [the boycott] was going to accomplish what we needed to accomplish."

As Meyer and Staggenborg (1996) note, institutional channels became less effective, talks with lawmakers stalled, and the policy window closed. Indeed, as thousands of protestors stood on the capitol steps, former governor Bill Owens signed S.B. 90, requiring law enforcement officials to report suspected illegal immigrants to immigration officials. When asked why the marches did not have a more powerful impact on this legislation, several organizers indicated that their energies were so tied up with events at the national level, including H.R. 4437, they lost sight of what was taking place locally. John, the AFSC organizer, said:

All of us, every single person, every single planner, every single organizer that was there, thought it was a serious mistake to ignore S.B. 90. That should have been at the forefront. S.B. 90 and everything else that happened, that should have been there. We didn't do it, we didn't discuss it. But we were so focused on the Senate and the federal level that we forgot about our own home. Did we help our people or not? I mean, yes, we blew it on S.B. 90, no doubt. But the other activity [around H.R. 4437] was a more vicious law that we helped contain. That happened because all of us were walking in the streets.

I asked Manuel, another organizer, about S.B. 90 and the lessons learned from the marches. He was more incensed than John, especially because CBOs bowed to pressures to change frames after the public reacted harshly. Ultimately, he said, it made little difference because they were unable to defeat S.B. 90. He was especially irritated with Democrats because they supported the legislation:

> So we had a bunch of American flags and what do the Democrats do? Pass anti-immigrant legislation. So if we would have had Mexican flags they would have passed *more* anti-immigrant legislation? So the reality is to have a different discussion. Let's not have a discussion about the Mexican flags versus the American flags, as the topic of discussion, let's talk about immigration reform. The political reality is if we would have had Mexican flags, American flags, Irish flags, didn't matter. The people making the decisions were going to push anti-immigrant legislation, Democrats and Republicans alike.

Manuel was angry with Democrats for giving in to Republicans and to public pressure from constituents who opposed immigration reform. He recognized that it was a politically motivated move. Democrats were eager to push such restrictive legislation because they had just regained power and had to prove to Republicans, to constituents, and to themselves that they could "be as tough on immigration as Republicans." He went on:

> The biggest [lesson learned] is that we were so caught up on the national scene that we weren't paying close attention to the local scene. And so as our rally was going on [and] the government was signing S.B. 90. If we would have paid more attention to being more on top of the local scene, that would have been the perfect opportunity to call around, because we had all these thousands . . . close to 200,000 [people at the May 1 march] . . . but that many people there and we didn't even think about S.B. 90 . . . it was a tremendous error, a missed opportunity.

CBO leaders were not encouraged by what was taking place at the national level, either. They felt the Kennedy-McCain bill (S. 2611) was a half-hearted attempt by Senator Kennedy to respond to the mobilizations by pushing legislation that seemed most progressive given the other proposals; they later analyzed the bill and realized that it was not as helpful to immigrant communities as they originally thought. Moreover, because CBOs were so caught up in the national movement, they lost sight of the local context. Lily, of the human/immigrant rights group, noted that national CBOs were eager to pass any legislation that was even slightly favorable to immigrant communities. National leaders encouraged local CBOs to focus on federal legislation as well, reasoning that, if it passed, state-level initiatives would be moot. This ultimately hurt the CBOs' ability to mobilize against S.B. 90, as they did not have the resources to do so:

> It [Kennedy-McCain] was not good, but they [CBOs] were like, we need something, anything, please! The reality of our system is that the mobilizations had an impact on what was happening in Washington, but mobilizations have to be connected to base building and power analyses and short-term, medium-term, and long-term strategy, and building from the ground up. . . . The national immigrant rights movement, whom we were deferring to, thought they were playing on an even playing field [as lawmakers] and I don't believe that. . . . I remember speaking with another organizer saying that S.B. 90 was coming down the pike, and I called around and I talked to people who were more policy lawyer-likes but were not connected to immigrant communities, and they were like, "Oh, this is just codifying what already exists." We realized we couldn't take on this other campaign and we were tragically optimistic that if we won at the national level, S.B. 90 would be moot.

Despite the differences over tactics and strategies, most CBO leaders agreed that the 2006 mobilizations energized the Latino base in ways never seen before. Several were optimistic that they would be able to sustain movement momentum into future political action. Still others were cautiously optimistic and recognized that, in order for the movement to be truly effective, there would have to be an additional component that focused on changing public policy, changing "hearts and minds" of the moveable middle, and increasing electoral participation among those eligible to vote.

THE AFTERMATH OF THE MARCHES

Data from fifty-five interviews about the three major Denver events show that the mobilizations were carefully coordinated by a coalition of immigration and human rights CBOs, the SEIU, the Colorado Catholic conference, and community activists. The temporal aspect of the data allows me to show how CBOs changed in response to shifting political opportunities. As events progressed, however, organizational differences about tactics and strategies created divisions among coalition members. Using Meyer and Staggenborg's framework (1996) as an analytical tool, I show that the mobilizations were fairly successful given the context in which they took place. The Denver case is one where CBO leaders had to contend with the state and, to a lesser degree, with anti-immigrant activists, and yet they were able to demonstrate that social change was possible through political action. Even as targets and frames changed, the number of protestors grew so that, by May 1, turnout in Denver rivaled that of other large cities.

Still, several CBO leaders noted that for every action there is a reaction. The mobilizations galvanized anti-immigrant activists and watchdog groups such as the Colorado Minutemen, Save Colorado Now, and the Federation for American Immigration Reform (FAIR). The challenge for community organizers and activists is to maintain the momentum stemming from the mobilizations and, also, to find a way to translate the symbolic importance of the mobilizations into power in the electoral and public policy arenas.

Also, despite differences among organizers, the immigrant rights coalition that emerged in Colorado worked to successfully stage four major events, including the Day without an Immigrant event that brought a total of approximately 150,000 protestors to the steps of the Colorado state building on May 1, 2006. They learned to work together and, even if some were ideologically opposed to certain aspects of the marches, they supported each other in order to combine their resources. They also learned important lessons about how best to garner public support for their movement, recognizing they had to reframe challenges that were unappealing to the moveable middle.

The 2006 mobilizations did not begin with or result in a unified social movement characterized by similar ideologies, goals, or strategies. Nor did they challenge legislation, which explains why they were unable to oppose anti-immigrant legislation and maintain the momentum of the marches immediately after May 1. In a context with few political resources, many CBOs were competing for the same funding and constituents, which hindered their efforts to appeal to legislators who might otherwise oppose anti-immigrant measures. Once the marches were over, CBO leaders had to find ways of translating the symbolic importance of the marches into political power for Latinos and immigrants. This would prove difficult, as Latinos grew increasingly dissatisfied with electoral politics and elected officials, especially given lawmakers' response to the marches. One activist said, "It's no wonder Latinos don't vote, because they have been betrayed by members of both political parties time and time again. . . . You think Latinos are going to go out and vote for them after they pass the most restrictive legislation? They're not going to do that, why would they?"

On the policy side, House Bill 1017 (which requires employer verification) and H.B. 1023 (which denies some government services to illegal immigrants) have made it more difficult for immigrants to work in Colorado, despite the need for immigrant labor (Selvin 2008), pushing some into the shadows and others out of state. Today, some of the Denver-based CBOs are agitating for social change within the electoral arena, hoping that this will result in more comprehensive immigration reform, while others are continuing their work within the realm of contentious politics. Still others are focusing their efforts on the Development,

Relief, and Education for Alien Minors (DREAM) Act,[7] while others are developing proceesses for dealing with racial profiling incidents and the Immigration and Customs Enforcement (ICE) raids, which have become more common since 2006.

Lastly, the marches brought attention to the immigration issue but also galvanized opposition from anti-immigrant groups. As proof, members of the pro-immigrant community noted that, in the months following the marches, ICE agents took part in a raid of meatpacking plants in December 2006, including one in Greeley, Colorado, just northeast of Denver. In six states, nearly 1,300 workers were arrested and detained, and many were deported. Officials at the meatpacking plant in Greeley opposed the raid and said that most of their workers were U.S. citizens or were working legally with work visas. ICE officials defended the raid as a means to arrest people suspected of engaging in identify theft; of the nearly 1,300 people arrested, 65 were charged with criminal offenses (Leinwand 2006). Still, that day, hundreds of children came home to find their parents were gone, and many were placed in the child welfare system when relatives could not be located. Some organizers in Denver believe the Greeley raids were a direct response to the marches; while raising awareness about the plight of immigrants, they also fueled anti-immigrant sentiments, which created pressure on government officials to do something about the immigration problem (Leinwand 2006).

The one-year anniversary of the national call to action in May 2007 brought protestors to the streets of Denver for a second time (Aguilera 2007).[8] Turnout, at ten thousand, was lower than the year before, mostly because immigrants had been driven underground or were fearful of deportation. Colorado CBOs were not deterred, however. At the time of this writing, they are continuing their efforts to bring attention to immigrants' lives by dispelling myths about immigration and continuing to work on comprehensive reform. For example, some CBOs have intitiated a campaign on behalf of day laborers, most of them immigrants, who have been ticketed and harassed for soliciting work on street corners in the Denver suburb of Aurora. Others have focused their efforts on the DREAM Act, which could potentially open up a path for immigrant children to attend colleges and universities in the state despite their documentation status. Still, much work along this front is needed, as the incidence of raids continue across the country and legislation targeting immigrant communities continues to be proposed at the local and state levels.

There are also mixed feelings about the prospect for immigration reform at the national level. On the downside, although immigration was cited as the most important problem facing the United States in 2006 (USA Today 2006), there was little mention of reform during the 2008 presidential election. This was especially surprising given the fact that John McCain, who eventually became his party's nominee, cosponsored the Kennedy-McCain bill in 2006. Among its provisions, the bill would have called for a worker visa program that would allow employers to temporarily hire foreign citizens to fill jobs not filled by U.S. laborers (National Immigration Forum n.d.). During the Republican presidential debates, however, Senator McCain said he would not vote for his own bill and, during the general election, he and then-senator Obama rarely mentioned the immigration issue as the looming mortgage crisis shifted the public's concerns to the state of the economy. And although President Obama vowed to push comprehensive immigration reform as president (Gillman 2006), when asked about the top issues for his first hundred days in office, immigration reform was not at the top of the list.

The one possible upshot is that President Obama will have many opportunities to incorporate Latino communities into reform efforts, especially given his overwhelming support among Latinos during the election (Lopez and Minushkin 2008a). Although significant electoral turnout does not guarantee unwavering support, Latinos have the president's ear. He would do well to demonstrate a commitment to listenting to their concerns, including about immigration reform, as it will continue to be a pressing issue. Many Latinos feel the Obama administration is committed to addressing possible solutions to our nation's immigration system and is best-equipped to bring about reform that is sensitive to the realities of an increasingly globalized economy and society (Ferris 2008). Still, only time will tell if the president truly believes the motto he adopted on the campaign trail: ¡Sí, se puede!

NOTES

1. Colorado's S.B. 90, which became law in 2006, forbids city and local governments from implementing sanctuary policies for undocumented immigrants. The measure also requires law enforcement officials to report to U.S. Immigration and Customs Enforcement officials any person who is believed to be an illegal alien. Cities and counties must state in writing to law enforcement officials their obligation to comply, and they must file annual reports to the state indicating the number of illegal immigrants that were reported to immigration officials.

2. Ron Unz is a California-based political activist known for sponsoring Proposition 227, which aimed to dismantle bilingual education programs.

3. Conservative organizations also opposed Amendment 31 but on different grounds. They were opposed to the prospect of children with limited English proficiency being placed in classrooms with Anglo, English proficient children. I thank the anonymous reviewer for pointing this out.

4. Estimates varied but police told organizers that the crowd totaled 70,000 because the crowd spilled over into the streets surrounding the park. The *Denver Post* reported 50,000 protestors.

5. One estimate suggests the crowd totaled 15,000.

6. Television and news stories show a pattern of immigration opponents increasingly defining the issue in ethnic terms, using "illegal aliens" and "Mexicans" interchangeably (Martinez 2008a).

7. Proponents of the bill argue that the DREAM Act offers a potential path to citizenship for the hundreds of thousands of undocumented youth across the country. It would also allow states to determine their own policies for granting in-state tutition to undocumented students (Sherry 2007). In October 2007, the bill failed to pass the Senate by eight votes.

8. Authorities policing the event estimated the crowd to be 2,000 strong. Organizers claim to have counted between 10,000 and 15,000 people. The *Denver Post* estimates 10,000 people were at the event.

7

Migrant Civic Engagement

Jonathan Fox and Xóchitl Bada

The spring 2006 wave of immigrant rights mobilizations represents a watershed in the history of civic engagement in the United States. Never before had so many foreign-born literally "come out" for the right to be included in the United States. Indeed, in many cities, never before had so many taken to the streets for *any* cause. Practitioners involved in the policy debate, scholars who measure immigrant political opinion, and migrant leaders themselves were all caught off guard. This raises questions about the social foundations of the marches—what kinds of social and civic practices, networks and organizations made them possible?

To provide at least part of the answer, this chapter introduces the concepts of *civic binationality* and *migrant civil society,* which provide frameworks for understanding the already existing patterns of migrant organization that came together at this unusual historical turning point. Civic binationality refers to practices that are engaged both with U.S. civic life and with migrants' communities and countries of origin. The related concept of migrant civil society refers to migrant-led membership organizations and public institutions (which may not be engaged with communities of origin). The goal of this latter concept is to underscore the significance of migrant capacity for self-representation.

The recognition of practices of migrant civic binationality, grounded in an emerging migrant civil society, helps us to understand the patterns of civic engagement and repertoires of action that inform migrant participation in U.S. society. The point of departure here is that, at least for many adult migrants, their initiation into civic life either takes place in their country of origin or is oriented toward their country of origin. As many analysts of civic engagement have long noted, the best predictor of civic involvement of any kind is past involvement—

even if in a completely different arena.[1] Apparently, some people are more likely to be joiners than others—across cultures. From this perspective, the kind of civic engagement witnessed on a mass scale in the spring of 2006 was in part grounded in long-standing, often low profile practices of migrant civic binationality. At the same time, the 2006 marches constitute a powerful indicator that millions of immigrants have also been fully transplanted into the U.S. public sphere, followed by subsequent increases in naturalization and voter turnout among "new Americans" in 2008.

CIVIC BINATIONALITY

The spring 2006 marches revealed a process that has been taking place often silently but consistently: the emergence of Latin American migrants as actors in American civic and political life. They have created new migrant-led organizations, such as hometown associations, nonprofits, faith-based organizations, indigenous right groups, community media, and their own workers' organizations— and they *also* have joined existing U.S. organizations, such as community associations, churches, unions, business associations, civil rights organizations, and media groups (Bada, Fox, and Selee 2006; J. Fox 2005b, 2007). In the process, they are transforming these U.S. institutions, as other immigrant groups have done throughout American history.

At the same time, many Latin American migrants also remain simultaneously engaged as part of their national societies. As we know, some migrants remain civically engaged with their home communities, a process that scholars describe as "translocal" engagement.[2] Many tens of thousands of *paisanos* work together to promote "philanthropy from below," by funding thousands of hometown development initiatives.[3] In addition, through their consulates, Mexican migrants elect representatives to their home government's Advisory Council for the Institute for Mexicans Abroad, to provide input into the policy process.[4] For the first time, Mexican migrants also exercised their newly won right to cast absentee ballots, in the 2006 presidential election (and for the first time in a governor's race, in the state of Michoacán in 2007). Other Mexican migrants have become more engaged with their U.S. communities, working with the PTA, faith-based initiatives, neighborhood organizations, and trade unions as well as participating in canvassing and other efforts in support of candidates for election for school boards and city councils.[5] Until recently, many assumed that this question of whether to be involved here or there was inherently dichotomous. Yet in practice, many Mexican migrants are becoming full members of *both* U.S. and Mexican societies at the same time, constructing practices of what we could call civic binationality that have a great deal to teach us about new forms of immigrant integration into the United States.[6]

Yet some scholars and opinion makers firmly believe that having more than one civic identity is inherently contradictory. In contrast to the civic binationality approach, their assumption is that civic engagement is *zero-sum*—and therefore civic binationality is seen as illegitimate, analogous to bigamy. For example, Huntington (2004) does not deny that second-generation Mexican immigrants learn English. Indeed, the empirical evidence is overwhelming.[7] In his view, the problem is that many of them continue to *also* speak Spanish. The threat to the U.S. social fabric is not the lack of English acquisition; it is bilingualism. In this view, the question is not whether or not migrants can and do identify with more than one country and language; the issue is that binationalism or biculturalism are seen as evidence of divided loyalties and therefore such civic identities are a potential threat.[8] Indeed, Huntington is much more concerned about legal than he is about illegal immigration, since legal immigrants can become citizens and therefore can be politically enfranchised. In contrast to other restrictionists, who primarily deploy the "rule of law" argument, Huntington's main concern is about democracy: what will happen when the number of bilingual *citizens* grows? Curiously, *democracy* does not figure in his list of the ostensible core characteristics of the American "creed."

In contrast to this ideologically driven claim, the empirical evidence shows that, rather than producing a contradiction of divided loyalties, migrants' dual commitments tend to be mutually reinforcing. Specifically, for many Mexican migrant organizations, efforts to help their hometowns in Mexico often *lead* to engagement in U.S. society through similar civic and political efforts in their new hometowns in the United States (e.g., de la Garza and Hazan 2003). As a result, generalizations based on migrants' initial priorities and activities in the 1980s and 1990s, when many *were* more "inward-looking," focused more exclusively on their home communities (e.g., Waldinger and Fitzgerald 2004)—do not necessarily apply to the early twenty-first century, when many more engage actively with a wide range of U.S. civil society actors and elected officials. By the turn of the century, many Latin American migrant organizations pursued two-track strategies, sustaining their commitments to their communities of origin while working to improve their home communities in the United States. This is the kind of dual engagement that can be understood in terms of practices of civic binationality.

While many anthropologists and sociologists have documented the contours and processes of binationality, often through ethnographic methods and the conceptual lens of transnational communities, other scholars use large-scale survey research methods to assess the breadth and intensity of migrants' transnational activities and commitments.[9] Based on the findings from a 2006 Pew Hispanic Center telephone survey of 2,000 Latinos, including more than 1,400 foreign-born, Waldinger (2007) posited that those who participate in three different activities—

weekly phone calls, sending remittances, and return travel in the previous two years—can be considered those who are "highly attached to their country of origin." Only one in ten immigrants surveyed reported engaging in all three activities.[10] A strong majority of 63 percent showed "moderate attachment" by engaging in one or two of those three activities (more prominently among those who have been in the United States for less than a decade). Yet 28 percent of the foreign-born reported not being involved in any of these activities. This finding should give pause to those who would make broad generalizations based on research that concentrates on the transnational commitments of a minority of the immigrant community. Indeed, active binational practices appear to be most widespread among community leaders, established business leaders, organic intellectuals, and educators—especially those with the formal immigration status and economic means needed for easy cross-border travel.[11] Many hometown association members, and certainly leaders, either managed to join the middle class in the United States or were previously members of the politically engaged middle class in Mexico. They are also disproportionately male and tend to be either permanent residents or naturalized citizens. Their premigration civic roots are only recently receiving more systematic research attention. For example, most migrant leaders from Oaxaca and Puebla had previously been active in Mexico's teachers' movement or were politically active in their communities of origin prior to their migration, and they continue to be active in California (Franzoni Lobo 2007; Rosas-López, 2007).

The same Pew Hispanic Center survey also documented rates of involvement in immigrant civic and social organizations: Overall, "only 9% report belonging to a civic organization, social club or sports team of people from their native land" (Waldinger 2007, 10). Among more recent arrivals, the rate rises to 12 percent. Reported participation also varies significantly by national origin, with one in five Dominicans reporting involvement with immigrant civic or social organizations, 14 percent among Salvadorans, 12 percent among Colombians, falling to 6 percent for Mexicans. Whether these rates are considered high are low would depend on the comparative frame of reference. For example, to assess the 6 percent rate for Mexicans, one would need to compare that to participation rates in Mexico for people of similar socioeconomic status.[12] Yet this otherwise comprehensive survey did not assess the question of whether cross-border and U.S.-oriented repertoires of participation are mutually reinforcing or mutually exclusive, since it did not address participation in U.S.-oriented kinds of organizations, such as faith-based civic or social organizations, PTAs, or union locals.

Another recent survey supports the view that U.S.-oriented and homeland-oriented civic engagement can be mutually reinforcing. In their analysis of a panel survey of Mexico–to–United States migrants who were interviewed in the United States in advance of the July 2, 2006, Mexican presidential election, and again following the U.S. midterm elections in November of the same year, McCann, Cornelius, and Leal (2006) find that there is a positive and highly significant correlation between engagement in the public affairs of Mexico and of the United States (see DeSipio 2006 for similar results).

Civic binationality increasingly involves engagement with U.S. elected officials and elections, notably in Southern California, where hometown federations have worked closely with Latino civil rights groups and immigrant worker-based trade unions to campaign for voter registration and for state legislation on drivers' licenses. For years before the 2006 marches, for example, Los Angeles labor unions worked to promote civic engagement among their vast immigrant membership, including noncitizen campaigning for higher rates of citizen voting and the national Immigrant Workers Freedom Ride in 2003 (Jamison 2005; Milkman, this volume; Varsanyi 2005). For another example, Mexicanos for Political Progress in Chicago was created as a direct result of hometown association interest in U.S. electoral politics. In June 2006—as a consequence of hometown association participation in the spring marches—a group of Chicago-based hometown association leaders decided to form a nonpartisan political action committee with the goal of supporting candidates for state and local office who commit to address the agenda and demands of Mexican immigrants. Moreover, they registered 150 volunteers to participate in voter registration, canvassing, and logistical support on election day (Federación de Clubes Michoacanos en Illinois 2007). The group hosted gatherings in Chicago's Casa Michoacán to watch the U.S. Democratic presidential debates in order to analyze which candidate was the most committed to defending immigrant rights (Mexicanos for Political Progress 2007).

A survey by the Institute for Latino Studies of the University of Notre Dame sheds additional light on this dynamic. The 2003 face-to-face survey of 1,512 foreign-born and U.S. Latinos in the Chicago metropolitan area found that 6 percent of foreign-born Latinos belong to hometown associations. In addition, however, the findings suggest that membership in binational community organizations does not lower the probability of being civically engaged in local U.S. community groups. The authors find that "70 percent of members of hometown associations belong to at least four additional Chicago-based community organizations . . . [and] foreign-born Latinos are much more likely to belong to a community or civic organization than are the U.S. born; 53 percent of the foreign born belong to one or more community or civic organizations compared to only 37 percent of the U.S. born" (Ready, Knight, and Chun 2006, 3). In other words, joiners tend to join *both* U.S.-oriented and cross-border organizations.

Nevertheless, there still appears to be a disconnection between reported rates of participation in home country–oriented organizations and the massive turnout for the 2006 immigrant rights marches. Overall, the scope of pre-2006 cross-border civic or political engagement does not come close to accounting for the scale of mass participation in the marches. The Pew Hispanic Center survey strongly supports the view that most Latin American migrants see their future in the United States, which is quite consistent with the massive turnout in the streets in the spring of 2006 (Waldinger 2007). Another comparative reference point is to look at the turnout of Mexican migrants in the 2006 Mexican presidential election, in which for the first time they were permitted to cast absentee ballots. The low turnout was a major surprise to voting rights advocates, who had campaigned for a decade to encourage the government to carry out a commitment made in principle in a 1996 constitutional reform.[13] Previous large-scale surveys of relatively recent migrants had reported high levels of interest in the Mexican elections (Suro and Escobar 2006a). It is certainly true that the administrative obstacles to voting were significant. In the end, of the approximately 4 million people the Mexican government estimated were eligible to vote, just under 33,000 Mexicans in the United States managed to cast valid ballots (IFE 2006). Similarly, in the precedent-setting migrant vote in the Michoacán governor's election of November 2007, less than 1,000 had tried to register by the July deadline.

While voting rights advocates campaign for more accessible voting procedures in the future, recent survey evidence suggests that approximately four or five out of ten Mexican migrants "would likely be out of reach, regardless of the procedures established for future absentee voting. This would be true not only because they live in out-of-the-way locations like north-central Indiana, but because they pay practically no attention to affairs south of the border. Yet this still leaves a vast amount of transnational 'civic potential'" (McCann, Cornelius, and Leal 2006). Indeed, few national experiences with new processes for diasporic voting have led to much higher participation rates. Yet even taking into account all of the obstacles, the number of migrants who voted by absentee ballot was still remarkably small, especially when one considers Mexico's difficult transition to a competitive electoral system. Recall that in the late 1980s and early 1990s, several hundred Mexicans were killed in campaigns for electoral democracy. In summary, the contrast between the low turnout in Mexico's long-distance voting and the scale of the spring 2006 protests suggests that many more migrants have entered the public sphere in the United States than have sustained homeward-looking civic engagement.[14]

MIGRANT CIVIL SOCIETY

While civic binationality is a relevant concept for understanding participation trends among core groups of migrant "joiners," other approaches are needed to explain why such a vast number of migrants who are usually nonparticipants chose to engage in coordinated collective action in the spring of 2006.[15] Another reason why the concept of civic binationality is not sufficient to capture the full range of migrant collective action is that their engagement often takes forms that are not binational; many migrants who are engaged in civic life focus primarily on U.S. issues and organizations. Yet, it can be difficult to recognize and analyze the dynamics that are specific to migrant collective action when the foreign-born are subsumed into U.S. ethnic and racial categories. One way to address this issue is to look at patterns of migrant collective action through the conceptual lens of migrant civil society.

Simply put, migrant civil society refers to *migrant-led* membership organizations and public institutions. This includes four very tangible arenas of collective action: membership organizations, nongovernmental organizations, media, and autonomous public spheres. Migrants may organize around their identities as workers, their neighborhoods of residence, their community of origin, their ethnicity, or their faith. Sometimes, these potentially multiple identities overlap, as in the cases of specifically Oaxacan Catholics who reproduce their distinctive public rituals in Los Angeles or religious farmworkers in the Midwest, where union leaders preside over weddings and baptisms. In terms of the concerns of this volume, reflecting on what was new and different about the 2006 marches, one of the most important factors was the exercise of migrant civic and political leadership. Migrants were representing *themselves,* rather than having advocates speak for them. This emphasis on self-representation makes the notion of migrant civil society distinct from (though often overlapping with) broader U.S. Latino civil society. The rationale for this concept is that it helps us see where and how migrants exercise leadership in U.S.-based organizations and institutions, which in turn draws our attention to processes of immigrant integration that are otherwise not visible.

The first of these four arenas, involving migrant membership organizations, includes both those that are home country–oriented and those that are engaged primarily with U.S. issues. The first includes hometown clubs and federations, indigenous rights groups, and expatriate voting rights advocacy networks. Migrant-led membership organizations also include faith-based organizations, PTAs, majority-migrant trade union locals, worker centers, as well as broad-based community organizations, such as those networked through the Industrial Areas Foundation.[16]

Hometown associations (HTAs) are among the best known, bringing migrants together from shared communities of origin. They represent the "paradigm case" of civic binationality. Hometown clubs often begin as informal associations, such as soccer clubs, but over time many have not only become formal organizations, they have also "scaled up" to form federations that represent communities of origin from the same "sending" state. Though many have rural origins, HTAs are predominantly concentrated in metropolitan areas in the United States.[17] Among Latin American migrants, Mexican and Salvadorans have focused the most on coming together around these territorially based collective identities. Together, they involve the active participation of many tens of thousands of migrants who are sufficiently well-established in their U.S. lives to participate in regular meetings and fund-raising and civic activities in support of cross-border "philanthropy from below" (see, e.g., Merz 2006; Portes, Escobar, and Walton Radford 2007).

Until recently, these forms of self-organization were largely invisible outside the migrant community—and were primarily engaged with their communities of origin, rather than with their communities of residence. Increasingly, however, over the past decade, HTAs have become more involved with civic life in the United States, and they were among the many previously low-profile forms of organization that "came out" in the spring 2006 marches. Indeed, the three states that experienced the largest turnouts in the marches, by far—California, Texas, and Illinois—are also the three states that together account for the vast majority of Mexican HTAs in the United States and Canada: 69 percent of those registered with the Mexican consulates (see table 7.1; also table 1.1, in chapter 1 of this volume). The concentration of the HTA repertoire of civic action in Chicago, Los Angeles, and Dallas is clearly disproportionate to these cities' share of the Mexican-born population overall. Notably, in these cities, hundreds of HTAs have taken the civic binationality path. By 2006, at least in Chicago and Los Angeles, HTAs and their federations were fully engaged with both their respective city halls and with their state legislatures—not to mention with trade unions and mainstream Latino civic organizations.

In Chicago, Mexican HTAs had a long history of focusing their efforts on campaigning for the right to vote absentee in Mexican elections. Just as they were confronting the many practical obstacles imposed by the Mexican government's administrative requirements of the "remote vote," the Sensenbrenner bill (H.R. 4437) emerged as the number one threat to immigrant rights. In response, Chicago's HTAs redirected the momentum generated by their home country right-to-vote campaign and began to focus their meetings at Casa Michoacán on discussing strategies to challenge the Sensenbrenner bill. Their simultaneous engagement with issues of representation in policy processes *both* in Mexico *and* in Chicago offers supporting evidence for McCann, Cornelius, and Leal's survey-based observation (2006) that there is a positive and highly significant correlation between migrant engagement in the public affairs of Mexico and of the United States.

In January 2006, Mexican HTAs and their umbrella confederation (CONFE-MEX) joined with labor unions, radio personalities, the Illinois Coalition for Immigrant and Refugee Rights, the Catholic Campaign for Social Justice, religious

TABLE 7.1 Mexican Hometown Associations (HTAs) in
Selected U.S. Cities

City	Number of HTAs
Los Angeles •	84
Dallas •	64
Chicago •	52
Houston •	50
San Jose •	22
San Bernardino	20
Las Vegas •	19
San Antonio •	17
Santa Ana	17
Atlanta •	15
Miami •	15
Denver •	14
San Francisco •	14
Sacramento	14
New York City •	12
Omaha •	12
San Diego •	11
Fresno •	10
Phoenix •	8
Austin	7
El Paso	4
Oxnard	4
Washington DC •	2
Presidio	2
Brownsville	1
Del Rio	1
Laredo	1
MacAllen	1
Detroit •	1
Other (United States and Canada)	81
Total HTAs	575

SOURCE: Authors' elaboration using the Directory of Mexican Organizations, 2008, http://www.ime.gob.mx.
• Cities with large marches

congregations, and traditional Latino organizations to call for a March 10 rally to
demand dignity for undocumented workers.[18] For many HTAs, direct involvement
in the organization of immigrant rights marches in 2006 was a new development. For most of them, organizing public protests *in* the United States had not
previously been part of their repertoire (even though their leadership included
migrants who were also labor organizers). In the March 10 demonstration, some
leaders participated in the organizing committee, sharing the podium as speak-

ers during the rally and rubbing elbows with local politicians, long-established Latino activists, and migrant leaders from different nationalities.[19]

With more than 100,000 in the streets, Chicago's March 10 protest was the second major march of the spring 2006 cycle of mobilization and by far the larg- est up to that point (Ávila and Olivo 2006; Bada, Fox and Selee 2006). Encour- aged by the turnout, some Latino labor coalitions and immigrant-led labor orga- nizations decided to hold their planning meetings for the May 1 protest at Casa Michoacán—the headquarters of the Illinois Federation of Michoacán HTAs and Chicago's flagship public space for Mexican civic binationality. In addition, the March 10 movement leadership quickly understood that their demands needed the support of other communities.

The first planning meetings to organize the marches were almost entirely in Spanish. But in a creative and sophisticated adjustment, immigrants from Ire- land, Poland, Pakistan, Cambodia, and elsewhere were able to access simultane- ous English translations through special headsets (Ávila and Martínez 2006). The HTAs were even able to obtain moral support from African American organiza- tions such as the Rainbow/Push Coalition and some sectors of the Chicago Mus- lim community (Konkol 2006).[20] At one of the organizing meetings at Casa Mi- choacán in Pilsen, for Chicago's May 1 march, Jesse Jackson said, "There is real fear among blacks about the loss of jobs. But it's not because of the undocumented workers that are the cause. It's cheaper wage jobs" (Konkol 2006, 48). He further said that the struggle for decent pay also has to do with the exodus of manufactur- ing jobs that are being exported overseas to avoid labor rights and living wages (Ayi 2006; Konkol 2006). The African American turnout in the May 1 march was modest but inspiring. According to the only large-scale survey of marchers car- ried out during the entire spring 2006 cycle of mobilization, conducted by re- searchers at the University of Illinois in Chicago, an estimated 3 percent of the May 1 marchers in Chicago's downtown were African American (Pallares and Flores-Gonzáles 2010). Among the most visible organized groups with large Afri- can American constituents were community-based organizations such as ACORN and STOP (Student/Tenant Organizing Project) (Ginsberg-Jaeckle 2006).

After the marches, many HTAs, along with other migrant-led organizations, added a new focus to their advocacy efforts: working to encourage higher rates of naturalization among the large permanent resident population and to increase Latino electoral participation. In the case of Chicago, CONFEMEX participated in the New Americans Initiative, a state government–sponsored campaign to promote citizenship among legal permanent residents.[21] In the 2008 presidential election, CONFEMEX registered voters and promoted turnout in the city's sur- rounding counties, which had transformed from white Republican strongholds to multicultural immigrant communities within just a few years. These electoral mobilization strategies did not have the same visibility as the marches; but their ultimate goal was to follow up on one of the marches' central slogans: "Hoy marchamos, mañana votamos" (Today we march, tomorrow we vote).

Across the United States, Mexican immigrants have not only come together based on their shared home communities; they have come together around collective identities grounded in their spirituality or their ethnicity. The case of New York's Tepeyac Association is a high-profile model of binational faith-based immigrant community organizing. Each October, Tepeyac organizes the Antorcha Guadalupana, a two-month relay race from Mexico City's Basílica de Guadalupe to Manhattan's Saint Patrick's Cathedral. On their way north, the runners cross numerous states in Mexico and the United States, demanding social justice for immigrants and a new legalization program for undocumented workers (e.g., Rivera-Sánchez 2004).

In addition, the distinct experiences of indigenous Mexicans have grounded ethnically based membership and advocacy organizations, most notably in California. At least one in ten Mexicans is of indigenous origin, and they represent a growing share of the migrant population in the United States as well. While some seek to evade discrimination by eliding ethnic difference, others bring politicized ethnic identities with them, or their experience of racialization as migrants in northern Mexico and the United States politicizes their ethnicity. The most prominent Mexican indigenous organization in the United States is the Binational Front of Indigenous Organizations, formerly the Oaxacan Binational Indigenous Front and still known as the FIOB (Fox and Rivera-Salgado 2004; Fox 2006). This membership organization is both binational and panethnic, with five Mexican languages spoken among its elected leadership council. The FIOB works in diverse coalitions, advocating both for immigrant rights and for indigenous rights, both in the United States and in Mexico—where the FIOB plays a pioneering role in speaking out against abuses of Central Americans in transit. In Los Angeles, for example, the FIOB works closely with the broad-based Coalition for Humane Immigrant Rights of Los Angeles as well as with many of the Mexican federations of hometown associations. In several regions of California, the FIOB works closely with the flagship immigrant rights defenders of California Rural Legal Assistance. In Fresno, the FIOB played a leading role in convening that city's spring 2006 march, which drew by far the largest protest turnout ever in that city (e.g., Martínez-Nateras and Stanley 2009).

The second arena of migrant civil society involves migrant-led media. Nonprofit media range from local and binational newspapers to radio networks and programs, independent video, and now numerous Internet discussion forums oriented to hometowns or regions. Beyond the nonprofit media lies the huge world of commercial Spanish-language media. Though for-profit enterprises fall outside most definitions of civil society, these media nevertheless play key civic roles, not only informing their publics, but also encouraging public service.

Spanish-language media have systematically encouraged both U.S. citizenship and voter turnout (A. Rodríguez, 1999, 2005).

The civic role of Spanish-language media personalities has yet to be fully documented but was quite significant even before their widely recognized role in the mass mobilization of the spring of 2006. (e.g., Ramírez, this volume) Again, it probably is no coincidence that Los Angeles and Chicago are both major centers of national Spanish-language media and that they experienced the largest marches in 2006. The experience of Chicago radio talk-show host El Pistolero is especially important, since that city was the first of the spring 2006 protest wave to experience a truly enormous immigrant march. When later interviewed in English on National Public Radio, El Pistolero revealed the relevance of his own family's Mexican political history for understanding his current civic commitments to immigrant rights:

> I grew up in a very active, pro-immigrant valley. I come from Fresno, California, the Central Valley, and to be honest, I lost my father in Mexico and that's how I ended up in Central California, because my father was in politics in Mexico and he lost his life because of it. And I've always promised myself that I would never get into politics. But you know, you hear the call and it is the moral responsibility when you're behind a microphone, not just to entertain people, but to inform people of what's going on around their lives. (Block 2006)

Indeed, El Pistolero's experience indicates that, at least in Chicago, migrant-led media and religious leaders were more significant than the HTAs in building the momentum prior to the spring 2006 marches. El Pistolero led, together with Marco Cárdenas, a priest at Our Lady of Fátima, a July 2005 mobilization in Chicago's Mexican neighborhoods of Pilsen and Little Village to protest the actions of local Minutemen, foreshadowing the central role that migrant media and religious leaders would later play nationwide. The march attracted tens of thousands of protesters and was the first organized attempt to gain momentum to promote a legalization campaign after the tragic events of September 11. The HTAs did not participate in this action, arguing that the march was not going to be covered by the media if it was convened by two people and was not going to be held downtown. Clearly, they did not anticipate that so many would turn out, that Representative Luis Gutierrez would join the march, nor that Senator Ted Kennedy would call organizers to offer his support to the cause (Martínez and Piña 2005).

The third arena constituting migrant civil society involves nongovernmental organizations. Many nonprofits *serve* migrant communities, but in this approach only those that are *migrant-led* would be considered part of migrant civil society. Here one must keep in mind the clear distinction between nonprofits or NGOs and membership organizations—a distinction that is side-stepped by the fuzzy U.S. term *community-based organization*. While many U.S. community

development organizations are quintessentially U.S. Latino nonprofits, an un-
counted number are in fact migrant-led, as in the cases of Fresno's Binational
Center for Oaxacan Indigenous Development and Chicago's Little Village Community Development Corporation (an affiliate of the National Council of La Raza).
This Chicago nonprofit is led by a pioneer of civic binationality, Jesús García—a Mexican immigrant who is also both a former Illinois elected official
and a founder of a Chicago-based, home state–oriented organization, Durango
Unido (Bada, Fox, and Selee 2006).

The fourth arena involves autonomous public spheres, which refer to large
migrant-led gatherings where *paisanos* can come together to interact and to express themselves with relative freedom and autonomy, whether around culture,
religion, sports, or recreation. For example, in California, indigenous Oaxacan
migrants organize huge annual music, dance, and food festivals known as
Guelaguetzas. They are the embodiment of the imagined cultural and civic space
known as Oaxacalifornia (Fox and Rivera-Salgado, 2004). Specifically, Oaxacan
migrant civil society in California is sufficiently dense that migrants put on at
least seven *different* Guelaguetza festivals each year. They are held in parks, high
school auditoriums, college campuses and civic centers, and the largest is held in
the L.A. Sports Arena—the former home of the Los Angeles Lakers basketball
team. In each one, hundreds volunteer their time so that thousands can come together and parents can share their culture with their children. Indeed, probably
few had had the opportunity to see such a festival when they were living in
Oaxaca—in part because the official Guelaguetza is Oaxaca's peak official tourist
event, with ticket prices to match. With so much activity, California's multigenerational Oaxacan migrant dance groups are in high demand, and they represent
yet another network of membership organizations. Each of the seven annual festivals reveals an X-ray of the social networks and organizational styles present in
the web of Oaxacan civil society in California. Most Guelaguetza festival conve-
ners work with local U.S. politicians, school districts, and student organizations
in their cities of residence. Some also collaborate with the Oaxacan state government, while others keep their distance.

Figure 7.1's conceptual diagram attempts to capture some of the dynamics underlying the role of migrant civil society in the 2006 marches, stressing the mutually reinforcing synergy between these four arenas. In this view, the marches were
grounded by a remarkable "virtuous circle" of mutual support between membership organizations, nonprofit support organizations, and the migrant-led media,
which in turn permit the construction of autonomous public spheres—in this case,
throughout the streets of U.S. cities.

When seen in the light of the increased Latino voter turnout in the 2008 presidential election, the 2006 slogan "Today we march, tomorrow we vote" does indeed
appear prescient. At the time, it was not clear whether those words constituted a

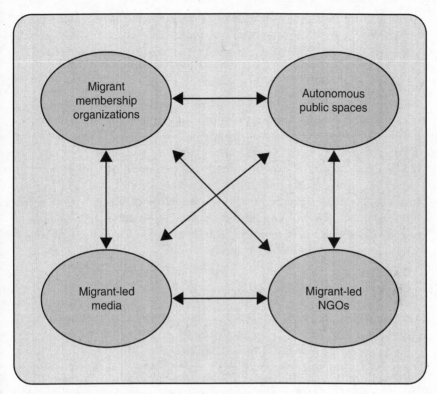

FIGURE 7.1. Migrant civil society: pathways of synergy.

prediction, a threat, or wishful thinking. Though the response to calls for street marches in 2007 and 2008 went largely unheeded, it appears that many key immigrant rights activists had reoriented their mobilization to promote electoral engagement. Naturalization rates for Mexican permanent residents had already been on a steady rise since the late 1990s, in the aftermath of the 1996 tightening of immigration laws, and they appear to have increased substantially since 2006 (Passel 2007). The total number of citizenship applications doubled in the year ending September 30, 2007, compared to the previous year, reaching 1.4 million (Preston 2007b). In addition to the mobilization against the Sensenbrenner bill, the government's doubling of application fees for naturalization also caught the attention of many permanent residents. Major Latino institutions, like Univision and the National Association of Latino Elected Officials, led their most successful citizenship and voter turnout efforts ever, under the catchy slogan "Now is the time" (Ayón 2009). In the 2008 elections, the Latino vote reached 9 percent of the electorate, its highest share ever, and made a difference in swing states such as Florida, Nevada, and Colorado to an unprecedented degree (Lopez 2008). Thanks to competitive primary elections, the presidential race even provoked intense Latino voter mobilization in California, which otherwise would have not been considered "in play."

Latinos voted Democratic by a margin of 67 to 31 percent in 2008, in sharp contrast to their 40–44 percent support for George W. Bush in 2004 (Lopez 2008). Specifically, Spanish-dominant Latinos, who had supported John Kerry over Bush only by 52 to 48 percent in 2004, reportedly went 75 percent for Obama in 2008 (Sharry 2008). Remarkably, Latinos surveyed were hopeful looking forward. In January 2009, more than seven in ten (72 percent) reported that they expected Obama to have a successful first term (Lopez and Livingston 2009). Whether this civic optimism will persist in spite of the deepening economic crisis and uncertainty as to whether the Obama administration will pursue comprehensive immigration reform remains to be seen.

CONCLUSIONS

In conclusion, extensive prior practices of civic binationality and the emerging institutions of migrant civil society both help to account for the remarkable "civicness" of the spring 2006 mobilizations. Millions of people, with little organized direction, followed a shared protest repertoire, very much operating within the conventional terms of engagement of U.S. civil society. Millions stayed remarkably "on message," displaying U.S. flags in large numbers for the first time, wearing white, systematically avoiding violence or destruction of property, building coalitions across sectors and ethnic groups, creating new public spaces, and leaving them clean when they were done.[22] Virtually no arrests were reported, which made the protests more peaceful than many large sporting events.[23]

In retrospect, it would be easy to take this civicness for granted. Yet a historical and comparative perspective suggests that this would be a mistake. Consider the violent protests in France, primarily by second-generation immigrant youth. They erupted just a few months before the U.S. protest wave, during the fall of 2005. During three weeks of nationwide rioting, more than 2,900 people were arrested and nine thousand cars were burned (Caldwell 2007). The U.S. media did not begin to cover the events until the weekly numbers of car burnings were in the hundreds. Yet in the spring of 2006, had a *single* car been burned by immigrant protesters in the United States, one can be sure that the televised image would have been repeated so many times on Fox News that viewers would have gotten the impression that hundreds of cars were burned.

More recently, following the harsh anti-immigrant rhetoric in the broadcast media and in the 2008 Republican presidential primary campaign—arguably a backlash in response to the 2006 marches—a major pundit warned for the first time of a backlash against the backlash. Indeed, influential *Miami Herald* commentator Andres Oppenheimer (2007) warned darkly of a potential looming "Latino intifada." He argued that, as the undocumented are increasingly vilified and forced further underground, after their efforts to "work within the system" are spurned, "many of them will become increasingly frustrated, angry, and some of them eventually may turn violent." He concluded, "The millions of undocumented among us will not leave. They will only get angrier."

One can further underscore the significance of the marches' civicness by taking into consideration a relevant U.S. historical precedent that Oppenheimer did not mention: the 1992 Los Angeles uprising. This wave of violent protest led to at least fifty-three deaths, the most costly episode of rioting in recent U.S. history. While the dominant U.S. media frame projected this conflict in black-white terms, the events on the ground reveal that this mass expression of dissent and alienation also included large numbers of Latino immigrant participants. Recall that the immediate trigger was the "not guilty" verdict in the trial of police officers who were caught on videotape beating an unarmed African American man. Yet underlying economic tensions and a lack of civic representation help to explain the specific patterns of violence and participation that emerged. The most intense property damage was found to have occurred in neighborhoods whose population had recently become almost majority Latino (Pastor 1993, 7; 1995) and that had experienced rapid ethnic succession (Bergesen and Herman 1998). While the historically Mexican American neighborhoods of East Los Angeles experienced very little disorder, most of the looting and arson took place in areas of recent migrant settlement (South Central, Koreatown, Westlake). The most striking indicator of the Latino role is evident in the pattern of police arrests, which involved substantially more Latinos than African Americans. Of the total of 5,633 arrests, "Latinos constituted 50.6% and African Americans comprised 36.3%" (Pastor 1993, 9). Approximately one-third of the Latinos arrested were deported. Of those interviewed, 78.2 percent were of Mexican origin, and the rest were Central American. The Immigration and Naturalization Service called them "riot aliens" (Pastor 1993, 12).

One possible explanation of the striking difference between the collective expression of alienation and resentment in Los Angeles in 1992 and the civicness of 2006 is that, in the interim, tens of thousands of immigrants had created their own social and civic organizations. In the areas of recent settlement that exploded in 1992, migrant civil society was thin. The 2008 presidential election offered a major test of immigrants' capacity to translate their social and civic energy into actual political representation, as millions of naturalized citizens and permanent residents attempted to turn "Today we march, tomorrow we vote" into more than a slogan. Hopes have been raised, but it is not clear how long they will last. If the conventional pathways to political representation "within the system" fail to produce a viable path to regularization for the unauthorized over the next several years, then less civic forms of protest may follow. What will the immigrant politics of the future look like: the riots of 1992 or the marches of 2006? The answer depends in part on the U.S. political system's capacity to create viable channels for the integration of millions of immigrants into U.S. society. But the answer also depends on immigrants themselves, who have demonstrated their willingness and capacity to act like citizens regardless of their status. In the process, they have built a migrant civil society that has demonstrated an unprecedented potential to be recognized in the future.

NOTES

1. Political economist Albert Hirschman (1984) described this as "the transformation and mutation of social energy."

2. On distinctions between translocal and transnational engagement see, among others, Fitzgerald (2004), Waldinger and Fitzgerald (2004), and Fox (2005a).

3. On Mexican hometown associations, see, among others, Bada (2004, 2007, 2008) on Michoacán organizations and Smith and Bakker (2008) on Zacatecas-related experiences.

4. See Institute for Mexicans Abroad, www.ime.gob.mx. For background on the Mexican government's outreach to the diaspora, see Ayón (2005), among others.

5. On Latino faith-based political actions supported by the Catholic Church, see Heredia (this volume). For historically grounded analyses of Latino immigrant participation in California's labor unions, see Milkman (this volume) and Shaw (this volume). On Latino immigrant participation in Chicago's labor movement, see Fink (2010)

6. For conceptual discussion, see Fox (2005a). To follow current discussions among binationally oriented Mexican civic and political activists in the United States, see Huellas Mexicanas, http://www.huellasmexicanas.com.

7. For critiques of Huntington's empirical assumptions, see Citrin and colleagues (2007) and Fraga and Segura (2006), among others. Huntington implies that the expansion of the Spanish language is such a threat to the U.S. social fabric that nationalist backlash is understandable, even alluding to Bosnian-style ethnic cleansing.

8. The contours of the public debate suggest that, in practice, this is a particularly Mexican problem, as *immigrant* is often treated as a synonym for *illegal,* and *illegal* often becomes used as a synonym for *Mexican.* These critics do not apply the same logic to other forms of binationalism, such as the many American Israeli dual citizens (who often serve in the armed forces of another country).

9. For detailed bibliographic references, see Fox (2005b, 2007).

10. The methodology here would appear to underrepresent the transnational attachments of undocumented migrants, since migrants would be less able to engage in return travel and they would be much less likely to have a land line.

11. At the same time, one could argue that our understandings of transnational or binational identities should not be limited to tangible cross-border activity, since people can identify with their countries and communities of origin, and with a corresponding sense of peoplehood, without necessarily calling or going home. People can be transnational where they are.

12. This comparison of different national origin groups is very instructive, yet it is insufficient. To understand the diverse patterns and repertoires of migrant civic engagement, researchers need to bring to bear an additional comparative lens. Most often in migration research, the term *comparative* refers to the comparison of different national origin groups. Yet the Mexican population in the United States is so large and so diverse that national origin averages can mask key variables, such as region of origin, region of settlement, and ethnicity. A comparative approach also means looking *both* at how migrants are organizing themselves in relationship to Mexico and other Mexican migrants *and* at how they are organized in the United States in community groups or as workers, parents, naturalized voters, or members of faith-based communities.

13. The 1996 reform involved both citizenship for migrants and the "non–loss of nationality"— two concepts that are distinct in Mexican law (A. Castañeda 2006). For analyses of the Mexican political debate over expatriate rights, see Badillo (2004), among others. For estimates of the size of the migrant electorate, see Marcelli and Cornelius (2005).

14. This interpretation is also implied by the provocative title of former foreign minister Jorge Castañeda's book, *Ex Mex: From Migrants to Immigrants* (New Press, 2007).

15. This section draws on more detailed discussions in Fox (2005b, 2007).

16. On recent IAF faith-based programs trying to engage Latino migrant communities in Charlotte, North Carolina, see Deaton (2008)

17. For discussion of the hometown civic-political impacts of HTAs, see Bada (2008), Fox (2007), Fox and Bada (2008), and Smith and Bakker (2008), among others.

18. For more information about the activities of this confederation, see Confederación de Federaciones Mexicanas, http://www.confemexusa.com, and Vonderlack-Navarro (2007).

19. This coalition is still active. The March 10th Movement Committee was created in early 2006 in Chicago to organize a series of protests against the Sensenbrenner bill and to demand legalization, dignity, and respect for the millions of undocumented migrants. During the summer of 2006, the committee organized a National Strategy Convention in Hillside, Illinois, to coordinate the efforts of several immigrant advocacy organizations interested in creating an emergency response team to fight against local anti-immigrant ordinances. In 2007, this coalition decreased its activities, but it reactivated in the summer of 2008. At the time of this writing, several local members of this coalition meet every Tuesday in Chicago to continue the fight for immigrant rights. Their activity included fundraising to support the worker occupation of the Republic Windows and Doors factory, a manufacturing plant with a predominantly immigrant labor force that tried to close without offering severance pay and was ordered to compensate the workers after all the media attention brought by the occupation.

20. In the early 1980s, the Chicago Rainbow/Push Coalition inaugurated a Latino chapter with modest Mexican immigrant representation. Today, the Rainbow/Push Coalition and CONFEMEX (Confederación de Federaciones Mexicanas), the largest Mexican HTA umbrella in Chicago, collaborate regularly on immigration and labor rights issues.

21. Note that by 2004, Illinois already had one of the highest rates of citizenship among Mexican-born permanent residents, where more than 31 percent of those eligible had naturalized. This contrasted with 28 percent in California and only 20 percent in Texas (Bada, Fox, and Selee, 2006, 12). This wide range of interstate variation is also seen within states, notably in California—suggesting that national origin is a variable of limited usefulness for understanding the determinants of naturalization.

22. The shift in the public display of flags was especially rapid and remarkable. For example, as the *Atlanta Journal-Constitution* reported, "Though there were Mexican, Salvadoran and Guatemalan flags sprinkled in the crowd, most of the marchers carried American flags, a response to critics

who had denounced marchers in previous events for carrying Mexican flags, saying the flags showed they were unwilling to integrate into U.S. culture" (Borden and Rockwell 2006).

23. This implicit pact of civility was broken in Los Angeles on the first anniversary of the marches in 2007, when unprovoked riot police attacked peacefully assembled families (while the mayor was abroad).

8

Regarding Family

New Actors in the Chicago Protests

Amalia Pallares and Nilda Flores-González

In spring 2006, immigrants and their supporters staged the largest mobilizations in Chicago's history.[1] In this chapter we look at the participation of new actors who united their voices with more seasoned activists to demand immigrant rights in Chicago. Because these mobilizations combined the efforts of more traditional community and immigrant organizations with those of loose political and social networks of groups and individuals, we argue that they were informed by a *variety* of ideological and political tendencies, and not only one. Further, we argue that the conceptual framework guiding immigrant activism in Chicago was not a cohesive body of shared meanings that might characterize what we traditionally have considered social movements. Rather, this framework is best characterized as a set of common referents provided by the lived experiences of communities of immigrants, their nonimmigrant family members, and Latinos at large. These common referents are informing their political identifications and visions and enabling certain *coyunturas,* or coming together for specific purposes. Specifically, in this chapter we focus on how the common referent of family has become a source of political identification and mobilization among mixed-status families and youth. In particular, we claim that ideas about the sanctity of family preservation and the injustice of family separation are being used by movement activists to produce a new collective action frame that explains and justifies these new actors' mobilization.

The work presented here is part of the larger Immigrant Mobilization Project at the University of Illinois, Chicago, which we codirected and which involved about two dozen faculty and graduate students studying different aspects of the mobilizations in Chicago from diverse interdisciplinary perspectives (see

Pallares and Flores-González 2010). This initiative examined the immigrant mobilizations in Chicago starting in the spring of 2006 and focused on unraveling the political conditions, resources, and ideological frames that led to this mass movement. We investigated the role of different social, cultural, and political institutions and new political actors in shaping and framing the movement and in mobilizing participants.

The Immigrant Mobilization Project used mixed methods to gather data on the mobilizations in Chicago. Our mixed-data approach included the use of surveys, participant observation, interviews, oral histories, and archival research. Two surveys were conducted during the May 2006 and May 2007 marches using a multistage block-sampling design to give participants an equal chance of being selected for the study (Flores-González et al. 2006). Interviewers were assigned "block numbers" within two rallying sites at the beginning and end of the marches: Union Park and Grant Park. Within those blocks, they were instructed to approach every tenth person as a potential respondent for the survey. This sampling process yielded 410 surveys for the May 2006 march and 376 for the May 2007 march.

As seen in table 8.1, these surveys indicate that the Chicago marchers in both 2006 and 2007 were predominantly Latinos. More than half of those who turned out in 2006 (58 percent) were foreign-born, although unlike what may have been the case in other cities, nearly three-quarters (74 percent) of those who responded to our survey were U.S. citizens, either by birth or naturalization. Additionally, half of all respondents were young, between the ages of 15 and 28, and the majority of these young marchers (65 percent) were second-generation U.S. citizens.

In 2007 we added questions about family composition to our surveys. Respondents indicated that although most were U.S. citizens, nearly half (47 percent) lived in mixed-status families, measured as having at least one undocumented member as well as a legal resident or citizen member. Thus, a significant number of marchers had family ties to undocumented immigrants, even when they themselves were U.S. citizens. In addition, as table 8.2 suggests, marchers with family ties to an undocumented immigrant were more likely to have marched at least once before.

Other data collected in the surveys similarly suggest greater politicization on the part of marchers from mixed-status families. As Pallares (2009) reports, marchers from mixed-status families were more concerned about legalization issues than respondents who did not belong to mixed-status families, and they were also more likely to support unconventional political strategies such as sanctuary.

Based on the survey responses, we set out to better understand the motivations for participation in the marches as well as the significance people attached to their

TABLE 8.1 Characteristics of Chicago Marchers, 2006 and 2007

	2006 (%)	2007 (%)
Race/Ethnicity		
Latino	78	84
White	16	6
African American	4	6
Asian and other	5	4
Foreign Birth and Legal Status		
Foreign-born	58	60
U.S. citizen	74	69
Non–U.S. citizen	27	31
Family Composition		
Mixed status	n/a	47
Citizen and permanent resident members only	n/a	41
Undocumented members only	n/a	9
Legal permanent resident members only	n/a	3
Youth Characteristics (for marchers aged 15–28)		
Youth as % of all marchers	51	54
U.S. citizens as % of youth	79	81
Second-generation U.S. citizens as % of youth	65	n/a
(at least one foreign-born parent)		
Youth in mixed-status families	n/a	45
U.S. citizens in mixed-status families	n/a	37

TABLE 8.2 Frequency of March Participation by Family Composition, 2007 Survey

	First-Time Marcher (%)	Occasional Marcher (1–2 prior marches) (%)	Frequent Marcher (3 or more marches) (%)
All marchers	24	49	27
Mixed status	19	53	28
Non–mixed status	27	47	26

activism. Thus, we conducted over two hundred in-depth interviews and oral histories with participants, organizers, and leaders of organizations and institutions that participated in the mobilizations. These were complemented by published materials and other written documents related to the events and the organizations involved in the marches. We also were participant observers during the marches and at other immigrant rights–related events. In this chapter, we bring together data from the surveys, our participant observation, and our in-depth interviews to focus on mixed-status families who are resisting family separation and on youth participants in the marches.

THE FAMILY AS A COMMON REFERENT

The notion of family, its preservation, unity and continuity, has become an increasingly common referent for immigrants and their descendants. The defense of family stems from the shared lived experiences of immigrants since the late 1990s as well as from culturally resonant values that are considered more broadly American. Benford and Snow (2000, 624) explain that frame amplification idealizes, clarifies, or invigorates existing values. They suggest that activists engaged in frame amplification are more likely to tap into existing cultural values than to create alternative, countervalues.

Clearly, the defense of family resonates with the preexisting legal history and politics of the United States. The prioritizing of family unity is not an immigrant invention, as it has been reinforced by post-1965 family reunification policies and laws. However, the most recent politicization of family and family unity is something that can be traced to the early to mid-1990s. The religious right's political platform of family values elevated the sanctity of family as something to be preserved and placed in direct opposition to abortion and lesbian, gay, bisexual, transgender rights. The effectiveness of this discourse is not only visible in local and national public policies designed to curb reproductive freedom and LGBT rights, but both major parties have adopted and appropriated much of the language and goals of the family values movement (see Coontz 1992, 1998; Gillis 1997). The politicization of family unity among immigrants gained relevance in the mid-1990s, with the California referendum for Proposition 187 and other local initiatives, the Illegal Immigration Reform and Immigrant Responsibility Act of 1996, and the Personal Responsibility and Work Opportunity Reconciliation Act of 1996. It continued and became exacerbated after 9/11, when national security became a new framework of justification for further immigration enforcement and border control.

These changes in immigration and national security laws have increased the number of family separations as a consequence of increased deportations (more than a 200 percent increase, from 50,924 in 1995 to 208,521 in 2005), stricter border enforcement, deportations of legal immigrants with criminal records, and the creation of expedited removals.[2] These changes have also severely restricted the legal options once available to undocumented immigrants. Examples are the decline in immigrations judges' discretion, the elimination of Section 245i of the Immigration and Nationality Act, and the termination of suspensions of deportation.[3] All these changes have led to an increased visibility of family separation cases both among immigrant communities and among the general population. One immediate consequence of these state-led processes is that the concept of family has become politicized in new ways and has acquired political meaning for undocumented immigrants and their families, legal immigrants, and for the wider Latino communities in which they reside.

It is not enough to state, however, that immigrants mobilized around the notion of family. We must also explain how family actually gets constructed and signified in the process of collective action. The specific claims, arguments, and counterarguments that are made in the process of struggle rely on specific meanings that are grafted onto concepts of family, expanding what the notion of family can represent in specific contexts. In the following sections, we explicate how two distinct groups in Chicago have politicized the notion of family. The first example focuses on our work with an organization of mixed-status families in which at least one parent has a pending order of deportation. The second example focuses on how youth (as a cohort) politicize the family. We argue that despite important differences between the groups, in both cases, the family is a common referent and conduit through which questions of citizenship and democracy become publicly articulated, ultimately informing the goals and political strategies pursued.

While this case study focuses on Chicago, other research in this volume suggests that the use of the family frame has nationwide resonance. Martinez (this volume) poses that the discourse on family was engaged by activists in Denver to denounce the threat to families posed by H.R. 4437 and to present a more humane view of immigration. And while concern over the impact of immigration policies on family unity and preservation may be expected of members of immigrant families, Suro (this volume) cites national data to claim that second- and third-plus-generation Latinos share these concerns.

MIXED-STATUS FAMILY ACTIVISM: DEMOCRACY, CIVIC RESPONSIBILITY, AND CITIZENSHIP

In recent years a number of different campaigns and organizations in Chicago and throughout the country have played a central role in calling attention to the issue of deportation and its effects on families.[4] Differing from social service models, in which organizations designed to serve immigrants assist them, these groups are characterized by two principal features: they focus on the rights of people who have been deported or face the threat of deportation, and they consist primarily of individuals directly affected by deportation.

In Chicago, La Familia Latina Unida (LFLU) is a campaign focused on stopping deportations and fighting for the reunification of families that have been separated through deportation. The campaign is housed in the Centro sin Fronteras organization based in Pilsen, and its president is undocumented immigrant Elvira Arellano, who was detained in 2002 and who, after being in sanctuary in a Methodist church for one year, was arrested in Los Angeles in August 2007 and deported. Single mother Arellano and her minor son, Saul, a citizen of the United States, are one of thirty-five families who faced losing one or more family members to deportation when LFLU was launched. All of the families had experienced a prior deportation. In most of the cases, the deportation occurred when an undocumented family member who left the United States to visit a very sick or dying relative was stopped and deported upon his or her return, and then banned from attempting to enter the United States for ten years or more. However, despite the ban all returned to reunite with their children and spouses in the United States.

In the face of disempowerment and the almost impossibility of self-representation as individuals, members of LFLU have pursued stand-in representation through the focus on children. They have also pursued collective representation by deploying the family as a political subject and by organically linking themselves to the broader immigrant movement (both as mobilizers and as symbols), allowing the details of their pain to be made public, rendering the private public in novel ways. Since 2004, LFLU has pursued two major goals: (1) raising public awareness of the problems of deportations and raids and their effect on families by addressing communities, churches, and local, national, and foreign politicians and NGOs; and (2) lobbying for a private bill that would benefit thirty-five families who have been separated or are facing imminent separation due to deportation of one of the family members. Originally sponsored by Representative Luis Gutierrez and Senator Dick Durbin, the bill has been regularly reintroduced but not discussed in committee.

As noncitizens and therefore nonconventional political actors whose civil and political rights as individuals are frequently questioned, members of LFLU have opted to frame their struggle as a family issue, making the family, its continuity, unity, and integrity a central axis of identification and resistance. This form of political subjectivity that focuses on the preservation of family is simultaneously inclusive and exclusionary. It is inclusive because it incorporates the rights, needs, and desires of the adults, be they citizens, residents, or undocumented parents and grandparents. It refers not only to the welfare of the children but also to the welfare of the adults and to the survival and continuity of the interpersonal relationships that have historically sustained marginal populations experiencing racial, social, and economic oppression. But it is also exclusionary insofar as it relies on a conventional model of the traditional family, reproducing both the moral ideals of the Christian right, in a competition of sorts over who has most family values, as well as traditional gender norms.[5] What is critiqued is not the model itself but the fact that undocumented immigrants and their relatives are not included in the imagined community of these traditional families. Nonetheless, relying on these conventional models, undocumented immigrants in LFLU attempt to raise important unanswered questions about a political system that is willing to import labor but not recognize its civil, social, and human rights.

In extensive participant observation and in-depth interviews with members of LFLU, (undocumented individuals facing deportation and their resident and citizen spouses and children), we have identified two themes or different ways in which family is politicized: supporting family unity is viewed as a civic responsibility and as a way to uphold and defend democracy. Discourse on family unity and separation is deeply intertwined with these two notions, both for adults and children interviewed.

Civic Responsibility: An Engagement with Family First

For many of the interviewees, civic responsibility is measured first and foremost by one's loyalty and commitment to family. For parents, parenting is a social responsibility, and their ability to carry it out ensures a better and more secure society and more responsible future citizens. The families we interviewed measure their contributions to U.S. society not only in terms of their work and their financial weight but also in terms of their own family values. It is this commitment to the idea of family (however idealized) that they frequently use to distinguish themselves from others and to explain why they had to break the law (by leaving to visit ailing or dying relatives). Several of them understand caretaking as a form of social citizenship that benefits not only one's children but society as a whole. We often encountered arguments explaining how, in caring for her children in low-income urban neighborhoods, an undocumented mother is ensuring that her children will not be involved in gangs or become criminals; or how, in being a hard worker and also a constant presence in his children's lives, an undocumented father keeps his children motivated and off the streets. In aiming to deport them, the state interrupts parents' task of making children socially responsible citizens. Therefore, in the view of LFLU members, the state is not only disrupting their families but is disrupting society and undermining social order.

This discourse is not that dissimilar from a dominant family values discourse that regularly draws a relationship between the decline of family and social disorder (see Gillis 1997). It is intimately connected to a self-presentation of these undocumented parents as morally ideal individuals (law-abiding, tax-paying, non-government-dependent individuals). Extending this image in a more collective direction, the discourse introduces the notion of an ideal protocitizen as a community-building, church-attending, model parent and example for her or his children. For example, Benjamin, a citizen father of three citizen kids and husband of a woman facing deportation, talked about his wife's case:

> She has never worked. She has always stayed home and taken care of the kids. No one can say anything bad about these kids. They are very good. I work so that my salary is enough so that she can stay home and take care of her children, instead

of them being with somebody bad or becoming involved in gangs. But this is something the government does not recognize. . . . The work she does is probably not well-recognized but it is something very noble and she is a good person. We are proud of her. So what happens? We want our kids to be better citizens, having their mother in the house, to take them to school, pick them up from school.

As suggested by Benjamin, civic responsibility also entails a personal morality that privileges loyalty to family above all other principles, laws and concerns. It is this primary responsibility that many parents use to explain their activism under such difficult and tenuous conditions. LFLU parents often define their struggle first as being about and for their children. Several interviewees contended that if they were individuals alone they would have given up long ago and somehow gotten by in Mexico. For the children and youth of LFLU, their main responsibility lies in doing well in school, obeying their parents, staying out of trouble, and both protecting and advocating for their deportable parent(s). Many of the LFLU children have been increasingly active in public forums and events in Chicago, the United States, and abroad. When asked why they are engaging in these activities, many of the LFLU children and youth stated that they could not imagine doing otherwise and that they would feel useless and powerless if they felt they could not do anything.

For both adults and children, activism around this issue is understood as the next logical step for them, the ultimate assumption of responsibility that is part and parcel of being a family. Interestingly, LFLU members are now expanding this notion of civic responsibility to include not only their own families but also the broader community of families who cannot or do not speak for themselves. When faced with the question of whether they actually represent the undocumented, they argue that because many of the undocumented cannot speak for themselves, they must speak for many more families than their own.

While the notion of taking care of one's family as a civic act may run counter to the notion of a distinct public/private divide between state and family that is more prevalent in Anglo liberal (and Protestant) political theory, this divide is not so clear in Catholic views of state/family relation or in Latino political thought and activism.[6] Further, some continental political theory has also questioned the state/family divide. On his work on governmentality, Foucault claims that by the nineteenth century the family becomes an element of government and that serving the family is serving the state or public life, because family is a crucial node of governmental practice.[7] Finally, movements ranging from the feminist movement to the contemporary Christian right have questioned the separation between the personal and the political and have politicized family in very different ways.

Democracy

LFLU activists argue that a real democracy would value all families equally. Instead, they point out that while state policies support some families, they destroy others. They frequently refer to dominant political discourse on family values to point out the inconsistencies between what that discourse supposedly stands for and the separation of their own families. They frequently refer to this discrepancy in their speeches and literature. For example, the "Family Book" created by LFLU, with photos and stories of all the families facing deportation, has a cover page photo of George W. Bush, citing a speech in which he stated, "Family values don't stop at the Rio Grande." In our initial interview with Elvira Arellano, when she was on hunger strike in the summer of 2006, she discussed the case of Marta Jimenez, who was detained when she was four months pregnant. Elvira stated, "They speak of family values but when they shackled Mrs. Jimenez and chained her pregnant stomach, where were their family values? Are not our families worth as much as theirs?"

LFLU parents consistently raise the question of whether it is fair and democratic to have different levels of protections for mixed-status families than exist for families in which all members are citizens. They argue that, in a democracy, citizen children should extend their protections to noncitizens, instead of noncitizen parents extending their legal vulnerabilities to their children.[8] While this view has been argued in different ways, but never upheld by U.S. immigration courts, it is consistent with the Convention on the Rights of the Child (never ratified by the United States), which supports a child's right to family, as well as with the principles of U.S. family law that advocate keeping families together excepting extreme cases of negligence and abuse.[9] Additionally, this use of family as a political subject with rights raises problems similar to the plural self posited by anti–abortion rights activists in a liberal political framework. It is not possible in this view to separate a deportable parent from his or her citizen child. Hence, this issue presents a new challenge to liberal democracy that has not been fully addressed in previous constitutional debates and that is not yet incorporated into broader questions about the relationship between democracy and social inequalities in the United States.

Other aspects of democracy that are present in the discourse of LFLU activists concern the rights of citizen children, specifically the loss of their future opportunities, as well as the schism that these children experience between the promise of democracy and the reality of exclusion of their parents. LFLU members emphasize the rights of children as birthright citizens who are in a country where they can be denied their citizenship if they have to follow a deported parent. Often the children's educational accomplishments and strong feelings of belonging in the United States are emphasized, and their departure is expected to lead to a decline of their well-being, a possible loss of accomplishment, and a denial of opportunity.

Activists in LFLU argue that children are placed in the impossible situation of having to choose between their country and their family. Even remaining in the country would also mean a decline in accomplishments, opportunity, and well-being, as they would suffer the emotional, physical, and financial effects of being separated from one or both parents. LFLU parents stress the trauma that a previous deportation or the threat of deportation already places on their kids. They speak with great emotional difficulty about the effect this has on their performance in school, their temperament, their relationship to their parents, and their feelings about justice and democracy in the United States. One LFLU child, 11-year-old Cristina, spoke of her feelings about reciting one particular section of the Pledge of Allegiance in school: "When I am in school I don't say it [liberty and justice for all] and my teachers get angry. They say they will send me to the office if I don't say it. I don't believe in what it says because there is no justice for my mother and they are saying that there is justice. It's a lie. I don't want to say it on any day. Sometimes I don't say it when my teachers aren't looking."[10]

Children like Cristina experience the possibility of their parent's deportation as an ever-present schism between their allegiance to country and to family and as a reminder that the ideals their country stands for do not apply to the people they most love. Children who have birthright citizenship are also faced with the question of whether they will be able to stay or have to leave without ever having had a choice in the matter. Their birthright citizenship that in many respects is just like the citizenship of others, but in one fundamental way is not, has led LFLU activists and their children to raise the banner of human rights and children's rights as crucial issues that are deeply intertwined with their own personal struggles, and to pursue legal and political strategies that stress the rights of citizen children in a democratic system.[11] For many march attendants and immigration movement activists the issue of family resonates not only as a human rights issue but because many of them have very painful histories of family separation in their own families. To the extent that other immigrants and descendants of immigrants identify strongly with this liminality, this betwixt and between discussed by Chavez (1997) that characterizes the immigrant experience, these questions about the rights of citizen children will resonate among a broader public.

BROADENING THE DEFINITION OF FAMILY: YOUTH, CIVIC RESPONSIBILITY, AND DEMOCRACY

Many of these same themes and understandings were behind young people's participation in the marches. While youth are frequently characterized as politically apathetic, hundreds of thousands of youth participated in the largest demonstrations in Chicago's history. As shown in table 8.1, slightly over half of the people we surveyed during the May 1, 2006, and May 1, 2007, marches were between the ages of 14 and 28. We conducted in-depth interviews with almost one hundred of these young marchers and found out that most of them had not been politically active prior to their participation in the marches. Only about a third had ever voted or signed a petition, and only 20 percent had engaged in other political activities. However, those who were politically involved prior to the marches were engaged primarily around the immigration issue. Moreover, a significant number of the young marchers we interviewed had volunteered for organizations that provide services to immigrants, such as ESL and citizenship workshops. Similar to the youth in Bloemraad and Trost's study (this volume), many of our interviewees engaged in discussions about immigration issues with parents, other family members, and friends, and their engagement was firmly tied to immigration and seldom translated into other social or political issues.

Both the surveys and the interview data show that many young people who attended the marches view immigrant rights as intricately connected to the defense of family in at least two distinct ways: in their own personal familial affiliation, and in a broader community that they identify as being part of their people or collective family. While immigration is a family issue among the youth we studied, the concept of the family is not limited to immediate or nuclear family. For these youth, the concept of family extends to real as well as imagined family; they specifically mention their communities, their "people" *(la raza),* and the marginalized. This broader concept of family is informed by their experiences as racialized people who, regardless of their place of birth or legal status, are viewed and treated by others as "immigrants," and particularly "illegal immigrants" (Chavez 2008). Thus, family is an elastic concept that sometimes alludes only to relatives but that can also include community members, coethnics, and panethnics, all of whom share a common racialized classification. Because both racialization and interpersonal relationships link them to the undocumented, most second-generation youth interviewed feel that their "family" has been affected directly or indirectly by immigration issues. They attended the marches to denounce proposed immigration laws as unfair to families and disruptive of the unity, stability, and continuity of the family. Their denunciation involves a sharp critique of democracy as well as a claim of rights for their families and broader communities of families. Like members of LFLU, the youth have politicized the concept of family. Moreover, our research suggests that the defense of family is playing a central role in the youth's formation as political subjects, the place they are assigning to themselves in the immigration struggle, and their visions about democracy and its limits.

Civic Responsibility: A Broader Notion of Family

Similar to members of LFLU, many of the youth we interviewed measure civic responsibility in terms of degree of loyalty and commitment to family. We pose here that, for young people, participation in the immigrant protests is a form of collective brokering and an extension of their civic duty to represent their families and communities. For many of the youth, representing their family starts early in life. Studies show that the children of immigrants, particularly when parents do not speak English, become representatives of the family as they broker or mediate interaction between the family and outsiders (Portes and Rumbaut 2001; Zentella 1997). In what becomes a role reversal, as soon as children gain enough fluency to read or converse in English, they begin translating written and spoken language to and from their parents. Children whose Spanish-language skills are disregarded by their schools occupy an important position within the family precisely because they know Spanish and English (Valenzuela 1999). While outside of the family they occupy such marginal positions, their status as brokers for their families strengthens their loyalty, commitment to, and responsibility for their family and community. Bloemraad and Trost (this volume) describe similar practices that cement familial bonds between youth and their immigrant parents.

Immigrant and second-generation youth are frequently members of mixed-status families made up of citizens, legal residents, and undocumented or any combination of these. As shown above, 45 percent of the youth we surveyed in 2007 are from mixed-status families where at least one member is undocumented. Youth in mixed-status families live with the constant threat of the disruption of their family unity due to deportation. For them, representing the undocumented members of their family is a must in order to preserve the family unit intact. Some of these youth had already endured long separations from their parents. For these young people, there is an obvious and direct connection with the claims of the undocumented.

For other youth, the connection to the undocumented is much looser, as they may not have any family member who is undocumented. Many of them take a more encompassing definition of family that includes notions of "my people." This notion is mostly based on nationalistic or ethnic terms and it is the equivalent to the use of *la raza* by Mexicans in the Southwest. The notion of "my people" means in most cases Mexicans or Latinos. One of our interviewees, 16-year-old Kimberly, makes this clear when she says, "And it was important for me to stay united with my people. Not only with my family and community, but my people as a whole." Youth often used *my people* as an all-encompassing term that includes coethnics, other U.S.-born Latinos, and immigrants of any legal status. One consequence of adopting this broader notion of family is that youth develop an understanding that most Latinos are affected by immigration. As a young citizen we interviewed put it, "Whether you were documented or not, it affected you. Even if you are documented you have family or friends, your whole neighborhood, affected by the issue" (Joshua, 21 years old).

In a city with high residential segregation, it is not surprising to find that most of the youth in our study live in predominantly ethnic communities with large populations of immigrants. There they come into daily contact with people who are undocumented and these daily interactions strengthen a sense of loyalty and commitment to them. The undocumented are an integral part of their communities and their deportations threaten the very core of community life.

The integration of the undocumented as "my people" also has to do with the racialization of the term *undocumented* and its indiscriminate use. In the public imagination, *undocumented immigrant* has come to mean Mexican and is applied to anyone who looks Mexican regardless of legal status or ethnic origin (Chavez 2001, 2008; Santa Ana 2002). Indeed, Suro (this volume) suggests that the second and third-plus generation may have felt demonized along with the undocumented population. Many young people in our study allude to their inclusion or the inclusion of others in this category by the media and the public. They resent the ways in which they are associated with criminality, as the language of illegality is applied to them and others who, like them, look Mexican. Lori, 20 years old, stated, "They [non Latinos] like to categorize people regardless of their race. If you look Mexican you are automatically an immigrant no matter if you were born here or not." Like Lori, the youth we interviewed vehemently question the criminalization of Mexicans, and other Latinos, by insisting, "We're not criminals [just] because we came here illegally" (Lucia, 21 years old).

Additionally, many young marchers like Lucia claim the undocumented as "my people" because they identify as "immigrants" even when they and/or their parents are U.S.-born (see Flores-González 2010). Assuming an immigrant identity is their response to the broader marginalization and racialization of the Latino community where people happen to have different legal and national origin status. For instance, many Puerto Rican youth participated in the marches because, although they are citizens, they share the immigrant experience and a similar racialization process in this country. Jacquelyn, a 23-year-old Puerto Rican, said, "The migration for Puerto Ricans wasn't an easy migration. It was very hard and it was very traumatic for some people and either they returned to the island or they stayed but I feel like those struggles that they went through we cannot forget and those are similar struggles that the undocumented are going though and we shouldn't forget." Similar racializing experiences that cut across generations, national origin, and legal status may be leading young Latinos to find common bonds and to develop a broader and unifying identity, as suggested by Suro (this volume).

Furthermore, when questioned about their support for immigrants, young people articulate a rationale for participation derived from their belief that the opportunities they enjoy were gained at the expense of earlier immigrants who sacrificed. Perhaps Armando, a 25-year-old interviewee, best captured the feelings of loyalty and commitment to the real and imagined family and of civic responsibility to represent and pay back the debt:

> My family, we're immigrants. They came here legally but nonetheless they are immigrants. My community, my neighbors are immigrants. These are people that I know. These are people who are good people. . . . These sacrifices that they made so that I can flourish and I am here where I am because of that . . . me as a citizen, who grew amongst immigrants, who can represent them without fear of being deported. I don't see it as doing anyone a favor. I see it as my responsibility. You know, if people made sacrifices for people like me to be where I am now, it's time that I give back and I do my part.

Democracy: Creating a Discourse on Rights

In our interviews, young people voice a strong critique of democracy that is based on their expanded notions of family. They explicitly point to the contradictions of U.S. democracy when it comes to immigrant families. They argue that rights that are granted to, and taken for granted by, most American families do not apply to undocumented families. At the core of this contradiction are the unity, stability, and continuity of the family to which the undocumented have no right. As 16-year-old Laura said, "to say that the United States is about keeping families, it's like when you deport somebody you're separating the whole entire family, you destroy a whole family." Our interviewees talk about how deportations tear at the financial security and family unity. One young woman was distraught by the plight of her best friend's family, which was facing the imminent deportation of the family breadwinner: "My one friend, her dad was in the process of getting deported and it was terrible. I hated seeing what my friend was going through and her whole family was just getting separated just like that and it was not good because her dad is the one that brings in all the money and if they took him away my friend has to go too because they can't survive without him" (Lucia).

Many youth link the lack of rights for immigrant families to the invisibility that this society renders to the undocumented. They maintain that dominant images of the "illegal" are abstract and dehumanizing and do not convey the reality lived by the undocumented and their families. Young people are critical of a democracy purportedly based on equality for all that nevertheless allows the dehumanization of this segment of society. Many of the youth seek to "put a face" on the undocumented to make them real and to show that they are ordinary people who might be your neighbors or classmates. They believe that if others could "see" the undocumented, they would be more likely to extend rights to them:

The marches humanize the undocumented. Suddenly, the undocumented people have a face and sometimes you are shocked to find out somebody who is undocumented. Like there was a girl in one of my classes who was undocumented. It made me sad because I know pretty well that after she graduates what's gonna happen. She has a college diploma, yet she can't use it anywhere. And it's really important that we give the undocumented a face, give them an identity, give them a name because then these human rights seem reasonable. (Jorge, 22 years old).

Youth are particularly critical of a democracy where place of birth determines access to opportunities. They consider the concept of citizenship that is solely based on place of birth as a very limited one. Many have personal stories of lost opportunities that they view as simply unfair or absurd, and they especially question laws that restrict educational opportunities for undocumented youth. It is troubling for some of these young people to witness how other youth who have lived most of their lives in the United States, and for whom it is the only country they know, are marginalized, criminalized, and excluded because they were born on the other side of the border. Our interviewees view these youths to be as American as those who were born in the United States.

Finally, the criminalization of the undocumented as well as those who assisted them—most notably family members—was another factor that made young people both question U.S. democracy and argue for the need to act publicly and urgently in order to empower themselves as well as others. Specifically, they frequently mention the Sensenbrenner bill (H.R. 4437) as an undemocratic proposal that threatened the preservation, unity, and continuity of family by making undocumented relatives, friends, coworkers, or clients a criminal liability.

The critique of American democracy expressed by the young marchers we interviewed extends to the role the government and those in power play in making these anti–immigrant family laws. Many of the youth we talked to blame President George W. Bush, Congress, and/or the Republican Party for supporting laws that would have a devastating effect on immigrant families. For our young interviewees, there are more pressing social and political issues that "they should be worrying about other than breaking families up" (Carmen, 14 years old). By marching, young people hoped to

communicate to Congress, to the lawmakers, to the president that they [the undocumented] are people that deserve to live in the US and that the laws that are trying to be passed are wrong and they're not here alone, and they're not gonna be . . . they're going to be represented no matter what. As much as they'd like for them to kind of be able to just deport them or you know push them to the country that they came from, that they can't do that. It's not as easy for them to do something like that. That people will stand up for human rights. (Jacquelyn, 23 years old)

This quote speaks of the broader family, the solidarities and coalitions between the undocumented (who are not alone) and the legal residents and citizens, as a model for democratic empowerment. Because people will stand up, the undocumented will gain representation and not be pushed out. Clearly, the young marchers we interviewed are simultaneously critiquing the exclusions that exist in the current model of U.S. democracy and using democratic principles to demand rights for the undocumented, to engender a more expansive democratic vision, and to assign a forceful role to themselves as representatives of those who cannot represent themselves. Youth attended the marches to exercise their right to protest and to question unfair laws and practices, but most of all they marched to represent their families (real and imagined) that they feel have been excluded by this democracy.

CONCLUSIONS

In this chapter we have argued that family is a crucial common referent used by both undocumented families and young protesters to explain their politicization along two lines: to justify their own activism and to articulate why their struggle is a democratic one. We have attempted to find the political in the familial by not simply assuming that peoples' activism can be explained solely by the fact of being in a mixed-status family, and thus being directly affected by the issue of illegality. After all, millions of people who did not participate in the protests have undocumented family members. Instead, we have shown that, for those who did march, ideological factors came into play as they articulated narratives about themselves, their families, and their communities that helped produce the political aspirations and visions that were necessary for sustained mobilization. In Chicago, we have underscored the ways in which both LFLU members and youth link family unity, and the activism to preserve it, to notions of civic responsibility and democracy. Moreover, we have argued that the family frame has the potential to politicize and mobilize a broader segment of the population that is not undocumented or directly affected by immigration policy.

This chapter also aims to contribute to current debates on ethnic as well as cross-ethnic or Latino solidarity (Latinidades). D. Gutierrez (1995) has aptly shown that communities that share a national origin or descent (specifically Mexicans) have historically never agreed on the question of immigration or immigrant policy toward the undocumented. Taken to its full extent, Gutierrez's cautionary claim that we should not assume intraethnic solidarities leads us to suggest that when intraethnic solidarities do occur they need to be adequately explained, and not merely assumed. Hence, when Mexicans and Latinos of different generations, ages, and legal statuses come together in support of the rights of the undocumented, we need to ask why and how this could happen, and what are the social, political, and cultural common grounds that may be supporting these coalitions.

These shared identifications are visible not only in the signs the marchers carried in the 2006 demonstrations; they help explicate the significant levels of support that members of LFLU have received locally and nationally since the convergence of the marches and Elvira Arellano's seeking sanctuary in a Chicago church. These shared identifications also help explain the second- and third-generation youth who acted as bodyguards for Elvira and who have worked consistently to support and promote her cause. For a small organization like LFLU, the marches presented a political opportunity that the organization's members seized, rendering themselves and their cause visible to a much broader public. But their ability to ride this opportunity and keep their agenda alive also depends on the resonance of their claims about the importance of family, and a wider acceptance of this notion of the family as a political subject among a plethora of immigrant-identified communities.

For many young people, these marches were their public initiation as political actors. The current federal debate about immigration has profound implications for their lives, not only because many are the children of the undocumented, but also because young protesters interpret the Sensenbrenner bill and similar legislative initiatives as an attack on communities and groups with whom young people identify. The overwhelming participation of youth in the 2006 and 2007 immigrant rights marches show that youth care deeply about immigrant rights and that this may be the "common cause" that will lead to the political engagement of naturalized and U.S.-born Latino youth.

Since 2006, when our field research was first initiated, the focus on family has spread from the LFLU's discourse and that of the young marchers we interviewed to acquire a broader resonance among several social and political actors. In the 2007 and 2008 marches, family motifs were much more visible in activists' literature and signs. Spanish-language television programs ranging from *Don Francisco* to *Cristina* to *Veredicto Final* have covered several cases of family separation. Human Rights Watch and the National Council on La Raza have published reports on the effects of raids on children and families. The new sanctuary movement, a growing (and multiracial) national coalition of faith-based groups and organizations designed to assist families facing deportation and to end deportations, has defended the importance of family in its major events and publications. In 2008, LFLU and Centro sin Fronteras, as well as youth in the organizations Zocalo and Batey Urbano, played a central role in founding Ya Basta, a coalition of several Chicago organizations that demand a moratorium on deportations and raids in order to end family separation. In October of that year, the Chicago City Council unanimously approved a resolution to support such a moratorium, after hearing moving testimonies in which family separations were emphasized. Finally, in December 2008, Representative Luis Gutierrez, in conjunction with the Ya Basta coalition, initiated a campaign in several churches to collect names of citizens willing to adopt a relative or friend who is undocumented. This campaign went national, in an attempt to present President Barack Obama with thousands of signatures in defense of a moratorium, and concluded on Mother's Day 2009. The participation of evangelical churches, including Chicago's El Rebaño, in this campaign (with five thousand people attending one related event) evidences the adoption of this issue by groups that have not previously been active in the immigrant movement and that were not considered likely to become involved.

While these other actors use somewhat different rationales to resist family separation than LFLU and youth (the sanctity of marriage is one frequently mentioned reason), their recrafting of the family frame at this stage does not appear to contradict or challenge previous frames but is instead expanding support among Latinos. It remains to be seen if these faith-based initiatives will lead to increased visibility, more cross-racial awareness, and a wider support for this issue among non-Latinos, all key goals in activists' quest to convince a broader public that all families are created equal.

NOTES

Parts of this chapter draw from Amalia Pallares's "Representing La Familia: Family Separation and Immigrant Activism in Chicago" and Nilda Flores-González's "Immigrants, Citizens or Both? The Second Generation in the Immigrant Rights Marches," both chapters in ¡Marcha! Latino Chicago and the National Immigrant Movement (University of Illinois Press, 2010).

1. The March 10 mobilization drew 300,000 marchers while the May 1 march had over 500,000.

2. Expedited removal, enacted in the 1996 law, involves the processing and immediate deportation of people stopped at the border without granting them a hearing in front of a judge.

3. In suspension of deportation hearings, immigrants could go before a judge and argue that their deportation would lead to extreme hardship. However limited, it was a possibility that was eliminated after 1996, leaving almost no legal room for undocumented immigrants to appeal or for immigration judges to make exceptions (Coutin 2003). Additionally, Section 245i allowed immigrants seeking permanent residency to apply to remain in the United States without returning to their country of origin and applying through the U.S. Consulate. When applied, this prevented family separation. This was also terminated by the 1996 bill.

4. In addition to the Chicago campaign of La Familia Latina Unida housed in the organization Centro sin Fronteras, other important organizations are Families for Freedom based in New York, and American Families United based in Pennsylvania.

5. For more on immigrants' use and performance of morality, see Coutin (2003).

6. For works in political theory that make this distinction, see Georg H. W. Hegel's Philosophy of Right, translated by S. W. Dyde (Cosimo Classics, 2008), and John Locke's Second Treatise of Government (1690; Barnes and Noble, 2004). For more on political familism among Latinos, see Zinn (1975), Chabram-Dernersesian (1999), and Gutiérrez (2008).

7. We thank political theorist Stephen Engelmann for helpful observations on this matter. For more on this perspective see Michel Foucault and Paul Rabinow's *Foucault Reader* (Pantheon, 1984) and Jacques Donzelot's *Policing of Families* (Johns Hopkins University Press, 1997).

8. In terms of the citizen children's rights angle, no court has ever agreed that citizen children have a constitutional right to remain with their parents, as federal immigration law tends to trump state-level family law. Nor has any court agreed that deporting a parent is a de facto deportation of the child, as the child is purportedly free to stay in the country or to return at a later stage. Courts have repeatedly established that undocumented immigrants cannot use the citizenship of their child to prevent their own deportation. While immigration law has historically favored family reunification, this is based on the parents' right to use their status as a means to legalize their child, and not vice versa. Children's rights are derivative of their parents'; and to complicate things further, children are not recognized as having legal agency in their own right but as being under tutelage of their parents. For a more extensive discussion of the legal angle, see Thronson (2007).

9. The International Covenant on Civil and Political Rights, the European Convention of Human Rights, the Universal Declaration of Human Rights provision on family unity, the Council of the European Union, the American Declaration of the Rights and Duties of Man, and the American Convention on Human Rights also protect a person's right to a private life and/or a family.

10. For Cristina and other interviewees, we use pseudonyms.

11. Some of these strategies include a legal suit filed by Saul Arellano, which was dismissed by a judge in 2006; the "4 Million Kids" collective lawsuit filed by several children throughout the country; marches and demonstrations staged by citizen children in 2007; and the Citizen Children Bill sponsored by Representative Jose Serrano.

9

It's a Family Affair

Intergenerational Mobilization
in the Spring 2006 Protests

Irene Bloemraad and Christine Trost

From March 10 to May 1, 2006, between 3.5 and 5 million people across the United States participated in immigrant rights rallies (Fox, Selee, and Bada 2006). As Suro (this volume) points out, many of the faces in the crowd were those of children and adolescents (see also Flores-González et al. 2006; Fox, Selee, and Bada 2006; Wang and Winn, this volume). One report of the May 1 rally in Oakland, California, claims that a quarter of marchers were school-age children and teenagers (Rauh 2006). If this estimate is accurate and representative of other demonstrations, 1 million youth may have participated in the demonstrations, boycotts, and other immigrant rights events of spring 2006.[1]

Compared to other metropolitan areas in the United States, mobilization against H.R. 4437, the Border Protection, Antiterrorism, and Illegal Immigration Control Act of 2005, and in favor of legalization and immigrant rights was slower and less concentrated in the San Francisco Bay Area. As early as March 10, 2006, between 100,000 and 300,000 people marched in Chicago, while on March 25 anywhere from 200,000 to 1 million people rallied in Los Angeles.[2] In the Bay Area, the first sizeable mobilization only occurred on April 10, the National Day of Action, bringing together an estimated 25,000 people in San Jose.

On May 1, tens of thousands of Bay Area residents participated in marches and boycotts, but events were dispersed throughout the region. The largest rally occurred in San Jose, where an estimated 100,000–125,000 people participated. Numbers were lower in San Francisco, where the crowd was put at about 30,000. These figures, representing the two largest cities in the Bay Area, understate participation, however, since dozens of rallies occurred in smaller cities and towns. In Oakland, police estimated that 15,000–17,000 people congregated in the downtown area, although organizers put the figure much higher, at 50,000, noting that not all participants in the hundred-block march were able to get to the final destination in front of city hall and the Ronald V. Dellums Federal Building (Bender and MacDonald 2006). In Richmond, between 2,000 and 8,000 people marched from three Catholic churches to converge on the city's Civic Center (Simerman 2006). These figures suggest that perhaps 35 and 15 percent of the Latino population in Oakland and Richmond, respectively, participated in local May 1 rallies.[3] Others participated through boycotts. Throughout the region, schools reported dramatic reductions in attendance and employers with significant numbers of Latino workers closed their businesses or opened with reduced staff.

This impressive youth mobilization demands study and explanation. There are a number of literatures that could be used to speak to this question, focused on political behavior, political socialization, social movements, and school-based civic education. However, an in-depth look at these research traditions shows that they tend not to consider immigrant families, often offer a narrow view of political and civic engagement, and rest on data from thirty to forty years ago.[4] Theorizing and understanding youth participation in 2006 requires new theories and new data. This chapter offers a step toward that goal, providing an account of youth engagement and family political socialization during the spring 2006 immigrant rights protests. It builds on an emerging empirical and theoretical literature that shows how children influence parents' political attitudes and activities, particularly in immigrant families (Bloemraad 2006; Wong and Tseng 2008). We draw on early findings from the Immigrant Families' Political Socialization Project, which conducted in-depth multigenerational interviews of Mexican-origin families in Richmond and Oakland, California, to make three claims.

First, our data confirm that the protests of spring 2006 mobilized large segments of the Mexican-origin population, both adults and youth, and that among these individuals a significant number had never before engaged in any political activity. We argue that such large-scale mobilization was, in part, due to the intergenerational sharing of information and opinions as well as mobilizing efforts by some family members of others in the household. Put simply, the protests were a family affair, and accounts that fail to examine family and youth participation miss a critical part of the story of the 2006 immigrant rights demonstrations.

We also make the case for a bidirectional, parent *and* child, model of political socialization. Youth played an active and independent role in these mass mobilizations. Especially within immigrant families, youth engagement opens the possibility that political socialization—the process of acquiring or developing attitudes, values, beliefs, skills, and behaviors related to public affairs and politics—occurs in two directions: from parent to child, as conceived by the traditional literature on this topic, *and* from child to parent, as children with greater access to the English language and mainstream institutions provide political information to their parents and encourage them to participate.[5]

Finally, we suggest that a focus on families helps us to see and conceptualize the family as a particularly useful site for political mobilization. As different family members access and pool together different information sources, networks, and institutional experiences, intergenerational communication and interaction can increase all members' knowledge and participation. In the context of the immigrant rights marches, adolescents drew on new technologies, peer networks, and resources from schools and youth organizations, while parents drew on experiences in workplaces and churches and exposure to ethnic media. When information, opinions, and experiences were shared, the possibilities for widespread participation increased.

Our analysis is a complement to that of Pallares and Flores-González (this volume), who demonstrate how framing and rhetorical strategies around families has become a key part of the immigrant rights movement (see also Heredia, this volume). We heard very similar messages from those we interviewed. Here we focus on intergenerational mobilization: the processes by which people acquired information, were spurred to participate, and joined in the protests because of family interactions.

THEORIZING YOUTH ENGAGEMENT AND POLITICAL SOCIALIZATION

We know that young people can be political actors. College students are often singled out for their consequential participation in contentious political action, ranging from the U.S. civil rights and feminist movements (Freeman 1975; McAdam 1988; Morris 1984) to democratization movements in Eastern Europe and China (Calhoun 1997; Zhao 1998). Less has been written about high school students, but, particularly within the history of the Chicano movement, they played an important role. Muñoz argues that the walkouts by Mexican American high school students in East Los Angeles in 1968 signaled "the entry of youth of Mexican descent into the history of the turbulent sixties" (1989, xi).

According to social movement scholars, youth are particularly apt to get involved due to biographical availability, "the absence of personal constraints that may increase the cost and risks of movement participants such as full-time employment, marriage and family responsibilities" (McAdam 1986, 70). Put simply, youth participate because little stops them, costs are modest, and they have time on their hands. Yet, while the idea of biographical availability has appeal, comparisons of social movement joiners with those who sit out find little support for this proposition: the middle aged are more likely to participate than those in their teens and early twenties, and those with school-age children (arguably an impediment to biographically availability) participate more than others (Beyerlein and Hipp 2006; Rosenstone and Hansen 1993; Verba, Schlozman, and Brady 1995).

The familial nature of the spring 2006 protests—when youth came out *with* their parents to marches and rallies—suggests an alternative account of youth mobilization within the context of family politicization.[6] Prior research on political socialization contends that parents transmit both general orientations about politics (e.g., political efficacy and trust) and more specific attitudes (e.g., political ideology and partisan identification), as well as the propensity to be politically active (Beck and Jennings 1975, 1991; Jennings and Niemi 1981; Verba, Schlozman, and Brady 1995). According to García Bedolla (2005), parents can also help their children develop a strong, positive group identity as Latino, which further enhances political engagement. Such effects might vary by urban location (Sánchez-Jankowski 1986). Research shows that even though intergenerational transmission of attitudes and behaviors from parent to child is far from perfect, family members provide direct political stimulation through family discussion and they model political behaviors, such as when they go to vote.[7] Children with politically active parents are more likely to become politically engaged (Jennings and Niemi 1974; Verba, Schlozman, and Brady 1995).

Significantly, these findings are almost entirely based on research with native-born America citizens. Parents are assumed to have much greater knowledge about and experience with the political system than children or adolescents. Left unquestioned is the assumption that parents hold relatively developed views of American politics, have access to political information, and have the legal status to engage in acts such as voting.

These assumptions become much more tenuous in the case of immigrant families. U.S.-born children often have more direct access to the mainstream's dominant language and culture than immigrant parents. Numerous studies document how the children of immigrants find themselves in the position of translator for their parents during medical exams, in interactions with public officials (including school employees and police), or during disputes with others, such as landlords (e.g., Bloemraad 2006; Kibria 1993; Orellana 2001; Portes and Rumbaut 2001). In a pilot study of child to parent political socialization in immigrant families, Wong and Tseng (2008) found that college students with immigrant parents report acting as translators of political materials, as teachers of political concepts and institutions, and as opinion shapers, discussing political stances with their parents. There is solid ground to believe that processes of political socialization from parents to children might be attenuated in immigrant families and that the reverse process—child to parent political socialization—might also occur.

We argue that we must reformulate old top-down models of political socialization into interactional models of family socialization and mobilization. Different family members may draw on different institutions when sharing information, viewpoints, and opportunities for participation. Clearly schools play an important part in the lives of children, and research shows that school-based political learning activities can also augment parents' political socialization (McDevitt and Chaffee 2000, 2002). Both parents and children gain skills and information from participation in community associations and religious institutions, but their patterns of membership may well differ. Media also affect both parents and children, but the types of media older and younger family members access likely differ, particularly as youth adopt new communication tools, such as social networking sites like MySpace.com and Facebook.com. In immigrant families, in particular, adults may rely on non-English media, while children are more likely to access mainstream, American media sources. Parents and children also draw on different networks of friends and acquaintances, depending on social ties, organizational affiliations, employment, and school attendance. In immigrant families, adults' social ties may be more firmly rooted in coethnic networks while children may have greater interethnic friendships, widening their networks of information and mobilization. In cases where parents and children have strong, positive, and frequent interactions, family members can "pool" sources of political mobilization and socialization. The possibility of such pooling underlies the need to shift our conceptualization of political socialization and engagement away from the individual and toward the family as a unit.

DATA AND METHODS: MULTIGENERATIONAL IN-DEPTH INTERVIEWS

We draw on data collected as part of the Immigrant Families' Political Socialization Project.[8] The project team interviewed members of forty Mexican-origin families living in the cities east of the San Francisco Bay, largely in Richmond and Oakland, California. For each family, we interviewed one youth and at least one parent.[9] The youth were U.S.-born citizens between the ages of 14 and 18.[10] The parents held one of three legal statuses: undocumented, noncitizen legal permanent resident, or naturalized citizen, with approximately similar numbers across these statuses. We also recruited four families with U.S.-born citizen parents as a control group, for a total of seventy-nine individual interviews. All but four interviews were conducted between March 21, 2006, and August 10, 2006, with 97 percent occurring after the large wave of May 1 rallies.[11] Respondents were asked general questions about the respondent's current and past civic and political engagement, and we asked specific questions about participation in and attitudes toward the spring 2006 events. Interviewers were encouraged to follow up on respondents' answers to learn about the process by which people became involved in the marches, rallies, and boycotts as well as the conversations respondents had with others about these events.[12]

A FAMILY AFFAIR: UNPRECEDENTED CROSS-GENERATION MOBILIZATION

The first striking finding from our research is respondents' unprecedented degree of participation in the spring 2006 events and its cross-generational nature. At the outset, we sought to recruit families with modest economic and educational resources for civic and political engagement, and to recruit some families that face barriers due to noncitizen or undocumented status. Of those we interviewed, fully 61 percent attended a march, participated in a boycott, or engaged in some other direct action activity around immigrant rights between March and May 2006.[13] Among parents, 62 percent participated in some way, and among teens the proportion was 61 percent. Despite the potential risk associated with participating in public demonstrations, almost all the undocumented parents interviewed participated in some manner (8 out of 9), compared to 6 of 13 naturalized citizens and 7 of 13 legal permanent residents. Those lacking legal status had the most to fear from H.R. 4437, but, supporting the idea that the protests were not just a manifestation of self-interest, 3 of the 4 U.S.-born parents interviewed also participated. Among the teens, all of whom are U.S. citizens, about two-thirds of the children of undocumented parents or of noncitizen permanent residents participated (6 of 9 and 8 of 12, respectively), compared to about half of the teens whose parents are naturalized citizens (7 of 13) or U.S.-born (2 of 4). These findings suggest that undocumented parents do become involved in political activity, albeit within the context of an arguably unique moment of mobilization, and they may play a role in helping their U.S.-born children become engaged citizens despite their own legal status. The data also support the proposition, elaborated below, that some youth encouraged their parents' participation.

The widespread participation in spring 2006 protest activities stands in contrast to more modest engagement in other political activities. We asked our respondents a series of questions about their prior political participation, inquiring whether they had ever worked on a candidate campaign; worked on a ballot proposition or ballot initiative campaign; signed a petition; sent a letter or e-mail to a public official; attended a political meeting; attended a neighborhood meeting; participated in any protest or march *other than* the spring 2006 immigration rallies; and (only for parents) whether they had ever made a financial contribution to a political campaign. Among parents, the median number of political activities was only one out of eight possible activities; sixteen of the parent respondents had never engaged in any of these activities prior to the spring of 2006. Among the teens, the mean number of political activities was also one, as was the median. Nine of the thirty-eight teen respondents reported never having engaged in any sort of political activity. Of the parents and teens who had never engaged in any prior political activity, over half (56 percent) participated in an immigrant rights activity in the spring of 2006. Put another way, of all those who did participate, almost a third (30 percent) told us that this was the first political activity in which they had *ever* participated in the United States.

A recurring theme in our interviews was the essential role played by social networks of friends, family, and acquaintances in mobilizing respondents to participate. This highlights the importance of studying political socialization and participation as an interactive process rather than an atomized one (Bloemraad 2006, 79–101). In a number of cases, parents and teens were hesitant, even scared, about their first-time participation. Señora Sanchez,[14] a legal permanent resident who participated in an April 10 march, explained:

> There were a lot of people and they invited me. I took my daughter, the older one, and she told me, "Mami, I do not like to be doing this." I think because there were a lot of people. And I am not like that either [someone who participates], not at all. . . . I did not think there would be so many people and my older daughter could not believe what she was doing. I told her that there is nothing bad and we are just supporting people. To tell you the truth, I am very scared of the kids that do bad things [attending the rally]. I feel like I will end up in prison for being there [giggling].

The personal encouragement of others helped overcome initial fears—in Señora Sanchez's case, her child's babysitter urged her to go, as did the desire to be part of what quite a few described as a movement of solidarity. Critically, from the perspective of familial political socialization, Señora Sanchez did not attend the march alone but convinced her eldest daughter to attend too.

Teens were also mobilized into political participation for the first time in spring 2006, most often through friends at school. The teenage daughter of a legal permanent resident, who had previously never participated in any political activity, attended two demonstrations, one on April 10 and another on May 1. Abril explained, "At first I had no clue what was going on, but then all my friends were like, 'Yeah, the immigrants. . . . They're trying to kick everybody out. Like, if they find someone that is an immigrant, they're going to kick them out.' I was like, 'Oh, that's not fair,' so they told us what days [the protests would be] through text messages on the phone and stuff." Like Señora Sanchez, Abril was mobilized through personal networks, though in her case this was not only through face-to-face contact but also through the medium of text messaging, something the teenage respondents reported frequently.

As with Abril, various respondents reported much more exposure to political information because of the marches. In some cases, participation changed their attitude and behaviors toward politics. One single mother, an undocumented migrant, had never before engaged in political activities, but she now watches the news and follows current events regularly, activities that she did not do before her participation in two Oakland marches. To the extent that mobilization is easier once people have participated at least once in an event or activity, the broad participation in the events of 2006 holds out the possibility of greater future engagement among Mexican-origin residents.

Another common theme was the familial nature of participation in the marches and boycotts. Señora Sanchez went to the April 10 march with her daughter, and Abril attended the May 1 march with her family. Abril's participation with her parents is especially noteworthy since she told us that her interactions with her parents are quite limited. Abril does not know how to read or write in Spanish, and she does not speak the language fluently, creating communication problems. Both parents also work long hours. When we asked Abril whether she talks to her parents about politics or current events, she told us no, the same answer her mother gave when asked the same question. This lack of communication even extends to talking about school. As Abril explained, "I really don't talk to them. When I get home, I go to my room. Usually they're never around, they're always working." Abril's mother said that she was unsure whether her daughter and she share similar political views, but "the only thing we agree on is the protests that have taken place, because the people need papers and we agree on that, totally." Reinforcing the notion that the protests were a strong expression of collective solidarity and identity, as a number of other contributors in this volume have argued, we found that the rallies brought together some parents and children who often seem to live lives apart from each other.

The rallies also carried a strong emotional importance for families with close parent-child interaction, uniting family members of different generations and legal statuses within a generalized "Latino" community and reinforcing family bonds. The youth we interviewed, all of whom had U.S. citizenship, overwhelmingly expressed solidarity with the plight of undocumented immigrants, in a manner similar to that reported by Pallares and Flores-González (this volume). In some cases the concern was personal, because of their parents' status or that of family members. Yet not all teens knew their parents' legal status. These teens and others not directly motivated by family circumstances felt solidarity with other Latinos and other immigrants.[15]

Parents similarly participated for personal and collective reasons. Señora Pacheco is an undocumented immigrant whose only previous political activity was signing a petition to extend her children's elementary school through to the eighth grade. She participated in one of the local marches after her 11-year-old U.S.-born son convinced her to attend. She found the experience a powerful one "because I felt a great emotion when the mass of people met. . . . In that corner, there were three masses of people and when they all met, they clapped and I felt a great emotion, very nice, because as they were coming over, we were all united. And then we went together and left, all united." She talked to her children about the marches and protests, including her older son, who participated in demonstrations with friends at school on May 1. Discussion of and attendance at the protests occurred across generations.

Dual Political Socialization

The earlier example of Señora Sanchez, who encouraged her daughter to participate in the protests, shows a traditional example of political socialization where the parent directly influences her child's participation and tries to influence her views on the issue of immigrant rights and legalization. We see the same dynamics in the case of Isabel, the 18-year-old daughter of a naturalized U.S. citizen. Isabel attended the May 1 protest in Richmond with her father and sister. Asked whose idea it was to participate, Isabel responded:

> Well, I guess my dad you can say . . . he went through that, he didn't have papers so he wanted me to go and be part of that. 'Cause he came from Mexico like that, and he wants a better life for the immigrants. He already had the chance. He came and he's already a citizen, and he wants that to be given to the immigrants. . . . Sunday, we started talking about it. My dad was the one who said, "I want to go," and my sister and me, were like, "Oh well, we'll go with you."

In line with existing political socialization literature, Isabel's father shared his views and experiences, influencing his daughters, and he modeled a particular political behavior, which encouraged his daughters' participation.

Yet we also heard repeated instances of teens influencing their parents or becoming active participants on their behalf. One single mother who is a naturalized U.S. citizen, Señora Huerta, explained that her daughters often provide translation and interpretation help. Señora Huerta provided an example from the week before, when one of her daughters came to the doctor's office to assist her and then also helped another person facing language barriers. This sort of help naturally spills over into political "translation": Señora Huerta's daughters not only translate election ballots and state propositions from English to Spanish, they also provide substantive interpretations and their political viewpoints. As she explains, "My daughter helps me: 'Mom, check this, this proposal this, and this proposal that. Mom, this one is good for you!' [laughs] She helps me out, both of them help me." In this role, her daughters provide her with a type of political socialization, a role that the teen confirmed in our interview with her. As with the college students interviewed by Wong and Tseng (2008), the high school students in our study at times translate, teach, and try to shape their parents' opinions.

Teen to parent socialization can occur because of teens' better English skills but also because of their legal status. U.S.-born children, unlike their undocumented or noncitizen legal resident parents, hold citizenship. This provides them with protection and more tools for political participation than their parents. These children might even feel a greater need and responsibility to participate for their parents' sake. For example, Maria's mother is unauthorized while her father only received his permanent residency papers three years earlier, after many years in the United States without documents. Both parents did not attend the marches, wary of mass protest and violence. Maria's mother explicitly told her daughter and son not to go—"I was afraid that they [marchers] could cause a riot instead of marching and there was going to be violence"—although Maria's father, who also worried about the dangers of massive crowds, was less categorical and more open to having his children attend.

From Maria's perspective, there was little question about the need to participate. She explained, "At my school, there are a lot of Hispanic students . . . I guess their parents are immigrants and some of them are immigrants, too. And so since my parents are immigrants, I was like, well, I needed to do something about it." She participated in the April march in Richmond and noted that, while it was fun and the thing to do, "I also believed that it was something that I needed to do." Teens at times participated (and boycotted school) against the express wishes of their parents, often justifying their acts as helping their parents and others in the community like them.

Sites of Mobilization

The size of the mass mobilizations from March to May 2006 was made possible in part because many Latinos were receiving information and encouragement from numerous sources. Among those we interviewed, most mentioned the role of the ethnic media, including Spanish-language television and two nationally syndicated radio DJs, Renán Almendárez Coello ("El Cucuy") and Eduardo Sotelo ("El Piolín"). Both parents and teens said that friends and acquaintances talked about the marches as people tried to figure out whether they should go and who else was going. The strong push to participate from the ethnic media combined with interpersonal conversations to help convince many that they should join in too. These dynamics were readily apparent among both teens and their parents.

Yet teens and parents also experienced mobilization pressures and political interactions unique to each generation. Taking a family-based, bidirectional approach to political socialization allows us to see families as places where diverse sources of information, social networks, institutional influences, and opportunities for mobilization are brought together by different family members. To the extent that youths and adults access different institutions, organizations, and networks, parent-child interactions expand the opportunities for all members of the household to become more politically knowledgeable and engaged. This should be particularly evident in immigrant families, where immigrant members might be more oriented to coethnics while U.S.-born children may be more focused on a diverse, "American" set of networks and institutions. Here we very briefly consider some of the knowledge, networks, and institutions upon which different generations drew during the 2006 marches and boycotts.

Teen Mobilization: Schools, Youth Groups, and Peers.   Not surprisingly, schools played a crucial role in the narratives that teens gave of their participation in the marches. Schools provide sites where teens come together to talk with each other and a physical location at which to rally. Adults in positions of authority at school, especially teachers but also administrators, counselors, and others, at times helped organize marches, facilitated the diffusion of information about the proposed immigration legislation, and provided legitimacy to the protests, though in some cases authorities worked to dissuade students from participating by demanding that students remain in school. Maria's account of the first march she attended in April, which started at her school, shows the uncertainty around the early protests and suggests that, without the support of key individuals at school, adolescents such as she could have been demobilized rather than encouraged to participate:

> In the morning, we went [to school] and there were people with posters and stuff, and they were like, "What are we going to do, what are we going to do?" I guess they just wanted to stand there and hold the signs and wait for people to pass or something. . . . So we were standing outside and the security guard came outside and he was like, "You guys have the right to protest but only at lunchtime. You can't do it during school hours." And he said that he would start suspending people, so then I did not want to get suspended. . . . I guess the people organizing it said, "We are going to walk to [downtown]," and we [Maria and her friend] are like, "Should we go? Or should we stay?" And then we decided to go, so we marched all the way [downtown] . . . a couple of hours. It was fun because you and your fellow classmates are part of something and so then we had signs and people would honk at us and people were taking pictures. Oh, and one of the principals went with us, so it was like all protected, and the police was with us, too. And when we got there, the superintendent [of the school district] was there, and some people spoke about what they believe and then afterwards there was a bus there that took us back to school.

Students at Maria's school played a key role in mobilizing and organizing this early march, but the support of school authorities gave it added legitimacy and made it appear safe to students like Maria.[16] Participation itself was a positive experience, setting the stage for participation at future rallies such as the May 1 protest.

The importance of schools in mobilizing teens can be seen in the case of a young woman who did not attend the marches, though she sympathized with the goals of the protests. When asked why she decided not to attend, she responded that friends had gone but "they didn't even tell me" about the marches or that they were planning to go. If they had asked, she said, she would have gone. Importantly, this young woman also told us that "I kind of got sidetracked last year, I kind of dropped out, you can say." The teen reported hearing about the immigration debates on television, but media reports alone were not enough to spur her to participate, absent the invitation from her friends. Since she skips classes frequently, she was less likely to be mobilized by school networks.

Having children at school also mobilizes parents, either because children bring home information acquired at school or because of parents' own direct contact with their children's school. A number of the parents said that they participated in the marches because someone at their child's school encouraged them to do so. Interestingly, elementary schools seemed particularly important in this regard, perhaps because parents came into more regular contact with teachers, counselors, and school officials.

The influence of teens on parents is thus direct, as discussed earlier, and indirect, by bringing parents in contact with new networks through the activities of children. We see both of these dynamics in the case of Eduardo's family. Eduardo, a 17-year-old soccer enthusiast, plays in an organized team that includes a number of friends from school. His mother also volunteers for the team.

Eduardo explains that he took the lead in his family in becoming part of the spring 2006 protests. He and his friends got together to organize a group of youth to participate in a March 25 rally. Although his parents did not participate—indeed, they were initially unenthusiastic about his activities—Eduardo encouraged his parents to participate in later events. Before the May 1 march, "I told them, like, how me and my friends are going to go and, if they go, it would be better 'cause at least if one more person [goes], that can make a difference." He initially met with resistance, "they weren't that into it," but after a while, "they were agreeing with me, then they started to talk to me, like, about the other stories of how they worked." Both of Eduardo's parents are now legal residents, but the protests played an important role in encouraging his parents to discuss more openly their history as undocumented migrants and the hardships they encountered.

From the perspective of Eduardo's mother, her son's encouragement and, importantly, the fact he plays soccer led her to participate in the marches. Eduardo's mother reported that she heard about the marches through TV and at church, but the main push was through the soccer team. The marches were announced at practices and games, and then friends from soccer would talk about how important it was to support the protests, and they would ask each other whether they planned to attend, mutually reinforcing the importance of participation.

Finally, almost all the teens interviewed mentioned hearing about or coordinating participation in the marches through new technologies such as social networking sites like MySpace.com and cell phone text messaging. No parents reported using such technologies, although in a few cases parents mentioned that teens would do Internet searches for them or talk about information gleaned from the Web. With new technologies, teens clearly have the edge over their immigrant parents, allowing them to serve as a conduit of information for their parents.

Parents' Mobilization: Work, Church, and Ethnic Media.   The experiences of the parents we interviewed echo other studies of adults' civic and political engagement. As Verba, Schlozman, and Brady (1995) argue, workplaces are important sites for skill acquisition, mobilization, and political information. Señor Rivera, a custodian at a large East Bay employer, participated in a series of demonstrations at his workplace two years prior to the 2006 immigrant rights rallies. These demonstrations ultimately led to a successful union organizing campaign. The union was able to address some long-standing grievances and, in spring 2006, it was pressing for better wages for the custodial staff. According to Señor Rivera, these past organizing successes partially shaped his positive attitude toward participation in the immigrant rights marches, since "you can see how the process is going, because sometimes it is by a process . . . it is by steps." Señor Rivera was one of only a few respondents to explicitly mention the role of unions, but he was not the only one to talk about how workplaces served as sites of information, political experience, and mobilization. Another parent, who worked for a large company of over four hundred people, discussed the marches with others during work. These workers came together to request time off on May 1, and they were accommodated by their employer.

Few of the adult respondents could speak English fluently, so parents were more likely to rely on coethnic organizations where the dominant language of discussion was Spanish. Such organizations included the Catholic Church, which played an important role in Richmond, in a manner like that reported by Heredia (this volume) in Los Angeles. The May 1 rallies began at three Richmond Catholic churches, and a number of the respondents mentioned hearing about the protests through acquaintances at church or from the priest.

Some teens were also active in church, but the number mentioning church as a source of influence was lower than among parents. Similarly, while some teens paid attention to ethnic media, almost all parents relied on Spanish-language media for information. These "ethnic" influences sometimes spilled over to children, as when a parent would be watching the evening news on Spanish-language television and the teen would listen in. Parents thus widened their children's sources of information about immigration beyond mainstream American institutions.

A POST-2006 CODA: YOUTH AND FAMILIES
AFTER THE MARCHES

Our research suggests that the breadth of participation in the protests of 2006 was due, in part, to family dynamics. Families act as sites where information, networks, and institutional experiences can be pooled; they allow bidirectional political socialization across generations; and they facilitate the interactive process of political learning, opinion formation, and mobilization. While child to parent political socialization has been documented in native-born American families (McDevitt and Chaffee 2000, 2002), we speculate, in line with Wong and Tseng (2008), that such dynamics are even more pronounced in immigrant families. Immigrant adults' access to "mainstream" media and institutions can be limited by language, legal status, and other obstacles of foreign birth. U.S.-born citizen children face fewer of these barriers, and they enjoy legally guaranteed political rights as well as the symbolic legitimacy of citizenship. The phenomenon of child translators and language brokers is regularly identified in studies of the second generation, often to highlight the negative repercussions for child psychology and parental authority of having children forced to take adult roles.[17] We know much less about second-generation political and civic integration. Without downplaying the concerns around "parentified" children, our data suggest, at least in the context of the 2006 spring protests, that political discussion and reciprocal interaction served to tighten family bonds, facilitated intergenerational communication (including in some cases where it was limited to begin with), and led to numerous instances of family participation in rallies and marches.

But will the spring 2006 protests have lasting effects? The immigrant rights marches were extraordinary for the breadth and depth of participation by millions of individuals across the United States. In this chapter we use the terms *political socialization* and *mobilization* interchangeably, but it is possible that the collective effervescence in opposition to H.R. 4437 was an extraordinary, one-time *mobilization,* not an event with real power to influence long-term political *socialization.* Many of the respondents in this study described their participation as positive and even empowering. Did these feelings persist, and if so, did these experiences provide the groundwork for further activism around immigration issues or other public concerns?

Based on follow-up interviews with 31 of our original respondents (17 parents and 14 teens), the evidence for long-term effects are mixed. These interviews, conducted between March and August 2008, asked study participants questions about civic and political engagement similar to those asked in 2006. On average, civic engagement for both teens and parents declined in the two years since the 2006 protests.[18] A worsening economy affected some, who needed to dedicate time to making ends meet rather than participating in civic activities. Among youth, transitions out of high school and into work and parenting appeared to decrease both time and opportunities to participate. Thus, a teen who had participated in a wide range of activities while in school, from sports and youth groups to the debate team, now balanced full-time work with impending motherhood. Her transition to adulthood left her with little time or energy for other activities beyond attending meetings over equal pay in solidarity with other workers in her workplace.

Yet levels of reported political activism remained the same, despite economic challenges and life-course transitions, offering some evidence for a socialization effect and challenging the idea of a single "flash in the pan" moment of political mobilization. Of the 11 parents we reinterviewed who reported participating in the 2006 protests, 4 said they joined in an immigrant rights protests in 2007 and/ or 2008, while 3 of 7 teens reported the same. Also noteworthy, 7 of the 9 parents eligible to register to vote in 2006 had registered in 2008, and all 7 reported voting in an election over the preceding two years. Among youth, of 8 respondents old enough to register, 5 had done so by summer 2008 and 2 reported voting in the prior two years. Since these data were collected *before* the last months of the 2008 election campaign, a high point of recent electoral participation in the United States, they provide some indication that cries of "Today we march, tomorrow we vote!" might become a reality.

We also found continued evidence of intergenerational exchange. There is speculation that increased U.S. Immigration and Customs Enforcement (ICE) raids have damped civic and political participation in immigrant communities, particularly among Mexican migrants. While this seems a logical conclusion, we found little direct evidence of this among those we reinterviewed. One undocumented woman continues to be highly active, attending protests against ICE raids, working with unions, and meeting with elected representatives. Children of undocumented parents appear to have become much more aware of the danger to their families and have engaged in ICE protests as well as supportive activities around related immigration initiatives, such as the DREAM Act. Among those parents who are naturalized, a number reported that kids continue to translate ballots or help with absentee registration and that, as their children turn 18, they pushed their parents to become citizens and vote. As suggested in other contributions to this volume, lines that might have previously demarcated child citizens from noncitizen parents seem more blurred. One father, a legal permanent resident who cannot vote, asked his daughter, "Who are *we* going to be voting for?" The daughter, who sees her vote not only for herself but also her parents, gave her "I voted!" sticker to her father after casting her ballot; her father wore the sticker the whole day. For this mixed-status immigrant family, voting was a family affair.

The long-term effects of the 2006 immigrant rights protests will only be known over the coming decades. Already, Latino youth turnout for presidential elections has increased substantially, from 10 percent in 2000 to 17 percent in 2008.[19] We suspect that first-time participation in events such as the 2006 marches has a greater effect in the formative moments of one's life, such as the transition from adolescence to young adulthood. If this is the case, then the widespread participation of minors in spring 2006 may mark the beginning of a generational shift in American and Latino politics and a new era of heightened political activism among the youngest citizens of our democracy.

NOTES

We would like to acknowledge the generous financial support of the Russell Sage Foundation and excellent research assistance by Edwin F. Ackerman, Vanessa Cruz, Abril Díaz, Monica Gudino, Sara Levine, Angela Fillingim, Ricardo Huerta Niño, Heidy Sarabía, and Robert Vargas. Feedback and suggestions from Tomás Jiménez, Lisa García Bedolla, Kim Voss, and attendees at the conference "Understanding the Immigration Protests of Spring 2006: Lessons Learned, Future Trajectories," held at the University of California, Berkeley, in April 2007, helped improve this chapter. This chapter is a revised and updated version of Bloemraad and Trost (2008).

1. In California, urban school districts reported absentee rates of about one in five in the public K-12 system: 20 percent in San Diego, 18 percent in San Francisco, and 16 percent in San Jose (Sebastian, Knight, and Asimov 2006). Among Los Angeles middle and high school students, the absentee rate climbed to 27 percent. One heavily Latino West Contra Costa high school, used in this research to recruit study participants, reported an absentee rate of about 70 percent.

2. Participation numbers cited here and below are drawn from newspaper reports collected by the author as well as those collected and compiled by Fox, Selee, and Bada (2006) and Wang and Winn (2006).

3. We make this estimate by taking the midpoint between the lowest and highest estimate of the number of protestors at the Oakland and Richmond rallies, and then we divide this by the number of Latino residents in each city. Such a rough calculation clearly has problems, since not all participants were Latino or city residents, and not all Latinos in these cities participated in a local protest. (Indeed, some interviewees attended rallies in San Francisco or even Los Angeles.) It nonetheless gives a rough sense of participation.

4. Models of adult participation map poorly onto the experience of children and teenagers, and none would have predicted the high level of youth participation in the spring 2006 protests. Research on adults' civic and political participation emphasizes the influence of education, workforce participation, occupation, income, and marital status in explaining differences in individuals' civic or political engagement (Putnam 2000; Rosenstone and Hansen 1993; Verba, Schlozman, and Brady 1995). Given children's and teenager's age and stage in their life course, none of these measures work very well for youth. Most have not yet reached the end of their educational trajectory; few work full-time; personal incomes are modest if not nonexistent; and few are married or have children. Studies of political socialization, while of impressive pedigree, became largely marginalized in the early 1980s, with only recent hints of renewed vitality (Jennings and Niemi 1968, 1974, 1981; Niemi 1999; Niemi and Hepburn 1995; Verba, Schlozman, and Brady 1995; Jennings, Stoker, and Bowers 2009). Social movement scholars, who document young people's participation in the protests of the 1960s

and 1970s, do not usually examine contemporary youth participation nor consider it within the context of family participation (McAdam 1988; Morris 1984). Finally, current research on school-based civic education and community-service learning focuses predominantly on schools and programmatic interventions, offering a rich but narrow slice of youth citizenship that speaks little to immigrant experiences (McDevitt and Chaffee 2000, 2002; McNeal 1998; Yates and Youniss 1998; Youniss, McLellan, and Yates 1997; Youniss et al. 2002).

5. Sociologists of childhood express reservations about the term *socialization*: socialization implies that children have little or no agency in the present and that they are unformed and continuously preparing (or developing) for the future, when they can begin their productive lives as workers, parents, voters, and so on (e.g., Orellana 2001; Thorne 1987). We retain this term since it is the dominant way of talking about political learning, but we argue that this socialization occurs at all stages of life and can work in multiple directions across generations.

6. The 2006 protests also differ from prior Chicano youth protests in two other respects: the 2006 marches were, on the whole, more focused on a particular issue than a broad societal critique, and they were immigrant-focused rather than centered on protesting racism and discrimination faced by the long-standing U.S.-born Mexican American population. Indeed, today's Latino youth are much more likely to be living in mixed-status families, our focus here, than were youth in the 1960s. In 1970, those born in Mexico made up less than 17 percent of the total Mexican-origin population in the United States, while in 2000, over 40 percent of Mexican-origin residents were themselves born in Mexico (Bean and Stevens 2003, 54).

7. An important part of intergenerational political socialization also occurs indirectly: adult family members shape children's opportunities to acquire education, jobs, and income, which in turn affects political engagement.

8. More details on methodology are reported in Bloemraad and Trost (2008).

9. In three of the forty families, we were only able to complete an interview with one family member, either the parent or teen, but not both. In two other families, both parents (not always of the same legal status) were interviewed, either separately or together. All youth and parent interviews were conducted separately, to preserve confidentiality.

10. In two cases, we interviewed youth born in Mexico who migrated to the United States as small children (one was 7 months old, the other was 7 years old). Both acquired U.S. citizenship through a parent's naturalization.

11. The origins of this project predate the spring 2006 protests, but as the momentum of the protests built through March and April 2006, we modified the interview schedule to include questions on these events.

12. Families were recruited through four public high schools with large Latino populations in Oakland and Richmond, California, and through snowball sampling to include a few families with students at private (often religious) schools. To understand how immigrants of modest economic backgrounds and limited schooling learn to participate in the associational and political life of their new homes, we restricted participation in the study to families where the interviewed immigrant parent had less than a high school education. Seventy percent of Mexican-born U.S. residents do not hold a high school diploma (U.S. Bureau of the Census, n.d.). Prior research overwhelmingly demonstrates that socioeconomic status, and especially education, correlates strongly with civic and political engagement (Miller and Shanks 1996; Rosenstone and Hansen 1993; Verba, Schlozman, and Brady 1995).

13. This figure is much higher than the estimate of 15–35 percent Latino participation in the May 1 rallies in Oakland and Richmond. In large part, this is because we included participation in *any* demonstration between March and May 2006 as well as participation in the boycott by not going to work or school. It is also possible that families willing to participate in a research study such as ours

are more willing to participate in activities such as immigrant rights rallies. Given the nonrandom sampling employed, such a possibility must be taken seriously and precludes statistical significance tests of our findings. Yet, as we discuss later in the chapter, most of the study's families did not appear inordinately politically engaged; many respondents reported the events of spring 2006 as the first political activities in which they ever engaged.

14. All names are pseudonyms.

15. Many youth were also caught up in the idea that everyone was participating and they should not be left out. A number liked the idea of skipping school to do something very different from their normal day-to-day routine. In some cases, this caused conflict with parents, who wanted children to attend school.

16. This is in stark contrast to the experience of Chicano students during the 1960s walkouts, when school authorities harassed students and, in some cases, had student leaders jailed (Muñoz 1989). The schools we studied also might not be representative of all U.S. schools. Neumann-Ortiz (2008), for example, writes of school employees facing sanctions in Wisconsin due to their participation in the marches.

17. Interestingly, this same negative view of disruption and breakdown in family structure also rests at the heart of some studies of political socialization in native-born families (McDevitt and Chaffee 2002).

18. Civic engagement activities declined for 10 parents, remained the same for 3, and increased for 4. Among teens, civic engagement activities declined for 8, remained the same for 2, and increased for 4.

19. CNN National exit poll data for 2000 and 2008, and Pew Hispanic Center data, cited by the organization Nonprofit Vote, http://www.nonprofitvote.org/voterturnout2008.

Looking Forward

*Whither American Politics and Immigrant
Rights Mobilization?*

May Day march, Chicago, 2009. Courtesy of Xóchitl Bada.

10

L.A.'s Past, America's Future?

The 2006 Immigrant Rights Protests and Their Antecedents

Ruth Milkman

The nation's streets have been relatively quiet since the massive immigrant rights marches of spring 2006, but the aftereffects of that unexpected burst of protest activity are evident on multiple fronts. On the one hand, U.S. Immigration and Customs Enforcement (ICE) dramatically stepped up its workplace raids and deportations of undocumented immigrants soon after the marches, while intensifying its efforts to police the U.S.-Mexico border. As if orchestrated to maximize media exposure, ICE's displays of force, along with other efforts to intimidate and expel foreign-born residents in some localities, seemed calculated both to strike fear into the hearts of unauthorized immigrants and their families and to placate the xenophobic political constituency within the Republican base. On the other hand, and with much less fanfare, immigrants themselves have been actively pursuing all available opportunities for greater political incorporation. Among those eligible, naturalization applications along with new voter registrations soared in the immediate aftermath of the marches, directly contributing to the expanded and heavily Democratic Latino vote in the 2006 and 2008 elections. Although it has attracted far less media attention than the ICE raids and the scattered grassroots mobilizations of anti-immigrant activists, this political shift among Latino immigrants may prove more significant in the long run. As more and more naturalized citizens become voters and as immigrant birth rates continue to outpace those of the native-born, Latino voters are emerging as a new force on the U.S. political landscape.

Efforts to pass comprehensive immigration reform under the Bush administration were repeatedly stymied by divisions within the Republican Party and may well be postponed further in light of the economic crisis that began in 2008.

Still, it is unlikely that the genie can be put back in the bottle. Not only immigrants and those who advocate on their behalf, but also organized labor and a growing number of employers (strange bedfellows indeed!) strongly support reforms that would create a path to legalization for the nation's twelve million undocumented immigrants. In general, elites are far more positively inclined toward expansive immigration policies, but polling data suggest that legalization for the undocumented also has extensive public support.[1] If and when immigration reform is achieved, it will further magnify the political influence of the foreign-born population. And insofar as anti-immigrant animus remains strongly associated with the Republican Party, the growing Latino vote will be harvested primarily by Democrats—with vital assistance from organized labor, whose political reach remains far more substantial than its relentlessly declining membership might suggest.

These political dynamics, which helped fuel the spring 2006 marches and were reinforced in their wake, were prefigured a decade earlier by events in California. That state not only has the nation's single largest concentration of unauthorized immigrants but also has been on the leading edge of immigrant worker organizing and immigrant rights advocacy for decades. In coalition with organized labor, Latino immigrants have become a formidable force in California politics, especially in the years since 1994, when a large majority of the state's voters endorsed the anti-immigrant Proposition 187. That ballot measure would have denied public services (including schooling) to undocumented immigrants had it not been struck down by the courts as unconstitutional.

In a pattern strikingly similar to the impact of the Sensenbrenner bill (H.R. 4437) passed by the U.S. House of Representatives in December 2005, Proposition 187 deeply alarmed both authorized and unauthorized immigrants and sparked large-scale popular protests. In Los Angeles, the anti-187 street demonstrations in 1994 were (at the time) the largest since the Vietnam War. But Proposition 187 had other—albeit unintended—consequences as well, most importantly stimulating a wave of reactive naturalization that greatly increased the proportion of citizens among California's legal immigrants. The newly eligible voters thus created landed overwhelmingly in the Democratic column, thanks to the widely publicized endorsement of Proposition 187 by Republican governor Pete Wilson, who also signed the measure into law. Especially in Los Angeles, the organized labor movement quickly seized this opportunity to extend its influence into the electoral arena by actively helping newly naturalized immigrants register to vote and then encouraging them to go to the polls and to vote for labor-friendly candidates.

The parallels between the grassroots reaction to Proposition 187 and that to H.R. 4437 eleven years later suggest the prospect that the political drama that unfolded in California in the mid-1990s might now be reenacted on the more spacious national stage. As if to signal precisely that outcome, many of the May 1, 2006, demonstrators carried signs declaring, "Hoy marchamos, mañana votamos" (Today we march, tomorrow we vote). Shortly afterward, the We Are America Alliance and a host of other organizations—including organized labor—launched naturalization and voter registration drives, which had already begun to yield fruit by the 2006 midterm elections and also contributed to the outcome of the 2008 presidential contest. The trajectory of immigrant organizing and political incorporation in California over the past decade, then, offers a guide to the likely national implications of the 2006 marches—or at least to one possible scenario.

IMMIGRANT UNION ORGANIZING

That trajectory began with the unionization efforts of Latino immigrant workers in Southern California, a development that took nearly everyone by surprise when it first emerged in the late 1980s. Most observers had presumed that the massive stream of undocumented Mexicans and Central Americans who entered California after the passage of the Hart-Celler Act in 1965 would have little or no interest in or impact on the organized labor movement.[2] With union density plunging at the time, both nationally and in California, organized labor's obituary already had been written many times over. Early on, moreover, many union leaders expressed hostility to the new immigrants, who were regarded as a threat to hard-won labor standards.

Yet, by century's end, the labor movement had been unexpectedly revitalized in the nation's most populous state, with union density inching upward there even as it continued to decline relentlessly in the United States as a whole. A wave of Latino immigrant unionization efforts in Southern California starting in the late 1980s was among the key ingredients contributing to this shift.[3] The iconic example is the Justice for Janitors campaign launched by the Service Employees International Union (SEIU), an effort that made its first major breakthrough in Los Angeles in 1990 and went on to consolidate its gains thereafter. Foreign-born workers in other industries and occupations—from construction to manufacturing and hospitality to home health care and other service industries—also organized in the 1990s, when many thousands joined union ranks. To be sure, even in the aftermath of these organizing successes, the unionization rate among immigrants remains lower than among U.S.-born workers for a variety of reasons (most importantly, because so few immigrants are employed in the highly unionized public sector).[4] But the potential for recruiting low-wage immigrant workers into unions is widely recognized inside the labor movement today—as was the case well before the spring 2006 marches.

As immigrant unionization gained traction in Los Angeles and elsewhere in California, another kind of organizing among foreign-born workers was also taking shape. The "worker center" movement began in the 1990s, offering low-wage immigrant workers assistance in pursuing their legal rights, using a community-oriented approach that eschewed conventional unionism and was sometimes in tension with it. The growth of worker centers was a national phenomenon, but from the outset they had a strong presence in California. As Fine (2006) and Gordon (2005) have documented, worker centers are structured differently from conventional membership-based unions; they are community-based organizations that advocate for, provide services to, and also organize low-wage immigrant workers. Worker centers also systematically engage unauthorized immigrants in various forms of civic and political participation, notwithstanding their inability to vote and lack of official citizenship rights.

At first, the emergence of immigrant organizing, both in traditional unions and in worker centers, surprised both labor movement activists and outside observers. The newcomers, especially the undocumented, were seen as vulnerable, docile persons intensely fearful of any confrontation with authority and thus as poor prospects for recruitment into unions or other worker organizations. The dominant view in the early 1980s was, "No, you can never organize those guys. You're beating your head against the concrete," as one union organizer put it (Milkman 2006, 115). Friend and foe alike wondered why the burgeoning population of Latino immigrant workers—most of whom had minimal formal education and few economic resources, and many of whom were undocumented—would dare to take the risks involved in organizing. The majority were sojourners who intended to return home after a short stay in the United States, the conventional wisdom went, and in any case U.S. wages and working conditions compared favorably with the jobs that they had left behind in their home countries. For the undocumented, moreover, organizing might lead to apprehension by the immigration authorities or even deportation.

Such assumptions were by no means limited to the labor movement; indeed, as Delgado (1993) reported in the early 1990s, among academic and other commentators as well, "the unorganizability of undocumented workers because of their legal status has become a 'pseudofact.'" But this once-conventional wisdom was overturned later in the 1990s, as foreign-born Latinos emerged as protagonists in one workplace campaign after the next. Evidence rapidly accumulated to suggest that immigrant workers generally, and Latinos in particular, were actually *more* receptive to organizing than native-born whites. "It's not true that immigrants are hard to organize," a San Francisco hotel union organizer declared. "They are more supportive of unions than native workers" (Wells 2003, 120). An L.A. janitors' union activist was more emphatic: "We Latino workers are a bomb waiting to explode" (Waldinger et al. 1998, 117).

Not only was this the common impression of organizers, but it was confirmed by attitudinal surveys, albeit in a fragmentary way. In the 1994 Worker Representation and Participation Survey (WRPS), for example, 51 percent of Latino respondents nationwide (regardless of nativity) who were not union members indicated that they would vote for a union if a representation election were held in their workplaces, compared to 35 percent of non-Latinos.[5] And in California, 67 percent of Latino respondents to a 2001–2 statewide survey indicated that they would vote for unionization, double the rate for Anglo respondents (33 percent). Only African Americans showed stronger prounion preferences (74 percent). Whereas few previous studies examined such attitudes by nativity, the 2001–2 California survey found far more prounion sentiment among immigrants (most of them Latino) than among natives: 66 percent of noncitizen respondents, regardless of ethnicity, expressed a prounion preference, compared to 54 percent of foreign-born citizens and 42 percent of native-born respondents (Weir 2002, 121).[6]

By century's end, then, the once-dominant view of immigrants as unreceptive to unionization efforts had been largely replaced by its opposite. Several factors underlay immigrants' newly recognized "organizability." One was the strength of social networks among working-class immigrants—networks that are essential to basic survival for foreign-born newcomers and that can help galvanize union drives as well as political mobilization efforts. In Southern California, with its relatively homogenous immigrant population, largely Mexican and Central American, these networks were especially vibrant.

In addition, class-based collective organizations like unions are highly compatible with the past lived experience and worldviews of many Latino immigrants. There is evidence to suggest that, as a group, these immigrants are more inclined to view their fate as bound up with that of the wider community; whereas native-born workers tend to have a more individualistic orientation. And crucially, the shared experience of stigmatization among immigrants, both during the migration process itself and often continuing for many years thereafter, means that when unions or worker centers offer a helping hand it is often welcomed with gusto.

Southern California was the primary laboratory for the workplace organizing efforts that emerged among immigrants in the 1990s. The L.A. metropolitan area is home to the nation's largest concentration of undocumented immigrants (Fortuny, Capps, and Passel 2007) and, as I have argued elsewhere, the region had additional comparative advantages that helped foster union revitalization there in the late twentieth century (Milkman 2006). More recently, immigrant union organizing has begun to spread across the nation, even as the immigrant population itself has become increasingly geographically dispersed. The Houston and Miami Justice for Janitors campaigns are among the many recent examples.[7] Union drives among foreign-born workers have been launched in a wide variety of settings, albeit with uneven success, and the worker center movement is a nationwide phenomenon as well.

The spring 2006 marches finally liquidated any remaining doubts about immigrant "organizability." Few would dispute that a sense of stigmatization, and of being under siege in a hostile environment, rather than generating passivity and fear as many commentators once presumed, instead can foster solidarity and organization among the foreign-born. Like immigrant union organizing, this response to political attacks on immigrant rights was foreshadowed in California. Building on the workplace organizing sketched above, the community response to Proposition 187 became a crucial stimulus to immigrant political mobilization in the late 1990s in the nation's most populous (and immigrant-rich) state.

PROPOSITION 187 AND IMMIGRANT POLITICAL MOBILIZATION

Proposition 187, thanks to the endorsement of then-governor Pete Wilson, instantly linked the anti-immigrant political backlash with California's Republican leadership, an association that remains powerful to this day. As a result, the unprecedented political mobilization among immigrants stimulated by Proposition 187 became a bonanza for the Democratic Party, with which organized labor already had a long-standing relationship. Latino immigrants naturalized and then voted with a strong Democratic tilt in California's supercharged political environment during the 1990s, a pattern that was absent at the time in other states with large Latino populations (Pantoja, Ramírez, and Segura 2001).

The fears that Proposition 187's passage provoked among immigrants in 1994 galvanized the entire Latino community. Households often included a mix of native-born and immigrant members and of documented and undocumented immigrants. Even the previously apolitical Mexican hometown associations, whose local activities had previously revolved around beauty pageants and sporting events, became involved. But above all, the L.A. labor movement, fresh from the success of the Justice for Janitors campaign and similar immigrant organizing efforts in the years just before Proposition 187 came before the voters, seized this extraordinary moment of opportunity. As in workplace organizing, so in politics; Southern California had a comparative advantage. The weakness of traditional political machines in Los Angeles (thanks to a wave of political reform a century ago), as well as the relatively small number of political offices and the high costs of mounting electoral campaigns in the city, had created a vacuum that the newly strengthened L.A. labor movement was destined to fill (Mollenkopf 1999).

Starting in the early 1990s, the L.A. County Federation of Labor was transformed from a junior partner of the local Democratic Party establishment into an independent force with its own capacity for grassroots field mobilization. The County Fed began to devote extensive resources to helping immigrants eligible for naturalization become citizens and then to mobilizing them at the polls.

L.A.-based Latino community organizations and immigrant rights groups had already laid the groundwork for these efforts in the aftermath of the 1986 Immigration Reform and Control Act, which provided amnesty for thousands of undocumented immigrants. Building on that effort, and spurred by Proposition 187, the labor movement began to assume a key role. Miguel Contreras, a union organizer who became the political director of the County Fed in 1994 and then rose to its top leadership post in 1996, was the leading architect of the city's labor-Latino alliance, which built on the SEIU's immigrant worker membership as well as that of the hotel workers' union, where Contreras previously had been on staff.

Under his leadership, which emerged alongside and was then reinforced by the Latino community reaction to Proposition 187, the County Fed deployed its massive economic and human resources into direct mail, phone banks, precinct walking, and worksite outreach efforts that targeted union members as well as new immigrant voters. Candidates that the federation supported, mostly Latinos, began to win contest after contest in congressional, legislative, and city council races, rapidly displacing the old-line political insiders.[8] An early example was the 1994 election of union organizer Antonio Villaraigosa to a state assembly seat representing northeast Los Angeles. Two years later, the County Fed helped Democrats regain control of the state assembly. Then in 1999, Villaraigosa became speaker of the assembly, going on to become mayor of the nation's second-largest metropolis in 2005.

The County Fed had not only the capacity to undertake this kind of grassroots political mobilization but also the economic and organizational resources to be politically influential in Los Angeles, and eventually statewide. Given the extraordinarily high cost of California political campaigns, and the limited resources of the Latino immigrant community, virtually no other organized entity representing this constituency could even aspire to play such a critical role. Writing on the eve of the political transition that occurred when the County Fed began to operate as a major player in the mid-1990s, one incisive analyst of L.A. ethnic politics concluded, "Mexicans remain on the sidelines and have yet to position themselves to be part of any new governing coalition" (Skerry 1993, 81; see also Frank and Wong 2004). But that observation was quickly rendered obsolete as the County Fed moved into the electoral arena in the mid-1990s. Labor-sponsored candidates rapidly displaced the small political clique of Mexican Americans who had long aspired to build on their ethnic community's growing demographic weight but who lacked the necessary resources.

The new cadre of labor-backed elected officials went on to win living-wage ordinances and other measures that aimed to benefit L.A. low-wage workers generally and immigrants in particular. Their efforts also fostered union-friendly community development efforts—for example, by making city subsidies for new hotels and other major development projects contingent on "community benefits agreements" under which employers agreed to pay a living wage and/or to be neutral in union organizing campaigns among the workers who would later be employed on the sites (Gottlieb et al. 2005). Labor's political clout also helped secure the passage of state legislation that directly benefited union organizing efforts. A case in point was a bill sponsored by state assembly member Gil Cedillo, passed in September 2000, prohibiting employers from using state money to promote or deter unionization efforts (Logan 2003). Although it was enjoined and later struck down by the courts, this bill was a telling reflection of labor's enhanced political clout.

More generally, the relationship between labor's growing political influence and its ongoing efforts to unionize unorganized workers took the form of a virtuous circle in these years. In one stunning example, the SEIU added 74,000 L.A. home health-care workers to its ranks in 1999 after engaging in a long political campaign to change state law to create an "employer of record" for this growing occupational group. Although labor's influence was somewhat diminished after the 2003 recall election that thrust Arnold Schwarzenegger into the governorship, the basic political infrastructure built in the late 1990s remains largely intact.

The conditions that fostered Latino immigrant organizing in California in the 1990s emerged from the peculiarities of the state and its largest metropolis, but they gradually began to influence the national landscape as well. For example, unionists in California led the effort to change organized labor's official position on immigration policy, mobilizing at the AFL-CIO's fall 1999 national convention.[9] In February 2000 the same forces successfully promoted the passage of an AFL-CIO Executive Council resolution officially reversing labor's long-standing support for employer sanctions and calling for a new immigrant legalization program. Over the months that followed, the U.S. labor movement, again with leadership from California, mounted a national campaign for immigration reform, an effort that seemed to be on the verge of success prior to September 11, 2001, when it went into the deep freeze.

As the immigrant rights movement began to recover from that setback, California's influence once again helped to position organized labor nationally as a leading advocate of immigration reform. The 2003 Immigrant Workers Freedom Ride, chaired by Maria Elena Durazo (Miguel Contreras's spouse and then-head of the L.A. hotel workers' union who, after Contreras's death in 2005, rose to head the County Fed), deepened the ties between labor and the immigrant rights movement and helped expand those ties beyond California to the national level. As Randy Shaw argues in his chapter in this volume, the Freedom Ride helped lay the groundwork for the 2006 marches.

Today the labor movement again has the potential to play a pivotal role, again pioneered by California unionists but now national in scope, in immigrant political mobilization. Although unauthorized immigrants can participate in street demonstrations and other forms of "noncitizen citizenship," as Gordon (2005, 275–78) calls it, acquiring formal citizenship is the key hurdle they must overcome in a society where the meaning of political participation is largely restricted to voting.[10] A century ago, naturalized citizens were more likely to vote than their native-born counterparts; today the opposite is true. National voting rates among Asians and Latinos (regardless of citizenship status) are lower than those of other ethnic groups (DeSipio 2001). However, thanks in large part to the efforts of California's labor movement (along with Latino and immigrant rights groups) to naturalize those eligible and to increase Latino electoral participation, the gap in voting rates between the state's Latinos and whites virtually disappeared in the post–Proposition 187 years. If one controls for age, citizenship, and socioeconomic status, Latino turnout rates in the state were only one percentage point lower than those of comparable whites from 1994 to 2000; in the 1998 election, when labor mobilized especially energetically against an antiunion proposition on the state ballot, Latino turnout was four percentage points higher (Citrin and Highton 2002, 28–29; see also Ramakrishnan 2005, esp. chap. 6).

Latinos in California not only vote; they mostly vote for Democrats. Some Latinos did cast their ballots for Arnold Schwarzenegger in the 2003 recall election, but when he launched a broad antiunion attack in the form of a series of referenda on the November 2005 ballot, the Latino vote again turned against him, in yet another California election where labor's political mobilization played a critical role. The standard comparison is to Texas, George W. Bush's home state, where at least until recently Republicans still captured much of the Latino vote. That divergence is partly the legacy of former Republican governor Pete Wilson's sponsorship of Proposition 187; organized labor's weakness in Texas is the other key factor (Skerry 1993; Pantoja, Ramírez, and Segura 2001; Meyerson 2004).

In California, then, and especially in Los Angeles, the labor movement has been a potent vehicle of Latino immigrant mobilization, both in the workplace and the voting booth. That helps explain why Los Angeles became the epicenter of the national immigrant rights movement, with a reported 500,000 marchers in the streets on March 25, 2006, and even more on May 1, when protests against H.R. 4437 surged across the nation. The labor-Latino coalition that developed in California after Proposition 187 has continued to flourish over the years since, stacking up huge electoral successes, winning hearts and minds in the immigrant community, and building lasting organizational capacity. The big question now is whether that coalition can expand into a national one.

PROPOSITION 187 REDUX?

Organized labor can claim at best partial credit for organizing the massive spring 2006 marches. The Catholic Church, immigrant hometown associations, a variety of immigrant rights advocacy groups, student organizations, and perhaps most importantly (and least expected) the ethnic media—all played critical roles. Even some employers quietly supported the effort. Union staff and activists participated actively in planning the protests in many cities around the country, with the SEIU in particular assuming responsibility for providing security—a successful undertaking in that the crowds were extremely peaceful despite the fact that they swelled to a volume far beyond expectations. In Chicago, a committee of local unions helped plan the May 1 marches, and unionists participated in many other cities as well, as part of a wider coalition led by immigrant rights organizations and activists.[11]

Although it was but one force among many in planning the marches, afterward the labor movement was uniquely positioned to become an important player in immigrant political mobilization at the national level. Despite declining union density, organized labor remains a potent force in U.S. politics, with voter mobilization capacity that far outstrips its level of direct influence in the workplace (Dark 1999). The ties between organized labor and the immigrant rights movement were greatly strengthened by their interaction in planning and participating in the marches, so that a national labor-Latino coalition like the one that emerged a decade ago in California is within the realm of possibility.

The vast geographical scope of the demonstrations—which were largest in Los Angeles, Chicago, and other long-standing immigrant gateway cities but also surprisingly substantial in places like Nebraska and North Carolina—reflects the many changes that have taken place in the geographical distribution of immigration over recent years. Not only has the overall size of the nation's undocumented population grown dramatically, but both authorized and unauthorized immigrants have become much more widely dispersed, for reasons Massey, Durand, and Malone (2002) have documented. Once concentrated in Southern California, as well as in other traditional destinations like New York, Texas, Illinois, and Florida, immigrants have increasingly settled in communities throughout the nation. And crucially, immigrant-focused labor organizing—by unions as well as worker centers—has sprung up in many parts of the country where it was once unimaginable.

In this regard the congruence between the geography of the spring 2006 marches and that of the worker centers themselves is especially striking.[12] Nor is it an accident that, in the aftermath of the marches, the worker centers acquired a far higher profile than they had before, and they built new ties to organized labor, which had shown limited interest in worker centers previously. A few months after the marches, for example, the National Day Laborer Organizing Network formalized a relationship with the AFL-CIO and soon after entered into an alliance with the Laborers' union (then a Change to Win affiliate) as well.

Meanwhile, precisely echoing the history of what unfolded after Proposition 187 in the mid-1990s, the Sensenbrenner bill stimulated not only the marches but also a new wave of reactive naturalization among eligible immigrants. In the fiscal year that ended on September 30, 2007, applications for naturalization soared to a level 55 percent higher than in the previous fiscal year, with over 1.1 million "initial receipts" among an estimated total of 8.5 million legal permanent residents who are eligible to become citizens (U.S. Bureau of Citizenship and Immigration Services 2007).[13] The number of naturalization applications exceeded 100,000 in every month from March to July 2007. After that, a substantial fee hike and changes in the citizenship exam led to a brief lull, but by September 2007 the upward trend had resumed. Only in two other years in the past century—not coincidentally, both in the mid-1990s, following Proposition 187—did total naturalization applications exceed 1 million.[14]

Efforts to promote naturalization and voter registration have continued steadily since the spring 2006 marches, led by Spanish-language media organizations and immigrant rights coalitions like the We Are America Alliance.[15] There is evidence that the unprecedented spate of ICE workplace raids and deportations that followed the marches helped to galvanize and accelerate these campaigns, although this was surely not the Bush administration's intent. A mid-2008 survey by the Pew Hispanic Center found that both U.S.-born and foreign-born Latinos overwhelmingly disapproved of the raids and of criminal prosecution of unauthorized immigrants; fully 35 percent of *native-born* Latino respondents indicated that they were worried that a family member or close friend could be deported. The same survey found growing Latino support for Democratic political candidates (Lopez and Minushkin 2008, 4, 6, 11).

As in post–Proposition 187 California in the late 1990s, immigrants across the United States have been voting more than they did in the past, and voting disproportionately for Democrats. According to exit polls, Latinos (not all of them foreign-born) made up a (then) record 8 percent of all voters in the November 2006 midterm elections, held just six months after the marches. Fully 69 percent of Latino voters cast their 2006 ballots for Democratic congressional candidates, compared to only 47 percent of white voters (Ayón 2006). In that very close electoral contest, arguably the Latino immigrant vote was a decisive factor in ending Republican control of the U.S. Congress.

Voter registration and get-out-the-vote (GOTV) efforts aimed at the 2008 elections began to take shape shortly afterward, led by the We Are America Alliance as well as campaigns like Ya Es Hora (Now Is the Time), sponsored by a coalition of Latino advocacy organizations and Spanish-language media, which have also been engaged in recent efforts to promote naturalization (NALEO 2007). Eleven million Latinos voted in 2008, a 38 percent increase over 2004. Even in the context of the generally high voter turnout in the presidential contest that led to the election of Barack Obama, Latinos increased their share of the total to 9 percent, a new record. And according to exit polls, 67 percent of all Latinos voted for Obama, compared to 43 percent of whites. The figure was even higher—78 percent—among Latino immigrants, who made up about 40 percent of all Latino voters. Latino votes were crucial in some battleground states that shifted into the Democratic column, including Nevada, Colorado, and New Mexico as well as Florida and Virginia. The success of the mobilization effort is also reflected in the fact that 15 percent of 2008's Latino voters had never voted before, according to postelection surveys. As conservative commentator Richard Nadler (2009) observed shortly afterward, "The fear and the fury engendered in the broader Hispanic community has destroyed conservative prospects in the Southwest, weakened them in the West, and wiped them out in New England" (see also Preston 2008c; *Daily Labor Report* 2008; Lopez 2008; NALEO 2008a).

Obama's campaign actively worked to win support from and mobilize Latino voters, an effort led by Obama's field director Cuauhtémoc Figueroa, a former union official, with assistance from Marshall Ganz, former political director of the United Farm Workers union. Organized labor also devoted significant resources to GOTV efforts in support of Obama and other Democrats in the 2008 campaign, including an estimated $4.5 million specifically targeting Latino voters. The SEIU was the big player here, contributing about $3 million to groups like the We Are America Alliance, Ya Es Hora, and the union's own Mi Familia Vota effort, which focused on battleground states like Colorado and Arizona as well as Texas.[16] However, those figures pale relative to the estimated $450 million that unions and their political action committees spent on the 2008 election, not including the time devoted by union volunteers who made millions of phone calls and home visits (Greenhouse 2008a).

These developments suggest that the labor-Latino coalition that first developed in California in the 1990s is now beginning to be replicated on a national scale. That has several potential ramifications. One is that it could boost renewed efforts to achieve comprehensive immigration reform. In the wake of the political stalemate that developed in the waning years of the Bush administration, it was to the Democrats' advantage to preserve the image of the Republican Party as deeply hostile to immigrant rights—an image that the Sensenbrenner bill had indelibly impressed on the immigrant community. Yet Democrats were wary of openly embracing the cause of immigrant rights during the 2008 election campaign, fearful of alienating their own native-born constituents. Further delay could result from the deep economic crisis that began in 2008, although immigrant advocacy groups have been pressing the Obama administration to launch a new effort.

Apart from immigration reform itself, further developing the embryonic national labor-Latino coalition could benefit both immigrants and the labor movement. Unions nationally could become the midwife of political mobilization and social transformation for today's Latino immigrants, replicating the dynamic that emerged in California after 1994. Organized labor, with its extensive financial resources and political capacity, together with the Latino and immigrant advocacy organizations, is now poised to assume this agentic role. It has done so before, most importantly for the massive wave of working-class immigrants from southern and eastern Europe, when a surge of unionization in the 1930s and 1940s and accompanying political incorporation helped narrow the inequalities between the haves and have-nots and propelled many first- and second-generation immigrants into the middle class—and into the Democratic Party. As Mark Twain reportedly put it, history may not repeat itself, but sometimes it rhymes.

NOTES

1. For a summary of recent polling data, see http://www.pollingreport.com/immigration.htm. These data suggest some volatility in attitudes and that a substantial minority disapproves of legalization. On elites, see Schuck (2007).

2. Asian immigrants have been much less studied, and a smaller proportion of them are low-wage workers. Yet many of the same assumptions were made about them, and they too have actively organized in recent years. This chapter, however, focuses on Latino immigrants, the dominant group within California's low-wage workforce.

3. I analyze these developments in Milkman (2006).

4. In 2008, 20.1 percent of California's U.S.-born workers, and 13.2 percent of the state's foreign-born workers, were union members (Milkman and Kye 2008).

5. African Americans were the only group among whom prounion attitudes were more widespread (see Freeman and Rogers 1999).

6. Although this survey, the 2001–2 California Workplace Survey (CWS), asked a question identical to the one in the WRPS, the results are not strictly comparable. The WRPS asked the question of all nonunion workers except high-level managers, while the CWS asked it only of nonunion nonsupervisory respondents, excluding a much larger group of middle managers. In both surveys the question was, "If an election were held today to decide whether employees like you should be represented by a union, would you vote for the union or against the union?"

7. On Houston, see Greenhouse (2008b, 254–58); on Miami, see Shaw (2008, chap. 4).

8. Redoubtable political commentator Harold Meyerson (2001) noted in mid-2001 that "the Fed has plunged itself into 23 hotly contested congressional, legislative, and city council races around Los Angeles in the past five years and has won 22 of them." See also Shaw (2008, chap. 7).

9. See Shaw (2008, 209–14) and, on the role of Northern California unionists, Hamlin (2008).

10. See also Gordon's recent proposal (2007) for a more expansive, labor-based form of citizenship.

11. See Randy Shaw's chapter in this volume on the SEIU's role in providing security at the marches. On labor's role in the Chicago protests, see Fink (2010). For an account that argues that labor's role in the planning of the protests was relatively marginal, see Narro, Wong, and Shadduck-Hernández (2007).

12. Compare Fine's map (2005) of the worker centers with the geography of the marches shown in Figure 1.1 of the introduction to this volume. As Randy Shaw notes in his chapter in this volume, that geography also echoes the route of the 2003 Immigrant Workers Freedom Ride. Also see Narro, Wong, and Shadduck-Hernández (2007), on the geographical spread of the protests.

13. The 8.5 million figure (for 2005) is from Passel (2007, iv). The 2006–7 naturalization application surge was especially sharp in Southern California, according to Gorman and Delson (2007). See also Preston (2007a).

14. Regarding the large numbers of applications in the mid-1990s, one recent journalistic account notes, "That's when many illegal immigrants who received amnesty in the 1980s became eligible for citizenship, and a political backlash against them motivated many to apply" (Watanabe 2007).

15. See http://www.weareamericaalliance.org.

16. The SEIU spent the most, but other Change to Win affiliates, specifically the United Food and Commercial Workers, the Laborers' union, the Teamsters, and UNITE HERE (which represents garment and hotel workers) also contributed substantially to this effort. The AFL-CIO also contributed a modest amount of funding (Monterroso 2009).

11

Drawing New Lines in the Sand

Evaluating the Failure of Immigration Reforms
from 2006 to the Beginning of the Obama
Administration

Louis DeSipio

When millions of immigrants, their U.S. citizen family members, and their supporters protested in the late winter and early spring of 2006, a new voice was raised in the national immigration debate and a new pro-immigrant organizational coalition coalesced. Many who marched expected—and many who watched the marches feared—that Congress would heed the demands of this new coalition and pass comprehensive immigration reform that would include among its provisions one of the central demands of the marchers: a path to permanent residence for the approximately twelve million unauthorized immigrants in the United States.[1] Indeed, among the most evocative imagery of the protests were signs seen nationwide—and pictured in many newspapers—saying "Today we march, tomorrow we vote."

Despite these expectations, neither 2006 nor 2007 saw a comprehensive immigration bill pass both houses of Congress, and the 2008 and 2010 elections saw little discussion of immigration reform, particularly after the end of the Republican primaries. The Senate did pass a bill in 2006 that included a path to permanent residence among its provisions, but the House rejected a comprehensive approach. Instead, Congress agreed on enforcement-focused legislation in 2006. In 2007, the Senate twice took up a comprehensive bill and could not find the votes to overcome a filibuster against a bill considerably more restrictive than the bill the same body had passed the previous year. Nor could it pass smaller pieces of the bill, such as the DREAM Act that would provide a path to permanent residence for some unauthorized immigrants.

In this chapter I assess the short- and medium-term effects of the 2006 immigrant rights protests on comprehensive immigration reform with an eye to the possibilities for such reform in the Obama administration. I evaluate three themes: public opinion on immigration, the electoral legacies of the protests (in the 2006, 2008, and 2010 races), and the emergence of a new organizational infrastructure that shapes the immigrant civic and political voice. My evaluation is that the protests spurred more rigid positions on all sides of the debate, which will make the compromises necessary to achieve "comprehensive" immigration reform more difficult to achieve. Advocates of an incorporative immigration policy have not yet been able to build on their remarkable organizational successes in 2006 to galvanize support in the general public or in Congress for immigration reform that includes a path to legal status for unauthorized immigrants resident in the United States.

THE SPRING 2006 IMMIGRANT RIGHTS PROTESTS AND 2006–2007 CONGRESSIONAL ACTION

The 2006 immigrant rights protests were unprecedented in their scope. Estimates suggest that these marches included as many as five million people who marched in more than 150 cities (Woodrow Wilson International Center for Scholars 2007). That many of these marchers were immigrants, including many unauthorized immigrants, made this accomplishment all the more significant.

This national mobilization was made possible by a new organizational coalition that included some traditional immigrant rights organizations but that added new institutional players: state federations of hometown associations, service unions, ethnic radio, and some religious organizations that had not previously been involved in immigrant organizing.

While numbers (and the organization and outrage that they reflect) are important in a democracy, they do not necessarily lead to policy outcomes. In the case of the 2006 protests, however, the short-term goal of the marches—blocking the enactment of H.R. 4437, which the U.S. House passed in 2005 and would have criminalized unauthorized status—succeeded. As the protests were taking place, House leaders publicly backed away from this most contentious aspect of the law. The Republican leadership had been privately circumspect about criminalization for months, but the rank and file were much more committed. The marches succeed in removing criminalization from the debate.

In legislative terms, the short-term consequence of the protests was even more positive. A bipartisan coalition in the U.S. Senate passed more inclusive legislation that explicitly rejected the criminalization provisions in the House legislation and provided, among other things, for several paths to permanent residence. For unauthorized immigrants who had been resident in the United States since April 2001, S. 2611 provided for an "earned adjustment" to legal status. Immigrants applying under this provision would have to work in the United States for six years after the bill's enactment, pass a background check, pay back taxes, learn civics and English, and pay a $2,000 fine. For unauthorized immigrants who had not been resident since April 2001, S. 2611 would have allowed for a three-year deferred mandatory departure status, at the end of which they could apply for permanent resident status. They would be subject to the same requirements as the applicants who had been resident longer. S. 2611 would also have created a final path to permanent residence. It would have allowed for up to 200,000 guest workers to enter the country annually, initially with three-year temporary visas. After being present (and working) in the United States for four years (after having renewed the temporary visa once), S. 2611 would have provided the opportunity to establish permanent residence. These opportunities for guest workers were narrowed somewhat in floor debates.

The bipartisan coalition that proposed S. 2611 held firm and the bill passed the Senate with only minor amendments, 62–36. The supporters included twenty-three Republicans. Most of the amendments were unrelated to the issue of permanent residence. The exception limited permanent residence for guest workers to those sponsored by an employer, who in turn would have to show that there was no native worker to fill the position.

The House held firm (and tapped popular sentiment to add to border enforcement), leading to a stalemate. After the passage of the Senate bill, House leaders convened twenty hearings nationwide that spoke to the hard-line immigration-enforcement constituency and came across more as an election-year ploy than a serious policy discussion.

As the 2006 elections neared, Republican leaders in both houses of Congress (including supporters of the more inclusionary bill in the Senate and exclusionary bill in House) realized that they needed to pass some immigration legislation focused on border enforcement. Each chamber broke up its bills into smaller pieces. The only one of these to pass both the House and Senate was P.L. 109–367, which authorized a seven-hundred-mile fence on the southern border. P.L. 109–367 passed overwhelmingly—80 to 19 in the Senate and 283 to 138 in the House.

The election of Democratic House and Senate majorities in the midterm elections raised expectations that Congress would be able to pass a comprehensive immigration bill in 2007 (well enough in advance of the 2008 races to insulate some members from their votes). Congressional leaders, seeing that the debate in the House would likely be more contentious, scheduled debates on the legislation first in the Senate (S. 1348).

This bill was the result of ongoing conversations between Democratic and Republican senators and representatives of the Bush administration. Overall, it was considerably more restrictionist (and, arguably, proposed more fundamental changes) than the 2006 bill. Most profoundly, it would have changed the allocation of visas for immigration leading to permanent residence to a system that would reward education, job skills, and English-speaking ability and diminish the importance of family ties to U.S. citizens and permanent residents. This would represent a significant change in the structure of immigration to permanent residence established in the 1965 Immigration and Nationality Act.

The S. 1348 bill did include provisions for legalization of unauthorized immigrants but would have held this legalization in abeyance until enforcement provisions were in place. These enforcement provisions included building at least 370 miles of border fence and developing a fraud-proof system to verify worker eligibility as well as a doubling of the size of the Border Patrol. The legalization provisions were more restrictive than in the 2006 Senate bill. Immigrants resident in the United States on January 1, 2007, would be eligible for legalization. They would have one year to register with the government. During this period, they could work legally in the United States but could not travel internationally. Once the triggers were in place, applicants could apply for a temporary visa that would last for eight years, at which point they could apply for permanent residence. Each of these transitions would require the payment of fees and fines that would amount to several thousand dollars per immigrant. In order to attain legal permanent resident status, applicants would need to demonstrate that they could speak English. This legislation, then, would require a wait of at least thirteen years for an unauthorized immigrant to be eligible for application for naturalization. S. 1348 also provided (initially) for at least 400,000 temporary-worker visas, and these temporary workers would be allowed to work in many sectors of the economy where they cannot currently. These temporary workers would *not* have a direct path to permanent residence, as did temporary workers under the 2006 bill.

Ultimately, the bill failed to overcome a filibuster. The vote in favor of cloture was just forty-six votes, suggesting that even in a purely majoritarian system the bill was facing an uphill struggle in the Senate (not to mention in the House, where it would have faced a more difficult path). Senators proposed 351 amendments to the bill, many of which were designed to reduce the likelihood of Senate passage.[2]

The presidential race moved comprehensive immigration reform off the congressional agenda in 2008. Later in this chapter I discuss the 2008 campaign in greater depth, as part of my assessment of the electoral legacies of the 2006 protests, but the absence of immigration reform legislation from the congressional docket in 2008 can be seen as a tactical calculation by leaders of both parties to remove a controversial issue from the debate in an election year. This served members facing reelection bids as well as the presidential candidates, whose positions on many controversial aspects of immigration were more similar than different.

PUBLIC OPINION ON IMMIGRATION

The failure to translate the massive immigrant rights protests into incorporative policy changes (or substantive policy change in areas other than enforcement) rests in part with the American public's response to the protests and, more generally, to their ambivalent and internally contradictory views on immigration and immigrants. Mass opinion on immigration has followed a similar pattern through much of U.S. history (Tichenor 2002; Zolberg 2006). The American public generally think that immigration at current levels is too high but that immigrants already resident in the United States are an asset. They strongly oppose unauthorized migration and support increasing barriers to unauthorized migration, but they support a path to legal residence over deportation for unauthorized migrants resident in the United States. Although this summary oversimplifies public opinion on this complex subject, it highlights the internal inconsistency in U.S. attitudes toward immigration and explains, in part, why Congress is slow to act: there are strong constituencies for either incorporation or exclusion, but neither dominates public opinion.

The 2006 immigrant rights protests did not alter this pattern and may have strengthened it. Gallup conducted ten polls with a question on the volume of immigration in the George W. Bush years, including two during the period of the protests (see table 11.1). Between June 2002 and June 2008 (with the exception of June 2006), between 39 and 49 percent of poll respondents reported that the level of immigration should be decreased, and 33 to 39 percent said that it should be maintained at its current level. Support for increasing immigration levels hovered between 12 and 18 percent. These results, including the slightly anomalous June 2006 findings, offer support for all sides in the immigration debate. New allies did not appear in the general public, by any means, but the protests did not alienate the American public either. While small changes may have appeared at the margins from poll to poll, this series of polling data shows little change in public opinion on this issue between 2000 and 2010. Probably most importantly, these results reflect a division in public opinion, one in which the best organized group can disproportionately influence policy.

Surveys during the period of the protests attempted to gauge public opinion on legalization, not a topic extensively examined before 2006. The specific questions asked varied based on pollsters' assessments of what was being discussed in Congress. Seven such polls were conducted during the period of the protests. Majorities, sometimes large majorities, supported allowing unauthorized migrants residing in the United States to stay in the United States. This response appeared both when staying was discussed in terms of a guest-worker program or as a "path to citizenship." Of these, a poll by the Pew Research Center for the People and the Press and the Pew Hispanic Center (2006b) asked the most rigorous

TABLE 11.1   Attitudes toward Level of U.S. Immigration, 2000–2010

In your view, should immigration be kept at its present level, increased, or decreased?

	Sept. 2000 (%)	June 2001 (%)	June 2002 (%)	June 2003 (%)	June 2004 (%)	June 2005 (%)	April 2006 (%)	June 2006 (%)	June 2007 (%)	June 2008 (%)	June 2009 (%)	Ju 20 (
Present level	41	42	36	37	33	34	35	42	35	39	32	3
Increased	13	14	12	13	14	16	15	17	16	18	14	1
Decreased	38	41	49	47	49	46	47	39	45	39	50	4
Decreased minus present level	−3	−1	13	10	16	12	12	−3	10	0	18	

SOURCES: J. Jones 2008b; Morales 2010.

Note: "No opinion" excluded, so columns do not add up to 100 percent. Respondents with no opinion declined from 8 perc in 2000 to 3 percent in 2008.

battery of questions, which discouraged respondents from taking mutually contradictory positions. It found that approximately one-third of respondents felt that unauthorized immigrants should be allowed to stay permanently, one-third said they should be allowed to stay as temporary workers, and slightly less than one-third thought they should be forced to return to their countries of origin. Again, these results can be read by leaders to support many different policy outcomes.

The Pew Hispanic Center (2006b) reviewed surveys during the period of the protests and found little change resulting from the demonstrations. Survey results (from a variety of sources, some more scientific than others) found that the American public were divided on the question of whether immigrants help or hurt the economy. Overwhelmingly, Americans perceived unauthorized migration as a "very" or "extremely" serious issue for the United States but believed that unauthorized immigrants took unwanted jobs. These views were similar to those found before the immigrant rights protests (National Immigration Forum 2006).

The protestors were viewed somewhat less favorably. A Rasmussen Reports survey (2006b) conducted in late April found that respondents were twice as likely to view the protestors unfavorably as favorably. Interestingly, these same respondents supported "earned citizenship" by a 53 to 31 percent margin. Thus, even if the protestors alienated some in the nonimmigrant community, this did not alter underlying attitudes. Over the course of the protests, favorable opinions of the protestors did grow slightly, topping out at 29 percent as the marches were ending (Rasmussen Reports 2006a).

Opinions about immigration vary by state and region (Rasmussen Reports 2006c). The sampling methodology of this Rasmussen survey should caution against overinterpreting these data, but the findings add to the complexity of American views on immigration. They also add to the complexity of crafting a legislative solution for an issue such as this that cuts across party lines.

One group in U.S. society did show some change of opinion in response to the immigrant rights protests. Latino adults generally supported a legalization program that leads to permanent residence (and were even more supportive of a guest-worker program) (Latino Policy Coalition 2006a, 2006b, 2006c). In the past, Latino *citizens* have not been as strong in their support for pro-immigration policies, particularly for legalization of unauthorized immigrants. The protests galvanized immigration as a civil rights issue for the vast majority of U.S. citizen Latinos (Latino Policy Coalition 2006b). The marches and the accompanying policy debate also appear to have raised the salience of immigration for Latinos, including Latino U.S. citizen voters (Carroll 2007b). The greater support for inclusive immigration reform among Latinos indicates that the protests began the process of building an ethnic coalition in support of such reform.

My reading of these admittedly contradictory data suggests that public opinion, with the exception of Latino public opinion, was not moved dramatically by the 2006 immigrant rights protests. The public continued to want to have their cake and eat it too when it came to immigrants. This has contributed to an environment in which elected leaders have a great deal of discretion in policy making, influenced by the best organized interests in the debate. Through 2006 and 2007, the loudest voice in the immigration debate advocated restrictionist policies. The polling evidence, however, offers some encouragement for advocates of inclusive policies. Such policies can generate a great deal of public support as long as they are balanced by new tools of enforcement to reduce future unauthorized migration (in a sense, it was this balance that the Senate sought to achieve in 2006).

The pool of Americans for whom immigration is the most salient issue (and who generally oppose inclusive immigration reforms) does not appear to have grown. In 2006, several Gallup polls reported that between 10 and 15 percent of respondents said that "immigration/illegal aliens" should be one of the top two issues that the president and Congress should deal with. This share increased to 29 percent in 2007 (while Congress was debating immigration reform) but declined to between 6 and 8 percent in 2008 (Saad 2006; Carroll 2007a; J. Jones 2008a). Other measures—such as the growth of the Minutemen or support for Representative Tancredo's presidential candidacy—suggest that this stridently anti-immigrant sector of the American public is growing.

ELECTORAL CONSEQUENCES

The immigrant rights protests and popular concerns about immigration policy undoubtedly shaped the federal elections in 2006, 2008, and 2010. The outcomes of these elections, however, have not been consistent, either with advocates of comprehensive reform or restriction winning nationally. Overall, advocates of comprehensive immigration reform have won more seats. The threat of primary challenges by single-issue anti-immigration reform candidates, however, has caused many immigration moderates, particularly Republican moderates, to take more hard-line positions. Perhaps as importantly, the immigration issue divides each party, so congressional and senatorial leaders cannot rely on party discipline to overcome members' reluctance to debate immigration. This is particularly apparent among Democrats in the U.S. House who won seats previously held by Republicans.

The election of Barack Obama in 2008 and the surge in Democratic majorities in Congress created the potential for a compromise, assuming the Obama administration took a leadership role on the issue that the Bush administration initially was unwilling to do and increasingly became unable to do. That said, other issues—particularly the economy—eclipsed immigration in the first years of the Obama administration (J. Jones 2008a). It is unclear if the network of immigrant rights and civil rights organizations that coordinated the 2006 marches will be able to apply sufficient pressure on the administration or Congress to raise the legislative salience of immigration reform. They were able to do this in 2006 (and were responsible for the elimination of criminalization from the policy debate), but immigrant rights groups and their supporters have not been able to influence the legislative debate since.

Candidates, Campaigns, and the Protests

By the time immigrants and their families began to protest, it was largely too late to influence the 2006 midterm elections. Immigration was central to the outcomes of a few races, but—with few competitive races in the general election—these outcomes did not change the balance of support for comprehensive reform in the Senate or House. Immigration was slightly more relevant in the 2008 races, particularly in the Republican presidential primary. The influence of immigration as an issue in congressional races in this period, ultimately, was to make compromise more difficult. Many of the new seats won by the Democrats, the seats that added to the party's legislative majority, were in areas where Democrats had previously been at an electoral disadvantage. In these parts of the country, Democrats have since taken positions on comprehensive immigration reform that range from cautious to outright opposition.

The 2005–6 election cycle and the midterm and later elections that followed offer three models for ways in which immigration influences the outcomes of congressional races, which in turn have guided the thinking of members of Congress. This first of these elections that proved instructive to other candidates preceded the protests—the fall 2005 special election in California's 48th Congressional District to fill the remainder of Christopher Cox's term after his appointment to the Securities and Exchange Commission. This Orange County district is safely Republican, but its constituency reflects Republican divisions over immigration. In a crowded primary, the establishment Republican candidate (who had no strong history on immigration or, evidently, much concern about the issue prior to the primary) faced a surprising challenge from Jim Gilchrist, the founder of the Minutemen. Ultimately, the Republican—John Campbell—won in a runoff. In the process, though, his positions on immigration hardened. In his subsequent reelection races (in November 2006, 2008, and 2010), he faced no serious challenge in part because his opposition to immigration reform topped his campaign agenda.

This lesson was not lost on Republicans who, though they were unlikely to face serious challenges in a general election, might face primary challenges from single-issue anti-immigrant candidates. The national consequence was to reduce the number of Republican immigration moderates who would support a compromise bill in the U.S. House.

Candidates closer to the Republican establishment than Jim Gilchrist learned how to use immigration to undermine moderate Democrats in swing districts. In another California special election just after the spring 2006 marches, former representative Brian Bilbray ran a stridently anti–immigration reform campaign. In a runoff against a moderate Democrat, Bilbray cancelled a fundraising event with Senator John McCain—at the time the front-runner for the Republican presidential nomination—and criticized McCain's immigration bill as an "amnesty bill."

Running against immigrants did not guarantee success, however, even in Republican-leaning districts, offering a second, less common model for the role of immigration in contemporary congressional races. In Arizona's 8th Congressional District, Randy Graf defeated Steve Huffman in the 2006 Republican primary. Graf's candidacy was based largely on immigration as an issue and support for enhanced enforcement. Huffman was more to the center of the party and was endorsed by the retiring incumbent, Jim Kolbe. In the general election, the Democratic candidate Gabrielle Giffords defeated Graf. Analysis attributed the Democratic victory in the Republican-leaning district to the general Democratic tide in the election and the rejection by the district's moderates of Graf's single-issue candidacy.

Off-year elections in 2007 and 2008 provide a final model for the role of immigration in contemporary congressional races. Democratic victories, particularly in areas of traditional Republican dominance, do not guarantee increased support for comprehensive immigration reform. Equally important, nominally safe Democrats can face serious challenges from Republicans who focus their campaigns primarily or exclusively on the Democrat's support for legalization. Congressional races in Massachusetts, Mississippi, Louisiana, and Illinois each elected Democrats, three of whom were surprise victors in seats previously held by Republicans. In each of these races (Travis Childers in Mississippi, Don Cazayoux in Louisiana, and Bill Foster in Illinois), the victorious Democrat ran on pledges to oppose legalization. Both Childers and Cazayoux accepted the rhetorical gambit of the immigration restrictionists by opposing "amnesty." Foster, the most moderate of the three, called for noncitizens to pay "impact fees" until they qualify for citizenship (a proposal that would seemingly include legal permanent residents as well as unauthorized immigrants).

In a safely Democratic seat in Massachusetts, Niki Tsongas (the widow of Senator Paul Tsongas) faced a serious challenge from a Republican taking a hard line on immigration who directly challenged Tsongas's support for benefits for unauthorized immigrants. Tsongas ultimately won but by a narrow margin (51 to 45 percent). The result of this race was to caution Democrats in safe districts in a manner similar to the Gilchrest challenge to Campbell in a safe Republican district.

As should be evident, neither the 2006 nor 2008 congressional elections substantially changed the dynamics of support for immigration reform in either the U.S. House or Senate. While they certainly made some moderates more cautious (I offer some tangible evidence of this below), both the House and Senate remained divided, with a sizeable minority supporting enforcement and a sizeable minority supporting comprehensive reform that would include legalization. In the 2006 elections, immigration moderates replaced enforcement hard-liners in Arizona, Indiana, Iowa, Colorado, and Pennsylvania, but immigration was just one of several issues that distinguished the winning candidate. Several of the surprise Democratic victors in the 2006 Senate races—such as Virginia's Jim Webb, Missouri's Claire McCaskill, and Montana's John Tester—ran on strongly proenforcement platforms and had little or nothing to say about a path to permanent residence.

One of the systemic changes in the 2006 and 2008 elections was a function of the immigration debate. Latinos supported Democrats at rates comparable to previous elections (Gimpel 2007). How one interprets this depends on one's assessment of the degree to which Latinos voted more Republican in 2004 (Leal et al. 2005). But assertions that Republicans have been making inroads among Latinos have declined as the Latino voting population has come to see attacks on immigrants as a more general attack on Latino civil rights (Latino Policy Coalition 2006c).

The electoral lessons of 2006 appeared to affect some senatorial votes in 2007. On the key June 2007 cloture vote that doomed comprehensive reform, opponents included the three Democrats first elected in 2006—McCaskill, Tester, and Webb—as well as independent Bernie Sanders (VT), who was also elected in 2006. Five of the eleven Democrats who were up for reelection in 2008 voted against cloture; four of these five opponents had supported S. 2611 in 2006—Max Baucus (MT), Tom Harkin (IA), Mary Landrieu (LA), and Mark Pryor (AR). Eighteen of the twenty-one Republicans who were up for reelection in 2008 also voted against cloture. Of these, seven had voted in favor of S. 2611—Norm Coleman (MN), Susan Collins (ME), Pete Domenici (NM), Mitch McConnell (KY), Gordon Smith (OR), Ted Stevens (AK), and Mark Warner (VA).

Although a comprehensive bill never went to the House in 2007, the 2006 elections left a legacy in that body as well. Some of the surprise 2006 Democratic House victories came in southern and border states. These new Democratic officeholders included Nancy Boyda (KS) and Heath Shuler (NC), who joined the Congressional Immigration Reform Caucus, the legislative caucus that was the source of H.R. 4437 and that sees immigration reform only in terms of enforcement. Boyda and Shuler joined 4 incumbent Democratic members and 104 Republicans. This caucus increased its membership by several members between 2005 and 2009.

After the failure of the 2007 bill in the Senate, Shuler joined the Republican chair of the Congressional Immigration Reform Caucus, Brian Bilbray, to introduce a bipartisan border security bill that would require employers to screen new employees for work eligibility using a national database (E-Verify) and to expand the Border Patrol by eight thousand agents. Critics note that E-Verify has failed many tests and would likely exclude many eligible workers. The Bilbray-Shuler legislation had forty-two Democrats and thirty-six Republicans as cosponsors, indicating the divisions over immigration policy present in both parties in the House.

Immigration concerns were muted in the 2008 presidential race. The clearest effect of ongoing national debates about immigration policy appeared in the Republican presidential primaries, where candidates moved steadily to more restrictionist positions. John McCain initially paid a price for his support for comprehensive immigration reform. In 2007, McCain fell from front-runner status in part because his support for immigration reform alienated many Republican primary voters (Nagourney 2007). McCain's main rivals linked him to moderation on immigration; his response was to distance himself from his earlier positions. The Mitt Romney campaign aired ads declaring that "amnesty is not the answer." Rudy Giuliani spoke of the 2007 Senate bill as "a great example of why

Washington doesn't work." For Romney and Giuliani, however, these criticisms reflected a shift in their positions on immigration. Romney moved from support for a "path to citizenship" to opposition (Przybyla 2007). In 1996, then–New York mayor Giuliani filed suit to challenge provisions of a 1996 immigration bill that treated, he believed, unauthorized immigrants inhumanely by denying them access to public hospitals and education. At the time, he denounced "the anti-immigration movement in America" as "one of our most serious public problems" (Hook 2007).

The general movement of Republican presidential candidates toward restrictionist positions reflected their readings of the policy preferences of Republican primary voters but also Tom Tancredo's presence in the race. A November 2007 *Wall Street Journal* poll found that 38 percent of Republicans identified "illegal immigration" as one of the top two issues facing the nation (Kronholz 2007). The issue was less salient for Democrats, with just 14 percent identifying it among the top two issues. Representative Tancredo based his candidacy largely on anti-immigrant positions, which served to remind the front-runners for the Republican nomination to focus on restriction in order to reach the Republican base.

Even though McCain backpedaled on support for comprehensive immigration reform, he ultimately benefited from his prior advocacy for reform. The economic conservative wing of party backed him, which both kept his campaign alive financially and generated votes in several of the early competitive primary races. With four serious candidates in play (McCain, Huckabee, Romney, and Giuliani), McCain was able to stand out in part because of his previous positions on immigration. He was also able to position himself as a candidate who could win the votes of moderates in the general election.

The Democrats were quieter on immigration issues, perhaps reflecting the lower salience of the issue to Democratic voters. While the candidates' positions varied somewhat, all endorsed comprehensive reform. They demonstrated, however, that there were limits to this support. Senator Hillary Clinton had to quickly reverse herself when she seemed to endorse New York governor Eliot Spitzer's proposal to issue driver's licenses to unauthorized immigrants. Still, Democratic candidates only had so much latitude to backpedal. Several primaries in large immigrant-receiving states occurred quite early into the electoral season, and Latino votes were particularly important in these races.

The modest discussion of immigration present in the 2008 presidential primaries largely disappeared in the general election. Both Senators McCain and Obama sought to reach Latino voters by criticizing the other candidate's tepid support for comprehensive immigration reform. This outreach appeared largely in Spanish-language advertising in battleground states and was not repeated in English advertising or on the stump. Also, because the salience of immigration declined for the electorate in 2008, neither candidate was pressed to discuss his position on the issue, and ultimately neither candidate would have benefited from doing so. Their positions were relatively similar and would have faced opposition from a sizeable minority of the electorate. This was more a problem for Senator McCain because immigration as an issue was more important to Republican voters; but it also presented problems for Obama in his attempt to win in nontraditionally Democratic states such as Virginia, North Carolina, Indiana, and Missouri.

The 2008 contests repeated the pattern of the 2006 elections in the U.S. Senate. Several Democrats who won competitive races were critical of comprehensive reform. Kay Hagan (NC), for example, promised to "strengthen the borders, enforce and upgrade laws that crack down on employers who knowingly hire illegal workers, and eliminate the shadow economy that drives down wages and working conditions" (Kay Hagan for U.S. Senate 2008). Nowhere did she mention a legalization program as part of a comprehensive immigration solution. The appointment of Kirsten Gillibrand to replace Hillary Clinton in the Senate added a Democrat to the body who had voted against comprehensive reform in the House. Certainly, other Democratic Senate victors did speak more positively of comprehensive reform, but as with 2006, Democratic victories did not guarantee an easier path to legislative compromise on immigration reform.

The 2010 congressional elections saw many of these 2006 and 2008 Democratic gains reversed. When Congress convened in January 2011, Republicans controlled the majority of the House seats and the Democratic majority in the Senate narrowed. The new composition of the House and Senate considerably reduced the likelihood that Congress would debate comprehensive immigration reform. Aside from the unlikelihood that a Republican-majority House of Representatives would dedicate its energies to immigration legislation other than enforcement-focused bills, 2010 saw the election of several members for whom immigration control was the primary issue driving their candidacies. Most prominent among these was newly elected Representative Lou Barletta (R-PA), who came to national prominence as mayor of Hazleton, Pennsylvania. He led efforts in Hazleton to pass ordinances to deny business permits to companies employing unauthorized immigrants, to fine landlords who rented to the unauthorized, and to require tenants to register and pay for rental permits. Many other Republicans in the new majority learned, whether consciously or not, the lesson of California's John Campbell and wanted to avoid primary challenges from single-issue anti-immigration reform candidates. While the post-2010 U.S. Senate might seem to offer a venue for a debate over immigration reform, no member of either side of the aisle signaled a willingness to assume a leadership role. Republicans who in 2006 were divided on immigration—creating an opportunity for Senate passage of a comprehensive immigration bill—moved to near unanimity against comprehensive reform. And though the majority of Democrats continued to support reform, a sizeable minority on the Democratic side took positions closer to the Republican members than to their own caucus.

In the absence of congressional action, both the executive branch, through regulation and administration of immigration law, and the courts, which are increasingly being asked to evaluate the constitutionality of state efforts to manage immigration policy, are at the center of the immigration policy-making process. Neither of these branches of government, however, have the ability or responsibility that Congress does to set the parameters of national immigration policy and to balance the needs of employers, the states, immigrants (authorized and unauthorized), and the nation.

A Changing Electorate

The 2006 immigrant rights marches were partially responsible for a second electoral change: the increase in naturalized citizens, who can then vote. Perhaps not surprisingly, immigrant applications for naturalization increased in the months of the rallies. This increase is actually nested in a more general increase in naturalization applications (and naturalization awards). In 2005, 602,972 permanent residents applied for naturalization, slightly higher than the average number of new applications between 2000 and 2005. New applications increased to 730,642 and 1,132,073 in fiscal years 2006 and 2007, respectively, before declining in fiscal year 2008 to 525,786 (U.S. Bureau of Citizenship and Immigration Services 2007, 2008). As is often the case with increases in demand for naturalization, there was no single cause (DeSipio 1996b). During the final six months of 2006, immigrant service organizations offered more naturalization assistance and word circulated in immigrant communities of two changes in U.S. naturalization policies: a significant application fee increase and a redesign of the naturalization civics exam (Gorman and Delson 2007). The precipitous increase in applications in March and April 2006, however, must be seen as a direct consequence of the attention that the demonstrations focused on immigrant status and the need for an immigrant/ethnic political voice.

Although there were some processing delays, many of these applicants naturalized in time to register for the 2008 elections. In the period between the 2004 and 2008 elections, approximately three million immigrants naturalized, increasing the adult naturalized population to approximately sixteen million (author's estimates based on U.S. Department of Homeland Security 2008; U.S. Bureau of Citizenship and Immigration Services 2008; U.S. Bureau of the Census 2005b).

This increase in naturalizations needs to be put into context. Certainly, an increase of this magnitude is a positive sign, not just of immigrant interest in citizenship (which has been consistently high in the modern era; see Pachon and

DeSipio 1994), but more importantly of immigrant willingness to brave the bu- reaucratic hurdles of naturalization and to pay the increased fees. It also is reflec- tive of what has been a general pattern of increasing rates of naturalization. Ap- plications even at these relatively high levels by historical standards, however, will not seriously erode the pool of nearly 8.5 million legal permanent residents eligible for U.S. citizenship who have not naturalized (Passel 2007).

Naturalized citizens turned out at lower rates in the 2008 election than did U.S.-born citizens (U.S. Bureau of the Census 2009). This reinforces the pattern from recent elections in which naturalized citizens are less likely to vote than comparably situated U.S.-born coethnics (DeSipio 1996a; Shaw, de la Garza, and Lee 2000; Mollenkopf, Olson, and Ross 2001). (An exception to this pattern may have appeared in California beginning in the mid-1990s; see Pantoja, Ramírez, and Segura 2001.) In 2008, approximately 64.4 percent of U.S.-born adults turned out to vote, compared to 54 percent of naturalized citizen adults (U.S. Bureau of the Census 2009, table 13). Among Hispanics, however, the Census Bureau finds that turnout is higher among the naturalized (54 percent compared to 48 percent for the U.S.-born in 2008).

With these caveats in mind, naturalized citizens undoubtedly contributed to the Obama victory, a victory that resulted from strong majorities won among black, Latino, and Asian American voters despite the loss of support from the non-Hispanic white electorate. Thus, the 7 million naturalized voters who turned out in 2004 increased to at least 8.3 million (the national electorate numbered approximately 126 million). Preelection polling indicated that the naturalized citizen Asian Americans and Latinos were more likely to vote for Democrats than were their U.S.-born coethnics, so the naturalized citizen vote amplified the strong minority vote for Obama. With one exception, the naturalized electorate tends to be concentrated in states that were noncompeti- tive in the Electoral College. The exception is Florida, where naturalized citi- zen voters undoubtedly contributed to Obama's narrow 205,000-vote victory margin.

NEW RESOURCES FOR COMMUNITY MOBILIZATION IN IMMIGRANT COMMUNITIES

The coalition that brought together the 2006 immigrant rights marches—and particularly the new players involved: state federations of hometown associations, service unions, ethnic radio, and some religious organizations—offers a founda- tion for a new immigrant-led political movement in the United States. To date, however, and in part for very predictable reasons, this coalition has not been able to sustain the energy and creativity that it showed in early 2006. Ultimately, for the immigrant voice to be heard on the immigration debate, this coalition must reinvigorate itself.

In previous eras of intense immigrant community focus on immigrant status and/or naturalization (the late 1920s, World War II, the late 1980s, and the late 1990s), new immigrant-support infrastructures emerged. In both of the recent eras—the late 1980s' effort to ensure that unauthorized immigrants eligible for legalization were able to meet administrative requirements and the late 1990s' record numbers of citizenship-eligible immigrants pursuing naturalization— this community-based infrastructure included direct service organizations, the ethnic media, the philanthropic sector (including loan programs for paying application fees), and, to a limited degree, INS district offices. A similar community- service infrastructure has yet to emerge in the current era.

Despite the rhetoric of support for naturalization at the marches and after, the provision of services has been more sporadic. Organizations that have long served as naturalization resources—such as the National Association of Latino Elected Officials—have been able to increase the number of immigrants they serve; unions have also added immigrant/naturalization services for their members (and their families). To make a significant dent in the pool of citizenship-eligible immigrants, however, a rich new infrastructure (and a funding base to nurture it) would need to emerge in order to ensure that the current era's high immigrant interest in naturalization can be translated into higher numbers of new U.S. citizens.[3]

So, in terms of this final measure of the medium- and long-term consequences of the 2006 immigrant rights protests, the best grade that can be offered in incomplete. Immigrants are applying for naturalization in greater numbers. Immigrant community-based organizations, however, have not significantly increased the resources needed to move more immigrants into the application process. As a result, naturalization will continue to be biased toward potential applicants who have more resources or who have resided in the United States for longer. Looking to the future, the picture is potentially more dire. Immigrant communities have not begun the institutional growth that will be necessary to help unauthorized immigrants move toward legal status should Congress offer this opportunity.

CONCLUSIONS

The medium- and long-term objectives of the marchers for comprehensive immigration reform ultimately rest on congressional action and organizational activity. Reform must start with a compromise between advocates of enforcement and advocates of incorporation. Mass opinion on immigration will not drive policy in this area, and legislative positions appear to be moving to the margins rather than toward compromise. This quandary is not all that unusual. The last time Congress faced popular pressures to "do something" about unauthorized migration it took nearly a decade to craft a compromise solution (the Immigration Reform and Control Act of 1986) (Gimpel and Edwards 1990).

The election of Barack Obama to the presidency and the increase in the size of Democratic majorities in Congress enhanced the opportunity for comprehensive reform. This opportunity dimmed, however, as focus shifted to other issues—most notably the economy, health care, energy and the environment, and the ongoing wars in Iraq and Afghanistan. Even without these issues, Obama's 2008 campaign did not clearly signal that he saw comprehensive immigration reform as one his most pressing concerns.

The president is not the only agenda setter, of course. But Congress has not shown an inclination to lead in this area either. The instigators of the 2006 effort—Senators Kennedy and McCain—shifted their focus to other issues and no other senators or House leaders have replaced them. The death of Edward Kennedy, in August 2009, silenced one of Congress's staunchest defenders of immigrants.

Unlike the 1980s, when Congress last faced demands for comprehensive immigration reform, there is a potentially new set of community-based organizations that will seek to place such reform on the congressional agenda. The coalition of immigrant support organizations that formed to coordinate the 2006 marches remains, but it is not clear how vibrant it is. Particularly interesting among the coalition partners are the state federations of Mexican hometown associations. They were critical to turning people out in 2006, but their long-term investment in the immigration issue is not so clear.

What role can this coalition play in the medium term? The various groups' decision to move away from repeated mass marches is undoubtedly wise; it is not possible to repeatedly go to the well, particularly when there are no immediate decisions being made in Congress that can mobilize people. But the immigrant rights coalition has a unique opportunity in the current political environment to ensure that a voice traditionally overlooked in immigration debates remains in the debate—that is, the voice made up of immigrants and their families. The marches gave backbone to immigration-moderate Democrats who had been sitting on the sideline of the immigration debate, perhaps enjoying the fights within the Republican party, and this could happen again. The marches reminded these immigration-moderate Democrats that legalization needed to be part of a debate increasingly focused on enforcement. This effect was evident in 2006 in the Senate, which moved quickly to pass its version of immigration reform after the protests. With the move of Latino voters toward explicit support of the goals of the 2006 demonstrations, Democrats face an additional pressure. So, the goal for these immigrant rights groups is to find a strategy to reinvigorate the mass dimension of immigrant demand making and to use this pressure target the White House, Democrats in the Senate, and, particularly, Democrats in the House.

With limited experience in this sort of organization, however, it is not clear that this new leadership coalition can repeat the great successes of 2006.

NOTES

1. The popular debate constructed this as a "path to citizenship," but this is, quite simply, wrong. Congressional debates on legalization discussed a path to permanent residence (after a period of temporary residence or, perhaps, as a guest worker). After five years, these new permanent residents would have to go through a separate administrative process to naturalize. This is a long and winding "path" that in many cases—perhaps the majority—will *not* lead to U.S. citizenship. A study of immigrants who legalized under the 1986 Immigration Reform and Control Act (IRCA) finds that by 2002 less than half of IRCA legalizees had naturalized (Rytina 2002).

2. A filibuster is when a member or party in the Senate attempts to delay or prevent a vote on a bill by endlessly debating a bill. A vote for cloture ends debate on a bill, allowing the bill to move through the legislative process.

3. This critical need for community-based immigrant services will grow exponentially if Congress enacts a legalization program. If the 1986 law is any model, moving eligible applicants to legalized status will require a huge support network and a vast expansion of English-language and civics classes. In 1986–88, slightly fewer than three million immigrants legalized. Unlike the late 1980s, the unauthorized population is national, so this new service network will need to be developed not just in the traditional immigrant cities but also in small towns and rural areas throughout the nation.

12

The Efficacy and Alienation of Juan Q. Public

The Immigration Marches and Latino Orientations toward American Political Institutions

Francisco I. Pedraza, Gary M. Segura, and Shaun Bowler

Between March 10 and May 1, millions took part in the single largest coordinated protest action in American history, involving hundreds of cities on multiple occasions, affecting countless schools and businesses, and shuttering dozens of workplaces. The received understanding of minority participation in general, and immigrant participation in particular, would lead us to expect political passivity and nonparticipation. This would suggest that the marches were a surprising "one-off" experience with no broader lessons. But in examining attitudes toward the marches, we can gain some insight into how Latinos see the U.S. political system more generally. That is, attitudes toward the marches and what they might accomplish can be placed in the context of wider concerns about Latino political incorporation. The marches should not be dismissed as one-off events but, rather, should be seen as examples of political action that allow us to explore the degree to which Latinos, and Latino immigrants, are alienated from the U.S. political system.

In many ways the answer to the question of what the marches tell us about Latino attitudes toward U.S. politics is straightforward. In recent years Latinos have found themselves the focus of partisan politics and a series of policy measures that appear directly aimed at them. Beginning with a wave of English-only ballot initiatives in the 1980s, running through a subsequent wave of anti-immigrant measures such as California's Proposition 187 and its copies in other states, to the Sensenbrenner bill (H.R. 4437) of December 2005, an array of policy measures and political statements have targeted Latinos. Affirmative action programs, bilingual education programs, driver's licenses, state university tuition at the in-state rate, immigration fees, and rental policies were all issues debated at various levels of government

Advocates of the various policy changes—not all of them on the right of the political spectrum—argued that changes to immigration policy or access to government services were not aimed at the Latino community specifically or even aimed at immigrants as a group; they were really aimed at the illegal/undocumented population, regardless of ethnicity. Not surprisingly, however, the policies and policy discussions on immigration were keenly felt within the Latino community. Since 55 percent of the Latino adult population is foreign-born (Pew Hispanic Center 2008), the vast majority of Latinos in the United States—native-born, naturalized, and recently arrived—are directly connected to the immigrant experience, either because they themselves were legal immigrants, or illegal immigrants whose status was regularized after the Immigration Reform and Control Act (IRCA) in 1986, or because they are the children, spouses, in-laws, and neighbors of these very same people.

The role of government in these various debates is key. Somewhat at odds with the "small-government" tradition within conservative political thought, many conservatives saw government as a means of protection against a perceived threat of immigration (e.g., Huntington 2004) and lobbied for government action. If it is understandable that Latinos could feel themselves the target of many of the debates over immigration policies and issues (regardless of the intent of those who proposed those policies), it is also understandable to expect that the emphasis on government action and government enforcement would help shape Latino perception of government itself. It would not be surprising, therefore, if the majority of U.S. Latinos do not believe that the U.S. government works in their interest or at least did not believe so in 2006. The mobilizations of 2006 could therefore be understood as an act of defiance and push-back not just in terms of the policy debate over immigration but also as an expression of wider frustration with the political system itself.[1] The marches could be seen as an expression of opposition to a political system that seemed to make many of the marchers a target.

In this chapter, however, we offer an alternative, and less intuitive, interpretation of the marches. We explore the possibility that the mobilization marked not an expression of opposition to and alienation from the U.S. political system but an act of faith in that system and an expectation that the system will ultimately be responsive.[2] The marchers, in other words, believed that the system would hear their voices and would respond because the U.S. system of democratic government responds to popular concerns. To explore this interpretation we examine the general orientations of Latinos toward the U.S. political system, using the 2006 Pew Hispanic Center's National Survey of Latinos (Suro and Escobar 2006b).[3] Specifically, we measure Latino or Hispanic residents' beliefs regarding their influence on policy and whether government policy works on their behalf. We then use these measures to examine attitudes toward the 2006 protests and the immigration debate in general. We find that it is the *absence* of alienation that is associated with a positive assessment of the marches and the likelihood that they will result in a general social movement. We see that a sense of efficacy is a positive predictor of the belief that the immigration debate will be mobilizing for Latino voters. There is also some evidence that attitudes toward the marches were motivated by frustrations, but, taken together, our results challenge the interpretation of the marches as an act of defiance and instead can be seen as part of a growing body of evidence that suggests that immigrants, in particular, have a great deal of faith in the U.S. political system.

LATINO ORIENTATIONS TO THE POLITICAL SYSTEM

Much of our understanding of how Latinos as a group feel toward the government is gleaned from studies—some behavioral, some attitudinal—conducted over a decade ago. For instance, one of the earliest and major examinations of Latino attitudes toward government revealed that Latinos expressed somewhat low levels of trust in government officials, despite having generally strong levels of pride in and love for the United States (de la Garza et al. 1992, 79–81). Moreover, a sense of skepticism was seen among Latinos in response to questions about who government serves, with just under half of Latinos feeling that government is run by the few, in the interest of those few, and slightly more than half believing that government is run for the benefit of all (de la Garza et al. 1992, 81).

As is usually the case with studies of Latinos, these findings were further explored by national origin and across generation. Contrasts between Mexican Americans, Puerto Ricans, and Cuban Americans revealed that Cuban Americans generally hold higher levels of love for and pride in the United States, and a higher percentage believe that government is run for the benefit of all (de la Garza et al. 1992). Still other studies show that, over time, as Latinos are further removed from the immigrant experience and become more acculturated, their affect toward immigrants and support for policies perceived to benefit immigrants declines (Miller, Polinard, and Wrinkle 1984; Branton 2007). Our knowledge of Latino attitudes and orientation toward the system thus reflects the complexity of studying a group that includes multiple national origins and several generations of respondents, from new arrivals to second-, third- and fourth-generation respondents.

Perhaps more revealing than a within-Latino comparison is one drawn between Latinos and non-Latinos. In a study comparing support for economic individualism and patriotism between Mexican Americans and Anglos, de la Garza, Falcon, and García reported that "ethnic consciousness is statistically unrelated to economic individualism" (1996, 346). In the same study, Mexican Americans, specifically those measured as the "least acculturated" to the United States (native-born Spanish-dominant speakers and foreign-born Spanish-dominant speakers) were found to be statistically more patriotic than Anglos (de la Garza, Falcon, and García 1996, 347). The researchers reasoned that Mexican immigrants came to the United States looking for jobs and without expectations of the U.S. government providing services. In the case of patriotism, the authors cited works documenting the emotional experience of the naturalization process as a possible mechanism for higher levels of patriotism.

That research, however, was conducted at a time when the total Hispanic population was about half its current size and before the height of the recent policy changes we noted at the outset. More recently, a number of scholars have used newly collected survey data to specifically examine the behavioral effects of polices targeting Latinos in the 1990s. For instance, a rather large body of work details the effect of ballot initiatives, particularly those in California, that are perceived as targeting Latinos (Alvarez and Butterfield 2000). These studies show that the initiatives created a palpable sense of political threat among the Latino population, with clear—and potentially politically important—results. The initiatives increased political awareness and information among Latinos (Pantoja and Segura 2003; Ramakrishnan 2005) and contributed to Latino political mobilization (Barreto 2005; Bowler, Nicholson, and Segura 2006; Pantoja, Ramírez, and Segura 2001). Hostile policy proposals in the legislative or electoral arena are at least partially responsible for changes in levels of mobilization and information among Latinos. Whether there are *attitudinal* implications is another matter entirely.

While the changed political environment appears to have had mobilization effects, it is less clear whether it has affected how Latinos see their government. Hero and Tolbert (2005) suggest that as far as Latino political efficacy is concerned, the implications are limited. They examine the impact of direct democracy on political efficacy and find that blacks and Asian Americans indicate less confidence in government responsiveness than whites and Latinos. Even though Latinos are the most frequent "losers" in the California initiative process, they appear to have similar confidence in government to that of white non-Hispanics (Hero and Tolbert 2005, 183).

In summary, earlier work examined Latino attitudinal orientation toward the political system, but much has changed since those findings entered the literature. More recently, a variety of studies on the increasingly hostile political environment finds that the initiative process had a meaningful impact on Latino political behavior, specifically regarding information acquisition and voter registration and turnout. Its effect on attitudes is still an open question.

THE 2006 IMMIGRATION MARCHES

Latinos form a large and growing share of the U.S. population. If such a large and growing share of the population grows disaffected from politics and the representative process, this raises the potential for serious problems for the political system as a whole. It is plausible to suppose that Latinos will have distinctly lower regard for the current political system, especially in the midst of a particularly polemical immigration debate. We would expect that more recent immigrants would have lower regard for politics still.

The implications of low efficacy and satisfaction in government range from the mundane to the profound. On the one hand, low efficacy and high alienation are very likely to result in lower overall levels of political interest and engagement in traditional forms of political behavior such as voting. More seriously, a lack of faith in political institutions may encourage activity in opposition to the system and increase atypical and/or extraordinary acts of political participation, including boycotts, marches, strikes, and even political violence.

Understood through this lens, the immigration marches of 2006 may, not be seen so much a "one-off" event, but as the first example of a series of events that are a direct consequence of declining Latino support for representative institutions. How respondents see these marches, we believe, will provide insight into how they see the political process as a whole. If the preceding argument is correct, the marches may represent large-scale disenchantment with the political system and an extraordinary form of political participation designed to signal dissatisfaction.

On the other hand, participation in the marches and positive evaluations of the marches' subsequent impact may instead be a reflection of *faith* in the political system rather than disillusionment. More specifically, though Latinos generally and immigrants in particular likely find considerable cause for concern with the outputs of the political system, the act of attending a march and the accompanying belief that public demonstrations will affect policy outcomes presupposes a level of individual or group efficacy and a belief in the ultimate responsiveness in the political system. If respondents believed that the system and outcomes are beyond influence, and/or have a poor opinion of their own agency and empowerment, there would be little reason to take notice in the first place. Attitudes toward the marches may thus reflect one of two directly opposed interpretations: attitudes could be (1) an expression of resentment toward the political system or(2) an affirmation of belief in it. In the next sections we use public opinion data to examine which of these views is more accurate.

ANALYSIS

The Pew survey asked Latino respondents three questions that allow us to situate the marches in the wider political process and within a broader understanding of how Latinos view the political system. Respondents were asked to choose a viewpoint that most accurately reflected their own and to assess their likelihood of participating in future actions. These three questions were:

1) Which comes closest to your views: The immigrant marches are the beginning of a new Latino social movement that will go on for a long time; or, the immigrant marches were a one time event which will not necessarily be repeated?

2) Some people say that as a result of the debate over immigration policy in Washington, many more (Hispanics/Latinos) will vote in the November elections. Others say that the debate will not have much effect on political participation by (Hispanics/Latinos). Which comes closer to your views?

3) If there was going to be another of these marches in your home town this weekend, would you participate or not?

What is especially useful about these questions is that they assess orientations toward the political process in relation to concrete examples of political action and issues—the marches and immigration debate. They do not ask whether a respondent supports or opposes the marches. Instead, they ask the respondent to place the marches in the wider political process: whether the marches will be useful in the policy advocacy process, what the marches mean to the actors themselves, and whether the entire issue has motivated future participation. In looking to see what drives attitudes on these three questions we can see whether Latino respondents are motivated more by their frustration and possible alienation from the political system or, instead, are motivated more by their belief in the efficacy of political action.

We use standard statistical models to explain the variation in responses to the three questions. Responses to the three questions above become our dependent variables and our statistical models estimate the impact of factors that shape responses to those questions. First, our major items of concern are an individual's sense of alienation from the political system and that individual's sense of efficacy. These measures of efficacy and alienation tap into how an individual respondent sees herself in relation to the system. We expect that these views are related to, but distinct from, the first two outcomes we seek to explain, namely, how the individual perceives the impact of the marches and of the immigration debate on Latino *collective* efficacy. While individuals of Latin American ancestry make up the collective group we call Hispanics/Latinos, their sense of personal efficacy is not the same as their beliefs regarding the efficacy of the group. We can show

TABLE 12.1 Summary Statistics of Latino Evaluations of the 2006 Immigration Marches
and Correlated Attitudes

Dependent Variables		Sample Distribution (%)
Marches as social movement	1=Rallies are beginning of new Latino social movement	73
	0=Otherwise	27
Impact on Latino vote	1=More Latinos will vote	81
	0=Otherwise	19
Participate in future march	1=Will march	56
	0=Otherwise	44
Key Explanatory Variables		
Political alienation: "Political leaders do not care much what people like me think."	5=Agree strongly	35
	4=Agree somewhat	23
	3=Don't know	6
	2=Disagree somewhat	19
	1=Disagree strongly	18
Political efficacy: "In the United States, citizens can have an influence . . . by voting and engaging in other political activities."	5=Agree strongly	51
	4=Agree somewhat	27
	3=Don't know	7
	2=Disagree somewhat	7
	1=Disagree strongly	8

SOURCE: Suro and Escobar 2006b.

this by looking at descriptive data for the variables. Frequency distributions for the three outcome variables along with the two key explanatory variables, efficacy and alienation, are shown in table 12.1.

Second, to capture the consequences of contestation over Latinos and their place in society, we include respondents' attitudes on immigrants, perception of discrimination against Latinos, and dimensions of their self-identification—specifically, whether the respondents see themselves as a nationality-specific ethnic, use a panethnic identifier, or see themselves as "American." Compared to those who prefer to self-identify first as American, we expect those who see themselves as Latino or as a nationality-specific ethnic as more likely to view the marches as a social movement and to say they will march in the future. Third, the marches and surrounding issues plainly engaged some respondents as stakeholders in the debate. To capture the importance of having something personally at stake, we control for a number of demographic dimensions, including nativity, citizenship status, national origin group, and language use, which we measure using a five-point scale based on the language of interview (and which includes the possibility of using both English and Spanish). By including measures of perceived discrimination, nativity, identity, and language use, we can test whether the immigration policy debate had different impacts on various segments of the population, a possibility suggested in the literature described earlier and also explored by Suro in this volume.

We also include a measure for reliance upon Spanish-language radio news.[4] The role of Spanish-language radio in the mobilization efforts behind the marches has received considerable journalistic discussion, and we can test whether this effect carries over to how respondents perceive these marches. Though related, reliance on Spanish-language radio is conceptually distinct from the language of the interview; their bivariate correlation is sufficiently low to allay concerns that the estimated impact of one is confounded by its association with the other. [5] If the marches are associated with a particular orientation to the political system, it is important to understand how the means of political communication facilitates these views.[6]

All three dependent variables measure respondents' dichotomous evaluations of the marches and their impacts, with higher values indicating more positive assessments. Since the sample frame is entirely Latino and the sample size is $n = 2,000$, this allows us to reliably compare Latinos across a variety of demographic measures. Given dichotomous dependent variables, we use logistic regression in our statistical modeling. The statistical models estimate changes in probability of an individual holding a given opinion in light of a series of factors. In particular, the models allow us to see the effects of disillusionment with the political system upon attitudes toward the marches. We report summary results of the models in table 12.2 and identify factors statistically meaningful to each dependent variable, holding all other variables in the model constant. Readers interested in the detailed model results should turn to table 12.A in this chapter's appendix.

While the results and the models themselves are discussed more fully below, figures 12.1–12.3 summarize the changes in the predicted probabilities in the dependent variable given a full range of change in an independent variable, holding all other variables in the model constant. The bar charts in figures 12.1–12.3 are an easy way to see the estimated impact of a variable and compare that with the estimated impact for other statistically meaningful variables within each model.

Marches as a Social Movement

In the first column of table 12.2, we report results from our logistic regression, estimating the effects of each of the predictor variables on the propensity that respondents view the marches as the beginning of a social movement. The effects of specific interest—reported as changes in predicted probabilities moving from minimum to maximum values of each factor while holding all other predictors constant—are shown in figure 12.1.[7]

TABLE 12.2   Logit Models of Determinants of Latino Attitudes concerning the 2006 Immigration Marches

	Marches as Social Movement		Impact on Latino Vote		Participate in Future March	
Political efficacy	NS		+	***	NS	
Political alienation	−	*	NS		+	*
News from Spanish radio	+	**	+	***	+	***
Republican	−	***	NS		+	*
Registered to vote	NS		+	†	+	**
U.S.-born	+	*	NS		−	*
Naturalized	NS		−	†	−	*
Survey language	NS		NS		+	**
Immigrants help U.S. economy	+	*	+	***	+	***
Discrimination against Latinos	+	***	NS		+	***
Latino ID preferred	NS		NS		+	**
Country of origin ID preferred	+	*	NS		+	**
Mexican	NS		NS		+	*
Cuban	NS		−	*	−	***
Puerto Rican	NS		NS		NS	
Female	NS		NS		−	*
Age	NS		+	**	−	***
Education	NS		NS		NS	
Homeownership	NS		NS		−	*
Constant	NS		−	†	−	*
Percent predicted correctly	74.3	74.3	81.6	81.6	72.1	
PRE (proportional reduction in error) tau-c	0.348	0.348	0.386	0.386	0.426	
Observations	1,500	1,500	1,580	1,580	1,589	

SOURCE: Suro and Escobar 2006b.

NOTE: Two-tailed significance testing: † $p \leq 0.10$; * $p \leq 0.05$; ** $p \leq 0.01$. *** $p \leq 0.001$; NS indicates not statistically significant at levels indicated above.

In terms of our main concern, the coefficient for *political alienation* is negative and statistically significant. This suggests that, rather than understanding the 2006 marches as an expression of alienation from the system, more politically alienated respondents are *less* likely to view the marches as likely to have a meaningful impact (that is, the marches are less likely to be seen as an emerging social movement). Looking at figure 12.1, we see that our model predicts a 0.07 decrease in the probability that a respondent sees the marches as the start of a social movement when you move from those with the lowest value (1) of political alienation to the highest (5). The measure of *political efficacy* does not, however, obtain significance, but the result suggests that the marches are not viewed as a spasm of system opposition.

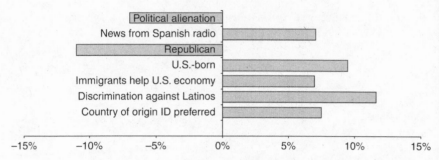

FIGURE 12.1. Estimated effects of variables of interest (from min to max values) on the probability that respondent views marches as the beginning of a social movement.

Spanish-language radio has been identified in other chapters of this volume as an important tool of mobilization, and our finding that Spanish-radio listeners hold more positive assessments of the impact of the marches is consistent with that observation. Further, U.S.-born Latinos express more optimism about the likely development of a social movement compared to foreign-born Latinos, a 0.09 estimated difference. Finally, respondents that perceive discrimination against Latinos and those who prefer to identify with their national ancestry or country of origin are more likely to view the marches as a social movement.

Anticipated Impact on Latino Vote

In the second column of table 12.2, we report estimates of our model on perceptions regarding the effects of the immigration debate on the propensity of Latinos to vote. For simplicity and the sake of comparison, we use the identical model specification as before. In general, our predictors perform modestly in mapping out the variation in respondents' perceptions of the *impact on Latino vote.*[8]

Looking at our two key predictors, *political efficacy* is both a positive and highly significant predictor of a respondent's view of the immigration debate's impact on future Latino voter turnout, while *political alienation* has no effect. Changes in predicted probabilities, illustrated in figure 12.2, show a 0.11 increase in the probability that a respondent will see the immigration debate as increasing future Latino voter turnout when going from the lowest to the highest value of *political efficacy.*

We also see that *Spanish-radio* consumption correlates positively with the view that the immigration debate will result in a higher turnout among Latino voters. The connection of Spanish radio to the mobilization efforts suggests that listeners were stimulated to take action in the immigration marches. Figure 12.2 shows that the remaining results are modest in effect. Respondents with positive assessments of immigration, as well as older respondents, are more likely

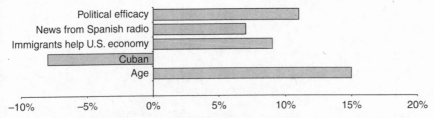

FIGURE 12.2. Estimated effects of variables of interest (from min to max values) on the probability that respondent views immigration debate as positively affecting Latino voter turnout.

to expect greater voter mobilization, while Cuban Americans are less likely to expect this.

Participate in a Future March

The Pew survey affords us the opportunity to explore respondents' interest in participating in future marches. Since the survey was taken in the wake of a previous wave of large and highly visible marches nationwide, participation in future efforts may, in fact, reflect a judgment regarding the efficacy of the past actions. With that in mind, our expectations with regard to the effects of alienation and efficacy are less clear.

We again use the same model specification to estimate a logit model of respondents' attitudes toward participation in future marches. The results are presented in the third column of table 12.2. In some respects, this model performs better than both of the previous estimations because many more of our predictor variables reach conventional levels of significance.[9]

Although the coefficient for *political alienation* is meaningful for predicting whether respondents would participate in a future march, we are surprised to see that the direction is positive, indicating that more politically alienated Latinos are more likely to participate in a march. The corresponding figure in figure 12.3 indicates a 0.08 increase in the predicted probability of expressing interest in joining a future march, going from the lowest to the highest value of *political alienation*.

At first glance, this result is less consistent with the claim that the 2006 marches are not necessarily an expression of system opposition. If participation in a march is more likely among those alienated from the political system, a more conventional "antisystem sentiment" explanation would appear to be in order. We believe, however, that such a conclusion would misunderstand the circumstances in which respondents are making this decision. In the wake of highly visible and extraordinarily large direct action, like the marches in the spring of 2006, respondents indicating a desire to march again are skeptics regarding the efficacy of the first actions. That is, we need not necessarily assume that those

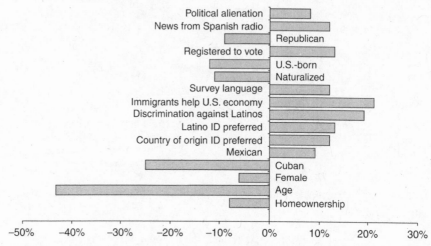

FIGURE 12.3. Estimated effects of variables of interest (from min to max values) on the probability that respondent expresses interest in participating in a future march.

interested in marching in the summer of 2006 are the same as those who actually took to the streets that spring. Rather, respondents less persuaded in the responsiveness of the system will underrate the importance of the earlier actions and, conceivably, believe more action is necessary.

Listening to Spanish radio has again the expected effect. Respondents who report getting some or all of their news from Spanish radio are more likely than those who get their news from other sources (or in English) to express interest in joining a future march. The mobilization effects of Spanish radio appear to have been long lasting, even into the summer after the marches.

An interesting set of differences can be identified regarding nativity and naturalization. According to figure 12.3, respondents that are *U.S.-born* are 12 percent less likely than their foreign-born counterparts to express interest in participating in a future march. Similarly, the relationship for *naturalized* respondents is negative and significant, suggesting that foreign-born respondents with citizenship are 11 percent less likely to express interest in marching in a future protest. By extension, it is the unexpressed category—foreign-born noncitizens—who express the greatest interest in joining a future march, an alternative mode of participation for those who cannot vote.

Those of Cuban background are again less likely to view the marches positively, in this case expressing less interest in participating, while Mexicans are more interested. The distinctive views of Cuban Americans—even after controlling for Republican partisanship—may be a consequence of differences in experience with immigration laws. Women, older voters, Republicans, and homeowners have less interest in future marches. By contrast, those interviewed in Spanish who hold a positive view of immigrants, who perceive anti-Latino discrimination, or who still cling to national origin expressions of identity are more likely to want to march.

CONCLUSION

In this chapter we have sought to use Latino attitudes toward the 2006 immigration marches as a window into Latino attitudes toward the political system more generally. Seen against the backdrop of a series of policy measures and debates, the marches could easily be understood as an expression of alienation and frustration. Yet the marches do not appear to reflect a broad-based Latino expression of system opposition. Rather, views of the marches reflect largely positive orientations to the political system. A sense of efficacy is positively associated with the belief that the immigration debate will mobilize the Latino electorate. Viewed in these terms, then, the marches reflect a confidence in American democracy rather than hopelessness or opposition. But there is some evidence that the marches did represent frustration and not simply optimism. Our third finding is that a desire to "march again" may, in fact, be more a reflection of frustration than confidence; though, coming in the wake of the previous wave of visible actions, interpretation of this desire is somewhat complex.

Nevertheless, from the point of view of the system as a whole, there are grounds for optimism. Immigrants see value in both the U.S. political system and the efficacy of political participation within the United States, at least at some stage in their life cycle as residents and citizens of the United States. This optimism among immigrants is also seen in a growing body of other evidence (e.g., Branton 2007; Michelson 2001, 2003).

This kind of optimism raises two questions. First, where does it come from? Why do immigrants have a rosier view of politics than the U.S.-born? Second, what happens to optimism once immigrants arrive? For some scholars, immigration is a process of self-selection that makes immigrants have more positive views of their new home: immigrants choose the system, which makes them more supportive of it. One consequence is that the large number of foreign-born within the Latino community results in Latinos being, on average, more trusting of government (Abrajano and Alvarez n.d.). The argument of self-selection is not entirely satisfactory, however. It does not fit easily with relatively low levels of political passivity of many immigrants (Ramakrishnan 2005). Nor, except for political refugees, does it accord well with the motives for immigration. Many immigrants are like people the world over—they have little concern for politics but a great concern for jobs and families. Perhaps a simpler explanation is that, despite its flaws, for many immigrants the United States offers an objectively more democratic and markedly less corrupt political system than that in their countries of origin. It is not surprising, then, that immigrants tend to see the U.S. political system in quite positive terms.

While academics still debate why immigrants may be more positive about the political system than those born in the country, there is greater consensus over what happens to that optimism: it becomes corroded by actual experience in the United States (e.g., Branton 2007; Michelson 2001, 2003; Abrajano and Alvarez n.d.). Acculturation seems to bring with it disappointment.

This point brings us back to the marches and their fallout. Our argument is that the marches need not be seen as unique and one-time events. Rather they help us understand how Latinos see and interact with the political system more broadly. In that sense, one of the important consequences of the marches will be their effect on the opinions of participants in the years ahead. Will participation in the marches itself be an act that shapes attitudes? Some of our evidence, relating to future participation, suggests that disappointment with the consequences of the marches could lead to wider disappointment in the system. The marchers' demands were not met (and still are not, as of this writing) and, if anything, the strategic circumstances of immigrants and their advocates worsened after spring 2006. Comprehensive immigration reform legislation in the summer of 2006 foundered on anti-immigrant sentiment in the ruling party. Attempts to resurrect an immigration package similarly failed a year later after Democrats took control of the legislative branch. During that same period, the administration expanded Immigration and Customs Enforcement efforts, specifically engaging in high-profile workplace raids, the newer practices of raiding homes, and the controversial policy of enlisting local police in enforcement actions. The expansion of these actions, coupled with the legislative setbacks, almost certainly has the effect of enhancing a climate of threat and fear for immigrants, and for Latinos in particular.

As we have discussed in this chapter, the increasing hostility of the social and political climate might lead one to believe that Latinos would hold pessimistic views of American political institutions and their role in the system, perhaps justifying a shift toward nonparticipation. Yet, the elections of 2006 and 2008 witnessed a *growth* in the number of Latino voters and their importance in the presidential contest. During the immigration rallies many Latino participants held signs that read, "Today we march, tomorrow we vote," leaving many observers to wonder whether such widespread participation in the rallies would lead to a surge in electoral participation among immigrants in general, and among Latinos in particular. No surge occurred in the 2006 midterm election, but the number of Latino voters did increase from 2002 by 800,000 (according to the Census Bureau's 2006 Current Population Survey), keeping pace with the relative growth of the electorate seen for Anglos and African Americans (Leal et al. 2008).

Additionally, Latinos increased their share of the electorate to 9 percent in the general election of 2008, up from 8 percent in 2004. According to CNN exit polls, the share of Latino voters saw an even larger increase in New Mexico (+9 percent), Colorado (+5 percent), and Nevada (+5 percent), states with sizable Latino populations that participated heavily in the immigration rallies of 2006. Rather than reflecting a deep-felt pessimism with American political institutions, we believe these electoral performances (and outcomes, since in all three Latinos moved from Republican to Democrat) square neatly with our conclusion that widespread participation in the rallies reflected faith in the ability of the political system to respond to changing circumstances and claims for redress. Consistent with previous work documenting responses to Proposition 187 (in California) and related measures, Latinos have responded to this adversity with engagement, not withdrawal. In seeing the 2006 immigration marches against a wider picture of political participation by new Americans, this is surely grounds for cautious optimism about the prospects for political incorporation.

APPENDIX

TABLE 12.A Estimated Effects of Variables of Interest on Latino Attitudes concerning the 2006 Immigration Marches

	Marches as Social Movement	Impact on Latino Vote	Participate in Future March
Political efficacy	0.0207 (0.05)	0.1720 *** (0.05)	0.0731 (0.05)
Political alienation	−0.1001 * (0.04)	−0.0068 (0.04)	0.0807 * (0.04)
News from Spanish radio	0.3478 ** (0.13)	0.5342 *** (0.15)	0.5190 *** (0.12)
Republican	−0.5186 *** (0.15)	−0.1005 (0.18)	−0.3585 * (0.16)
Registered to vote	−0.0197 (0.22)	0.3721 † (0.22)	0.5595 ** (0.20)
U.S.-born	0.5227 * (0.19)	0.0277 (0.26)	−0.5003 * (0.23)
Naturalized	0.1307 (0.23)	−0.1711 † (0.24)	−0.4478 * (0.21)
Survey language	0.0681 (0.05)	0.0482 (0.05)	0.1254 ** (0.05)
Immigrants help U.S. economy	0.3448 * (0.14)	0.5716 *** (0.15)	0.8594 *** (0.14)
Discrimination against Latinos	0.2855 *** (0.08)	0.1495 (0.09)	0.3802 *** (0.08)

(continued)

TABLE 12.A *(continued)*

	Marches as Social Movement	Impact on Latino Vote	Participate in Future March
Latino ID preferred	0.2340	0.0554	0.5688 **
	(0.19)	(0.21)	(0.18)
Country of origin ID preferred	0.3882 *	0.1353	0.5143 **
	(0.17)	(0.19)	(0.17)
Mexican	0.1253	−0.0052	0.3752 *
	(0.18)	(0.19)	(0.17)
Cuban	−0.1732	−0.4778 *	−1.0092 ***
	(0.21)	(0.24)	(0.23)
Puerto Rican	−0.0347	−0.0950	0.0668
	(0.19)	(0.21)	(0.18)
Female	−0.0503	−0.2040	−0.2441 *
	(0.13)	(0.14)	(0.12)
Age	−0.0055	0.0161 **	−0.0245 ***
	(0.00)	(0.01)	(0.00)
Education	−0.0658	−0.0316	−0.0922
	(0.06)	(0.07)	(0.06)
Homeownership	−0.0128	−0.0113	−0.3238 *
	(0.14)	(0.16)	(0.13)
Constant	0.2158	−0.8459 †	−1.0713 *
	(0.45)	(0.50)	(0.44)
Percent predicted correctly	74.3	81.6	72.1
PRE tau-c	0.348	0.386	0.426
Observations	1,500	1,580	1,589

SOURCE: Suro and Escobar 2006b.

NOTE: Two-tailed significance testing: † $p \leq 0.10$; * $p \leq 0.05$; $p \leq 0.01$. *** Statistically significant at $p \leq 0.001$. Figures in parentheses are standard errors.

NOTES

An earlier version of this chapter was delivered at the conference "The Immigration Protests of 2006," Institute for Industrial Relations, University of California, Berkeley, April 20, 2007.

1. See also the concluding remarks by Fox and Bada (this volume) for a contrast between the civicness of the 2006 immigration rallies and the 1992 L.A. race riots that were interpreted as system opposition.

2. Our argument that Latino participation was not motivated by system opposition but was inspired by positive orientations fits nicely with the observation highlighted by Suro (this volume) that resentment, anger, and violence were absent from the marches. Similarly, Bloemraad and Trost (this volume) point out that adults marched with their children and that many interviewees reported their march experience to be "positive and empowering."

3. For analysis of general public attitudes toward the marches see DeSipio (this volume).

4. For additional analyses on the role of Spanish-language radio in the immigration rallies, see the chapter by Ramírez that examines how non-English-language communications can enhance

participation, the chapter by Wang and Winn addressing the working relationship between activists and radio DJs, and the chapter by Fox and Bada situating Spanish-language radio as a component of migrant civil society, all in this volume.

5. A majority, 75 percent, of Latinos in the Pew 2006 survey completed the survey only in Spanish, while 21 percent completed it only in English. Some 4 percent of Latinos interviewed used one or the other language more or less equally. Tabulations between survey language and Spanish-language radio news reveals that two-thirds of those completing the interview only in Spanish did not rely on Spanish-language radio news. A test of correlation between survey language and reliance on Spanish-language news radio using Pearson's r reveals a coefficient of 0.29, suggesting a weak linear relationship between the two variables.

6. We also control for the usual factors of party identification, voter registration, and socioeconomic status.

7. Overall, the model performs well, with a Goodman-Kruskal tau-c of 0.348 and 74.3 percent of the cases predicted correctly.

8. Overall, the model does well, with a Goodman-Kruskal tau-c of 0.386 and 81.6 percent of the cases predicted correctly.

9. In addition, the model's fit is strong, with a Goodman-Kruskal tau-c of 0.426 and 72.1 percent of the cases predicted correctly.

13

Out of the Shadows, into the Light

Questions Raised by the Spring of 2006

Roberto Suro

"White T-shirts."

"Children everywhere."

Scrawled in a notebook I carried to the immigrant march on the National Mall in Washington DC on April 10, 2006, those notes remain lasting impressions of that extraordinary spring. They are clues for deciphering what happened then and for understanding what those events tell us about a nation that is coming to terms with a new wave of immigration.

The immigrant rights marches of 2006 were an unprecedented public mobilization in their size and character, but their lasting impact is not to be found through the measures usually applied to social movements: policies changed, candidates elected, organizations formed, and so on. The marches originated outside of formal political processes, as many other social movements have, but the participants have remained largely disengaged from those processes. We have to look elsewhere for the marches' ongoing significance, and, as this volume shows, many approaches are available.

My approach is to see the marches as a vivid public display of attitudes rarely expressed beyond Latino households and communities. From this perspective, the spring of 2006 offers a valuable window into powerfully felt sentiments in the Latino population that were developing before the marches and that have a long trajectory still to run. The marches gain added meaning, then, as an extraordinary means of communication. While the messages emerged from long trends, the medium seems unique to that historical moment. Examining both what the marchers were saying and how they expressed themselves is essential to understanding how the large and growing Latino population relates to American society as a whole.

The demographic, social, and political forces that produced the immigrant marches developed over decades, and the momentum will carry forward for decades to come. The extraordinary events of the spring of 2006 can be read in a broad context, but first we have to go back to the events themselves. I return to those two lasting impressions.

White T-shirts. Once the word spread, white T-shirts became the emblematic uniform of the marches. America's *descamisados* found a wardrobe in the absence of adornment, in the simplest of garments. White is the color of light. And through the marches, people turned the light on themselves. They showed themselves. People who live in the shadows came out into the light, a light they cast on themselves.

Children. Who brings children to a protest? The marchers came with children as if they were on an outing—children on their shoulders, in strollers. Instead of marches, you could have called these events the immigrant promenades.

With children in tow and wearing white, it is difficult to be angry, it is difficult to be confrontational, it is difficult to provoke. The mood was calm, sometimes almost festive, buoyant and affirmative. I compare these marches to protests that I have witnessed, the antiglobalization marches of recent years, or the antiwar marches of the Vietnam era, or the open-housing marches in Chicago in the early 1970s. The contrasts overwhelm the comparisons. There was no fear or hostility in the immigration marches, no sense of friction, and no sense of confrontation. I compare the 2006 marches to others that have involved a similar population group. I think of the student walkouts in Los Angeles called to protest Proposition 187. Those were acts of rebellion and indignation. I compare them to some of the early Justice for Janitor marches in Los Angeles in the mid-1990s. Those were loud events—people banged on water-cooler bottles. The protestors wore red, not white.

The immigrant spring of 2006 seemingly produced a new species. Given the mood—the absence of stridency or anger—you could hardly call them protests. The proper label for this new species comes from Spanish. They were literally *manifestaciones*. People manifested themselves. They rendered themselves visible. They did not have to say anything. They only had to be there, in the agora, in the space of civic dialogue. By simply appearing, and especially because they appeared with their children, they made an existential statement, powerful for its simplicity: "We are here. We are human, flesh and blood, parents and children."

And then there was the other message, "We are many." That was the message of the numbers: 500,000 here, 300,000 there, 100,000 in places where no such numbers were known to exist; numbers baffling to everyone including the organizers of the marches. Both the participants and potential beneficiaries of the marches—immigrant Latinos, especially those here without authorization—are a population with no prior history of mass public demonstrations or other forms of political activity organized on a national or even a metropolitan basis. But in the spring of 2006 they came forward with their families, friends, and allies.

From March 10 to May 1, 2006, a span of just eight weeks, marches occurred in at least 120 cites involving more than 3.5 million people, according to estimates by the Mexico Institute at the Woodrow Wilson International Center for Scholars (Bada, Fox, and Selee 2006). Given its brief duration, its geographic span, and the number of people who participated, this was perhaps the most intense and concentrated political mobilization in American history. But then it ended. Despite repeated efforts by some organizers, significant numbers of immigrant marchers never assembled again. Indeed, when new marches were called in September 2006 and then again in May 2007, the numbers were paltry by comparison.

And so was it a spring lightning storm? A very brief, very dramatic, atmospheric disturbance that came and went?

As noted in the introduction to this volume, specific developments in the immigration policy debate provided the immediate catalyst for the marches. But then the policy debate continued, and the marches did not. Moreover, the marches did not produce a clear agenda regarding immigration policy—organizers differed on key questions, such as how much compromise on the terms of a legalization program was acceptable. Though events in Washington DC were a significant stimulus, one has to look elsewhere, to broader developments, both to understand why the marches occurred and to assess their long-term impact.

Public opinion surveys conducted by the Pew Hispanic Center suggest that the marches reflected long-standing perceptions that discrimination is a problem for Latinos, perceptions that were heightened by the immigration policy debate.[1] Other data from the same surveys point to a growing sense of ethnic solidarity among Latinos, which was also seemingly enhanced both by the marches and the sometimes harsh anti-immigrant rhetoric that accompanied the policy debate. In light of these findings, the marches can be read as demonstrations of deep-seated feelings that had been building over time and that were prompted to move into the public arena by the policy debate and by the organizers and promoters of the marches. This reading emphasizes an element of communal protest, and in taking that approach it is important to remember the white T-shirts and children: the crowds manifested little anger or threat; they simply made their point by making their presence known. The atmosphere of the marches, then, powerfully illuminates the nonconfrontational character of the way Latinos perceived discrimination.

The Pew Hispanic Center surveys show that the proportion of Latinos who think that discrimination is preventing Latinos from succeeding in America has

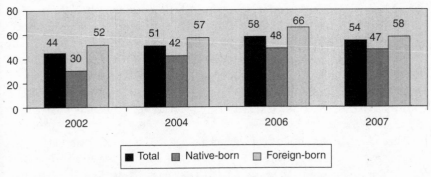

FIGURE 13.1. Percentage of Latinos who believe that discrimination is a major problem for Hispanics, by nativity. Early in the surveys, respondents were asked if they had a preference in the use of the terms *Hispanic* or *Latino,* and all subsequent references to these terms in the interviews reflected those preferences. Sources: Pew Hispanic Center/ Kaiser Family Foundation, *2002 National Survey of Latinos*; Pew Hispanic Center/Kaiser Family Foundation, *2004 National Survey of Latinos*; Pew Hispanic Center, *2006 National Survey of Latinos*; Pew Hispanic Center, *2007 National Survey of Latinos.*

been rising gradually in recent years, peaking in a survey taken shortly after the marches and then receding slightly in 2007 (see figure 13.1). Four surveys between 2002 and 2007 posed the question, "In general, do you think discrimination against (Hispanics/Latinos) is a major problem, a minor problem or not a problem in preventing (Hispanics/Latinos in general from succeeding in America?"[2] The rising perception of discrimination is most noticeable among the foreign-born. The share of immigrant Latinos who think that discrimination is a "major problem" stood at 52 percent in June 2002, when the first survey in the series was fielded. In the 2006 survey, conducted in the immediate aftermath of the marches, 66 percent of foreign-born Latinos responded the same way. A year later the response was 58 percent. Though the differences in responses among the native-born are somewhat smaller from one survey to another, the same basic trend is evident.

Overall, the surveys show a widespread and ongoing perception of discrimination in the Hispanic population. In all of the surveys, substantial numbers of Hispanics also picked the response "minor problem," so that no more than a fifth of the respondents in any of the four surveys said discrimination was "not a problem."

Other evidence from the 2006 Pew survey, which was conducted between June 5 and July 3, suggests that the events that spring could have contributed both to the breadth and the intensity of perceptions of discrimination among Latinos. All of the respondents who saw discrimination as either a major or a minor problem were then asked a follow up question: whether the immigration debate had worsened this discrimination. A little more than half (54 percent) responded that it had. So, the marches occurred at a time when a sense of grievance among large numbers of Latinos was particularly acute and was specifically linked to the matter of immigration policy. Given that widespread perceptions of discrimination predated the spring of 2006, it is clear that the events of that time period did not create these attitudes. But the policy debate appears to have heightened those feelings, and the marches offered a means of expressing them collectively and in public.

Moreover, the perception that the debate had had a negative impact on discrimination was shared equally by a majority of Latinos, regardless of gender, age, education, income, religious preference, or party affiliation. This held true regardless of whether Hispanics lacked a high school diploma or had a college degree or higher; whether they earned $30,000 or less or $50,000 or more. Examining responses by generation showed that Latinos far removed from the immigrant experience in their family histories perceived the debate as a source of greater discrimination every bit as much as the most recent arrivals. Among the first generation (the foreign-born), 51 percent saw more discrimination flowing from the immigration debate, compared with 47 percent of the second generation (the U.S.-born children of immigrant parents) and 60 percent of the third-plus generations (the U.S.-born children of U.S.-born parents). There is no statistically significant difference in those responses.

This constitutes a remarkably uniform response to a circumstance—the immigration policy debate—which ostensibly should have had different impacts on various segments of the population. Foreign-born Latinos obviously had a direct stake in the outcome of the deliberations in Washington DC, while native-born Latinos would not have been personally affected by the legislation in any manner, and for those in the third-plus generations the effects on family members would have been remote. Nonetheless, they all reacted similarly.

In the years after the marches, circumstances changed but many Latinos continued to see peril in U.S. immigration policies. Starting in mid-2006, federal authorities stepped up the pace of high-profile workplace raids designed to capture and deport unauthorized foreign-born laborers. Two years later, following a series of such enforcement actions, a Pew Hispanic Center survey found that a majority of all Latinos worry about deportation. Of course, the feeling was more widespread among the foreign-born, with nearly three-quarters (72 percent) expressing "some" or "a lot" of worry that they, a family member, or a close friend might face deportation. Interestingly, more than a third (35 percent) of native-born Hispanics offered the same views (Lopez and Minushkin 2008b).

In response to the crackdown, leaders of well-established Latino civil rights organizations like the National Council of La Raza (NCLR), which were not in the forefront of organizing the marches, increasingly posed the plight of undocumented migrants as a broader crisis for all Hispanics. For example, in her address to the NCLR annual convention in July 2008, Janet Murguía, president of the organization, said regarding the raids, "Our nation's immigration laws need to be enforced. But, what is happening today with these raids is an assault on civil rights, common decency and basic human dignity." And, decrying what she termed as hate speech about illegal immigrants, Murguía said, "Make no mistake. This is about all of us" (National Council of La Raza 2008).

Survey data collected by the Pew Hispanic Center over several years indicates a growing sense among Latinos that they share a common identity that arcs across differences in country of origin, social and economic status, language preferences, and citizenship or immigration status. Prompted by developments in the immigration debate, the 2006 marches offered an opportunity for the public expression of this still-developing identity.

This line of analysis has to start from a recognition that, while Latinos are often viewed as a single group by non-Latinos, among Latinos the perception of differences is at least as great or greater than the perception of commonalities. In other words, while it is common for journalists, policy makers, and ordinary citizens to see Hispanics as a single population, Hispanics see a lot of differences among themselves. The survey data, however, suggests that these views have been changing over time.

In the 2006 Pew survey, for example, the number of Latinos who said that Hispanics from different countries of origin were working together to achieve common political goals (58 percent) was strikingly higher than when the same question was asked in a 2002 survey (43 percent). And the biggest change was evident among the foreign-born: 62 percent versus 42 percent. (See figure 13.2.)

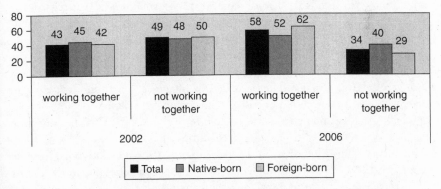

FIGURE 13.2. Percentage of Latinos who believe that Hispanics are working together toward common political goals, by nativity. Sources: Pew Hispanic Center/Kaiser Family Foundation, 2002 *National Survey of Latinos*; Pew Hispanic Center, 2006 *National Survey of Latinos*.

Another major survey, the 2006 Latino National Survey, conducted by a team of scholars from several major universities, also found a rising level of common identity. Probing the use of the labels *Hispanic* and *Latino* and measuring the strength of different panethnic identities rather than association with country of origin or the United States, the survey team concluded that expressions of an overarching identity had more than doubled since a similar survey was conducted in 1989.[3]

A growing sense of common identity could be relevant to understanding the marches in a number of ways. A greater sense of solidarity across the whole of the Hispanic population could help explain a willingness to mobilize on behalf of that portion of the population most affected by the immigration policy debate: the foreign-born and especially the unauthorized. Those same sentiments might have led some Latinos to feel that the entire population was being demonized by some of the harsh rhetoric being aimed at the unauthorized. Finally, the marches at some level might have been an expression of that broad identity itself, a public voicing of the developing sense that this is a group with common bonds. Indeed, growth in numbers is one of the defining characteristics of the Hispanic population, and perhaps the simplest and most powerful message conveyed by the marches was "We are many."

The survey findings do not show huge shifts in opinion taking place in 2006, and indeed there is no reason to think that the season of marches and policy debate fundamentally changed perceptions among Latinos. Rather, the survey data suggest that the marches tapped into well-established feelings that were expressed through acts of public assembly that spring.

Rather than standing out as an exception, or even as an aberration, in the history of the Latino population, the marches take on significance for what they say about long-term trends in attitudes and identity formation. In that regard, the marches highlight a broad and growing perception that Latino advancement in this country is hindered by discrimination and that this discrimination can grow more severe when restrictions on immigration are debated. In addition, the marches illuminated a broad and growing perception that Hispanics, despite a variety of cultural, social, economic, and civic difference, constitute a single group than can act with common purpose. Both of these attitudes appear to be on an upward trajectory and hence are likely to inform the ways that Latinos organize themselves and take political action in the future.

Perhaps the most striking characteristic of the Latino population has been its rapid growth in recent years (up by 22 percent between 2000 and 2005), and its greatest social and political impact derives from the fact that it is growing rapidly while the rest of the population is not (Hispanics accounted for more than half of overall population growth in those five years) (Pew Hispanic Center 2006a). But, because this growth has been driven by recent births and immigration, this is a population that is strikingly underrepresented in formal the political process. In 2007, eligible voters made up only 40 percent of the Hispanic population, compared to 77 percent of the non-Hispanic white population (Taylor and Fry 2007). The most disenfranchised portion of this population is found among the unauthorized migrants who were the primary subjects of the marches. Hence assembling in the streets was at one level an act of necessity because few other options were available for influencing the policy debate. But a mere default option is unlikely to have attracted so many participants. Instead, the marches served as effective means of voicing deeply felt attitudes, and the tone of the marches offers important insights into the character of these attitudes.

As noted in DeSipio's chapter in this volume, the Republicans under President George W. Bush made considerable gains among Latinos in the 2004 election, with Bush taking at least 40 percent of the Hispanic vote. That trend was reversed in both November 2006 and 2008, with the Republican share of the total Hispanic vote reverting to about 30 percent, according to the national exit polls (Lopez 2008). A variety of factors combined to produce Republican losses among Hispanics, just as they did in the general population. But, in the round of interviews conducted as he prepared to leave office in January 2009, Bush repeatedly expressed regret over the failure to pass immigration reform during his administration. In one session, after noting that "obviously we got whipped in 2008," he warned fellow Republicans that harsh rhetoric on immigration threatened to alienate Latino voters for the long term. He stated, "If the party is viewed as anti-immigrant—then another fellow may say, well, if they're against the immigrant, they may be against me" (White House 2009).

The lack of confrontation and the absence of palpable anger during the 2006 marches and in the years since then suggests that, while most Latinos see discrimination as a problem, this perception has not yet produced a sense of grievance or an attitude of opposition toward American society. The marches conveyed a plea for acceptance and an almost optimistic sense of inevitability. "We are here. We are part of you. We are many. We are not leaving." If there was one overarching demand advanced by the marchers, it was for defeat of the restrictionist measures enacted by the House of Representatives. (Indeed, the House bill eventually died.)

In effect, the marchers were pleading against prospective action that would have constituted a form of rejection. They were not really asking that anyone do anything on their behalf. There were no past wrongs that needed to be righted, no benefits that needed to be bestowed. Even in asking for a legalization program for unauthorized migrants, the marchers were arguing for what they perceived as the status quo: let these people continue to live and work here.

There has been considerable discussion over the years as to whether Latinos will eventually resemble a minority group, as in the African American model;

whether they will be more likely to follow the path of assimilation typical of many immigrants of the transatlantic era; or whether an entirely new model is necessary to understand this population (Suro 2006). It is not clear that the 2006 marches pushed Latinos in one direction or another. Rather than a turning point, I see the marches as a signal event that illuminates an important social process in identity formation that is still very much underway.

Adopting this perspective does not require discounting the importance of the marches as specific events. Even though the attitudes expressed were already developing, the marches represented an altogether new way of expressing those attitudes through collective public action. In this regard, the medium many have been more extraordinary than the message. But it was a message rarely spoken out loud and certainly never communicated so boldly before. And so the marches offer a window into the Latino psyche. They dramatically reveal a state of mind that is as important today as when thousands went into the streets.

NOTES

1. See the Pew Hispanic Center's website, http://www.pewhispanic.org, for access to reports, fact sheets, datasets, and other publications generated from the surveys.

2. Early in the surveys, respondents were asked if they had a preference for using the terms *Hispanic* or *Latino*, and all subsequent references in the interviews reflected those preferences.

3. The home page for the Latino National Survey, with links to several publications and data products, is http://depts.washington.edu/uwiser/LNS.shtml. The findings on panethnic identity were presented by the survey team at a conference at the Woodrow Wilson International Center for Scholars in Washington DC on December 7, 2006. A summary of the event and associated materials are available at the center's website, http://www.wilsoncenter.org/index.cfm?event_id=201793& fuseaction=events.event_summary.

Aarts, Kees, and Holli Semetko. 2003. "The Divided Electorate: Effects of Media Use on Political Involvement." *Journal of Politics* 65(3): 759–84.

Abraham, Yvonne. 2007. "As Immigration Raids Rise, Human Toll Decried." *Boston Globe*, March 20.

Abrajano, Marissa, and R. Michael Alvarez. N.d. "Why are Latinos More Politically Trusting than Other Americans?" *American Politics Research.*

Aguilera, Elizabeth. 2007. "Immigration at Heart of March." *Denver Post*, May 2.

Almada, Jorge Morales. 2006. "Da inicio hoy el Día de la Ciudadanía." *La Opinión*, July 1.

Althaus, Dudley, and Cynthia Leonor Garza. 2006. "Dreams of Many Ride on Boycott." *Houston Chronicle*, May 1.

Alvarez, Michael R., and Tara L. Butterfield. 2000. "The Resurgence of Nativism in California? The Case of Proposition 187 and Illegal Immigration." *Social Science Quarterly* 81:167–79.

America's Voice. 2008. "Latin American Immigrant Voters Swing from Republicans to Democrats." Press release, November 7. Available at: http://www.americasvoiceonline.org/press_releases/entry/latin_american_immigrant_voters_swing_from_republicans_to_democrats. Accessed January 28, 2009.

Anderson, Terry. N.d. "Hold Their Feet to the Fire Rally." Available at: http://www.youtube.com/watch?v=HQmdSZCOPho&mode=related&search.

Andrews, Kenneth T. 2004. *Freedom Is a Constant Struggle: The Mississippi Civil Rights Movement and Its Legacy.* Chicago: University of Chicago Press.

Andrews, Kenneth T., and Michael Biggs. 2006. "The Dynamics of Protest Diffusion: Movement Organizations, Social Networks, and News Media in the 1960 Sit-Ins." *American Sociological Review* 71:752–77.

Arbitron. 2007. *Hispanic Radio Today: How America Listens to Radio, 2007 Edition.* Available at: http://www.arbitron.com/study/grt.asp.

Archdiocese of Los Angeles. 2006a. "Cardinal Mahony Commemorates Migration Day by Launching Justice for Immigrants Campaign in Los Angeles." Press release, January 14. Carolina Guevara, personal files.

———. 2006b. "Cardinal Mahony Calls on Catholics, Archdiocese of Los Angeles." Press release, February 28. Carolina Guevara, personal files.

———. 2006c. "Hundreds of Farm Workers, Jornaleros, Braceros and Labor Union Members to Honor the Memory of Cesar Chavez." Press release, March 24. Carolina Guevara, personal files.

———. 2006d. "Cardinal Roger Mahony Urges Students to Stay in School Tomorrow." Press release, March 30. Carolina Guevara, personal files.

———. 2006e. "Cardinal Mahony Designates Wednesday, April 5, as Special Day of Prayer and Fasting for Just and Humane Immigration Reform." Press release, April 2. Joan Harper, personal files.

———. 2006f. "Justice for Immigrants: April 10th National Day of Action, Candlelight Vigil and Procession." Flyer. Joan Harper, personal files.

———. 2006g. "Positive Action for Positive Change: Suggestions Toward Promoting Immigration Reform on Monday, May 1st, 2006." Press release, April 16. Al Hernandez Santana, Director Hispanic Affairs for the California Catholic Conference, Sacramento, personal files.

———. 2006h. "Cardinal Mahony, Mayor and LAUSD Head Issue Joint Letter Asking Parents to Urge Students to Stay in School May 1." Press release, April 26. Carolina Guevara, personal files.

———. 2006i. "Archdiocese Ships Boxes to Senators Frist and Reid Containing More Than 150,000 Signatures Urging Senate to Pass Immigration Bill That Is Just and Humane." Press release, May 22. Carolina Guevara, personal files.

———. 2007. "Fast and Prayer for Comprehensive Immigration Reform." Press release, January 27. Joan Harper, personal files.

———. N.d. "Justice for Immigrants, Draft Work Plan." Justice for Immigrants Steering Committee, Archdiocese Office of Justice and Peace. Joan Harper, personal files.

Archibold, Randal. 2007. "Immigrant Rights Rallies Smaller Than Last Year." *New York Times,* May 2.

———. 2008. "Crowds Are Smaller at Protests by Immigrants." *New York Times,* May 2.

Armenta, Guillermo. 2006. Personal interview, September 23.

Ávila, Oscar, and Michael Martínez. 2006. "Immigrants at Crossroads; Stakes Are High for Legalization Campaign." *Chicago Tribune,* May 1.

Ávila, Oscar, and Antonio Olivo. 2006. "A Show of Strength; Thousands March to Loop for Immigrants' Rights; Workers, Students Unite in Opposition to Toughening of Law." *Chicago Tribune,* March 11.

Avrich, Paul. 1984. *The Haymarket Tragedy. Princeton: Princeton University Press.*

Ayi, Mema. 2006. "Jackson: We're All in This Immigration Battle Together." *Chicago Defender,* April 26.

Ayón, David R. 2005. "Mexican Policy and Émigré Communities in the U.S." Background paper presented at the Mexican Migrant Civic Participation in the United States seminar, Woodrow Wilson International Center for Scholars, Washington DC, November. Available at: http://www.wilsoncenter.org/migrantparticipation.

———. 2006. *Immigration and the 2006 Elections*. U.S.-Mexico Policy Bulletin no. 8. Washington DC: Woodrow Wilson International Center for Scholars, Mexico Institute, December.

———. 2009. *Mobilizing Latino Immigrant Integration from IRCA to the Ya Es Hora Citizenship Campaign, 1987–2007*. Research Series on Latino Immigrant Civic Engagement no. 1. Washington DC: Woodrow Wilson International Center for Scholars, January. Available at: http://www.wilsoncenter/migrantparticipation.

Bada, Xóchitl. 2004. "Reconstrucción de identidades regionales a través de proyectos de remesas colectivos: La participación ciudadana extraterritorial de comunidades migrantes michoacanas en el área metropolitana de Chicago." In *Organizaciones de mexicanos en Estados Unidos: La política transnacional de la nueva sociedad civil migrante*, edited by Guillaume Lanly and M. Basilia Valenzuela. Guadalajara: University of Guadalajara.

———. 2007. "The Binational Civic and Political Engagement of Mexican Migrant Hometown Associations and Federations in the United States." *Iberoamericana* 7(25).

———. 2008. "Transnational and Trans-local Sociopolitical Remittances of Mexican Hometown Associations in Michoacán and Illinois." PhD dissertation, University of Notre Dame, Sociology Department.

Bada, Xóchitl, Jonathan Fox, and Andrew Selee, eds. 2006. *Invisible No More: Mexican Migrant Civic Participation in the United States*. Washington DC: Woodrow Wilson International Center for Scholars, Mexico Institute. Available at: http://www.wilson center.org/migrantparticipation.

Badillo Moreno, Gonzalo, ed. 2004. *La puerta que llama: El voto de los mexicanos en el exterior*. Mexico City: Senado de la República, Gobierno de Michoacán.

Bailey, Melissa. 2007. "Mayor to Feds: 'Back Off.'" *New Haven Independent*, June 11.

Baker, Bryan C. 2007. *Trends in Naturalization Rates*. Washington DC: Office of Immigration Statistics, Department of Homeland Security. Available at: http://www.dhs.gov/xlibrary/assets/statistics/publications/ntz_rates508.pdf. Accessed April 9, 2008.

Balderrama, Francisco E., and Raymond Rodriguez. 1995. *Decade of Betrayal: Mexican Repatriation in the 1930s*. Albuquerque: University of New Mexico Press.

Banaszak, Lee Ann. 1996. *Why Movements Succeed or Fail*. Princeton: Princeton University Press.

Barlow, William. 1998. *Voice Over: The Making of Black Radio*. Philadelphia: Temple University Press.

Barnes, Gerald. 2006a. "Letter from Most Reverend Gerald Barnes to Parish Leaders." Parish kit, January. Justice for Immigrants. Available at: http://www.justiceforim migrants.org/parish-kit.shtml. Accessed January 2006.

———. 2006b. "Statement by Most Reverend Gerald Barnes, Bishop of San Bernardino, Chairman, USCCB Committee on Migration." September 12. Justice for Immigrants. Available at: http://justiceforimmigrants.org/files/+BarnescallforCIR.pdf. Accessed June 11, 2007.

Barr, Cameron W., and Elizabeth Williamson. 2004. "Women's Rally Draws Vast Crowd." *Washington Post*, April 26.

Barragan, Cecilia. 2007. Personal interview, January 21.

Barreto, Matt A. 2005. "Latino Immigrants at the Polls: Foreign Born Voter Turnout in the 2002 Election." *Political Research Quarterly* 58:79–86.

Barreto, Matt, Victoria DeFrancesco, and Jennifer Merolla. 2005. "Multiple Dimensions of Mobilization: The Impact of Direct Contact and Political Ads on Latino Turnout." Paper presented at the annual meeting of the Western Political Science Association. Oakland, CA.

Barreto, Matt, Sylvia Manzano, Ricardo Ramírez, and Kathy Rim. 2009. "Mobilization, Participation, and Solidaridad: Latino Participation in the 2006 Immigration Protest Rallies." *Urban Affairs Review* 44(5): 736–764.

Bauböck, Rainer. 1994. *Transnational Citizenship: Membership and Rights in International Migration.* Aldershot, UK: Edward Elgar.

Bean, Frank D., and Gillian Stevens. 2003. *America's Newcomers and the Dynamics of Diversity.* New York: Russell Sage Foundation.

Beck, Paul Allen, and M. Kent Jennings. 1975. "Parents as 'Middlepersons' in Political Socialization." *Journal of Politics* 37:81–107.

———. 1991. "Family Traditions, Political Periods, and the Development of Partisan Orientations." *Journal of Politics* 53:742–63.

Bender, Kristin, and Heather MacDonald. 2006. "Spirited Workers' Message Made Loud, Clear in Oakland." *Oakland Tribune,* May 2.

Benford, Robert D. 1993. "Frame Disputes within the Nuclear Disarmament Movement." *Social Forces* 71(3): 677–701.

Benford, Robert D., and David A. Snow. 2000. "Framing Processes and Social Movements: An Overview and Assessment." *Annual Review of Sociology* 26:611–39.

Benjamin-Alvarado, Jonathan, Louis DeSipio, and Celeste Montoya. 2009. "Latino Mobilization in New Immigration Destinations: The Anti–H.R. 4437 Protest in Nebraska's Cities." *Urban Affairs Review* 44(5): 718–35.

Bergesen, Albert, and Max Herman. 1998. "Immigration, Race and Riot: The 1992 Los Angeles Uprising." *American Sociological Review* 63(1): 39–54.

Beyerlein, Kraig, and Mark Chaves. 2003. "The Political Activities of Religious Congregations in the United States." *Journal for the Scientific Study of Religion* 42:229–46.

Beyerlein, Kraig, and John R. Hipp. 2006. "A Two-Stage Model for a Two-Stage Process: How Biographical Availability Matters for Social Movement Mobilization." *Mobilization* 11(3): 219–40.

Biggs, Michael. 2003. "Positive Feedback in Collective Mobilization: The American Strike Wave of 1886." *Theory and Society* 32(2): 217–54.

———. 2005. "Strikes as Forest Fires: Chicago and Paris in the Late 19th Century." *American Journal of Sociology* 110(6): 1684–1714.

Block, Melissa. 2006. "Spanish D.J. Organizes Immigration Reform Protests." Official transcript, *All Things Considered,* National Public Radio, March 28.

Bloemraad, Irene. 2006. *Becoming a Citizen: Incorporating Immigrants and Refugees in the United States and Canada.* Berkeley: University of California Press.

Bloemraad, Irene, and Christine Trost. 2008. "It's a Family Affair: Intergenerational Mobilization in the Spring 2006 Protests." *American Behavioral Scientist* 52(4): 507–32.

Bobo, Lawrence, and Frank Gilliam Jr. 1990. "Race, Socio-Political Participation, and Black Empowerment." *American Political Science Review* 84:377–93.

Bobo, Lawrence, and Mia Tuan. 2006. *Prejudice in Politics: Group Position, Public Opinion, and the Wisconsin Treaty Rights Treaty.* Cambridge, MA: Harvard University Press.

Borden, Teresa, and Lilly Rockwell. 2006. "Immigration Rallies Fill Nation's Streets, Latinos Test Political, Economic Muscle." *Atlanta Journal-Constitution,* April 11.

Bosniak, Linda. 2006. *The Citizen and the Alien: Dilemmas of Contemporary Membership.* Princeton: Princeton University Press.

Boston Globe. 2007. "Needed: Immigration Policy." Editorial, March 9. Available at: http://www.boston.com/news/globe/editorial_opinion/editorials/articles/2007/03/09/needed_immigration_policy. Accessed November 12, 2007.

Bowler, Shaun, Stephen P. Nicholson, and Gary M. Segura. 2006. "Earthquakes and Aftershocks: Tracking Partisan Identification amid California's Changing Political Environment." *American Journal of Political Science* 50:146–59.

Branton, Regina. 2007. "Latino Attitudes toward Public Policy: The Importance of Acculturation." *Political Research Quarterly* 60(2): 293–303.

Briggs, Vernon M., Jr. 2004. "Immigration Policy and American Unionism: A Reality Check." Briggs Papers and Speeches, Vernon M. Briggs Jr. Collection, Kheel Center for Labor-Management Documentation and Archives, School of Industrial Relations, Cornell University, Ithaca. Available at: http://digitalcommons.ilr.cornell.edu/briggsIV/13.

BBC. 2003. "Millions Join Global Anti-War Protests." February 17. Available at: http://news.bbc.co.uk/1/hi/world/europe/2765215.stm. Accessed April 9, 2008.

Brockett, Charles D. 2005. *Political Movements and Violence in Central America.* Cambridge: Cambridge University Press.

Broder, John M., and Susan Sachs. 2002. "The Tightening Border; Facing Registry Deadline, Men from Muslim Nations Swamp Immigration Office." *New York Times,* December 17.

Broder, Tanya. 2007. *State and Local Policies on Immigrant Access to Services: Promoting Integration or Isolation?* National Immigration Law Center, Los Angeles. Available at: http://www.nilc.org. Accessed November 15, 2007.

Brown, R. Khari, and Ronald E. Brown. 2003. "Faith and Works: Church-Based Social Capital Resources and African American Political Activism." *Social Forces* 82(2): 617–41.

Brownell, Peter. 2005. "The Declining Enforcement of Employer Sanctions." *Migration Information Source.* Migration Policy Institute, Washington DC. Available at: http://www.migrationinformation.org/Feature/display.cfm?ID=332. Accessed April 16, 2008.

Burns, Nancy, Kay Lehman Schlozman, and Sidney Verba. 2001. *The Private Roots of Public Action.* Cambridge, MA: Harvard University Press.

Caesar, Stephen. 2009. "Mass Marks Start of Catholic Ministry to Help Deportees to Mexico." *Tucson Citizen,* January 18. Available at: http://www.tucsoncitizen.com/ss/border/107977.php. Accessed January 28, 2009.

Calavita, Kitty. 1992. *Inside the State: The Bracero Program, Immigration, and the I.N.S.* New York: Routledge.

Calderon, Jose. 1992. "'Hispanic' and 'Latino': The Viability of Categories for Panethnic Unity." *Latin American Perspectives* 19(4): 37–44.

Caldwell, Christopher. 2007. "Rioters vs. State in a Test of Will." *Financial Times,* December 1–2.

Calhoun, Craig. 1997. *Neither Gods nor Emperors: Students and the Struggle for Democracy in China.* Berkeley: University of California Press.

Calvo, Maria Antonia, and Steven J. Rosenstone. 1989. *Hispanic Political Participation.* San Antonio, TX: Southwest Voter Research Institute.

Carens, Joseph H. 1987. "Aliens and Citizens: The Case for Open Borders." *Review of Politics* 49(2): 251–73.

Carroll, Joseph. 2007a. "Americans Divided on Need for New Immigration Laws." Gallup News Service, July 16.

———. 2007b. "About One in Three Hispanics Say Immigration in Nation's Top Problem." Gallup News Service, July 19.

Castañeda, Alejandra. 2006. *The Politics of Citizenship of Mexican Migrants.* New York: LFB Scholarly Publishing.

Castañeda, Jorge. 2007. *Ex Mex: From Migrants to Immigrants.* New York: New Press.

Castañeda Paredes, Mari. 2003. "The Transformation of Spanish-Language Radio in the U.S." *Journal of Radio Studies* 10:5–16.

Center for New Community. 2007. "Indecent Proposals: Top 10 Most Offensive Quotes from Anti-Immigrant Groups." Available at: http://www.buildingdemocracy.org/Press _Center/Press_Releases/%22Indecent_Proposals%3A_Top_10_Most_Offensive_Quotes %22_from_AntiImmigrant_Groups_200706191082. Accessed November 12, 2007.

Chabram-Dernersesian, Angie. 1999. "En-countering the Other Discourse of Chicano-Mexicano Difference." *Cultural Studies* 13(2).

Chavez, Leo. 1997 [1992]. *Shadowed Lives: Undocumented Immigrants in American Society.* New York: Wadsworth.

———. 2001. *Covering Immigration: Popular Images and the Politics of the Nation.* Berkeley: University of California Press.

———. 2008. *The Latino Threat: Constructing Immigrants, Citizens, and the Nation.* Stanford: Stanford University Press.

Chertoff, Michael. 2006. "Operation Return to Sender." Press release, June 14, Department of Homeland Security. Available at: http://www.dhs.gov/xnews/releases/press _release_0926.shtm. Accessed on December 2, 2007.

Chinchilla, Norma Stoltz, Nora Hamilton, and James Loucky. 2009. "The Sanctuary Movement and Central American Activism in Los Angeles." *Latin American Perspectives* 36(6): 101–26.

Cacho, Lisa Marie. 2008. "The Rights of Respectability: Ambivalent Allies, Reluctant Rivals, and Disavowed Deviants." Pp. 190–206 in *Immigrant Rights: In the Shadows of Citizenship,* edited by Rachel Ida Buff. New York: New York University Press.

Cho, Eunice Hyunhye. 2008. "Beyond the Day without an Immigrant: Immigrant Communities Building a Sustainable Movement." Pp. 94–121 in *Immigrant Rights: In the*

Shadows of Citizenship, edited by Rachel Ida Buff. New York: New York University Press.

Cicchetti, Charles J., A. Myrick Freeman III, Robert H. Haveman, and Jack L. Knetsch. 1971. "On the Economics of Mass Demonstrations: A Case Study of the November 1969 March on Washington." *The American Economic Review* 61:719–24.

Citrin, Jack, and Benjamin Highton. 2002. *How Race, Ethnicity and Immigration Shape the California Electorate*. San Francisco: Public Policy Institute of California.

Citrin, Jack, Amy Leman, Mike Murakami, and Kathryn Pearson. 2007. "Testing Huntington: Is Hispanic Immigration a Threat to American Identity?" *Perspectives on Politics* 5(1)(March).

Colias, Mike. 2006. "Immigrant Rally Chiefs Ponder What's Next." *Seattle Post-Intelligencer,* May 2.

Columbus Telegram. 2006. "Schuyler Marchers Number 3,000 Plus." April 11.

Congressional Quarterly. 2006. "The Democratic Takeover Up Close: Open Seats." December 6.

Coontz, Stephanie. 1992. *The Way We Never Were: American Families and the Nostalgia Trap*. New York: Basic Books.

———. 1998. *American Families: A Multicultural Reader*. London: Routledge.

Cordero-Guzman, Hector R. 2005. "Community-Based Organizations and Migration in New York City." *Journal of Ethnic and Migration Studies* 31:889–909.

Cornelius, Wayne A. 2001. "Death at the Border: Efficacy and Unintended Consequences of US Immigration Control Policy." *Population and Development Review* 27(4): 661–85.

———. 2005. Controlling 'Unwanted' Immigration: Lessons from the United States, 1993–2004." *Journal of Ethnic and Migration Studies* 31(4): 775–94.

Coutin, Susan Bibler. 1993. *The Culture of Protest: Religious Activism and the U.S. Sanctuary Movement*. Boulder, CO: Westview Press.

———. 2003. *Legalizing Moves: Salvadoran Immigrants' Struggle for U.S. Residency*. Ann Arbor: University of Michigan Press.

Daily Labor Report. 2008. "Immigrant Role in Obama's Election Win Boosts Expectation for Immigration Changes." November 10.

Dallas Morning News. 2006. "No Turning Back." April 10.

Dark, Taylor E. 1999. *The Unions and the Democrats: An Enduring Alliance*. Ithaca: Cornell University Press.

Das Gupta, Monisha. 2008. "Rights in a Transnational Era." In *Immigrant Rights in the Shadows of United States Citizenship*, edited by Rachel Ida Buff. New York: New York University Press.

Davenport, Christian, Hank Johnston, and Carol Mueller. 2005. *Repression and Mobilization*. Minneapolis: University of Minnesota Press.

Davila, Arlene. 2000. "Mapping Latinidad: Language and Culture in the Spanish TV Battlefront." *Television New Media* 1(1): 75–94.

Deaton, Joyce. 2008. *Charlotte: A Welcome Denied*. Reports on Latino Immigrant Civic Engagement no. 1. Washington DC: Woodrow Wilson International Center for Scholars, November. Available at: http://www.wilsoncenter.org/migrantparticipation.

de Graauw, Els. 2008. "Nonprofit Organizations: Agents of Immigrant Political Incorporation in Urban America." In *Civic Hopes and Political Realities: Immigrants, Community Organizations, and Political Engagement,* edited by S. Karthick Ramakrishnan and Irene Bloemraad. New York: Russell Sage Foundation.

de la Garza, Rodolfo. 2004. "Latino Politics." *Annual Review of Political Science* 7:91–123.

de la Garza, Rodolfo, Louis DeSipio, F. Chris García, John A. García, and Angelo Falcon. 1992. *Latino Voices: Mexican, Puerto Rican and Cuban Perspectives on American Politics.* Boulder, CO: Westview Press.

de la Garza, Rodolfo O., Angelo Falcon, and F. Chris García. 1996. "Will the Real Americans Please Stand Up: Anglo and Mexican-American Support of Core American Political Values." *American Journal of Political Science* 40:335–51.

de la Garza, Rodolfo, and Miriam Hazan. 2003. *Looking Backward, Moving Forward: Mexican Organizations in the US as Agents of Incorporation.* Claremont, CA: Tomas Rivera Policy Institute. Available at: http://www.trpi.org.

Delgado, Hector. 1993. *New Immigrants, Old Unions: Organizing Undocumented Workers in Los Angeles.* Philadelphia: Temple University Press.

DeSipio, Louis. 1996a. "After Proposition 187, the Deluge: Reforming Naturalization Administration while Making Good Citizens." *Harvard Journal of Hispanic Policy* 9:7–24.

———. 1996b. *Counting on the Latino Vote: Latinos as a New Electorate.* Charlottesville: University of Virginia Press.

———. 1996c. "Making Citizens or Good Citizens? Naturalization as a Predictor of Organizational and Electoral Behavior Among Latino Immigrants." *Hispanic Journal of Behavioral Sciences* 18(2): 194–213.

———. 2001. "Building America, One Person at a Time: Naturalization and Political Behavior of the Naturalized in Contemporary American Politics." In *E Pluribus Unum? Contemporary and Historical Perspectives on Immigrant Political Incorporation,* edited by Gary Gerstle and John Mollenkopf. New York: Russell Sage Foundation.

———. 2006. "Transnational Politics and Civic Engagement: Do Home Country Political Ties Limit Latino Immigrant Pursuit of US Civic Engagement and Citizenship." In *Transforming Politics, Transforming America: The Political and Civic Incorporation of Immigrants in the United States,* edited by Taeku Lee, S. Karthick Ramakrishnan, and Ricardo Ramírez. Charlottesville: University of Virginia Press.

Diaz, Jesse. 2006. Personal interview and field notes, May 1.

———. 2010. "Organizing the Brown Tide: La Gran Epoca Primavera 2006 in Los Angeles, an Insider's Story." PhD dissertation, University of California, Riverside.

Diaz, Elvia, and Robbie Sherwood. 2005. "Prop. 200's Effect Minimal; Political Fallout May Loom Large in 2006 Races." *Arizona Republic,* June 5. Available at: http://www.azcentral.com/arizonarepublic/news/articles/0605Immigration-illegal05.html. Accessed November 15, 2007.

Doyle, Paula. 2006. "Coalition Lobbies Legislators for Human Immigration Reform." *The Tidings.* May 26.

Earl, Jennifer, Andrew Martin, John D. McCarthy, and Sarah A. Soule. 2004. "The Use of Newspaper Data in the Study of Collective Action." *Annual Review of Sociology* 30:65–80.

Eisinger, Peter K. 1973. "The Conditions of Protest Behavior in American Cities." *American Political Science Review* 67:11–28.

Emory Law Journal. 2002. Randolph W. Thrower Symposium. *Emory Law Journal* 52(3).

Escamilla, Kathy, Sheila Shannon, Silvana Carlos, and Jorge Garcia. 2003. "Breaking the Code: Colorado's Defeat of the Anti-Bilingual Education Initiative (Amendment 31)." *Bilingual Research Journal* 27:357–82.

Espinosa, Gaston, Virgilio Elizondo, and Jesse Miranda. 2003. *Hispanic Churches in American Public Life: Summary of Findings.* Interim Reports vol. 2. Notre Dame: University of Notre Dame, Institute for Latino Studies.

Faiola, Anthony. 2007. "States' Immigrant Policies Diverge." *Washington Post,* October 15.

Fantasia, Rick, and Kim Voss. 2004. *Hard Work: Remaking the American Labor Movement.* Berkeley: University of California.

Farr, James. 1995. "Remembering the Revolution: Behavioralism in American Political Science." In *Political Science and History: Research Programs and Political Traditions,* edited by James Farr, John Dryzek, and Stephen Leonard. Cambridge: Cambridge University Press.

Fears, Darryl. 2004. "Pollsters Debate Hispanics' Presidential Voting: Discrepancy in Estimates vs. Results Examined." *Washington Post,* November 26.

Federación de Clubes Michoacanos en Illinois. 2007. "Mexicanos for Political Progress (MX-PP): Un paso más en la participación política de la comunidad mexicana." In *Presencia Michoacana en el Medio Oeste.* Chicago: Federación de Clubes Michoacanos en Illinois.

Félix, Adrián, Carmen González, and Ricardo Ramírez. 2008. "Political Protest, Ethnic Media, and Latino Naturalization." *American Behavioral Scientist.* 52(4): 618–34.

Ferris, Susan. 2008. "Latinos Expecting Obama to Deliver on Immigration Promises." *Sacramento Bee,* November 21. Available at: http://www.sacbee.com/341/story/1416648 .html. Accessed January 13, 2009.

Fine, Janice. 2005. "Worker Centers: Community-Based and Led Worker Organizing Projects." Available at: http://www.epinet.org/content.cfm?id=2221.

———. 2006. *Worker Centers: Organizing Communities at the Edge of the Dream.* Ithaca: Cornell University Press.

Fink, Leon. 2010. "Labor Joins La Marcha: How New Immigrant Activists Restored the Meaning of May Day." In *¡Marcha! Latino Chicago and the National Immigrant Movement,* edited by Nilda M. Flores-González and Amalia Pallares. Urbana: University of Illinois Press.

Fitzgerald, David. 2004. "Beyond Transnationalism: Mexican Hometown Politics and an American Labour Union." *Ethnic and Racial Studies* 27(2).

Fix, Michael, ed. 1991. *The Paper Curtain: Employer Sanctions' Implementation, Impact and Reform.* Santa Monica and Washington DC: RAND Corporation and Urban Institute Press.

———. 2007. *Securing the Future: US Immigrant Integration Policy; A Reader.* Washington DC: Migration Policy Institute.

Fix, Michael, and Laureen Laglagaron. 2002. *Social Rights and Citizenship: An International Comparison.* Washington DC: Urban Institute.

Fix, Michael, and Jeffrey S. Passel. 2002. "The Scope and Impact of Welfare Reform's Immigrant Provisions." Discussion paper in the Assessing the New Federalism series. Washington DC: Urban Institute.

Fix, Michael, Jeffrey Passel, and Kenneth Sucher. 2003. *Trends in Naturalization*. Brief no. 3 in Immigrant Families and Workers: Facts and Perspectives series. Washington DC: Urban Institute. Available at: http://www.urban.org/url.cfm?ID=310847. Accessed September 16, 2005.

Flores, William V. 2003. "Undocumented Immigrants and Latino Cultural Citizenship." *Latin American Perspectives* (30)2: 87–100.

Flores-González, Nilda. 2007. "Representing Self and Others: Youth's Claims for Immigrant Rights." Unpublished manuscript.

———. 2010. "Immigrants, Citizens or Both? The Second Generation in the Immigrant Rights Marches." In ¡*Marcha! Latino Chicago and the National Immigrant Movement*, edited by Nilda M. Flores-González and Amalia Pallares. Urbana: University of Illinois Press.

Flores-González, Nilda, Amalia Pallares, Cedric Herring, and Maria Krysan. 2006. "UIC Immigrant Mobilization Project: General Survey Findings." University of Illinois, Chicago.

Foner, Philip S. 1986. May Day: A Short History of the International Workers' Holiday, 1886–1986. New York: International Publishers.

Fornek, Scott. 2006. "Chicago 'Giant' Put Rest of Country on Notice." *Chicago Sun Times*, April 2.

Fortuny, Karina, Randy Capps, and Jeffrey S. Passel. 2007. *The Characteristics of Unauthorized Immigrants in California, Los Angeles County, and the United States*. Washington DC: Urban Institute, March. Available at: http://www.urban.org/UploadedPDF/411425_Characteristics_Immigrants.pdf.

Four Freedoms Fund (FFF) and Grantmakers Concerned with Immigrant and Refugees. Available at: http://www.gcir.org/resources/gcir_publications/groundswell_report2_new.pdf. Accessed November 11, 2007.

Fox, Cybelle. 2007. "The Boundaries of Social Citizenship: Race, Immigration and the American Welfare State, 1900–1950." PhD dissertation, Harvard University.

Fox, Jonathan. 2005a. "Mapping Mexican Migrant Civil Society." Background paper presented at the Mexican Migrant Civic Participation in the United States seminar, Woodrow Wilson International Center for Scholars, Washington DC, November. Available at: http://www.wilsoncenter.org/migrantparticipation.

———. 2005b. "Unpacking Transnational Citizenship." *Annual Review of Political Science* 8:171–201.

———. 2006. "Reframing Mexican Migration as a Multi-Ethnic Process." *Latino Studies* 4:39–61.

———. 2007. *Accountability Politics: Power and Voice in Rural Mexico*. Oxford: Oxford University Press.

Fox, Jonathan, and Xóchitl Bada. 2008. "Migrant Organization and Hometown Impacts in Rural Mexico." *Journal of Agrarian Change* 8(2–3).

Fox, Jonathan, and Gaspar Rivera-Salgado, eds. 2004. *Indigenous Mexican Migrants in the United States.* La Jolla: University of California, San Diego, Center for Comparative Immigration Studies and Center for U.S.-Mexican Studies.

Fox, Jonathan, Andrew Selee, and Xóchitl Bada. 2006. "Conclusion." In *Invisible No More: Mexican Migrant Civic Participation in the United States,* edited by Xóchitl Bada, Jonathan Fox, and Andrew Selee. Washington DC: Woodrow Wilson International Center for Scholars, Mexico Institute.

Fraga, Luis Ricardo, Herman Gallegos, Gerald P. Lopez, Mary L. Pratt, Renato Rosaldo, José Saldivar, Ramón Saldivar, and Guadalupe Valdes. 1994. *Still Looking for America: Beyond the Latino National Political Survey.* Report prepared by the Public Outreach Group, Stanford Center for Chicano Research. Palo Alto: Stanford University.

Fraga, Luis Ricardo, and David Leal. 2004. "Playing the 'Latino' Card: Race, Ethnicity, and National Party Politics." *The DuBois Review* 1:297–317.

Fraga, Luis, and Gary Segura. 2006. "Culture Clash? Contesting Notions of American Identity and the Effects of Latin American Immigration." *Perspectives on Politics,* 4(2): 279–287.

Frank, Larry, and Kent Wong. 2004. "Dynamic Political Mobilization: The Los Angeles County Federation of Labor." *WorkingUSA* 8:155–81.

Franzoni Lobo, Josefina. 2007. "Migración internacional, organización social y poder político municipal: Estudio comparativo en Chinantla, Puebla y San Miguel Tlacotepec, Oaxaca." Paper presented at the Latin American Studies Association, Montreal.

Freeman, Jo. 1975. *The Politics of Women's Liberation: A Case Study of an Emerging Social Movement and Its Relation to the Policy Process.* New York: Longman.

Freeman, Richard, and Joel Rogers. 1999. *What Workers Want.* Ithaca: Cornell University Press.

Gamson, William. 1990. *The Strategy of Social Protest.* 2nd edition. Belmont, CA: Wadsworth.

Gandy, Oscar H., Jr. 2000. "Race, Ethnicity and the Segmentation of Media Markets." In *Mass Media and Society,* 3rd edition, edited by James Curran and Michael Gurevitch. New York: Arnold and Oxford University Press.

Ganz, Marshall. 2000. "Resources and Resourcefulness: Strategic Capacity in the Unionization of California Agriculture, 1959–1966." *American Journal of Sociology* 105(4): 1003–62.

———. 2007. Personal interview, February 28.

———. 2009. *Why David Sometimes Wins: Leadership, Organization, and Strategy in the California Farm Worker Movement.* New York: Oxford University Press.

García, Ignacio M. 1997. *Chicanismo: The Forging of a Militant Ethos Among Mexican Americans.* Tucson: University of Arizona Press.

Garcia, John A., and Carlos H. Arce. 1988. "Political Orientations and Behaviors of Chicanos." In *Latinos and the Political System,* edited by F. Chris Garcia. South Bend: University of Notre Dame Press.

García, Maria Christina. 2006. *Seeking Refuge: Central American Migration to Mexico, the United States, and Canada.* Berkeley: University of California Press.

García, Mario T. 1989. *Mexican Americans: Leadership, Ideology, and Identity, 1930–1960.* New Haven: Yale University Press.

———. 2005. "PADRES: Latino Community Priests and Social Action." In *Latino Religions and Civic Activism in the United States,* edited by Gaston Espinoza, Virgilio Elizondo, and Jesse Miranda. New York: Oxford University Press.

García Bedolla, Lisa. 2005. *Fluid Borders: Latino Power, Identity, and Politics in Los Angeles.* Berkeley: University of California Press.

Garland, Phyl. 1982. "The Black Press: Down But Not Out." *Columbia Journalism Review* 21(3): 43–50.

Garrow, David. 2004. *Bearing the Cross: Martin Luther King, Jr., and the Southern Christian Leadership Conference.* New York: Harper Perennial.

Gerber, Alan S., and Donald P Green. 2000. "The Effects of Canvassing, Direct Mail, and Telephone Contact on Voter Turnout: A Field Experiment." *American Political Science Review* 94:653–63.

Gillis, John. 1997. *A World of Their Own Making: Myth, Ritual and the Quest for Family Values.* Cambridge, MA: Harvard University Press.

Gillman, Todd J. 2006. "Immigration Won't Be Top Issue for Either Obama or McCain." *Dallas Morning News,* August 26. Available at: http://www.dallasnews.com/shared content/dws/news/politics/national/stories/DN-immig_26pol.ART.State.Edition1 .4d84092.html. Accessed January 13, 2009.

Gimpel, James. 2004. *Losing Ground or Staying Even: Republicans and the Politics of the Latino Vote.* Washington DC: Center for Immigration Studies.

———. 2007. *Latino Voting in the 2006 Election: Realignment to the GOP Remains Distant.* Washington DC: Center for Immigration Studies.

Gimpel, James G., and James R. Edwards. 1990. *The Congressional Politics of Immigration Reform.* Needham Heights, MA: Allyn and Bacon.

Ginsberg, Steve. 1994. "Ex-field Hands Score as Deejays on Hispanic Radio. *Los Angeles Business Journal,* February 21. Available at: http://www.encyclopedia.com/doc/ 1G1-15198620.html.

Ginsberg-Jaeckle, Matt. 2006. "Unity in the Community: Housing Activists March for Immigrants' Rights." *Fight Back!,* July-August.

Gold, Scott. 2006. "Student Protests Echo the '60s, but with a High-Tech Buzz." *Los Angeles Times,* March 31.

Goldstone, Jack, and Charles Tilly. 2001. "Threat (and Opportunity): Popular Action and State Response in the Dynamics of Contentious Action." In *Silence and Voice in the Study of Contentious Politics,* edited by Ronald R. Aminzade, Jack A. Goldstone, Doug McAdam, Elizabeth J. Perry, William H. Sewell, Sidney Tarrow, and Charles Tilly. Cambridge: Cambridge University Press.

Gómez-Quiñones, Juan. 1990. *Chicano Politics: Reality and Promise, 1940–1990.* Albuquerque: University of New Mexico Press.

Gonzalez, Daniel. 2007. "The Rush Is on for Citizenship." *Arizona Republic,* September 13. Available at: http://www.azcentral.com/community/chandler/articles/0913natural-izations0913.html. Accessed November 11, 2007.

Goodman, Amy, and Juan Gonzalez. 2006. "Immigrant Rights Protests Rock the County: Up to 2 Million Take to the Streets in the Largest Wave of Demonstrations in U.S. History." *Democracy Now*, April 11. Available at: http://www.democracynow.org/article .p1%sid/06/04/11/1426231.

Goodnough, Abby. 2006. "A Florida Mayor Turns to an Immigration Curb to Fix a Fading City." *New York Times*, July 10.

Gordon, Jennifer. 2005. *Suburban Sweatshops: The Fight for Immigrant Rights*. Cambridge, MA: Harvard University Press.

———. 2007. "Transnational Labor Citizenship." *Southern California Law Review* 80(3): 503–88.

Gorman, Anna, and Tami Abdollah. 2007. "Turnout Is Low at Immigration Rallies." *Los Angeles Times*, March 26.

Gorman, Anna, and Jennifer Delson. 2007. "Citizenship Requests Soar before Big Changes." *Los Angeles Times*, February 25.

Gottlieb, Robert, Mark Vallianatos, Regina M. Freer, and Peter Dreier. 2005. *The Next Los Angeles: The Struggle for a Livable City*. Berkeley: University of California Press.

Greenhouse, Steven. 2003. "Immigrants Rally in City Seeking Rights." *New York Times*, October 5.

———. 2008a. "After Push for Obama, Unions Seek New Rules." *New York Times*, November 9.

———. 2008b. *The Big Squeeze: Tough Times for the American Worker.* New York: Knopf.

Guarnizo, L.E., A. Portes, and W. Haller. 2003. "Assimilation and Transnationalism: Determinants of Transnational Political Action among Contemporary Migrants." *American Journal of Sociology* 108(6): 1211–48.

Gunnell, John. 1995. "The Declination of the 'State' and the Origins of American Political Science." In *Political Science and History: Research Programs and Political Traditions*, edited by James Farr, John Dryzek, and Stephen Leonard. Cambridge: Cambridge University Press.

Gurowitz, Amy. 1999. "Mobilizing International Norms: Domestic Actors, Immigrants, and the Japanese State." *World Politics* 51(3): 413–45.

Gutiérrez, David G. 1995. *Walls and Mirrors: Mexican Americans, Mexican Immigrants, and the Politics of Ethnicity.* Berkeley: University of California Press.

———. 1999. "Migration, Emergent Ethnicity, and the 'Third Space': The Shifting Politics of Nationalism in Greater Mexico." *The Journal of American History* 86(2): 481–517.

Gutiérrez, Elena. *Fertile Matters: The Politics of Mexican-American Women's Reproduction.* Austin: University of Texas Press, 2008.

Gutiérrez, Félix. 2006. Interview with Bob Garfield. *On the Media*, National Public Radio, WNYC, New York City, March 31.

Gutiérrez, Félix, and Jorge Reina Schement. 1979. *Spanish-Language Radio in the Southwestern United States.* Austin, TX: Center for Mexican American Studies.

Hagan, Jacqueline Maria, and Susan Gonzalez Baker. 1993. "Implementing the U.S. Legalization Program: The Influence of Immigrant Communities and Local Agencies on Immigration Policy Reform." *International Migration Review* 27(3): 513–36.

Hamilton, James. 2000. "Alternative Media: Conceptual Difficulties, Critical Possibilities." *Journal of Communication Inquiry* 24:357–78.

Hamlin, Rebecca. 2008. "Immigrants at Work: Labor Unions and Noncitizen Members." In *Civic Hopes and Political Realities: Immigrants, Community Organizations, and Political Engagement*, edited by S. Karthick Ramakrishnan and Irene Bloemraad. New York: Russell Sage Foundation.

Hardy-Fanta, Carol. 1993. *Latina Politics, Latino Politics: Gender, Culture, and Political Participation in Boston.* Philadelphia: Temple University Press.

Heredia, Luisa. 2008. "Faith in Action: The Catholic Church and the Immigrant Rights Movement, 1980–2007." PhD dissertation, Harvard University.

Hernandez, Daniel. 2007. "Year One of the Immigrant Rights Movement: Washington Drags Its Feet While the Rest of Society Adapts to a New Reality." *Los Angeles Times,* March 25.

Hero, Rodney, and Caroline Tolbert. 2005. "Exploring Minority Political Efficacy." In *Diversity in Democracy Minority Representation in the United States,* edited by Gary Segura and Shaun Bowler. Charlottesville: University of Virginia Press.

Hertzke, Allen D. 1991. "The Role of Churches in Political Mobilization: The Presidential Campaigns of Jesse Jackson and Pat Robertson." In *Interest Group Politics,* 3rd edition, edited by Allan J. Ciglar and Burdett A. Loomis. Washington DC: CQ Press.

Hidalgo, Ellie. 2006. "Legal Immigrants in L.A. begin Path to U.S. Citizenship." *The Tidings,* July 7.

Hing, Bill Ong, and Kevin R. Johnson. 2006. "The Immigrant Rights Marches of 2006 and the Prospects for a New Civil Rights Movement." *Harvard Civil Rights-Civil Liberties Law Review* 42. Available at: http://papers.ssrn.com/sol3/papers.cfm?abstract_id=951268. Accessed July 2, 2008.

Hirschman, Albert. 1984. *Getting Ahead Collectively.* New York: Pergamon.

Holtz-Eakin, Douglas. 2005. Letter to F. James Sensenbrenner, December 14. Available at: http://www.cbo.gov/ftpdocs/69xx/doc6980/hr4437MaAm.pdf. Accessed July 2, 2008.

Hondagneu-Sotelo, Pierrette, and Angelica Salas. 2008. "What Explains the Immigrant Rights Marches of 2006? Xenophobia and Organizing with Democracy Technology." Pp. 209–25 in *Immigrant Rights in the Shadows of Citizenship,* edited by Rachel Ida Buff. New York: New York University Press.

Hong, Chung-Wha. 2006. Telephone interview conducted by Ted Wang and Robert Winn, April 26.

Hook, Janet. 2007. "Giuliani's Migrating Position Is in Dispute." *Los Angeles Times,* September 23.

Hoyt, Joshua, and Fred Tsao. 2006. *Today We March, Tomorrow We Vote: The Untapped Power of over 14 Million Potential New Immigration Voters in 2008.* Chicago: Illinois Coalition for Immigrant and Refugee Rights.

Hughes, Jim. 2006. "Immigrant Marches Ongoing." *Denver Post,* April 3.

Huntington, Samuel P. 2004. *Who Are We? The Challenges to America's National Identity.* New York: Simon and Schuster.

IFE (Instituto Federal Electoral). 2006. "Informe final sobre el voto de los mexicanos residentes en el extranjero (Libro Blanco)." Mexico City: Instituto Federal Electoral, December. Available at: http://www.ife.org.mx/InternetCDA/estaticos/votoextranjero/ libro_blanco.

Immigration Law Reform Institute. N.d. Model Illegal Immigration Relief Ordinance, Version 5.

Immigration Policy Center. 2009. "2008 Election Results Lesson Learned: Conservative and GOP Leadership Calling for New Strategy on Hispanic Voters." January 28. Available at: http://www.immigrationpolicy.org/images/File/factcheck/GOPLeadersCal lforCIR1-28-09.pdf. Accessed January 28, 2009.

Iyengar, Shanto. 1991. *Is Anyone Responsible? How Television Frames Political Issues*. Chicago: University of Chicago Press.

Iyengar, Shanto, and Donald R. Kinder. 1987. *News That Matters: Television and American Opinion*. Chicago: University of Chicago Press.

Itzigsohn, Jose. 2000. "Immigration and the Boundaries of Citizenship: The Institutions of Immigrants' Political Transnationalism." *International Migration Review* 34(4): 1126–54.

Jacobson, David. 1996. *Rights across Borders: Immigration and the Decline of Citizenship*. Baltimore: Johns Hopkins University Press.

Jamison, Angela. 2005. "Embedded on the Left: Aggressive Media Strategies and Their Organizational Impact on the Immigrant Worker Freedom Ride." Theory and Research in Comparative Social Analysis, Paper 24, January 20. Department of Sociology, UCLA. Available at: http://repositories.cdlib.org/uclasoc/trcsa/24.

JBHE Foundation. 2003. "40 Years Ago: A. Philip Randolph's 1963 March on Washington." *The Journal of Blacks in Higher Education* 74.

Jennings, M. Kent, and Richard G. Niemi. 1968. "The Transmission of Political Values from Parent to Child." *American Political Science Review* 65:69–82.

———. 1974. *The Political Character of Adolescence: The Influence of Families and Schools*. Princeton: Princeton University Press.

———. 1981. *Generations and Politics*. Princeton: Princeton University Press.

Jennings, M. Kent, Laura Stoker, and Jake Bowers. 2009. "Politics across Generations: Family Transmission Reexamined." *The Journal of Politics* 71(3)(July): 782–99.

Jiménez, Tomás R. 2008. "Mexican-Immigrant Replenishment and the Continuing Significance of Ethnicity and Race." *American Journal of Sociology* 113(6): 1527–67.

Johnson, Dawn Marie. 2001. "The AEDPA and IIRIRA: Treating Misdemeanors as Felonies for Immigration Purposes." *Journal of Legislation* 27(2): 481–91.

Johnson, Martin, Robert M. Stein, and Robert D. Wrinkle. 2003. "Language, Residential Stability, and Voting among Latino-Americans." *Social Science Quarterly* 84(2): 412–24.

Johnson, Phylis. 2004. "Black Radio Politically Defined: Communicating Community and Political Empowerment through Stevie Wonder's KJLH-FM, 1992–2002." *Political Communication* 21(3): 353–67.

Johnston, Hank, and Jackie Smith. 2002. *Globalization and Resistance: Transnational Dimensions of Social Movements*. Lanham, MD: Rowman and Littlefield.

Jones, Arthur. 2001. "Catholic Hospital Organization Signs Accord with Union." *National Catholic Reporter*, April 20.

Jones, Jeffrey. 2008a. "The People's Priorities: Economy, Iraq, Gas Prices." Gallup poll, May 30.

———. 2008b. "Fewer Americans Favor Cutting Back Immigration." Gallup poll, July 10.

Jones-Correa, Michael. 1998. *Between Two Nations: The Political Predicament of Latinos in New York City.* Ithaca: Cornell University Press.

Jones-Correa, Michael, and David Leal. 2001. "Political Participation: Does Religion Matter?" *Political Research Quarterly* 54:751–70.

Jordan, Miriam. 2007. "Univision Gives Citizenship Drive an Unusual Lift." *Wall Street Journal,* May 10.

Jung, S. J. 2006. Telephone interview at Young Korean American Service and Education Center, May 8.

Justice for Immigrants. 2005a. "Justice for Immigrants: A Journey of Hope; the Catholic Campaign for Immigration Reform." Available at: http://justiceforimmigrants.org/learn_about_justice.html. Accessed December 7, 2007.

———. 2005b. "Justice for Immigrants Video Competition." http://justicef.startlogic.com/videocomp.html. Accessed January 28, 2009.

———. 2005c. "What's New." http://www.justiceforimmigrants.org/new.html. Accessed on January 28, 2009.

———. 2006. "Catholic Bishops' Call for Comprehensive Immigration Reform." Parish kit. Available at: http://www.justiceforimmigrants.org/parish-kit.shtml. Accessed January 27, 2006.

Kandel, William, and Douglas S. Massey. 2002. "The Culture of Mexican Migration: A Theoretical and Empirical Analysis." *Social Forces* 80(3): 981–1004.

Kay Hagan for U.S. Senate. 2008. "The Issues." http://www.kayhagan.com/issues. Accessed February 5, 2009.

Keck, Margaret E., and Kathryn Sikkink. 1998. *Activists Beyond Borders.* Ithaca: Cornell University Press.

Kerwin, Donald. 2005. "Justice for Newcomers: A Catholic Call for Solidarity and Reform." Catholic Charities 2005 Policy Paper. Mirna Torres, Catholic Legal Immigration Network, Washington DC, personal files.

Kibria, Nazli. 1993. *Family Tightrope: The Changing Lives of Vietnamese Americans.* Princeton: Princeton University Press.

Killian, Lewis M. 1984. "Organization, Rationality, and Spontaneity in the Civil Rights Movement." *American Sociological Review* 49(6): 770–83.

Kim, Thomas. 2007. *The Racial Logic of Politics: Asian Americans and Party Competition.* Philadelphia: Temple University Press.

Kirschten, Dick. 1997. "The Politics of Citizenship." Available at: http://govexec.com/features/0197s4htm.

Kondracke, Mort. 2007. "Despite Danger, GOP Tees Up Immigration as Wedge Issue." November 8. Real Clear Politics. Available at: http://www.realclearpolitics.com/articles/2007/11/despite_danger_gop_tees_up_imm.html. Accessed November 11, 2007.

Konkol, Mark J. 2006. "Chicago Immigration March Gets PUSH Support: Jackson Pledges Participants, Says Blacks Need Not Fear." *Chicago Sun Times,* April 26.

Koopmans, Ruud, and Paul Statham. 2001. *Challenging Immigration and Ethnic Relations Politics: Comparative European Perspectives*. New York: Oxford University Press.

Koopmans, Ruud, Paul Statham, Marco Giugni, and Florence Passy. 2005. *Contested Citizenship: Immigration and Cultural Diversity in Europe*. Minneapolis: University of Minnesota Press.

Krikorian, Mark. 2005. "Not Amnesty but Attrition: The Way to Go on Immigration." *National Review*, March 22. Available at: http://www.cis.org/articles/2004/markoped 032204.html. Accessed November 12, 2007.

Kronholz, June. 2007. "Immigration Is the Question: How '08 Hopefuls Answer Could Take Them Far, Perhaps." *Wall Street Journal*, November 19.

Laglagaron, Laureen, Cristina Rodríguez, Alexa Silver, and Sirithon Thanasombat. 2008. *Regulating Immigration at the State Level: Highlights from the Database of 2007 State Immigration Legislation and the Methodology*. Washington DC: Migration Policy Institute. Available at: http://www.migrationpolicy.org/pubs/2007methodology.pdf. Accessed June 15, 2009.

Latino Decisions. 2010. http://latinodecisions.wordpress.com/2010/11/02/latino-election -eve-poll-results-november-2-2010.

Latino Policy Coalition. 2006a. "Final Weighted Frequencies." April. Available at: http:// latinopolicycoalition.org/poll2006.htm. Accessed April 3, 2007.

——. 2006b. "Topline Results." June. Available at: http://latinopolicycoalition.org/ poll2006.htm. Accessed April 3, 2007.

——. 2006c. "Topline Results." October. Available at: http://latinopolicycoalition.org/ poll2006.htm. Accessed April 3, 2007.

Leal, David L. 2002. "Political Participation by Latino Non-Citizens in the United States." *British Journal of Political Science* 32:353–70.

Leal, David L., Matt A. Barreto, Jongho Lee, and Rodolfo O. de la Garza. 2005. "The Latino Vote in the 2004 Election." Apsnet.org, PS Online, January, 41–49.

Leal, David L., Stephen Nuño, Jongho Lee, and Rodolfo O. de la Garza. 2008. "Latinos, Immigration, and the 2006 Midterm Elections." *PS: Political Science and Politics* 41(2): 309–17.

Lee, Taeku. 2008. "Race, Immigration, and the Identity-to-Politics Link." *Annual Review of Political Science* 11:457–87.

Leighley, Jan E., and Arnold Vedlitz. 1999. "Race, Ethnicity, and Political Participation: Competing Models and Contrasting Explanations." *Journal of Politics* 61: 1092–114.

Leinwand, Donna. 2006. "Immigration Raid Linked to ID Theft, Chertoff Says." *USA Today*, December 13.

Lien, Pei-te. 1994. "Ethnicity and Political Participation: A Comparison between Asian and Mexican Americans." *Political Behavior* 16:237–64.

Logan, John. 2003. "Innovations in State and Local Labor Legislation: Neutrality Laws and Labor Peace Agreements in California." In *The State of California Labor 2003*. Berkeley: University of California Press.

Lopez, David, and Yen Lee Espiritu. 1990. "Panethnicity in the United States: A Theoretical Framework." *Ethnic and Racial Studies* 13:198–224.

Lopez, Mark Hugo. 2008. *The Hispanic Vote in the 2008 Election.* Washington DC: Pew Hispanic Center, November 7. Available at: http://pewhispanic.org/files/reports/98 .pdf.

Lopez, Mark Hugo, and Gretchen Livingston. 2009. *Hispanics and the New Administration.* Washington DC: Pew Hispanic Center, January 15. Available at: http://pewhispanic .org/reports/report.php?ReportID=101.

Lopez, Mark Hugo, and Susan Minushkin. 2008a. *2008 National Survey of Latinos: Hispanic Voter Attitudes.* Washington DC: Pew Hispanic Center, July 24. Available at: http://pewhispanic.org/files/reports/90.pdf. Accessed January 13, 2009.

———. 2008b. *2008 National Survey of Latinos: Hispanics See Their Situation in U.S. Deteriorating; Oppose Key Immigration Enforcement Measures.* Washington DC: Pew Hispanic Center, September 18. Available at: http://pewhispanic.org/reports/report.php ?ReportID=93. Accessed January 11, 2009.

Ludden, Jennifer. 2007. "Immigrants Rush to Seek Citizenship." National Public Radio, July 30. Available at: http://www.npr.org/templates/story/story.php?storyId=12260517. Accessed November 11, 2007.

LULAC (League of United Latin American Citizens). 2008. "Historic Latino Voter Turnout Helps Elect Barack Obama." Press release, November 5. Available at: http://www .lulac.org/advocacy/press/2008/obamaelected.html.

MacManus, Susan A., and Carol A. Cassel. 1988. "Mexican-Americans in City Politics: Participation, Representation, and Policy Preferences." In *Latinos and the Political System. Notre Dame,* edited by E. Chris Garcia. South Bend: University of Notre Dame Press.

Mahony, Roger. 2006. Cardinal Mahony statement, Postcard Campaign for Immigration Reform, May 9. Archdiocese of Los Angeles, Archdiocesan News Archive. Available at: http://www.archdiocese.la/news/story.php?newsid=744. Accessed June 11, 2007.

———. 2008. "Renewing Hope, Seeking Justice." Keynote address the National Migration Conference, Washington DC, July 28. Archdiocese of Los Angeles, Archdiocesan News Archive. Available at: http://laarchdiocese.net/news/pdf/news_998_RENEWING %20HOPE,%20SEEKING%20JUSTICE.pdf. Accessed January 28, 2009.

Manteca, Martin. 2007. Personal interview, February 27.

Marcelli, Enrico, and Wayne Cornelius. 2005. "Immigrant Voting in Home-Country Elections: Potential Consequences of Extending the Franchise to Expatriate Mexicans Residing in the United States." *Mexican Studies/Estudios Mexicanos* 21(2): 429–60.

Mariscal, George. 2005. *Brown-Eyed Children of the Sun: Lessons from the Chicano Movement, 1965–1975.* Albuquerque: University of New Mexico Press.

Martin, Philip L. 1994. "Good Intentions Gone Awry: IRCA and U.S. Agriculture." *Annals of the Academy of Political and Social Science* 534:44–57.

Martínez, Cindy, and Francisco Piña. 2005. "Chicago en marcha por reforma migratoria." *MX sin Fronteras,* no, 20 (August): 7–9.

Martinez, Lisa M. 2005. "Yes We Can: Latino Participation in Unconventional Politics." *Social Forces* 84(1): 135–55.

———. 2008a. "Framing Immigration: The Media and Competing Claims about the 2006 Immigration Protests." Unpublished manuscript.

———. 2008b. "The Individual and Contextual Determinants of Protest among Latinos." *Mobilization* 13:180–204.

Martínez-Nateras, Myrna, and Eduardo Stanley. 2009. *Latino Immigrant Civic and Political Participation in Fresno and Madera, California.* Reports on Latino Immigrant Civic Engagement. Washington DC: Woodrow Wilson International Center for Scholars. Available at: http://www.wilsoncenter.org/migrantparticipation.

Massey, Douglas S., ed. 2008. *New Faces in New Places: The Changing Geography of American Immigration.* New York: Russell Sage Foundation.

Massey, Douglas S., Joaquin Arango, Graeme Hugo, Ali Kouaouci, Adela Pellegrino, and J. Edward Taylor. 1998. *Worlds in Motion: Understanding International Migration at the End of the Millennium.* New York: Oxford University Press.

Massey, Douglas S., Jorge Durand, and Nolan Malone. 2002. *Beyond Smoke and Mirrors: Mexican Immigration in an Era of Economic Integration.* New York: Russell Sage Foundation.

McAdam, Doug. 1986. "Recruitment to High-Risk Activism: The Case of Freedom Summer." *American Journal of Sociology* 92(1): 64–90.

———. 1988. *Freedom Summer.* New York: Oxford University Press.

———. 1999 [1982]. *Political Process and the Development of Black Insurgency, 1930–1970.* Chicago: University of Chicago Press.

McAdam, Doug, John D. McCarthy, and Mayer N. Zald. 1996. *Comparative Perspectives on Social Movements: Political Opportunities, Mobilizing Structures, and Cultural Framings.* New York: Cambridge University Press.

McAdam, Doug, and Ronnelle Paulsen. 1993. "Specifying the Relationship Between Social Ties and Activism." *American Journal of Sociology* 3:640–67.

McCann, James, Wayne Cornelius, and David Leal. 2006. "Mexico's Voto Remoto and the Potential for Transnational Civic Engagement among Mexican Expatriates." Paper presented at the American Political Science Association, Philadelphia, August 31–September 2.

McCarrick, Theodore E. 2006. "Statement of Cardinal Theodore E. McCarrick, Archbishop of Washington, Comprehensive Immigration Reform." March 1. USCCB/MRS. Available at: http://www.nccbuscc.org/mrs/mccarrick.shtml. Accessed June 12, 2007.

McCarthy, John D., Clark McPhail, and Jackie Smith. 1996. "Images of Protest: Dimensions of Selection Bias in Media Coverage of Washington Demonstrations, 1982 and 1991." *American Sociological Review* 61:478–99.

McDevitt, Michael, and Steven Chaffee. 2000. "Closing Gaps in Political Communication and Knowledge: Effects of a School Intervention." *Communications Research* 27:259–92.

———. 2002. "From Top-Down to Trickle-Up Influence: Revisiting Assumptions About the Family in Political Socialization." *Political Communication* 19:281–301.

McDonnell, Patrick J., and Robert J. López. 1994. "70,000 March through L.A. against Prop. 187." *Los Angeles Times,* October 17.

McNeal, Ralph. 1998. "High School Extracurricular Activities: Closed Structures and Stratifying Patterns of Participation." *Journal of Educational Research* 91:183–91.

Medina, Eliseo. 2006. "The Birth of a National Movement." *Los Angeles Times,* May 2.
———. 2007. Personal interview, February 13.
Melber, Ari. 2006. "MySpace, MyPolitics." *The Nation,* May 30. Available at: http://www
.thenation.com/doc/20060612/melber. Accessed October 22, 2007.
Menjívar, Cecilia. 2000. *Fragmented Ties: Salvadoran Immigrant Networks in America.*
Berkeley: University of California Press.
———. 2006. "Liminal Legality: Salvadoran and Guatemalan Immigrants' Lives in the
United States." *American Journal of Sociology* 111(4): 999–1037.
Merz, Barbara, ed. 2006. *New Patterns for Mexico: Remittances, Philanthropic Living and
Equitable Development.* Cambridge, MA: Harvard University Press.
Mexicanos for Political Progress. 2007. "Líderes mexicanos invitan a presenciar y anali-
zar el debate presidencial demócrata." Press conference, September 8. Available at the
FREBIMICH online forum, Google Groups. Accessed October 3, 2007.
Meyer, David S. 2004. "Protest and Political Opportunities." *Annual Review of Sociology*
30:125–45.
Meyer, David S., and Debra Minkoff. 2004. "Conceptualizing Political Opportunity." *So-
cial Forces* 82(4): 1457–92.
Meyer, David S., and Suzanne Staggenborg. 1996. "Movements, Countermovements, and
the Structure of Political Opportunity." *The American Journal of Sociology* 101:1628–60.
Meyerson, Harold. 2001. "California's Progressive Mosaic." *The American Prospect,* June 18.
———. 2004. "A Tale of Two Cities." *The American Prospect,* June 7.
———. 2005. "The Architect." *LA Weekly,* May 12.
Michelson, Melissa R. 2001. "Political Trust among Chicago Latinos." *Journal of Urban
Affairs* 23:323–34.
———. 2003. "The Corrosive Effect of Acculturation: How Mexican Americans Lose Political Trust." *Social Science Quarterly* 84(4): 918–33.
Migration Policy Institute. 2007a. "Frequently Requested Statistics on Immigrants in the
United States." Available at: http://www.migrationinformation.org/USfocus/display
.cfm?id=649. Accessed April 15, 2008.
———. 2007b. "Top 10 Migration Issues of 2007, Issue #1: Political Paralysis; The Failure
of US Immigration Reform." *Migration Information Source.* Available at: http://www
.migrationinformation.org/Feature/display.cfm?id=659. Accessed December 7, 2007.
Milkman, Ruth. 2006. *L.A. Story: Immigrant Workers and the Future of the U.S. Labor
Movement.* New York: Russell Sage Foundation.
Milkman, Ruth, and Bongoh Kye. 2008. *The State of the Unions in 2008: A Profile of Union
Membership in Los Angeles, California, and the Nation.* Los Angeles: UCLA Institute
for Research on Labor and Employment, September. Available at: http://www.irle.ucla
.edu/research/unionmembership.html.
Milkman, Ruth, and Kent Wong. 2000. *Voices from the Front Lines: Organizing Immigrant Workers in Los Angeles.* Translated by Luis Escala Rabadan. Los Angeles: Center
for Labor Research and Education.
———. 2001. "Organizing Immigrant Workers: Case Studies from Southern California."
In *Rekindling the Movement: Labor's Quest for 21st Century Relevance,* edited by Low-
ell Turner, Harry Katz, and Richard Hurd. Ithaca: Cornell University Press.

Miller, Lawrence, Jerry Polinard, and Robert Wrinkle. 1984. "Attitudes toward Undocumented Workers: The Mexican American Perspective." *Social Science Quarterly*
65:482–94.

Miller, Warren E., and J. Merrill Shanks. 1996. *The New American Voter.* Cambridge, MA:
Harvard University Press.

Minkoff, Debra. 1995. *Organizing for Equality.* New Brunswick: Rutgers University Press.

Mollenkopf, John Hull. 1999. "Urban Political Conflicts and Alliances: New York and Los
Angeles Compared." In *The Handbook of International Migration: The American Ex-
perience,* edited by Charles Hirshmann, Philip Kasinitz, and Josh DeWind. New York:
Russell Sage Foundation.

Mollenkopf, John, David Olson, and Tim Ross. 2001. "Immigrant Political Participation
in New York and Los Angeles." In *Governing American Cities: Interethnic Coalitions,
Competition, and Conflict,* edited by Michael Jones-Correa. New York: Russell Sage
Foundation.

Monterroso, Ben. 2007. Interview conducted by Randy Shaw, February 14.

———. 2009. Telephone interview conducted by Ruth Milkman, January 8.

Mooney, Margarita. 2007. "The Catholic Church's Institutional Responses to Immigration." In *Religion and Social Justice for Immigrants,* edited by Pierrette Hondagneu-
Sotelo. New Brunswick: Rutgers University Press.

Morales, Lymari. 2010. "Amid Immigration Debate, Americans' Views Ease Slightly."
Gallup poll, July 27. Available at: http://gallup.com/poll/141560/Amid-Immigration
-Debate-Americans-Views-Ease-Slightly.aspx. Accessed November 2, 2010.

Morris, Aldon D. 1984. *The Origins of the Civil Rights Movement: Black Communities Organizing for Change.* New York: Free Press.

———. 1993. "Birmingham Confrontation Reconsidered: An Analysis of the Dynamics
and Tactics of Mobilization." *American Sociological Review* 58(5): 621–36.

Morris, Aldon, and Naomi Braine. 2001. *Oppositional Consciousness: The Subjective
Roots of Social Protest.* Chicago: University of Chicago Press.

Murguía, Janet, and Cecilia Muñoz. 2005. "From Immigrants to Citizens." Special report,
The American Prospect 16(11).

Muñoz, Carlos, Jr. 1989. *Youth, Identity, Power: The Chicano Movement.* New York: Verso.

Muñoz, Rosalio. 2008. "Get Ready to Fast for Our Future." ¡LatinoLA! October 8. Available at: http://latinola.com/story.php?story=6861. Accessed January 28, 2009.

Munson, Ziad. 2003. "'My Life Is My Argument': Reconceptualizing Religion in Understanding Social Activism." Paper presented at the Religion, Political Economy and
Society seminar, Harvard University, October 22.

Mutz, Diana C., and Joe Soss. 1997. "Reading Public Opinion: The Influence of News Coverage on Perceptions of Public Sentiment." *Public Opinion Quarterly* 61:431–51.

Myers, Norman. 1992. "The Anatomy of Environmental Action: The Case of Tropical
Deforestation." In *The International Politics of the Environment,* edited by Andrew
Hurrell and Benedict Kingsbury. New York: Oxford University Press.

Nadler, Richard. 2009. "At What Cost?" *National Review,* February 23, 28–30.

Nagourney, Adam. 2007. "G.O.P. Candidates Confront Immigration Politics." *New York
Times,* March 20.

NALEO (National Association of Latino Elected and Appointed Officials). 2007. "Latino Coalition Unveils Unprecedented Campaign to Increase the Latino Vote in 2008 Presidential Elections. " Press release, November 14. Available at: http://www.naleo .org/pr111407.html

———. 2008a. "Latino Votes in the 2008 Presidential Election: Post-Election Survey of Latino Voters." November 21. NALEO Educational Fund. Available at: http://www .naleo.org/pr11-21-08.html.

———. 2008b. "Post-Election Survey of Latino Voters." November 25. NALEO Educational Fund. Available at: http://www.immigration08.com/2008/poll/latino_vote. Accessed January 11, 2009.Narro, Victor, Kent Wong, and Janna Shadduck-Hernández. 2007. "The 2006 Immigrant Uprising: Origins and Future." New Labor Forum 16(1): 49–56.

National Conference of State Legislatures (NCSL). 2007. Available at: http://www.ncsl. org/programs/immig/index.htm. Accessed October 31, 2007.

National Council of La Raza. 2008. President and CEO Janet Murguía's remarks at the 2008 Annual Conference. Available at: http://www.nclr.org/content/viewpoints/ detail/53062.

National Immigration Forum. 2006. Polling Summary: Public Support for Comprehensive Immigration Reform. Washington DC: National Immigration Forum. Available at: http://www.immigrationforum.org/images/uploads/PollingSummary706.pdf. Accessed January 13, 2009.

———. N.d. "McCain/Kennedy/Kolbe/Flake/Gutierrez: The Secure America and Orderly Immigration Act, Section-by-Section Analysis." Available at: http://www.immigration-forum.org/documents/PolicyWire/Legislation/CongressionalStaffSummary.pdf. Accessed January 13, 2009.

Nepstad, Sharon Erickson, and Christian Smith. 1999. "Rethinking Recruitment to High-Risk/Cost Activism: The Case of Nicaragua Exchange." Mobilization 4:25–40.

Neumann-Ortiz, Christine. 2008. "¡Sí, Se Puede! Spaces for Immigrant Organizing." In Immigrant Rights in the Shadows of Citizenship, edited by Rachel Ida Buff. New York: New York University Press.

New American Media. 2006. Legal Immigrants: A Voice of Reason in the Immigration Debate. San Francisco: New American Media.

Newbart, Dave, and Monifa Thomas. 2006. "These People Are Americans." Chicago Sun Times, March 11.

Newton, Kenneth. 1999. "Mass Media Effects: Mobilization or Media Malaise?" British Journal of Political Science 29(4): 577–99.

New York Times. 2006. "The Gospel vs. H.R. 4437." Editorial, March 3.

———. 2007. "The Misery Strategy." Editorial, August 9.

Nie, Norman H., Jane Junn, and Kenneth Stehlik-Barry. 1996. Education and Democratic Citizenship in America. Chicago: University of Chicago Press.

Niemi, Richard G. 1999. "Editor's Introduction." Political Psychology 20(3): 471–76.

Niemi, Richard G., and Mary A. Hepburn. 1995. "The Rebirth of Political Socialization." Perspectives on Political Science 24:7–16.

Nostrand, Richard L. 1975. "Mexican Americans Circa 1850." Annals of the Association of American Geographers 65(3): 378–90.

Oberschall, Anthony. 1989. "The 1960 Sit-Ins: Protest Diffusion and Movement Take-Off." *Research in Social Movements, Conflict, and Change* 11:31–3.

Ochoa, Gilda. 2004. *Becoming Neighbors in a Mexican American Community: Power, Conflict, and Solidarity.* Austin: University of Texas Press.

Odmalm, P. 2005. *Migration Policies and Political Participation: Inclusion or Intrusion in Western Europe?* London: Palgrave Macmillan.

OECD/SOPEMI (Organisation for Economic Co-operation and Development/Système d'Observation Permanente des Migrations). 2007. *International Migration Outlook 2007.* Paris: OECD.

Office of Immigration Statistics, U.S. Immigration and Customs Enforcement. 2006. *Enforcement.* Washington DC: Government Printing Office.

———. 2010. *Immigration Enforcement Actions: 2009.* Annual Report. Washington DC: Department of Homeland Security. Available at: http://www.dhs.gov/xlibrary/assets/statistics/publications/enforcement_ar_2009.pdf.

Okamoto, Dina. 2004. "Towards a Theory of Panethnicity: Explaining Asian American Collective Action." *American Sociological Review* 68:811–42.

Oliver, Jeff. 2006. "A New Corps Mobilizes over Immigration." *Christian Science Monitor,* March 28.

Olivo, Antonio, Vanessa Bauza, and Carlos Sadovi. 2008. "Smaller March Still Spirited." *Chicago Tribune,* May 2.

Oppenheimer, Andrés. 2007. "Pressure on Immigrants Could Erupt in Anger." *San Jose Mercury News,* November 6.

Orellana, Marjorie Faulstich. 2001. "The Work Kids Do: Mexican and Central American Immigrant Children's Contributions to Households and Schools in California." *Harvard Educational Review* 71(3): 366–89.

Owen, Bruce M., and Steven S. Wildman. 1992. *Video Economics.* Cambridge, MA: Harvard University Press.

Pachon, Harry, and Louis DeSipio. 1994. *New Americans by Choice: Political Perspectives of Latino Immigrants.* Boulder, CO: Westview Press.

Padilla, Felix. 1985. "On the Nature of Latino Ethnicity." In *The Mexican-American Experience: An Interdisciplinary Anthology,* edited by Rodolfo de la Garza. Austin: University of Texas Press.

Pallares, Amalia. 2009. "Family Matters: Strategizing Immigrant Activism in Chicago." In *Series on Latino Migrant Civic Engagement,* Report no. 7, edited by Xóchitl Bada, Kate Brick, Jonathan Fox, and Andrew Selee. Washington DC: Woodrow Wilson International Center for Scholars, Mexico Institute.

———. 2010. "Representing La Familia: Family Separation and Immigrant Activism in Chicago." In *¡Marcha! Latino Chicago and the National Immigrant Movement,* edited by Amalia Pallares and Nilda Flores-González. Urbana: University of Illinois Press.

Pallares, Amalia, and Nilda Flores-González, eds. 2010. *¡Marcha! Latino Chicago and the Immigrant Rights Movement.* Urbana: University of Illinois Press.

Pantoja, Adrian D., Ricardo Ramírez, and Gary M. Segura. 2001. "Citizens by Choice, Voters by Necessity: Patterns in Political Mobilization by Naturalized Latinos." *Political Research Quarterly* 54:729–50.

Pantoja, Adrian D., and Gary M. Segura. 2003. "Fear and Loathing in California: Contextual Threat and Political Sophistication Among Latino Voters." *Political Behavior* 25:265–86.

Park, John S. W. 2008. "On Being Here and Not Here: Noncitizen Status in American Immigration Law." Pp. 26–39 in *Immigrant Rights: In the Shadows of Citizenship*, edited by Rachel Ida Buff. New York: New York University Press.

Parks, James. 2003. "Immigrant Workers Freedom Ride." Available at: http://www.aflcio .org/aboutus/thisistheaflcio/publications/magazine/0903_iwfr.cfm.

———. 2005. "Recognizing Our Common Bonds." Available at: http://www.aflcio.org/ aboutus/thisistheaflcio/publications/magazine/commonbonds.cfm.

Passel, Jeffrey S. 2005. *Unauthorized Migrants: Numbers and Characteristics*. Washington DC: Pew Hispanic Center.

———. 2007. *Growing Share of Immigrants Choosing Naturalization*. Washington DC: Pew Hispanic Center, March 28.

Pastor, Manuel. 1993. *Latinos and the Los Angeles Uprising: The Economic Context*. Claremont, CA: The Tomas Rivera Center.

———. 1995. "Economic Inequality, Latino Poverty and Civil Unrest in Los Angeles." *Economic Development Quarterly* 9(3): 238–58.

Pear, Robert. 2007. "Little-Known Group Claims a Win on Immigration." *New York Times*, July 15.

Perla, Héctor, Jr. 2008. "Si Nicaragua Venció, El Salvador Vencerá: Central American Agency in the Creation of the U.S.–Central American Peace and Solidarity Movement." *Latin American Research Review* 43(2): 136–58.

Peter, Jochen. 2004. "Our Long 'Return to the Concept of Powerful Mass Media'—A Cross-National Comparative Investigation of the Effects of Consonant Media Coverage." *International Journal of Public Opinion Research* 16:144–68.

Pew Forum on Religion and Public Life. 2007. "U.S. Religious Landscape Survey." Available at: http://religions.pewforum.org. Accessed July 2, 2008.

Pew Hispanic Center. 2006a. *Hispanics: A Statistical Portrait at Mid-decade*. Available at: http://pewhispanic.org/reports/middecade.

———. 2006b. *The State of American Public Opinion on Immigration in Spring 2006: A Review of Major Surveys*. Washington DC: Pew Hispanic Center.

———. 2008. *Statistical Portrait of Hispanics in the United States, 2006*. Available at: http://pewhispanic.org/files/factsheets/hispanics2006/hispanics.pdf. Accessed April 15, 2008.

Pew Research Center for the People and the Press and the Pew Hispanic Center. 2006. *No Consensus on Immigration Problem or Proposed Fixes: America's Immigration Quandary*. Washington DC: Pew Research Center for the People and the Press.

Piven, Frances Fox, and Richard Cloward. 1978. *Poor People's Movements: Why They Succeed, How They Fail*. New York: Vintage.

Polling Report. N.d. http://www.pollingreport.com/immigration.htm.

Portes, Alejandro, Cristina Escobar, and Renelinda Arana. 2007. "Bridging the Gap: Transnational and Ethnic Organizations in the Political Incorporation of Immigrants in the United States." Working Paper. Center for Migration and Development, Princeton University.

Portes, Alejandro, Cristina Escobar, Alexandria Walton Radford. 2007. "Immigrant Transnational Organizations and Development: A Comparative Study." *International Migration Review* 41(1): 242–81.

Portes, Alejandro, and Dag Macleod. 1996."Educational Progress of Children of Immigrants: The Roles of Class, Ethnicity, and School Context." *Sociology of Education* 69(4): 255–75.

Portes, Alejandro, and Rubén G. Rumbaut. 2001. *Legacies: The Story of the Immigrant Second Generation.* Berkeley and New York: University of California Press and Russell Sage Foundation.

Potter, Tom. 2007. "In My Opinion: Immigration Reform." *Oregonian,* August 12. Available at: http://www.portlandonline.com/mayor/index.cfm?c=36625&a=164966. Accessed November 12, 2007.

Preston, Julia. 2007a. "Sharp Rise Seen in Applications for Citizenship." *New York Times,* July 5.

———. 2007b. "Surge Brings New Immigration Backlog." *New York Times,* November 23.

———. 2008a. "In Reversal, Courts Uphold Local Immigration Laws." *New York Times,* February 10.

———. 2008b. "270 Illegal Immigrants Sent to Prison in Federal Push." *New York Times,* May 24, 2008.

———. 2008c."In Big Shift, Latino Vote Was Heavily for Obama." *New York Times,* November 7.

Prior, Markus. 2007. *Post-broadcast Democracy: How Media Choice Increases Inequality in Political Involvement and Polarizes Elections.* New York: Cambridge University Press.

Project for Excellence in Journalism. 2006. *The State of the News Media.* Available at: http://www.stateofthenewsmedia.org/2006/narrative_ethnicalternative_audience .asp?cat=4&media=10. Accessed November 15, 2007.

Przybyla, Heidi. 2007. "Romney Shifts on Immigration, Sharpening Contrast with McCain." *Bloomberg News,* March 29.

Putnam, Robert D. 2000. *Bowling Alone: The Collapse and Revival of American Community.* New York: Simon and Schuster.

Quintero, Fernando. 2007. "Bid for Citizenship Rise." *Rocky Mountain News,* September 1. Available at: http://www.rockymountainnews.com/drmn/local/article/0,1299,DRMN _15_5687548,00.html. Accessed November 11, 2007.

Radionotas. 2006. "Entrevista con El Peladillo" Available at: http://radionotas.com.

Ramakrishnan, S. Karthick. 2005. *Democracy in Immigrant America: Changing Demographics and Political Participation.* Palo Alto: Stanford University Press.

Ramakrishnan, S. Karthick, and Celia Viramontes. 2006. *Civic Inequalities: Immigrant Volunteerism and Community Organizations in California.* San Francisco: Public Policy Institute of California.

Ramakrishnan, S. Karthick, and Tom Wong. 2010. "Partisanship, Not Spanish: Explaining Municipal Ordinances Affecting Undocumented Immigrants." In *Taking Local Control: Immigration Policy Activism in U.S. Cities and States,* edited by Monica W. Varsanyi. Palo Alto: Stanford University Press.

Ramírez, Ricardo. 2002. "The Changing Landscape of California Politics, 1990–2000." PhD dissertation, Stanford University.

———. 2005. "Giving Voice to Latino Voters: A Field Experiment on the Effectiveness of a National Nonpartisan Mobilization Effort." *Annals of the American Academy of Political and Social Science* 601:66–84.

———. 2007. "Segmented Mobilization: Latino Nonpartisan Get-Out-the-Vote Efforts in the 2000 General Election." *American Politics Research* 35(3): 155–75.

Rasmussen Reports. 2006a. *Immigration Rallies Fail to Move Public Opinion.* Asbury Park, NJ: Rasmussen Reports.

———. 2006b. *24% Have Favorable Opinion of Protestors.* Asbury Park, NJ: Rasmussen Reports.

———. 2006c. *Views on Immigration Issues by State.* Asbury Park, NJ: Rasmussen Reports. Available at: http://www.rasmussenreports.com/04%2006%20State%20by%20State%20Immigration%20Questions.htm. Accessed February 10, 2007.

Rauh, Grace. 2006. "Oakland Schools Miss Thousands of Students." *Oakland Tribune,* May 2.

Ready, Timothy, Roger Knight, and Sung-Chan Chun. 2006. *Latino Civic and Community Involvement: Findings from the Chicago-Area Survey.* Notre Dame: University of Notre Dame, Institute for Latino Studies, 2006.

Reid, Tim. 2006. "See if You Can Cope without Us, Protesting Latinos Tell America." *The (London) Times,* May 2.

Rivera-Sánchez, Liliana. 2004. "Expressions of Identity and Belonging: Mexican Immigrants in New York." In *Indigenous Mexican Migrants in the United States,* edited by Jonathan Fox and Gaspar Rivera-Salgado. La Jolla: University of California, San Diego, Center for Comparative Immigration Studies and Center for US-Mexican Studies.

Rodríguez, América. 1999. *Making Latino News: Race, Language, Class.* Thousand Oaks, CA: Sage.

———. 2005. "Media and Migrant Civil Society." Background paper presented at the Mexican Migrant Civic Participation in the United States seminar, Woodrow Wilson International Center for Scholars, Washington DC, November. Available at: http://www.wilsoncenter.org/migrantparticipation.

Rodriguez, Gregory. 2004. "Tamed Spaces: How Religious Congregations Nurture Immigrant Assimilation." In *Immigrants, Religious Congregations, and the Civil Society.* Faith and Public Policy Report. Malibu, CA: The Davenport Institute and Pepperdine University School of Public Policy.

Rodriguez, Joseph. 1998. "Becoming Latinos: Mexican Americans, Chicanos, and the Spanish Myth in the Urban Southwest." *The Western Historical Quarterly* 29(2): 165–85.

Rogers, Rob. 2007. "Marin Supervisors Criticize Immigration Raids." *Marin Independent,* March 13. Available at: http://www.marinij.com/ci_5426759?source=rss. Accessed November 12, 2007.

Rojas, Aurelio. 2006. "From Farm Laborer to Potentate in Capitol." *Sacramento Bee,* May 19.

Rojas, Guillermo. 1975. "Chicano/Raza Newspaper and Periodical Serials Listing." *Hispania* 58(4): 851–63.

Romero, Victor. 2008. "Who Should Manage Immigration—Congress or the States?: An Introduction to Constitutional Immigration Law." *In Immigrant Rights in the Shadows of Citizenship, edited by Rachel Buff. New York: New York University Press.*

Rosas-López, María de Lourdes. 2007. "Prácticas políticas transnacionales y poder local: Cambio y continuidad en las estructuras municipales rurales de la mixteca poblana-oaxaqueña." Paper presented at the Latin American Studies Association, Montreal.

Ross, Fred, Jr. 2006. Interview conducted by Randy Shaw, July 25.

Roscigno, Vincent J., and William F. Danaher. 2001. "Media and Mobilization." *American Sociological Review* 66:21–48

Rosenstone, Steven J., and John Mark Hansen. 1993. *Mobilization, Participation, and Democracy in America.* New York: Macmillan.

Rytina, Nancy. 2002. "IRCA Legalization Effects: Lawful Permanent Residence and Naturalization through 2001." Paper presented at the Effects of Immigrant Legalization Programs on the United States: Scientific Evidence on Immigrant Adaptation and Impacts on the U.S. Economy and Society, National Institutes of Health, Bethesda, MD, October 25.

Saad, Lydia. 2006. "Public Increasingly Names Iraq as Top Priority for Congress, President." Gallup News Service, December 4.

Sachs, Susan. 2003. "U.S. Crackdown Sets Off Unusual Rush to Canada." *New York Times,* February 25.

Sánchez-Jankowski, Martín. 1986. *City Bound: Urban Life and Political Life Among Chicano Youth.* Albuquerque: University of New Mexico Press.

Santa Ana, Otto. 2002. *Brown Tide Rising: Metaphors of Latinos in Contemporary American Public Discourse.* Austin: University of Texas Press.

Sassen, Saskia. 2006. "The Bits of a New Immigration Reality: A Bad Fit with Current Policy." Available at: http://borderbattles.ssrc.org/Sassen. Accessed June 10, 2008.

Schuck, Peter H. 2007. "The Disconnect between Public Attitudes and Policy Outcomes in Immigration." In *Debating Immigration,* edited by Carol M. Swain. New York: Cambridge University Press.

Schwartzman, Paul. 2006. "Immigrant Bill Sends Chill through Rally." *Washington Post,* March 8.

Sears, David, and John McConahay. 1973. *The Politics of Violence: The New Urban Blacks and the Watts Riot.* New York: Houghton Mifflin.

Sebastian, Simone, Heather Knight, and Nanette Asimov. 2006. "Big Student Boycott All Across State." *San Francisco Chronicle,* May 9.

Selvin, Molly. 2008. "Colorado May Hire Mexican Farm Workers." *Denver Post,* February 2.

Sensenbrenner, James. 2005. Border Protection, Antiterrorism, and Illegal Immigration Control Act (H.R. 4437). Full text available at: http://thomas.loc.gov.

Sharry, Frank. 2008. "What the 2008 Elections Mean For the Future of Immigration Reform." December 3. America's Voice, Washington DC. Available at: http://www.americasvoiceonline.org.

Shaw, Daron, Rodolfo O. de la Garza, and Jongho Lee. 2000. "Examining Latino Turnout in 1996: A Three States, Validated Survey Approach." *American Journal of Political Science* 44(2): 338–46.

Shaw, Randy. 2008. *Beyond the Fields: Cesar Chavez, the UFW, and the Struggle for Justice in the 21st Century.* Berkeley: University of California.

Sherry, Allison. 2007. "Tuition Hurdle Tests Illegal Immigrant Kids." *Denver Post,* October 28.

Shingles, Richard D. 1981. "Black Consciousness and Political Participation: The Missing Link." *American Political Science Review* 75:76–91.

Shklar, Judith. 1991. *American Citizenship: The Quest for Inclusion.* Cambridge, MA: Harvard University Press.

Skerry, Peter. 1993. *Mexican-Americans: The Ambivalent Minority.* Cambridge, MA: Harvard University Press.

Skylstad, William. 2006. "Letter to President Bush from Most Reverend William Skylstad, President of the United States Conference of Catholic Bishops." October 10. Available at: http://justiceforimmigrants.org/files/+SkylstadHR6061.pdf. Accessed June 11, 2007.

Simerman, John. 2006. "Marchers Unite Efforts in Pursuit of 'Better Life'—Thousands of Immigrants Protest." *Contra Costa Times,* May 2.

Simonett, Helena. 2000. "Popular Music and the Politics of Identity: The Empowering Sound of Technobanda." *Popular Music and Society* 24(2): 1–24.

Singer, Audrey. 2004a. *The Rise of New Immigrant Gateways.* Living Cities Census Series, Center on Urban and Metropolitan Policy. Washington DC: The Brookings Institution.

———. 2004b. "Welfare Reform and Immigrants: A Policy Review." In *Immigrants, Welfare Reform, and the Poverty of Policy,* edited by Philip Kretsedemans and Ana Aparicio. Westport, CT: Praeger.

Smith, Christian. 1996a. "Correcting a Curious Neglect, or Bringing Religion Back In.'" In *Disruptive Religion: The Force of Faith in Social Movement Activism,* edited by Christian Smith. New York: Routledge.

———. 1996b. *Resisting Reagan: The U.S. Central America Peace Movement.* Chicago: University of Chicago Press.

Smith, Jackie. 2008. *Social Movements for Global Democracy.* Baltimore: Johns Hopkins University Press.

Smith, Michael Peter, and Matt Bakker. 2008. *Citizenship across Borders: The Political Transnationalism of El Migrante.* Ithaca: Cornell University Press.

Solis, Oscar. 2008. "2008 Lenten Message from the Most Reverend Bishop Oscar Solis . . ." March. Available at: http://www.laarchdiocese.org/ministry/justice/peace/documents/LentenMessage2008.pdf. Accessed January 28, 2009.

———. 2009. "Immigration from the Church's Perspective: What Would Jesus Do?" Talk sponsored by Social Justice Committee, Santa Barbara Region, Deanery 4. Archdiocese of Los Angeles. Available at: http://www.archdiocese.la/ministry/justice/peace/St.MaryMagdalenFlyer-BishopSolis.pub. Accessed January 28, 2009.

Somers, Laurie Kay. 1991. "Inventing Latinismo: The Creation of 'Hispanic' Panethnicity in the United States." *The Journal of American Folklore* 104(411): 32–53.

Somers, Margaret. 2005. "Citizenship Troubles: Genealogies of Struggle for the Soul of the Social." In *Remaking Modernity*, edited by J. Adams, L. Clemens, and A. Orloff. Durham: Duke University Press.

———. 2006. "Citizenship, Statelessness and Market Fundamentalism: Arendtian Lessons on Right to have Rights." In *Migration, Citizenship, Ethnos*, edited by M. Bodemann and G. Yurdakul. New York: Palgrave Macmillan.

Soysal, Yasemin N. 1994. *Limits of Citizenship: Migrants and Postnational Membership in Europe*. Chicago: University of Chicago Press.

Spagat, Elliot. 2006. "Veterans Drawn into Immigration Debate." *Washington Post*, April 24.

Squires, Catherine R. 2000. "Black Talk Radio: Defining Community Needs and Identity." *Harvard International Journal of Press/Politics* 5(2): 73–93.

Starr, Alexandra. 2006. "The Spanish-Language DJs behind the New Wave of Latino Activism." *Slate Magazine*.

Starr, Penny. 2008. "Illegal Alien Deportations on the Rise." CNSNews Wire, April 10. Available at: http://www.libnot.com/2008/04/10/illegal-immigrant-crackdown-deportations-on-the-rise-says-ice.

The State. 2006. "Thousands March for Immigrants' Rights." April 11.

Steinhauer, Jennifer, and Julia Preston. 2007. "Action by Police at Rally Troubles Los Angeles Chief." *New York Times*, May 4.

Stokes, Atiya Kai. 2003. "Latino Group Consciousness and Political Participation." *American Politics Research* 31:361–78.

Suro, Roberto. 2006. "A Developing Identity: Hispanics in the United States." *Carnegie Reporter* (Spring).

Suro, Roberto, and Gabriel Escobar. 1998. *Strangers among Us: How Latino Immigration Is Transforming America*. New York: Knopf.

———. 2006a. *Pew Hispanic Center Survey of Mexicans Living in the U.S. on Absentee Voting in Mexican Elections*. Washington DC: Pew Hispanic Center, February 22.

———. 2006b. *2006 National Survey of Latinos: The Immigration Debate*. Washington DC: Pew Hispanic Center, July.

Suro, Roberto, Richard Fry, and Jeffrey Passel. 2005. *Hispanics and the 2004 Election: Population, Electorate and Voters*. Washington DC: Pew Hispanic Center.

Swarns, Rachel. 2005. "Bill on Illegal-Immigrant Aid Draws Fire." *New York Times*, December 30.

Tarrow, Sidney. 1994. *Power in Movement: Social Movements, Collective Action, and Politics*. Cambridge: Cambridge University Press.

———. 1998. *Power in Movement: Social Movements and Contentious Politics*. Cambridge: Cambridge University Press.

———. 2005. *The New Transnational Activism*. Cambridge: Cambridge University Press.

Tate, Katherine. 1993. *From Protest to Politics*. New York: Russell Sage Foundation.

Taylor, Paul, and Richard Fry. 2007. *Hispanics and the 2008 Election: A Swing Vote?* Washington DC: Pew Hispanic Center, December 6. Available at: http://pewhispanic.org/reports/report.php?ReportID=83.

Thompson, Ginger. 2001. "U.S. and Mexico to Open Talks on Freer Migration for Workers." *New York Times,* February 16.

Thompson, Ginger, and Steven Greenhouse. 2001. "Mexican Guest Workers: Worth a Try." *New York Times,* April 3.

Thorne, Barrie. 1987. "Re-Visioning Women and Social Change: Where Are the Children?" *Gender and Society* 1(1): 85–109.

Thronson, David B. 2007. "Choiceless Choices: Deportation and the Parent-Child Relationship." *Nevada Law Review* 6 (2006): 1165–1214.

Tichenor, Daniel J. 2002. *Dividing Lines: The Politics of Immigration Control in America.* Princeton: Princeton University Press.

Tilly, Charles. 1978. *From Mobilization to Revolution.* Reading, MA: Addison-Wesley.

Tilly, Charles, and Sidney Tarrow. 2007. *Contentious Politics.* Boulder, CO: Paradigm.

Toner, Robin. 2001. "Civil Liberty vs. Security: Finding a Wartime Balance." *New York Times,* November 18.

Torres, Andres, and Jose Velasquez. 1998. *The Puerto Rican Movement: Voices from the Diaspora.* Philadelphia: Temple University Press.

Uhlaner, Carole J., Bruce E. Cain, and D. Roderick Kiewiet. 1989. "Political Participation of Ethnic Minorities in the 1980s." *Political Behavior* 11:195–221.

Unity Blueprint for Immigration Reform. 2007. *Unity Blueprint for Immigration Reform.* March 29. Available at: http://www.unityblueprint.org/_documents/3-29-07Unity BlueprintForImmigrationReform.pdf. Accessed December 7, 2007.

USA Today. 2006. "Poll: Immigration Concern Rising in USA." April 6. Available at: http://www.usatoday.com/news/nation/2006-04-09-poll-immigration_x.htm.

U.S. Bureau of Citizenship and Immigration Services. 2007. *N-400 Naturalization Benefits.* Washington DC: U.S. Bureau of Citizenship and Immigration Services. Available at: http://www.uscis.gov/files/article/N400%20NATURALIZATION%20BENEFITS _September07.pdf. Accessed November 21, 2007.

———. 2008. *N-400 Application Benefits.* Washington DC: U.S. Bureau of Citizenship and Immigration Services Accessed, February 3. Available at: http://www.uscis.gov/ files/article/Natz_Benefits_Oct2008.pdf.

U.S. Bureau of the Census. 2000. *Census 2000 Summary File 1.* Washington DC: Government Printing Office.

———. 2005a. *Current Population Reports.* Washington DC: Government Printing Office.

———. 2005b. *Voting and Registration in the Election of November 2004.* Detailed tables. Available at: http://www.census.gov/population/www/socdemo/voting/cps2004. html. Accessed November 21, 2005.

———. 2009. *Voting and Registration in the Election of November 2008.* Detailed tables. Available at: http://www.census.gov/hhes/www/socdemo/voting/publications/p20/ 2008/tables.html. Accessed November 2, 2010.

———. N.d. Data tables. Available at: http://www.census.gov/population/www/socdemo/ foreign/datatbls.html.

USCCB (U.S. Conference of Catholic Bishops). 1984. Newsletter from the Bishops Committee on Migration and Tourism 2(6)(June–July).

———. 2003. *Strangers No Longer: Together on the Journey of Hope; A Pastoral Letter Concerning Migration from the Catholic Bishops of Mexico and the United States.* Washington DC: U.S. Conference of Catholic Bishops.

———. 2006. "USCCB Migration Committee Chairman Calls Senate Immigration Bill 'A Good Start.'" Press statement, April 4. Available at: http://www.usccb.org/comm/archives/2006/06-069.shtml. Accessed June 12, 2007.

———. 2007a. USCCB Hispanic Affairs website, data from demographics section. Available at: http://www.usccb.org/hispanicaffairs/demo.shtml. Accessed December 7, 2007.

———. 2007b. USCCB Migration and Refugee Services website. http://www.usccb.org/mrs/mrsdescription.shtml. Accessed December 1, 2007.

———. 2009. "Bishops Urge President-Elect Obama, Mexican President Calderon, to Protect Rights of Migrants, Address Root Causes of Migration." January 12. Available at: http://www.usccb.org/mrs. Accessed January 28, 2009.

———. N.d. USCCB website. http://www.nccbuscc.org. Accessed September 30, 2007.

U.S. Department of Homeland Security. 2008. *2007 Yearbook of Immigration Statistics.* Washington DC: Office of Immigration Statistics, U.S. Department of Homeland Security. Available at: http://www.dhs.gov/xlibrary/assets/statistics/yearbook/2007/ois_2007_yearbook.pdf. Accessed February 3, 2009.

U.S. Immigration and Customs Enforcement. 2006a. "Department of Homeland Security Unveils Comprehensive Immigration Enforcement Strategy for the Nation's Interior." Press release, April 20. Available at: http://www.ice.gov/pi/news/newsreleases/articles/060420washington_2.htm. Accessed January 21, 2009.

———. 2006b. *Fiscal Year 2006 Annual Report.* Washington DC: Government Printing Office.

———. 2007. *Fiscal Year 2007 Annual Report.* Washington DC: Government Printing Office.

Valenzuela, Angela. 1999. *Subtractive Schooling.* Austin: University of Texas Press.

Valle, Victor M., and Rodolfo Torres. 2000. *Latino Metropolis.* Minneapolis: University of Minnesota Press.

van Hook, Jennifer, Frank Bean, and Jeffrey Passel. 2005. "Unauthorized Migrants Living in the United States: A Mid-Decade Portrait." *Migration Information Source.* Migration Policy Institute, Washington DC. Available at: http://www.migrationinformation.org/USfocus/display.cfm?ID=329. Accessed April 16, 2008.

Vargas, Sylvia R. Lazos. 2007. "The Immigrant Rights Marches (Las Marchas): Did the 'Gigante' (Giant) Wake Up or Does It Still Sleep Tonight?" *Nevada Law Journal* 780.

Varsanyi, Monica. 2005. "The Paradox of Contemporary Political Mobilization: Organized Labor, Undocumented Migrant and Electoral Participation in Los Angeles." *Antipode* 37(4).

Verba, Sidney, and Victor Nie. 1972. *Participation in America: Political Democracy and Social Equality.* Chicago: University of Chicago Press.

Verba, Sidney, Kay Lehman Schlozman, and Henry Brady. 1993. "Race, Ethnicity, and Political Resources: Participation in the United States." *British Journal of Political Science* 23:453–97.

——. 1995. *Voice and Equality: Civic Voluntarism in American Politics*. Cambridge: Harvard University Press.

Vigil, Maurilio E. 1987. *Hispanics in American Politics*. Lanham, MD: University Press of America.

Villarreal, Luz. 1995. "Group Seeks to Join INS Outreach Effort." *Los Angeles Daily News*, June 30.

Viramontes, Celia. 2008. "Civic Engagement Across Borders: Mexicans in Southern California." In *Civic Hopes and Political Realities: Immigrants, Community Organizations, and Political Engagement*, edited by S. Karthick Ramakrishnan and Irene Bloemraad. New York: Russell Sage Foundation.

Vonderlack-Navarro, Rebecca. 2007. *Chicago Mexican Hometown Associations and the Confederation of Mexican Federations: Experiences of Binational Civic Participation*. Woodrow Wilson International Center for Scholars, Mexico Institute.

Voss, Kim. 1996. "The Collapse of a Social Movement: The Interplay of Mobilizing Structures, Framing, and Political Opportunities in the Knights of Labor." Pp. 227–58 in *Comparative Perspectives on Social Movements: Political Opportunities, Mobilizing Structures, and Cultural Framings*, edited by Doug McAdam, John McCarthy, and Mayer Zald. Cambridge: Cambridge University Press.

Waldinger, Roger. 2007. *Between Here and There: How Attached Are Latino Immigrants to Their Native Country?* Washington DC: Pew Hispanic Center, October 25. Available at: http://www.pewhispanic.org.

Waldinger, Roger, Chris Erickson, Ruth Milkman, Daniel J. B. Mitchell, Abel Valenzuela, Kent Wong, and Maurice Zeitlin. 1998. "Helots No More: A Case Study of the Justice for Janitors Campaign in Los Angeles." In *Organizing to Win*, edited by Kate Bronfenbrenner, Sheldon Friedman, Richard W. Hurd, Rudolph A. Oswald, and Ronald L. Seeber. Ithaca: Cornell University Press.

Waldinger, Roger, and David Fitzgerald. 2004. "Transnationalism in Question." *American Journal of Sociology* 109(5): 1177–95.

Wall Street Journal. 2007. "Hispanics and the GOP." Editorial, September 15.

Wang, Ted, and Robert C. Winn. 2006. *Groundswell Meets Groundwork: Recommendations for Building on Immigrant Mobilizations*. Special Report. New York: Four Freedoms Fund and Grantmakers Concerned with Immigrants and Refugees. Available at: http://www.gcir.org/publications/gcirpubs/groundswell. Accessed October 25, 2010.

Ward, Brian. 2004. *Radio and the Struggle for Civil Rights in the South*. Gainesville: University Press of Florida.

Watanabe, Teresa. 2006. "Mahony's Lenten Message Irritates Some at Service." *Los Angeles Times*, March 2.

——. 2007. "Citizenship Applications Climb Despite Fee Hike." *Los Angeles Times*, November 4.

Watanabe, Teresa, and Hector Becerra. 2006a. "500,000 Pack Streets to Protest Immigration Bills." *Los Angeles Times*, March 26.

——. 2006b. "How DJs Put 500,000 Marchers in Motion." *Los Angeles Times*, March 28.

Watanabe, Teresa, and Nicole Gaouette. 2006. "NEXT: Converting the Energy of Protest to Political Clout." *Los Angeles Times*, May 2.

Watanabe, Teresa, Anna Gorman, and Ari B. Bloomekatz. 2008. "March Smaller, but Festive." *Los Angeles Times*, May 2.

Watanabe, Teresa, and Joe Mathews. 2006. "Unions Helped to Organize 'Day without Immigrants.'" *Los Angeles Times*, May 3.

Watkins, Mel. 1994. *On the Real Side: Laughing, Lying, and Signifying—the Underground Tradition of African-American Humor that Transformed American Culture, from Slavery to Richard Pryor*. New York: Simon and Schuster.

Watt, Brian. 2008. "Interfaith Immigrants' Rights Coalition Launches Week on Rights." *News in Brief*, KPCC, December 10. Available at: http://www.publicradio.org/columns/kpcc/kpccnewsinbrief/2008/12/interfaith-immigrants-rights-c.html. Accessed January 28, 2009.

We Are America Coalition. 2006a. "Today We Act, Tomorrow We Vote: April 10 National Day of Action, Candlelight Vigil and Procession." Flyer. We Are America Southern California. Available at: http://todayweact.org/en/April_10_National_Day_of_Actions #Downtown_L.A.2C_5:00_pm_.40_La_Placita. Accessed December 1, 2007.

———. 2006b. Media packet, May 1. Available at: http://todayweact.org. Accessed December 1, 2007.

———. 2006c. Postcard, attached to Cardinal Mahony statement, Postcard Campaign for Immigration Reform, May 9. Archdiocese of Los Angeles, Archdiocesan News Archive. Available at: http://www.archdiocese.la/news/pdf/news_744_Microsoft %20Word%20-%20PostcardWeAreAmerica-Archdiocese%20FinalEdited.pdf. Accessed June 11, 2007.

———. 2006d. "We Are America Launches Massive Citizenship Drive." Press release, June 27. Available at: http://todayweact.org/en/Media_Advisory_-_July_1%2C_2006. Accessed November 17, 2007.

We Are America Alliance. N.d. http://www.weareamericaalliance.org.

Weir, Margaret. 2002. "Income Polarization and California's Social Contract." In *The State of California Labor 2002*. Berkeley: University of California Press.

Wells, Miriam J. 2000. "Immigration and Unionization in the San Francisco Hotel Industry." In *Organizing Immigrants*, edited by Ruth Milkman. Ithaca: Cornell University Press.

White House. 2005. "President Applauds House for Passing Immigration Reform Law Bill." Office of the Press Secretary, December 16. Available at: http://www.whitehouse .gov/news/release/2005/12/2005/216-13.html.

———. 2009. "Interview of the President and Former President Bush by Brit Hume, Fox News." Office of the Press Secretary, January 11. Available at: http://www.whitehouse .gov/news/releases/2009/01/20090111-1.html.

Winton, Richard. 2007. "Police Panel Presses LAPD to Act on Officer Abuse during Melee." *Los Angeles Times*, October 31.

Wong, Janelle. 2006. *Democracy's Promise: Immigrants and American Civic Institutions*. Ann Arbor: University of Michigan Press.

Wong, Janelle, and Vivian Tseng. 2008. "Political Socialisation in Immigrant Families: Challenging Top-Down Parental Socialisation Models." *Journal of Ethnic and Migration Studies* 34(1): 151–68.

Wong, Kent. 2006. Personal interview, November 17.

Woodrow Wilson International Center for Scholars. 2007. "Immigrants' Rights Marches, Spring 2006." Available at: http://www.wilsoncenter.org/index.cfm?topic_id=5949& fuseaction opics.item&news_id=150685. Accessed February 5, 2007.

Worth, Robert F. 2002. "Man Detained After 9/11 Says Rights Were Ignored." *New York Times,* May 11.

Wuthnow, Robert. 1999. "Mobilizing Civic Engagement: The Changing Impact of Religious Involvement." In *Civic Engagement in American Democracy,* edited by Theda Skocpol and Morris P. Fiorina. Washington DC: Brookings Institution Press.

Ya es hora! N.d. http://www.yaeshora.info. Accessed November 11, 2007.

Yates, Miranda, and James Youniss. 1998. "Community Service and Political Identity Development in Adolescence." *Journal of Social Issues* 54(3): 495–512.

Yost, Ellen G. 1997. "Immigration and Nationality Law." *The International Lawyer* 31(2): 589–98.

Youniss, James, Susan Bales, Verona Christmas-Best, Marcelo Diversi, Milbrey McLaughlin, and Rainer Silbereisen. 2002. "Youth Civic Engagement in the Twenty-First Century." *Journal of Research on Adolescence* 12(1): 121–48.

Youniss, James, J. A. McLellan, and Miranda Yates. 1997. "What We Know about Engendering Civic Identity." *American Behavioral Scientist* 40:620–31.

Zald, Mayer N., and Bert Useem. 1987. "Movement and Countermovement Interaction: Mobilization, Tactics, and State Involvement." In *Social movements in an Organizational Society,* edited by Mayer N. Zald and John D. McCarthy. New Brunswick, NJ: Transaction.

Zaller, John. 1992. *The Nature and Origins of Mass Opinion.* New York: Cambridge University Press.

———. 1996. "The Myth of Massive Media Impact Revived: New Support for a Discredited Idea." In *Political Persuasion and Attitude Change,* edited by D. C. Mutz, P. M. Sniderman, and R. M. Brody. Chicago: Chicago University Press.

Zanotti, Rev. Richard. 2006. Personal interview, December 7.

Zentella, Ana Celia. 1997. *Growing Up Bilingual.* Malden, MA: Blackwell.

Zhao, Dingxin. 1998. "Ecologies of Social Movements: Student Mobilization During the 1989 Prodemocracy Movement in Beijing." *American Journal of Sociology* 103(6): 1493–1529.

Zinn, Maxina Baca. 1975. "Political Familism: Toward Sex Role Equality in Chicano Families." *Aztlan* 6(1).

Zolberg, Aristede R. 2006. *A Nation by Design: Immigration Policy in the Fashioning of America.* Cambridge, MA, and New York: Harvard University Press and Russell Sage Foundation Press.

Zúñiga, Victor, and Rubén Hernández-Léon, eds. 2005. *New Destinations: Mexican Immigration in the United States.* New York: Russell Sage Foundation.

CONTRIBUTORS

XÓCHITL BADA is assistant professor of Latin American and Latino studies at the University of Illinois at Chicago. Her research interests focus on transnational communities, race relations, migration and development, absentee voting rights for migrants, labor rights of undocumented workers, and migrant-led grassroots organizations. Her work on Mexican hometown associations has been published by the Americas Program of the International Relations Center, PBS, and in the books *Diáspora Michoacana* (El Colegio de Michoacán, 2003) and *¡Marcha! Latino Chicago and the National Immigrant Movement* (University of Illinois Press, 2010). She coedited the Woodrow Wilson International Center for Scholars' conference report, *Invisible No More: Mexican Migrant Civic Participation in the United States* (2006) and is a coauthor of *Context Matters: Latino Immigrant Civic Engagement in Nine U.S. Cities* (Woodrow Wilson International Center for Scholars, 2010).

IRENE BLOEMRAAD, associate professor in sociology at the University of California, Berkeley, studies immigration, political mobilization and citizenship, placing the U.S. experience in international context. Her book, *Becoming a Citizen: Incorporating Immigrants and Refugees in the United States and Canada* (University of California Press, 2006), argues that the United States' lack of general integration policies has led to lower levels of citizenship among immigrants in the United States compared to Canada, and to poorer outcomes in terms of political participation. Bloemraad has published articles on naturalization, dual citizenship, immigrant community organizations, and ethnic leadership in academic journals such as *Social Forces, International Migration Review, Social Science Quarterly,* and the *Journal of Ethnic and Migration Studies.* Her current projects, funded by the Russell Sage Foundation, examine the political and civic socialization of mixed-status Mexican American families and the role of organizations in facilitating immigrants' civic and political participation.

SHAUN BOWLER is a professor of political science at University of California, Riverside. He is author or coauthor of a number of books on citizen attitudes toward politics and the political system, including *Demanding Choices,* with Todd Donovan (University of Michigan Press, 1998); *Diversity in Democracy,* with Gary Segura (Virginia University Press, 2005); and *Losers' Consent,* with Chris Anderson, Todd Donovan, André Blais, and Ola Listhaug (Oxford University Press, 2005).

LOUIS DESIPIO is an associate professor in the Departments of Political Science and Chicano/Latino Studies at the University of California, Irvine. He is author of *Counting on the Latino Vote: Latinos as a New Electorate* (University Press of Virginia, 1996) and coauthor, with Rodolfo O. de la Garza, of *Making Americans, Remaking America: Immigration and Immigrant Policy* (Westview Press, 1998). He is also an author and editor of a seven-volume series on Latino political values, attitudes, and behaviors. The most recent volume in this series—*Muted Voices: Latinos and the 2000 Elections*—was published in 2005 (by Rowman and Littlefield). DeSipio's research focuses on Latino politics, on the process of political incorporation of new and formerly excluded populations into U.S. politics, and on public policies such as immigration, immigrant settlement, naturalization, and voting rights. DeSipio serves as chair of the UC Irvine Department of Chicano/Latino Studies.

NILDA FLORES-GONZÁLEZ is an associate professor of sociology and Latin American and Latino studies at the University of Illinois, Chicago. She studies race and ethnicity, identity, youth, education, and U.S. Latinos. Her publications include *School Kids/Street Kids: Identity Development in Latino Students* (Teachers College Press, 2002) and articles in journals and chapters in edited volumes. She coedited ¡Marcha! *Latino Chicago and the National Immigrant Movement* (University of Illinois Press, 2010).

JONATHAN FOX is a professor in the Department of Latin American and Latino Studies at the University of California, Santa Cruz. He began carrying out field research in Mexico in 1982 and began working with migrant organizations in California in 1997. He has numerous books to his credit, including *Accountability Politics: Voice and Power in Rural Mexico* (Oxford University Press, 2007), *Indigenous Mexican Migrants in the United States* (coeditor; UC San Diego Center for Comparative Immigration Studies and Center for U.S.-Mexican Studies, 2004), *Demanding Accountability: Civil-Society Claims and the World Bank Inspection Panel* (coeditor; Rowman and Littlefield, 2003), and *Cross-Border Dialogues: U.S.-Mexico Social Movement Networking* (coeditor; UC San Diego Center for U.S.-Mexican Studies, 2002). He also coedited *Invisible No More: Mexican Migrant Civic Participation in the United States* (Woodrow Wilson International Center for Scholars, 2006) and coauthored *Context Matters: Latino Immigrant Civic Engagement in Nine U.S. Cities* (Woodrow Wilson International Center for Scholars, 2010) and *Subsidizing Inequality: Mexican Corn Policy since NAFTA* (Woodrow Wilson International Center for Scholars/CIDE, 2010).

LUISA HEREDIA is a lecturer in the Department of Sociology at Harvard University. Her research interests include immigrant integration, racial and ethnic politics, social movements, and religion, with a focus on U.S. Latino communities. She is currently working on a book derived from her dissertation, "Faith in Action: The Catholic Church and the

Immigrant Rights Movement, 1980–2007," which examines the Catholic Church's involvement in the immigrant rights movement in Los Angeles.

TAEKU LEE is professor of political science and law and chair of the Department of Political Science at the University of California, Berkeley. His book, *Mobilizing Public Opinion* (University of Chicago Press, 2002), received the American Political Science Association's J. David Greenstone Award and the Southern Political Science Association's V.O. Key Award. He is also coauthor of *Why Americans Don't Join the Party* (Princeton University Press, 2011) and *Asian American Political Participation* (Russell Sage Foundation Press, forthcoming). He has coedited *Transforming Politics, Transforming America* (University of Virginia Press, 2006) and *Accountability through Public Opinion* (World Bank Press, 2011) and is completing the *Oxford Handbook of Racial and Ethnic Politics in the United States* (Oxford University Press, forthcoming). Lee has served in administrative and leadership positions at UC Berkeley and for several political science associations; he has also served in advisory and consultative capacities for academic presses and journals, research projects, nongovernmental organizations, think tanks, and private corporations. Prior to coming to Berkeley, he was assistant professor of public policy at Harvard's Kennedy School of Government.

LISA M. MARTINEZ is associate professor of sociology at the University of Denver and faculty affiliate of the DU Latina/o Center for Community Engagement and Scholarship (DULCCES). She holds master's and doctoral degrees from the University of Arizona and a bachelor's degree from the University of Texas. Her areas of expertise are political sociology, Latina/o sociology, immigration, and race, class, and gender. She has studied unconventional political participation among Latinos ("Yes We Can: Latino Participation in Unconventional Politics," *Social Forces*, vol. 84, no. 1, 2005) and is finishing a research project on the role of grassroots organizations in mobilizing Latinos for different forms of political action.

RUTH MILKMAN is professor of sociology at UCLA and the CUNY Graduate Center and academic director of the Murphy Institute for Worker Education and Labor Studies at CUNY. She writes frequently on workplace and labor issues. Her recent books include *L.A. Story: Immigrant Workers and the Future of the U.S. Labor Movement* (Russell Sage Foundation, 2006) and *Working for Justice: The L.A. Model of Organizing and Advocacy*, coedited with Victor Narro and Joshua Bloom (Cornell University Press, 2010).

AMALIA PALLARES is an associate professor in political science and Latin American and Latino Studies at the University of Illinois, Chicago. Her research focuses on indigenous and peasant movements, comparative social movements in Latin America and the United States, and Latino immigrants and political identity in the United States. Her publications include *From Peasant Struggles to Indian Resistance: the Ecuadorian Andes in the Late Twentieth Century* (University of Oklahoma Press, 2002) and *¡Marcha! Latino Chicago and the National Immigrant Movement* (coeditor; University of Illinois Press, 2010), several chapters in edited volumes, and articles in journals such as *LASA Forum* and *Latino Studies*.

FRANCISCO I. PEDRAZA is a doctoral student in the Department of Political Science at the University of Washington, studying American politics and race and ethnicity.

RICARDO RAMÍREZ is associate professor of political science at the University of Notre Dame. His broad research interests include political behavior, state and local politics, and the politics of race and ethnicity. His research is geared to understanding the transforma-tion of civic and political participation in American democracy by focusing on the effects of political context on participation, the political mobilization of and outreach to Latino immigrants and other minority groups, and the causes and consequences of increasing diversity among elected officials. He is principal investigator of a longitudinal study of gendered career paths among Latina/o elected officials since 1990 and coeditor of *Trans-forming Politics, Transforming America: The Political and Civic Incorporation of Immi-grants in the United States* (University of Virginia Press, 2006). His most recent writings include the following chapters and articles: "Why California Matters: How California Latinos Influence the Presidential Election," "Political Protest, Ethnic Media and La-tino Naturalization," "Latinos during the 2006 Immigration Protest Rallies," and "Seg-mented Mobilization: Latino Nonpartisan Get-Out-the-Vote Efforts in the 2000 General Election."

GARY M. SEGURA is professor of American politics and chair of Chicano/a studies in the Center for Comparative Studies in Race and Ethnicity at Stanford University. His work focuses on issues of political representation, most currently on the accessibility of gov-ernment and politics to America's growing Latino minority as well as a book-length project on the links between casualties in international conflict and domestic politics. He was the co–principal investigator of the Latino National Survey, a national poll of 8,600 Latino residents of the Untied States conducted in 2006. His work has appeared in the *American Political Science Review,* the *American Journal of Political Science, Journal of Politics.*

RANDY SHAW is a longtime activist who is the author of three books on how activists win social change: *The Activist's Handbook: A Primer* (University of California Press, 2001), *Reclaiming America: Nike, Clean Air, and the New National Activism* (University of Cali-fornia Press, 1999), and his most recent book on the ongoing legacy of the farmworkers' movement, *Beyond the Fields: Cesar Chavez, the UFW, and the Struggle for Justice in the 21st Century* (University of California Press, 2008). Shaw is also the editor of the daily alternative online news source *Beyond Chron* (Beyond-Chron.org), where he frequently writes about immigrant rights activism and Latino voting. The founder and executive director of the Tenderloin Housing Clinic in San Francisco, where for the past three de-cades he has assisted low-income tenants and drafted laws to preserve affordable housing, Shaw has designed and implemented programs providing housing for thousands of homeless single adults. He is coauthor of *There's No Place Like Home: How America's Housing Crisis Threatens Our Children* (Housing America, 1999), and his story for *In These Times* on the U.S. housing crisis was voted the ninth most censored story by Project Censored for 2001 and 2002.

ROBERTO SURO is a professor of journalism at the University of Southern California's Annenberg School for Communication and a noted researcher and commentator on the Hispanic population and immigration matters. Prior to his current position, he served as director of the Pew Hispanic Center from 2001 to 2007, a Washington DC–based research organization that he founded. At the center, he supervised the production of more than one hundred publications that offered nonpartisan information on the rapid growth of the Latino population and its implications for the United States. A former journalist, Suro has more than thirty years of experience writing on Hispanic issues and immigration for media such as *Time* magazine, the *New York Times,* and the *Washington Post.* He is author of *Strangers among Us: Latino Lives in a Changing America* (Vintage, 1999) as well as numerous reports, articles, and other publications regarding the growth of the Latino population. In addition to his appointment at USC, Suro is affiliated with the Brookings Institution and the Migration Policy Institute.

CHRISTINE TROST is assistant director at the Institute for the Study of Social Change (ISSC) at the University of California, Berkeley, where she also conducts research and codirects the Graduate Fellows Program. Her research interests include political ethics, democratic theory, and civic and political engagement and incorporation. She has authored journal articles on a variety of topics related to political ethics, campaign practices, campaign finance reform, and civic and political engagement. She is coeditor, with Alison Gash, of *Conflicts of Interest and Public Life: Cross-national Perspectives* (Cambridge University Press, 2008); coeditor, with Matthew Grossmann, of *Win the Right Way: How to Run Effective Local Campaigns in California* (Berkeley Public Policy Press, 2005); and coeditor, with Jonathan Bernstein and Adrienne Jamieson, of *Campaigning for Congress: Politicians at Home and in Washington* (Institute of Governmental Studies Press, UC Berkeley, 1995). Prior to her position at ISSC, she led the research arm of UC Berkeley's Institute of Governmental Studies' Improving Campaigns Project from 2001 to 2004, and she has taught American politics as a lecturer at UC Berkeley and as a visiting assistant professor at Mills College. She holds a PhD in political science from UC Berkeley.

KIM VOSS is professor and chair of sociology at the University of California, Berkeley. She studies labor, social movements, and inequality. Her recent books explore the politics of the contemporary American labor movement and include *Hard Work: Remaking the America Labor Movement* (with Rick Fantasia; University of California Press, 2004) and *Rebuilding Labor: Organizing and Organizers in the New Union Movement* (coedited with Ruth Milkman; Cornell University Press, 2004). She is also author of *The Making of American Exceptionalism: The Knights of Labor and Class Formation in the Nineteenth Century* (Cornell University Press, 1993) and coauthor of *Inequality by Design: Cracking the Bell Curve Myth* (Princeton University Press, 1996).

TED WANG provides public policy consulting services to foundations and nonprofit organizations on immigrant and civil rights issues. He previously spent fourteen years as a civil rights advocate, serving as the policy director of Chinese for Affirmative Action and as a staff attorney at the Lawyers' Committee for Civil Rights of the San Francisco Bay Area. In these positions, he litigated affirmative action and voting rights cases and drafted local and state laws promoting immigrant rights, racial justice, and employment opportunities for low-income communities. He is a graduate of Reed College and Yale Law School.

ROBERT C. WINN is a consultant and independent documentary filmmaker. A graduate of Yale Law School as well as the University of Southern California School of Cinema

Television, he focuses on documentary and other research projects that explore the human face of policy issues. His current areas of interest include immigration, language access, and social justice. Recent public television projects include *Grassroots Rising* (2005), about labor issues and the Asian Pacific Islander community in Los Angeles; and *Saigon, USA* (2003), about generational conflicts in the center of the Vietnamese American community. His current documentary project is *Childhood in Translation*, about language access issues through the eyes of immigrant children who are the linguistic and cultural brokers for their families. Recent consulting work for philanthropic organizations has focused on the grassroots dimensions of the immigration reform debate.

INDEX

Aarts, Kees, 64
ABC case, 14
Abdollah, Tami, 63
abortion, 164, 169
Abraham, Yvonne, 53
Abrajano, Marissa, 246
Abril (San Francisco Bay Area march
    participant), 186, 187
absentee ballots, 143, 147, 149
Acercamiento Hispano, 50
ACORN, 151
Active Citizenship Campaign (ACC), 88–89
activism, legacies of, 10–12, 119
advertising, 69, 70, 76
advocacy organizations, 33, 35, 49
affirmative action programs, 233–34
Afghanistan, U.S. invasion of, 17, 231
AFL-CIO: anti-immigrant policy of, 16, 26, 28,
    82, 86, 208; Executive Council, 208;
    immigrant rights movement supported by,
    86–88, 89, 91; as IWFR sponsor, 24;
    labor-Latino alliance, 214n16; pro-
    immigration policy of, 16, 26, 28, 87–88, 93,
    97, 208; UFW activism and, 41n28; worker
    center alliance with, 210
African Americans: black church, 103; black
    radio, 67–68, 74–76; immigrant rights
    movement and, 52, 151; Latinos and, 42n35;
    mobilizing structures, 41n25; political

participation of, 229; prounion sentiments
    among, 205, 213n5; as second-class citizens,
    5, 31–32, 42n33; U.S. institutions as viewed
    by, 236
African immigration, 18
Agricultural Labor Relations Act (1975), 84
Almada, Jorge Morales, 111
Almendárez Coello, Renán ("El Cucuy"):
    Latino identity activated by, 65–66;
    linguistic isolation employed by, 75; as
    mobilizer, 46–47, 49, 74, 77, 80n1, 94, 189;
    radio station founded by, 79, 80n6
Althaus, Dudley, 97
Alvarez, Michael R., 236
Alvarez, R. Michael, 246
Amalgamated Clothing and Textile Workers
    Union (ACTWU), 89
American Baptist Churches v. Thornburgh, 14
American Convention on Human Rights, 179n9
American Declaration of the Rights and Duties
    of Man, 179n9
American Families United (PA), 178n4
American Federation of State, County and
    Municipal Employees (AFSCME), 97
American Friends Service Committee, 23, 129,
    131
American Indians, 32
Americanism, 5, 31–33, 38–39, 95, 128, 134–35
America's Voice, 56

Maryland State and DC AFL-CIO, 91
Mason, Fred, 91
Massachusetts Immigrant and Refugee
Advocacy Coalition, 58n5
Massey, Douglas S., 13, 210
Mathews, Joe, 97
May Day rallies, 48, 96–97, 115, 131–37, 210
McAdam, Doug, 22, 28, 41n25, 42n33, 102, 182,
196n4
McCain, John, 37, 56, 99, 108, 223, 225, 226–27, 231
McCann, James, 146, 147, 149
McCarrick, Theodore E., 121n11
McCarthy, John D., 22, 102, 124
McCaskill, Claire, 224
McConahay, John, 20
McConnell, Mitch, 225
McDevitt, Michael, 184, 193, 196n4, 197n17
McDonnell, Patrick J., 15
McNeal, Ralph, 196n4
McPhail, Clark, 124
means, immigration rights rallies (2006) and,
20–21
media: alternative, 64–65, 184; community, 143;
corporatization of, 67; ethnic, 21, 24–26, 33,
45, 46–47, 49, 58n4, 85, 177, 189, 192, 210, 211;
frames employed by, 128; local groups
supported by, 4; migrant-led, 148, 152–53;
non-English-language, 64–65; political
behavior and, 64–67. See also radio,
Spanish-language
"media malaise," 64
Medicaid, 16
Medina, Eliseo, 83; ACC and, 88–89; AFL-CIO
anti-immigration policy and, 86–88;
immigration rights rallies (2006) and,
94–95, 97–98; labor-Church unity and, 89,
98; as negotiator on Senate immigration
legislation, 92; OLAW created by, 85–86; on
patriotic symbolism at rallies, 97
Meehan, Susan, 95
Melber, Ari, 46
Memphis (TN), 68
Menjívar, Cecilia, 14
Merolla, Jennifer, 41n24
Merz, Barbara, 149
Mexican Advisory Council for the Institute for
Mexicans Abroad, 143
Mexican American Legal Defense and
Eduction Fund (MALDEF), 22–23
Mexican Americans: backlash against, 134;
Chicano youth protests and, 196n6;

pan-ethnic "Latino" identity opposed by,
30; political cliques of, 207; Southwest
population of, 10; student walkouts, 182;
U.S. institutions as viewed by, 235–36
Mexican-American War (1846–48), 10
Mexican immigrants: backlash against, 134;
Catholic Church and, 120n3; Chicano civil
rights movement and, 40n12; civic
binationality of, 143, 145–46, 147; as
"family," 172; hometown associations
(HTAs) of, 149–51, 150 t. 7.1; IRCA
legalization provisions for, 40nn14–15; labor
movement and, 203; racialization of, 173;
social networks of, 205; subethnic
marketing strategies geared to, 70
Mexicanos for Political Progress (Chicago, IL),
146
Mexico: Catholic binational meeting involving,
107; "culture of migration" in, 13; economic
development in, 120n8; electoral democracy
campaigns in, 147; presidential election in
(2006), 143, 145–46, 147; teachers' movement, 145; undocumented migrants from, 17
Meyer, David S., 28, 34, 36, 126–28, 130, 135, 137
Meyerson, Harold, 85, 100n1, 209, 213n8
Miami (FL), 70, 91, 205
Michelson, Melissa R., 245, 246
Michoacán (Mexico), 143
Mi Familia Vota, 80n8, 212
migrant civil society: autonomous public
spheres, 148, 154; collective action areas in,
148; defined, 142, 148; media, 148, 152–53;
membership organizations, 148–52;
nongovernmental organizations (NGOs),
148, 153–54; political effect of, 154–56;
synergy in, and immigration rights rallies
(2006), 154, 155 fig. 7.1
migrant labor, 166
Migration Policy Institute, 17, 120n2
Milkman, Ruth, 26, 38, 85, 100n1, 146, 204,
213n4
Miller, Lawrence, 235
Miller, Warren E., 196n12
Million Man March (Washington, DC; 1995),
39n3
Minneapolis (MN), 91
Minushkin, Susan, 53, 211
Minutemen Civil Defense Corps, 96
Minutemen Project, 36, 54, 125, 130, 153, 221, 223
Miranda, Jesse, 104
Mississippi, 224

TEXT
10/12.5 Minion Pro

DISPLAY
Minion Pro

COMPOSITOR
Westchester Book Group

INDEXER
Kevin Millham

PRINTER AND BINDER
IBT Global